Naked Awareness

Practical Instructions on The Union of Mahāmudrā and Dzogchen

Naked Awareness

Practical Instructions on The Union of Mahāmudrā and Dzogchen

by
Karma Chagmé

with commentary by
Gyatrul Rinpoche

Translated by
B. Alan Wallace

Edited by
Lindy Steele & B. Alan Wallace

Snow Lion Publications
Ithaca, NY USA

Snow Lion Publications
P.O. Box 6483
Ithaca, NY 14851
607-273-8519
http://www.snowlionpub.com

Printed in Canada on acid-free, recycled paper.

ISBN 1-55939-146-4

Library of Congress Cataloging-in-Publication Data

Karma-chags-med, 17th cent.
[Thugs rje chen po'i dmar khrid Phyag Rdzogs zun 'jug thos pa don ldan. English] Naked awareness: Practical instructions on the union of Mahamudra and Dzogchen by Karma Chagmé; with commentary by Gyatrul Rinpoche; translated by B. Alan Wallace; edited by Lindy Steele & B. Alan Wallace.
p. cm.
Includes bibliographical references and index.
ISBN 1-55939-146-4
1. Avalokiteśvara (Buddhist deity)—Cult—Early works up to 1800. 2. Mahāmudrā (Tantric rite)—Early works up to 1800. 3. Rdzogs-chen (Rñiṇ-ma-pa)—Early works to 1800. 4. Meditation—Tantric Buddhism—Early works to 1800. I. Gyatrul, Rinpoche, 1924- II. Wallace, B. Alan. III. Steele, Lindy. IV. Title.

BQ4710.AK3813 2000
249.3'444—dc21 00-023802

Contents

Preface 7

1 An Oral Transmission on the Vows of Mahāyāna Refuge and the Spirit of Awakening 13
2 Narratives of Actions and Their Consequences 37
3 Actions and Their Consequences 57
4 An Introduction to Parables and Their Meanings 81
5 A Prose Identification 97
6 The Identification of Mahāmudrā 121
7 How to Follow the Path of the Leap-over 153
8 Guidance on the Path of Transference 179
9 An Introduction to the Ground, Path, and Fruition 201
10 The Four Stages of Yoga 221
11 How to Progress Along the Grounds and Paths 243
12 Conclusion 261

Notes 283
Buddhist Sanskrit and Tibetan Terms 289
Buddhist Terms in English Translation 295
Glossary of Names 303
Index of Texts Cited by the Author 307
General Index 319

Preface

The author of this text, Karma Chagmé Rinpoche, was born in 1613 in the Nyomtö region of Zalmo Gang in the Do-Kham region of eastern Tibet, as prophesied, according to Tibetan tradition, by Padmasambhava. His father was the renowned Mahāsiddha Pema Wangdrak, and his mother, Chökyong Kyi, was regarded as a wisdom *ḍākinī*. His father, who was his spiritual mentor until he reached the age of eleven, named him Wangdrak Sung, and immediately upon his birth gave him the longevity empowerment from the *termas* of Tertön Ratna Lingpa. During this spiritual apprenticeship with his father, Wangdrak Sung, who proved to be a brilliant student, learned to read and write, performed spiritual ceremonies, memorized texts, and sat in silent meditation for extended periods of time.

In his eleventh year, he encountered the contemplative Prawashara, from whom he received many empowerments, oral transmissions, and instructions, following which he received the oral transmissions for Avalokiteśvara and the lineage of Mahāmudrā from Kün-ga Namgyal of Drungpa Tserlung. At the age of nineteen, Wangdrak Sung resolved to enter the Buddhist monkhood, so he journeyed to the seat of the Karmapa, Tsurphu Monastery, to receive the vows of ordination. There he took the vows of refuge, novice ordination, and eventually full ordination. He then entered Thupten Nyingling Monastery of the Zurmang tradition.

Now known by his monastic name, Karma Chagmé, he performed his duties in the monastery and continued his studies by mastering all the major and minor texts on Buddhist logic. In the year of the dragon, the Karmapa and his two spiritual sons came to Zurmang Monastery. During their stay, Karma Chagmé received from the Karmapa many empowerments, oral transmissions, and instructions, including teachings on Mahāmudrā. He then accompanied the Karmapa for the next year and a half, at times remaining with him in retreat and receiving further instructions. In his twenty-first year he was given a public examination during the Great Prayer Festival of the Karma Kagyü order before a gathering of twelve thousand monks, which increased his already considerable renown as an outstanding scholar.

Karma Chagmé then devoted himself to a thirteen-year retreat during which he meditated on the form of Avalokiteśvara known as Jinasāgara (Tib. Gyalwa Gyatso) as his chosen deity. Near the end of this retreat, he recognized and enthroned the young *tertön*, or treasure-revealer, Min-gyur Dorje, to whom he imparted many empowerments and transmissions. Recalling countless past lifetimes, the young *tertön* Min-gyur Dorje began having visions of innumerable deities, which unveiled a storehouse of precious transmissions. Karma Chagmé, as the treasure-keeper, was the scribe who recorded them.

After concluding his retreat, Karma Chagmé bestowed the empowerments for the *Namchö*, or "Space Dharma," revelations of *tertön* Min-gyur Dorje and the revelations of the great *tertön* Ratna Lingpa. In addition, he wrote the text partially translated here, which combines the practical instructions he had received on Mahāmudrā and Dzogchen. The founder of the Payül tradition of the Nyingma order, the Vidyādhara Künzang Sherab, received all these transmissions directly from Karma Chagmé. Notably, this particular lineage of practice has become the very heart of the Payül tradition and has been practiced continuously to the present time.

Karma Chagmé passed away in the year 1678 after announcing to thousands of his disciples that the time had come for him to depart to another realm. He revealed amazing signs at his death. It is said that he dissolved his mind into the heart of Buddha Amitābha, and after the cremation of his body many images of Avalokiteśvara Jinasāgara were found to be embossed on his bones.

Gyatrul Rinpoche, the commentator for this volume, was born in Tibet in 1925, and was recognized by Jamyang Khyentse Lodrö Tayé as the incarnation of Sampa Künkyab, a Payül lineage meditator who spent his life in retreat and who later gave empowerments and transmissions from his retreat cave to multitudes of disciples. After being brought to Payül Dhomang Monastery, the young Gyatrul was educated by his tutor Sangye Gön. Sangye Gön received his name as a baby from the famous Gili Tertön (Düdjom Lingpa), who singled out the child while passing through his village, named him, and predicted his future.

During the many years that the young Gyatrul spent with his *lama*, he remembers him having regular visitations from a white man whom he felt to be Avalokiteśvara; and he recalls that Sangye Gön's own white hair turned black and new teeth appeared, replacing those that were missing. Most of Gyatrul Rinpoche's basic training occurred under the direction of his teacher Sangye Gön, including his lineage of Karma Chagmé's *Buddhahood in the Palm of the Hand, The Union of Mahāmudrā and Dzogchen,* and much supplementary material that he studied with his teacher for three consecutive years. Later Gyatrul Rinpoche entered retreat with the enlightened activity emanation of the Düdjom incarnations, Tulku Natsog Rangdröl, who became his primary spiritual mentor. Gyatrul Rinpoche also received oral transmissions from the great Payül Chogtrul Rinpoche, the primary spiritual mentor of H. H. Penor Rinpoche, the present head of both the Payül lineage and the Nyingma order as a whole, and from Apkong Khenpo.

Since arriving in America in 1976, Gyatrul Rinpoche has been the spiritual representative of H. H. Dudjom Rinpoche, and with him he has founded Pacific Region Yeshe Nyingpo centers on the West Coast, including Tashi Chöling, a Tibetan Buddhist center near Ashland, Oregon. There he has hosted many great *lamas,* including H. H. Dudjom Rinpoche, H. H. Penor Rinpoche, H. H. Khenpo Jigmé Phuntsok, and many other accomplished scholars and contemplatives of the various orders of Tibetan Buddhism. Since his arrival in America, Gyatrul Rinpoche has himself taught Dharma to thousands of students in the West.

Karma Chagmé presented his classic work *Meaningful to Behold: The Essential Instructions of Avalokiteśvara on The Union of Mahāmudrā and Dzogchen (Thugs rje chen po'i dmar khrid phyag rdzogs zung 'jug thos ba don ldan.* Bylakuppe: Nyingmapa Monastery, 1984) in its entirety as an oral teaching lasting thirty days. This is a more elaborate treatise by Karma Chagmé than his work translated as *Union of Mahamudra and Dzogchen,* with a commentary by Tulku Chokyi Nyima. The Venerable Gyatrul Rinpoche taught the first chapter and the concluding eight chapters of the main body of this text at his Buddhist center Orgyen Dorje Den in San Francisco during the period 1994-95. That portion of this classic treatise, together with Gyatrul Rinpoche's oral commentary, has already been published under the title *A Spacious Path to Freedom: Practical Instructions on the Union of Mahāmudrā and Atiyoga* (Snow Lion Publications, 1998). This present volume includes my translation of the concluding, supplementary chapters (*rgyab chos*) of this treatise by Karma Chagmé, with Gyatrul Rinpoche's oral commentary presented during the period 1995-96, also at Orgyen Dorje Den.

I have translated this text in close collaboration with Gyatrul Rinpoche, who went through it with me line by line. Afterwards, when he gave teachings on this treatise at Orgyen Dorje Den in San Francisco, I served as his interpreter. This oral commentary was transcribed by a number of his students in California and was then initially edited by Lindy Steele, with the assistance of Les Collins and Latif Harris. I then further edited the entire translation of the text and commentary. I am deeply grateful for the selfless efforts of the Dharma friends who joined me in this labor of love, without whom this volume could never have made its way to publication. I would also like to express my heartfelt thanks to Mimi Hohenberg, whose kindness and generosity made it possible for me to work closely with Gyatrul Rinpoche on this and other translation projects.

To the best of our knowledge there is presently only one extant edition of this text, which was published in India in 1984. Written in the *dbu med* script, many words are abbreviated, and the spelling is loose, to say the least. This made the translation particularly challenging, and I would not have taken on the task but for the constant encouragement and assistance I received from Gyatrul Rinpoche.

Karma Chagmé states that he composed this treatise so that many old mendicants and recluses may accomplish their eternal longing for happiness by practicing the union of Mahāmudrā and Dzogchen; and he speculates that no advanced scholars will be interested in this work, though they may be gratified by its many citations. Karma Chagmé concludes this work with his apology to scholars for any possible errors in the order of some of the citations. Despite our best efforts, there may still be errors in the translation. If these are detected by other scholars, I hope they will bring them to my attention. As Gyatrul Rinpoche strongly emphasized, this work is intended chiefly for those wishing to practice Mahāmudrā and Dzogchen in order to realize the essential nature of their own minds. It is our earnest prayer that our efforts will help make this profound contemplative path accessible to people in the modern world.

B. Alan Wallace
Santa Barbara, California

CHAPTER ONE

An Oral Transmission on the Vows of Mahāyāna Refuge and the Spirit of Awakening

Homage to Avalokiteśvara!

– While this text begins with teachings on the vows of Mahāyāna refuge and the spirit of awakening, please bear in mind that refuge, the Four Thoughts that Turn the Mind,[1] and the spirit of awakening itself are really the pivotal focus of the teachings and practice. Without them we're not even Buddhists, and liberation and enlightenment are out of the question. It's by means of refuge, the Four Thoughts that Turn the Mind, and the spirit of awakening that we actually accomplish our own ends, as well as serve the needs of others.

Before beginning to study this text, we must bring to mind the importance of cultivating a wholesome and meaningful motivation for both the teachings and the practice. Our motivation must be to attain enlightenment in order to be of benefit to all sentient beings. Without cultivating a wholesome motivation, this commentary, its translation into English, and reading this work will be pointless.

What if we do neglect our motivation? We must then ask, "Is it enough to simply become a Buddhist? Is taking the vows of refuge and thereby entering the door of Buddhadharma enough?" No, it's not. Nor is it enough to take the precepts of refuge and the *bodhisattva*[2] vows. Our goal is the attainment of the omniscient state of enlightenment. Why is this needed? It is to attain enlightenment and to liberate ourselves from suffering. And to achieve this, we must first focus on the Four Thoughts that Turn the Mind.

The first of these four topics is the precious human life of leisure and endowment. Now, to understand this in terms of an analogy, imagine that you're drifting in a vast ocean and come upon a small island overflowing with everything that you could possibly need. It has forests, excellent soil, water, and a fine climate. However, although this soil is so rich that you could grow anything in it, it hasn't been properly prepared. Boulders, thorns, and so on need to be cleared away, then you can sow any crop you wish, and it will bring a fine harvest. Our precious human life is like this island with its rich soil. The stones, thorns, and so forth are like the three poisons of the mind. Just as this soil can give rise to a harvest that can be enjoyed and shared with others, similarly, this human life with which we are presently endowed is replete with all the necessary causes, personal as well as public opportunities or endowments, to accomplish our own ends and the goals of others.

Now, imagine that you fall back into this vast ocean, and it's filled with dangerous animals, such as sharks and crocodiles. This ocean is like the cycle of existence, in which so many sentient beings devour one another. The moment you fall back into the ocean, your situation becomes virtually hopeless.

There are many islands in this ocean, some of them dry with poor soil and some with no forests. There are very few that are replete with such excellent soil and such ideal conditions for prospering. Moreover, since none are permanent, eventually they will all sink back beneath the water. These other islands are like the various types of human life. Among human beings, there are some people who have some kind of spiritual practice, while many others have none at all. Human life without spiritual practice is like living on a dry and barren island.

Right now in our present circumstances we are on a very fertile island. This is a good island—our present human life—yet we need to bear in mind that we have it for only a short time. Spend this time most effectively and meaningfully in order to recognize what is virtuous and what is nonvirtuous, adopting the former and avoiding the latter. Most importantly, once you have taken precepts or vows, keep them. If you break them, then recognize and confess this and carry on, restraining from such acts in the future. In the meantime it's important not to fall into erroneous views and misconceptions that can lead you away from the spiritual path. By following these very simple, basic guidelines, our human lives can be very meaningful.

Even if you are drawn to the teachings and practice of Dzogchen, the Great Perfection, it's important to proceed step by step in order to gain realization in such practice. First, establish a foundation in the Hīnayāna, or the Individual Vehicle. Take the precepts of individual liberation, such as the five precepts, for example. Upon that basis, you can then proceed to Mahāyāna and cultivate the two types of the spirit of awakening, the spirit of aspiring for awakening and the spirit of venturing towards awakening, each having its own precepts. Most importantly, within the context of Mahāyāna practice, never be separated from these two types of the spirit of awakening. In developing a spirit of awakening and taking the precepts, we need to counteract our long-standing tendency to act out of self-centeredness. We need to engage in the practice of Dharma for the sake of others.

The Great Perfection is included in the context of Buddhist *tantra*, for which one must receive an empowerment before engaging in the practice. Of the various empowerments given, the fourth is of special importance. With the stage of generation and the stage of completion practices as the basis, receive this empowerment, while paying special attention to the fourth initiation and its *samayas*, or pledges. When fully understood, each of the preliminary practices, such as taking refuge, Vajrasattva meditation, and *guruyoga*, contains both the stage of generation and stage of completion. For example, if you have a full understanding of the practice of taking refuge, all forms are seen as emanations of the field of refuge; and all sounds are heard as the speech of the objects of refuge. Taking refuge in this way becomes a complete tantric practice. Similarly, as you engage in Vajrasattva meditation, you will see all forms as the form of Vajrasattva and hear all sounds as the speech of Vajrasattva. This is also true of the practice of transference of consciousness,[3] which includes the stages of generation and completion. However, *transference* has the special purpose of preparing us for death, and therein is its special advantage.

Bestowing and receiving an empowerment is very important, so it's very important to maintain the proper attitude. Some people seem to go for empowerments as if they were simply making a collection, proudly telling their friends of their latest acquisitions. This attitude is like throwing all precepts and empowerments into the garbage. It's just a waste.

The practice of the Great Perfection clearly relates to the two stages of generation and completion. Let's look at the Dzogchen view. Sometimes I hear people say they have received teachings on the Great Perfection and have gained realization. It seems that most people who make these proclamations fall into one of two categories: (1) while they think they're realizing the meaning, they are still grasping onto a mental object, so the subject/object dichotomy is still being sustained; and they are also grasping onto the idea that they have realized something. We can decide for ourselves whether that is on the right track. (2) Other people who make such claims are really remaining simply with a blank mind while they are apparently meditating. If that were true Dzogchen practice, then the stages of generation and completion and all the teachings on the ten *bodhisattva* grounds and five *bodhisattva* paths would obviously be irrelevant. If Dzogchen practice consisted simply of stopping thoughts and remaining in a state of mental vacuousness, then the two stages of this practice—of the Breakthrough and the Leap-over—would also be irrelevant.

Sometimes we try to justify other peoples' conduct, saying they are *siddhas*,[4] or accomplished beings, who are beyond judgment. But Guru Rinpoche himself said that while his view was as vast as space, he was meticulous in terms of his conduct. If Guru Rinpoche felt this was necessary, why should we make exceptions for *siddhas* who may have lesser degrees of realization?

Whether you are grasping at an object or becoming spaced out, you are not free of conceptual elaborations, so you are not truly engaging in

Dzogchen practice. Grasping onto an object seems to entail the extreme of substantialism, while spacing out is associated with the extreme of nihilism. At the same time, it is one more error to spend one's time focusing on others' errors in practice instead of attending to one's own situation, for this is a kind of spiritual hypocrisy.

Both the preliminaries and the actual practice of Dzogchen are crucial. Without training in the Four Thoughts that Turn the Mind, even on the verge of death, we will still cling to all the things we're so accustomed to grasping onto, such as our possessions, home, environment, status, and reputation. It's so difficult to let them go. It's so easy to have the sense that you can't die yet because you haven't completed your projects. It doesn't work that way. If you're an old man like me, the Lord of Death has already half swallowed you, so if you still have no renunciation and don't think about future lifetimes, that means that you're not really disillusioned with cyclic existence. In this case, what's the difference between being a Buddhist and non-Buddhist?

It's also possible that once you have taken refuge and heard some teachings, you might become conceited and think you have thoroughly fathomed the teachings. You might even think of yourself as a teacher. Bear in mind, it's not so easy to be a teacher. First, you must purify and subdue your own mind. Only then may you be in a position to help others subdue their minds. For example, if one blind person tries to lead another, they're both out of luck. Consequently, in order to accomplish our own goals and the goals of others, it's important to go back to the beginning, to cultivate what the Zen tradition calls a "beginner's mind"—totally fresh, unknowing, wide open to everything. Go back to the Four Thoughts that Turn the Mind, because they are the key that opens up the great treasure house of Buddhist teachings. In order to become familiar with them, read them. And, as you read them, study them, and put them into practice. –

[524] These are the profound practical instructions of Avalokiteśvara. On your right side arrange an image of the Buddha, and Dharma volumes such as this text of instructions. If you have a *stūpa*,[5] place it there as well, and in front of all these lay out the sevens kinds of offerings, a *maṇḍala*,[6] and so on.

– The author initially gives instructions on setting up an altar as a direct preparation for taking the precepts of refuge and purifying the mind. The minds we bring to the practice are impure, so it's helpful to create an environment, with beautiful offerings and so forth, that is pure and induces a sense of gladness and faith. –

I shall offer a more extensive explanation of the meaning of refuge and the spirit of awakening than was presented earlier in the instructions on the preliminaries.[7] Once you have understood the meaning of this, if you again request these vows, they truly will arise in you; it is difficult for them to arise simply by engaging in recitations without understanding the meaning. In this supplementary Dharma, the vows will be bestowed.

– Some people may wonder whether it is enough to take the vows of refuge just once. If one has taken these vows and kept them, in one way this is sufficient. On the other hand, taking these vows is like eating: we need to eat every day to sustain our health. Likewise, until we attain perfect enlightenment, it's very important to continue taking these vows of refuge and to keep them. –

In terms of the vows of refuge, [525] there are those common to the different *yānas*[8] and there are the Mahāyāna vows of refuge; and now we are concerned with the latter. Here is the object from whom the vows are requested, according to the tradition of the present teachings: In the space in front of you there is a broad, vast, and mighty throne of jewels supported by lions. Upon it is a variegated lotus with a hundred thousand petals, on which rests a round moon-disk. In its center is your own primary spiritual mentor Amitābha, present in the garb of a *sambhogakāya*,[9] surrounded by Kagyü *lamas*.

– When visualizing the Kagyü *lamas*, you might be wondering which Kagyü lineage (the Karma Kagyü, Drukpa Kagyü, and so on) you should imagine. Actually in this reference to the Kagyü *lamas*, the syllable "Ka" means "teachings" and "gyü" means "lineage." The term "Kagyü *lamas*" here refers to all spiritual mentors who hold the lineage of the *kama*[10] and *termas*.[11] This includes Kagyü *lamas* as well as the Geluk, Sakya, and Nyingma *lamas*. –

In front of him is the chosen deity Avalokiteśvara surrounded by a myriad of chosen deities. On his right is Buddha Śākyamuni surrounded by a myriad of *buddhas* including [526] the thousand *buddhas* of this fortunate era. Behind him is *The Perfection of Wisdom Sūtra in One Hundred Thousand Stanzas*, surrounded by a myriad of treatises and volumes of sublime Dharma. On his left is Vajrapāṇi, surrounded by a myriad of the Mahāyāna and Hīnayāna Saṅgha, including the eight *bodhisattva* spiritual sons and the eight supreme *śrāvakas*.[12] All the cardinal and intermediate directions are filled with *vīras*[13] and *ḍākinīs*.[14] Beneath him are a myriad of Dharma-protectors, including the Four-armed Mahākāla, Six-armed Mahākāla, and Draklha Gönpo. On the crowns of their heads is *Oṃ*, at their throats, *Āḥ*, and at their hearts, *Hūṃ*. From the *Hūṃ* at their hearts rays of light are emitted in the ten directions, inviting all the spiritual mentors, chosen deities, *vīras*, *ḍākinīs*, and Dharma-protectors like gathering clouds. Imagine that they dissolve into the deities visualized in front of you.

With palms pressed together holding a stick of incense, the master and disciples invite them by chanting together:

> You are the protector of all sentient beings without exception, the unassailable, divine conqueror who defeats the hosts of *māras*, who knows all things as they are. Lord, please come to this place together with your retinue.
>
> Lord, for countless eons you have cultivated compassion for sentient beings, and you have made vast prayers to fulfill the needs of us all. Now, when the time has come, please dispense a myriad of miraculous blessings from your spontaneous palace of the absolute space of phenomena. In order to liberate limitless hosts of sentient beings, please come together with your entire retinue.
>
> You are the Lord of all Dharmas, your complexion is like pure gold, with a splendor more magnificent than the sun. Due to my faith, may you gaze upon me. Peaceful and compassionate, subdued and abiding in meditative stabilization, with your Dharma and primordial wisdom free of attachment, you possess inexhaustible power. Return, return, O being of the peace of purity. Omniscient sage, foremost of living beings, come to this place of offerings, which are presented like beautiful reflections.
>
> Lord, it is good for you to come here. We possess merit and good fortune. Please accept our offerings, attend to us, and grant your blessings.
>
> When we offer this eight-petalled lotus as vast as the galaxy, with joy and open-heartedness, [527] please remain as long as you please.

– Holding a stick of incense, a flower, or any other suitable offering, ask for blessings and for forgiveness for all of the downfalls and errors you have committed in the past. –

If you wish, you may expand on this by offering the ritual bath and the *maṇḍala*. This is the brief liturgy:

> Just as the gods bathed you as soon as you were born, so do I bathe you with pure, divine water. This is a glorious, supreme bath, with the unsurpassable water of compassion. With the water of blessings and primordial wisdom, grant me whatever *siddhis*[15] I desire. The body, speech, and mind of the *jinas*[16] are free of the

> obscurations of mental afflictions, but in order to purify the obscurations of the body, speech, and mind of sentient beings, I bathe you with pure water.

– The *buddhas* are free of all obscurations and defilements, so there is nothing that *devas*[17] or human beings can do to purify them. But in order to purify our own obscurations, negative actions and so on, this ritual bath is offered. For example, in terms of the usual offerings placed on an altar or offerings made during a *sādhana*[18] practice, there is the offering of water for drinking. The *buddhas* aren't really thirsty, so this offering is not something they need. Rather, we offer it for our own benefit. The second offering is water to bathe the feet. Once again the *buddhas* don't need their feet bathed, but for our purification, we offer this as a ritual bath. To perform this ritual more elaborately with two phases not included in this text, one would imagine drying the *buddhas* with a pure towel, and then make an offering of beautiful garments.

These offerings are followed immediately with the concise *maṇḍala* offering. You may instead recite the intermediate or extensive *maṇḍala* offering while either placing a *maṇḍala* on your altar or performing the *maṇḍala* offering *mudrā*[19] with your hands. –

And:

> The foundation of the earth anointed with perfumed water and strewn with flowers, adorned with Mount Meru, the four world-sectors, the sun, and moon I visualize as a pure realm of the *buddhas*. Due to this offering, may all beings experience this perfectly pure realm! *Idaṃ ratna maṇḍalakaṃ niryātayāmi.*

Thus, imagine that the objects of refuge are experientially present in the space in front of you. Indeed, they are actually present, for it is said, "For those who believe in the Buddha, the Sage is present before them," and "Like reflections of the moon in water, they appear wherever you look." So they are actually present. Moreover, the *buddhas* and *bodhisattvas* dwelling in the pure realms of the ten directions see you with their eyes of primordial wisdom, and they certainly hear you chanting. So this is the same as requesting the vows from all the *buddhas*.

– At this point, you don't need to have any doubts. By having faith, the *buddhas* are, in fact, actually present. *Buddhas* are not like rocks that can be present in only one place. Rather, they are like a hundred reflections of the moon in a hundred water-filled vessels. Wherever there is a vessel of water facing the moon, there you will find the reflection of the moon. *Buddhas* are present, not as material entities, but as forms of primordial wisdom, for all those who have faith in them.

Moreover be certain that all the *buddhas* and *bodhisattvas* hear you chanting. That is, as you take vows from Buddha Amitābha or your own spiritual mentor in the nature of Buddha Amitābha, since they are the synthesis of all of the *buddhas*, this is the same as taking the vows from all of the *buddhas*. –

With the representations of the enlightened body, speech, and mind that you have set out in front of you as the basis of your visualization, request me to be your mentor. Imagine requesting the vows of Mahā-yāna refuge. The objects of refuge [528] are of the nature of the three embodiments, and the blessed *buddhas* are the Jewel of the Buddha. Request them to be your fundamental refuge. The holy Jewel of the Dharma is of the nature of the Mahāyāna scriptures and insights. Request this as your refuge in terms of the path. The *bodhisattvas* abiding on the first ground and beyond are the Mahāyāna Jewel of the Saṅgha. Imagine requesting them to be your refuge by being your companions.

– Here Karma Chagmé Rinpoche is telling his students to request that he be their mentor from whom to take these vows. That is one way to proceed, but you don't necessarily need to have your spiritual mentor present to take the vows of refuge. If he's not available, it is still possible simply to set up your altar with the representations of the enlightened body, speech and mind of the Buddha, and take the vows on your own. As you do the visualization, moreover, the person that you visualize may be your own spiritual mentor or it may be Guru Rinpoche. The being in whom you have the greatest faith is your primary spiritual mentor and you visualize that person as being of the nature of Amitābha.

Moreover, Mahāyāna refuge involves entrusting oneself from this time until Buddhahood. This is the level of commitment. It's not like the common tendency of practicing Buddhism until you're bored and then throwing it away. Being fickle like this doesn't hurt the Three Jewels—the Buddha, Dharma and Saṅgha. Instead, it is detrimental to you. It's taking this altogether unique opportunity in which you have the possibility of attaining perfect enlightenment in one lifetime—all of these causes and conditions which have come together in this extremely rare and precious situation of your present life—and then throwing it into the garbage. That's not so appropriate, is it? Isn't it like spilling food all over yourself in an excellent restaurant? –

This does not entail going for refuge for our own sake alone. Seek refuge in order to bring all sentient beings to the state of spiritual awakening. This is not seeking refuge only for the duration of your life, as in the case of the Hīnayāna; rather think, "I seek refuge from today until I achieve spiritual awakening." On bended knee, with your palms pressed together, and with the single-pointed wish to request the Mahāyāna vows of refuge, recite this after me three times:

> All *buddhas* and *bodhisattvas* of the ten directions, please attend to me. Mentor, please attend to me. From this time until I am present in the essence of enlightenment [529], I take refuge in the blessed Buddha, the foremost among human beings. I take refuge in the holy Dharma, the foremost freedom from attachment. I take refuge in the *āryas* and[20] non-returning Saṅgha, the foremost community. (3 times)

– The *āryas* are those beings who have gained unmediated, non-dual realization of ultimate truth. The "non-returning Saṅghas" refers to those who do not return to *saṃsāra*.[21] –

Oh, now consider that the Mahāyāna vows of refuge have arisen in your mind-streams, and respond, "Well done," to which the mentor replies, "This is the method."

These are the benefits of receiving the Mahāyāna vows of refuge. You are protected from all harm and injury in this life (except that which comes as the fruition of previous actions), from bad omens, and from falling to the Hīnayāna. In the future you will be protected from the fears of the miserable destinations and the fears of the cycle of existence. *The Ornament for the Sūtras* states:

> Because it protects from all injuries, from miserable destinations, misdeeds, fears, and the Hīnayāna, it is the sublime refuge.

– Once you have taken the Mahāyāna vows, it would be a reversal to allow your motivation to deteriorate so that you strive only for your own welfare. Therefore, taking the Mahāyāna vows of refuge protects you from "falling to the Hīnayāna." If you take the Mahāyāna vows of refuge and keep them, you are also protected from all of the six states of sentient existence. –

Upon [530] receiving the vows of refuge, you must engage in the corresponding disciplines. With respect to those disciplines, there are (1) three general practices, (2) three specific practices, and (3) three affiliated practices, making nine altogether.

1. Always endeavor to make offerings to the Jewels, at least offering the first morsel of your meals. Do not abandon the Jewels at the cost of your life or for any reward; and frequently practice going for refuge by recollecting the excellent qualities of the Jewels.

– Especially here in the West, it's very good to make real and imaginary offerings upon an altar of all kinds of things you find attractive. Anything that you desire, including items in a mall and people whom you find attractive, offer up to the Three Jewels. Simply having attachment for people and material objects brings no benefit; it only makes you dissatisfied, frustrated, and unhappy. However, as soon as you offer anything to the Three Jewels for which you have attachment, you accrue merit, or spiritual power, and such offering also decreases your attachment to those objects.

Under the Chinese Communist domination of Tibet, many Tibetans have had their commitment to the objects of refuge put to the test, and some forsook their vows of refuge. On many occasions the Chinese Communists threatened torture and death if Tibetans didn't renounce Buddhism. Faced with that kind of threat—which the Chinese were perfectly willing to carry out and, in fact, did in many cases—some did renounce the Buddha, Dharma, and Saṅgha. Others said they abandoned the Three Jewels to protect themselves from torture, but didn't really give up their vows. Still others refused even to give such lip service but maintained in all ways their refuge in the Three Jewels. This doesn't imply that they were stupid or simply stubborn, but rather shows the depth of their insight into the importance of the vows of refuge—how deeply they had fathomed and internalized them.

In Tibet, many earnest Dharma practitioners recited the vows of refuge many hundreds of thousands of times, as is done in the traditional preliminary practices. This is done not just to maintain a tradition, but to receive the great benefits of irreversibly entrusting oneself to the Three Jewels. –

2. The three specific practices include: once you have gone for refuge in the Buddha, do not go for refuge in any other gods. *The Sūtra of the Great Liberation* states:

> One who has gone for refuge in the *buddhas* is a genuine *upāsaka*, and never does one seek refuge in other gods.

– The Buddha has abandoned the two types of obscurations and has brought all wholesome qualities to perfection. Having taken refuge in such a supramundane, transcendent object of refuge, you do not take refuge in any other gods. This is not because you are afraid they'll be jealous. Rather, other gods are still in *saṃsāra*, so they are not able to protect you or lead you to the freedom they themselves have not yet achieved. If you were blind, you wouldn't seek another blind person as a guide, but someone with vision. The Buddha is one who has eyes of wisdom due to having eliminated all the types of obscurations and to having gained the two types of knowledge, ontological and phenomenological. Gods who are within *saṃsāra* are still subject to self-grasping and are still bound in ignorance. Not having eliminated the two types of obscurations, they are not suitable as objects of ultimate refuge in whom we utterly entrust ourselves. –

Since you have gone for refuge in the Dharma, do not inflict injury upon sentient beings. A *sūtra* states:

> Once you have gone for refuge in the holy Dharma, be free of thoughts of inflicting harm and injury.

– One may be motivated to inflict injury for various reasons, including killing for sport, anger or hatred, or convenience. The precept of taking refuge in the Dharma means that you do not inflict injury upon others. More broadly speaking, you do not engage in any of the ten nonvirtuous actions, which directly or indirectly involve inflicting harm on others. Now, a highly realized *bodhisattva* has the freedom to inflict harm in cases in which one sees that this is for the benefit of sentient beings. But one must discern this with wisdom and be motivated by compassion. If you're not highly realized, be careful! –

[531] Since you have gone for refuge in the Saṅgha, do not devote yourself to extremists. A *sūtra* states:

> Once you have gone for refuge in the Saṅgha, do not veer towards extremists.

– Taking refuge in extremists means entrusting yourself to those who abandon, abuse, and ridicule the Dharma, or who abuse their spiritual mentor. Coming under the influence of such people can alter your mind in harmful ways, so it's better not to come under their sway. This includes being influenced by people with sectarian, prejudiced attitudes and so forth, including those who count themselves as Buddhists.

So, what should one do with such people? Disengage from them in a harmonious way. –

3. The three affiliated practices include: reverence towards images of the Tathāgata, which represents the Jewel of the Buddha, and even a *sāccha* fragment of such an image; reverence towards volumes of Dharma, which represent the Jewel of the Dharma, and even a single syllable of such texts; and reverence to the garments of the Revealer, which represent the Jewel of the Saṅgha, and even a yellow patch of such cloth.

– Images of the Buddha, including *sācchas,*[22] Dharma volumes, and so forth must be treated with respect. Don't treat them casually, leaving them on the ground or stepping over them. Any Dharma book, even a syllable that represents the Dharma, represents the Jewel of the Dharma and should be treated with respect.

Here in the West, we have many excellent Dharma books; we can purchase *thankas*[23] and statues, and there are representatives of the Saṅgha.

Having these many objects of refuge and devotion, it's important to know the proper way to relate to them. –

There are eight benefits of going for refuge: (1) you enter into the community of Buddhists; (2) this becomes a basis for all vows; (3) all your previous sins are extinguished; (4) you are not afflicted by human or non-human obstructive forces; (5) you accomplish everything you intend; (6) your mind-stream becomes endowed with great merit; (7) you do not descend to the miserable states of existence; and (8) you swiftly, manifestly achieve perfect enlightenment. [532]

– Within the context of Buddhism many ritual practices counteract a wide variety of adversities including illness and so forth. If you engage in these with faith, they can be very effective in enabling you to accomplish everything you intend.

Bear in mind that until now you have already spent many countless eons wandering in *saṃsāra*. Now, you have come to this present life and many of you know the prognosis for getting out of *saṃsāra* by means of the various vehicles of spiritual practice within Buddhism. You know how long it takes if you follow the Hīnayāna or the Sūtrayāna. Within Vajrayāna, you know how long it takes if you follow the outer versus the inner *tantras*. In the context of the present teachings, you know how long it takes if you follow Mahāyoga,[24] Anuyoga,[25] or Atiyoga.[26] Within this context, you are presented with the opportunity to achieve the perfect enlightenment of a Buddha. You can come to the culmination of the path in this very lifetime. In this very broad context, recognize the unparalleled value of this present opportunity and place a great emphasis on this—even greater than on your wallets! –

That is receiving the Mahāyāna vows of refuge.

– If you are wondering at this point about the universality within Buddhism of taking refuge, then check out other Buddhist traditions—Geluk, Sakya, and Kagyü. You will see for yourself that the nature of taking refuge, the precepts, and the benefits are exactly the same for all four Tibetan Buddhist orders, although there may be some differences in the visualization of the objects of refuge.

For both the Mahāyāna taking of refuge and the Mahāyāna spirit of awakening, you must first gain an understanding of the Four Noble Truths and the Four Thoughts that Turn the Mind. With that foundation, you truly will know the meaning of taking refuge in the Three Jewels—the Buddha, the Dharma and the Saṅgha. You will be able to develop the spirit of awakening. Without gaining some insight into the Four Noble Truths and the Four Thoughts that Turn the Mind, without knowing the qualities of the Three Jewels and the benefits of developing the spirit of awakening, your whole practice is reduced to blindly mimicking others, and there's no benefit in that. Even if you practiced Dharma like that for a hundred years, the level of your practice would be no more than that of a tiny baby.

The reason for this retardation of spiritual practice is one's insufficient understanding of the Four Noble Truths and the Four Thoughts that Turn the Mind. With no such understanding, you cannot turn away from *saṃsāra*, you cannot genuinely take refuge, and you cannot genuinely develop the spirit of awakening; instead your spiritual practice is basically crippled.

Why do we take Mahāyāna refuge? Because we have not gained liberation from suffering and the sources of suffering. What is the primary cause of this cycle of existence? It is nonvirtue, specifically the three nonvirtues of the body, the four of the speech, and the three of the mind.

Those of the body include intentionally killing any sentient being, sexual misconduct such as adultery, and stealing, or literally, taking that which is not given. Engaging in these gives rise to suffering, so they are to be abandoned.

Those that comprise the four of the speech include consciously telling that which is not true; abusive or harsh speech—true or false makes no difference; slanderous speech, whether false or true, which causes divisiveness and disharmony where harmony was once present; and idle chatter or gossip, motivated by any of the mental afflictions of attachment, anger, ignorance, pride, and jealousy.

Those of the mind include craving another person's possessions; the intent to inflict injury on another sentient being; and holding to false views, such as thinking that our actions have no ethical consequences.

Since they give rise to suffering, these ten are to be avoided. In this life alone we can see how this suffering occurs. As a result of the mind being prone to the five poisons, we suffer, as do our families and communities. Moreover, the ten nonvirtues give rise to suffering and disharmony which can even extend from one nation to another.

How do we overcome these poisons? How can we overcome the nonvirtues that arise from these mental afflictions? This can be done by hearing and contemplating the Dharma and, finally, by engaging in meditation. Upon this basis, one takes refuge in the Buddha, the Awakened One, who has eliminated all suffering and the causes of suffering and has brought to perfection all virtues. In Tibetan the word for Buddha is "sang gye." "Sang" means "awakened," in the sense of being awakened from suffering and the sources of suffering. "Gye" means "expanded" or "fulfilled," referring to the fulfillment of virtues.

First, you take refuge in the Buddha, not in other sentient beings. If someone has not gained liberation from suffering and the sources of suffering, how can he possibly lead anyone else to the liberation he hasn't yet achieved? The second source of refuge is the Dharma, which consists essentially of the causes that free yourself and others from suffering and bring your own virtues to perfection. Finally, you take refuge in the Saṅgha, the practitioners of the Dharma who are on the path—those on the various grounds and paths to enlightenment.

To take refuge in the Buddha, Dharma and Saṅgha, think: From this day until achieving enlightenment, for the benefit of all creatures, I take refuge in the Buddha, Dharma, and Saṅgha.

Once you have taken the vows of refuge, it's very important to keep them. Once you have taken refuge, it's deceitful to continue inflicting harm on other sentient beings, just as it is deceitful to entrust yourself to the Buddha, and later reject this refuge. Let alone serving anybody else's ends, by doing this we don't even accomplish our own goals. Likewise, if we abandon the Saṅgha, it is no different than abandoning all three objects of refuge.

If you don't know the liturgy for taking the refuge vows, just take refuge mentally. Entrust yourself to the Buddha, Dharma and Saṅgha from your heart and your mind. Bear in mind that it is not for your sake alone that you do this, but take refuge for the benefit of all living beings who like yourself are within the cycle of existence, who like yourself are unaware of what to adopt and what to reject in order to experience genuine happiness and be free from suffering. While they long for happiness, they don't know how to accomplish it. They don't even recognize true objects of refuge; they don't know who can lead them from this endless cycle of suffering. So, for these reasons all sentient beings are objects of compassion. –

Now I shall discuss the generation of the Mahāyāna aspiration. Generally, in terms of aspirations, there are Hīnayāna and Mahāyāna aspirations. The first is the generation of the aspiration for enlightenment for the sake of your own peace and happiness, which entails a small-scale path. It is said, "The [aspirations of the] *śrāvakas* and *pratyekabuddhas*[27] are fundamental obstacles to the attainment of enlightenment"; and "Devoid of skillful means and lacking wisdom, you descend to the level of *śrāvakas*." They may attain the states of enlightenment corresponding to their own paths, but they cannot achieve ultimate enlightenment. So here it is necessary to strive to generate the Mahāyāna aspiration.

– The Hīnayāna, or individual vehicle, may be likened to a rickshaw. Desiring peace and happiness for yourself only will act as an obstacle to achieving the perfect enlightenment of a *buddha*. Such people can attain only the liberation of a *śrāvaka* or a *pratyekabuddha*. The *śrāvakas* do realize personal identitylessness, and the *pratyekabuddhas* gain a partial realization of phenomenal identitylessness. We, on the other hand, lack both of those realizations. We don't even really have insight into the Four Noble Truths or the Four Thoughts that Turn the Mind. We grasp tenaciously to the sense of "I," which is central to our whole existence. With this strong self-centeredness, we pretend to have virtues, while covering up our faults like a kitten covering up its poop. Doing that, we fail to accomplish our own goals, let alone the goals of others. This attitude—this reification of the self and placing the highest priority upon the self—is the source of all our problems. It is also the source of the vacillation that we experience—the constant vacillation from good times to bad times, the constant ups and downs. All of these are attributed to our self-grasping, self-cherishing mentality. -

Regarding the generation of the Mahāyāna aspiration, there are divisions in terms of its essence, its characteristics, its causes and conditions, and its numerous levels. First there is the division between the Mahāyāna relative spirit of awakening and the ultimate spirit of awakening. *The Sūtra on Unraveling the Intention* states:

> There are two kinds of the spirit of awakening: the ultimate spirit of awakening and the relative spirit of awakening.

[533] The characteristic of the Mahāyāna relative spirit of awakening is an awareness focused on achieving perfect enlightenment for the sake of others. *The Ornament for Higher Realization* states:

> The generated aspiration is for genuine, perfect enlightenment for the sake of others.

Many causes and conditions are taught, but in brief they are: faith in the *jinas* and *jinaputras*,[28] a compassionate mind, and being cared for by a spiritual friend. It is said:

> Its root is asserted to be compassion, which entails the constant thought to be of benefit.

The Jewel Meteor Spell Sūtra states:

> By having faith in the Jina and the Dharma of the Jina, faith in the way of life of the *bodhisattvas*, and faith in supreme enlightenment, the mind of the supreme beings arises.

There are twenty-two divisions, ranging from the earthlike spirit of awakening to the cloudlike spirit of awakening.[29] As *The Ornament for Higher Realization* states:

> Earth, gold, moon...there are twenty-two kinds.

[534] Alternatively, there are the three kinds of the spirit of awakening of conducting oneself with appreciation, the spirit of awakening of the pure extraordinary resolve, and the spirit of awakening of maturation, which eliminate obscurations. *The Ornament for the Sūtras* states:

> Three levels of the generated aspiration are asserted: appreciation, the pure extraordinary resolve, and the maturation. They eliminate obscurations.

Among the twenty-two divisions discussed in *The Ornament for Higher Realization*, the earthlike, goldlike, and moonlike spirit of awakening are the states of us beginners. *The Ornament for Higher Realization* states that the three mentioned types of spirit of awakening are brought forth by appreciation, and they occur at the stage of beginners.

– "Appreciation" in this context means being aware of the excellent qualities of the object of your appreciation. In other words, you've appreciated it for yourself, and have not just taken someone else's word for it. Then with appreciation based on understanding, you aspire to that object. Appreciation in this context is therefore more than blind faith, for it entails understanding of that for which one is striving. –

The best is the shepherdlike spirit of awakening, with which one resolves not to attain spiritual awakening oneself until all sentient beings have been brought to that state. This is like the spirit of awakening of Avalokiteśvara, and it is difficult. The helmsmanlike spirit of awakening is middling, and with it one resolves to attain spiritual awakening oneself together with all other sentient beings. The least is the kinglike spirit of awakening. Consider, "Since all sentient beings without exception have been my father and mother, [535] I must fulfill their needs, but I cannot do so now. Therefore, I resolve first to attain spiritual awakening myself, then without needing to apply effort, I shall serve the needs of all sentient beings by means of effortless, spontaneous, enlightened activities until the cycle of existence is empty." This is important.

It is said that by cultivating a relative spirit of awakening in that way, when the first *bodhisattva* level is reached, the ultimate spirit of awakening arises. And it is said in the Mahāmudrā and Dzogchen traditions that realization free of conceptual elaborations is the ultimate spirit of awakening. There is the spirit of aspiring for spiritual awakening and the spirit of venturing towards spiritual awakening. An extensive way of cultivating each of these separately is presented in the lineage stemming from Maitreya through Ācārya[30] Asaṅga. For this, one must have any of the kinds of vows of individual liberation, and the [*bodhisattva*] vows do not arise without having a spiritual friend who knows the collection of the *bodhisattva sūtras*. The ritual for taking the precepts of the spirit of aspiring for awakening and of venturing towards awakening simultaneously is presented in the lineage stemming from Mañjuśrī through Nāgārjuna and Śāntideva. In this tradition the vows may arise in anyone, so that is our present tradition. [536]

– According to the lineage stemming from Maitreya through Ācārya Asaṅga, one must have taken at least one of the vows of individual liberation, that is, at least one of the lay vows or monastic vows to take the *bodhisattva* vows. But according to the lineage stemming from Mañjuśrī through Nāgārjuna and Śāntideva, you may simultaneously take the vows of the spirit of aspiring for awakening and of venturing towards awakening, without a teacher being present and without having taken any precepts of individual liberation. –

As the basis for the spirit of awakening it is necessary to accumulate masses [of merit]. In the past, very wealthy *bodhisattvas* offered ten million temples and wish-fulfilling gems, then generated the spirit of awakening; and those lacking wealth offered discarded clothes and straw lamps, then generated the spirit of awakening. Those who had no possessions at all generated the spirit of awakening simply while pressing their palms together.

– Even if you are homeless and have nothing to offer, you always have your body, speech, and mind, which can be offered to the objects of refuge as you take the *bodhisattva* vows. –

The principal ways to accumulate masses of merit are the sevenfold devotion. (1) Imagine emanating your body as many times as there are atoms in the earth and making prostrations with each one. (2) Using the offerings you have laid out here simply as the basis of your visualization, imagine them to be of the nature of your bodies, possessions, and roots of virtue, in the aspect of the cloudlike offerings of Samantabhadra, filling the entire universe. Offer them to all the *buddhas* of the ten directions. (3) In their presence, disclose and confess all the sins and downfalls you have committed since the beginningless cycle of existence until now. (4) Meditate on rejoicing in all the roots of virtue performed [537] by *āryas* and ordinary beings. (5) To those who have manifestly attained spiritual awakening in other realms of the universe and who remain without teaching Dharma, request that they turn the Wheel of Dharma. (6) To all those who are about to pass away into *nirvāṇa*, request them not to do so. (7) Dedicate such virtue to achieving perfect spiritual awakening for the sake of all sentient beings. If you wish, at this point the teacher and students may recite a short prayer, but if not, there is no need.

– In America, there are some holy *lamas* who choose not to teach Dharma. In fact, there are two that readily come to mind. I don't know whether they are *buddhas* or not, but they are certainly very highly accomplished teachers. When asked to teach, they say, "No, no, no." When pressed, they answer that they already tried it and found it to be a waste of time. They report that while the students did seem to want to learn, after taking the *lama's* time, they didn't practice. So these *lamas* say, "What's the point? There's no reason to waste my time with these people. Those whom I thought had the greatest potential to practice Dharma were the greatest disappointment." So, instead of teaching, they live quietly, perhaps translating texts, but they are not inspired to teach. –

Now recite after me three times: "Whatever little virtue I have accumulated by means of prostrations, offerings, confession, rejoicing, beseeching, and requesting, I dedicate for the sake of everyone's great, perfect spiritual awakening."

Then following the preparatory ritual of the spirit of awakening, there is the main practice. "Having taken the Mahāyāna Three Jewels as their refuge, *bodhisattvas* of the past developed the spirit of aspiring for and venturing towards spiritual awakening. [538] Likewise, since all sentient beings have been my kind father and mother, I too shall bring forth the aspiration to enlightenment for their sakes." With that thought, recite three times after me: "All *buddhas* and *bodhisattvas* dwelling in the ten directions, please attend to me. Teacher, please attend to me. From this time until I reach the essence of enlightenment, I take refuge in the *buddhas*, and I likewise take refuge in the Dharma and the community of *bodhisattvas*. Just as the *sugatas*[31] of the past developed the spirit of awakening and gradually engaged in the practices of the *bodhisattvas*, likewise, in order to serve sentient beings I shall develop the spirit of awakening, and I shall gradually engage in the practices." Recognize that by reciting in that way three times, the vows of the spirit of awakening arise in you, and then say, "Well done."

The concluding task is taking delight in oneself. "Having attained a human body, it is significant that I have not died up to this point. By obtaining the vows of the spirit of awakening today—like an elixir that transforms iron into gold—I have taken birth in the family of the *buddhas*, [539] and I have become a child of the *buddhas*." With this thought, recite after me three times: "Now my life is fruitful. Human existence is well obtained. Today I have been born in the family of the *buddhas*, and I have become a child of the *buddhas*."

– Having taken the vows of the spirit of awakening, you've taken birth in the family of the *buddhas*; you've become a child of the *buddhas*. If you don't delight in that, then what do you take delight in? Having attained this human life imbued with ten types of endowment and the eight types of leisure, and having the opportunity in this life to take the vows of the spirit of awakening and to develop the spirit of awakening, you are in a position to make this life meaningful. –

If one expands on the practices associated with receiving those vows, there is much to be said, but to be concise: revere Mahāyāna spiritual mentors, avoid the four negative deeds, apply yourself to the four positive deeds, and do not mentally forsake sentient beings. Briefly stated, the practice of the aspiring spirit of awakening is to resolve to attain spiritual awakening for the sake of sentient beings. With this thought, recite after me: "Now by all means I shall engage in deeds that accord with this family, and I shall not contaminate this flawless, noble family."

– The four negative deeds are: lying to or deceiving one's spiritual mentor; discouraging others in their practice of virtue; out of anger speaking harsh words to a *bodhisattva*; and misleading sentient beings out of a motivation other than the extraordinary altruistic resolve to lead others from suffering. The four positive deeds to be followed are: avoiding lying even if in jest; instilling others with delight in their practice and guiding them towards the Mahāyāna path; looking upon all sentient beings as *buddhas*; dealing honestly with all sentient beings out of altruism. –

This is taking delight in others: "Today, in the presence of all the *buddhas*, I have promised to serve and bring about the happiness of all sentient beings until you all have been brought to the state of spiritual awakening. [540] So you deities in the sky and all you sentient beings who possess mental extrasensory perception, rejoice!" With this thought, repeat the following: "Today, in the presence of all the Protectors, I have invited sentient beings to experience joy until they reach the state of the *sugatas*. So *devas* and *asuras*,[32] rejoice."

Now repeat this prayer: "May the precious spirit of awakening arise in those in whom it has not yet arisen, may it not decline in those in whom it has arisen, and may it grow greater and greater. May we not be separated from the spirit of awakening, may we enter the *bodhisattva* way of life, may we be cared for by the *buddhas*, and may we also be free of the deeds of Māra.[33] May the intentions of the *bodhisattvas* to serve sentient beings be fulfilled. May sentient beings receive whatever the Protectors intend. May sentient beings have happiness. May the miserable states of existence always be empty. Wherever the *bodhisattvas* dwell, may all their prayers be fulfilled." [541]

By those means the vows of the spirit of awakening are received. This is the training: "Not forsaking sentient beings, bearing in mind the benefits of the spirit of awakening, accumulating the two collections, again and again cultivating the spirit of awakening, following the four positive actions and avoiding the four negative actions—those five comprise the training of the spirit of aspiring for spiritual awakening."

The training of the spirit of venturing towards awakening is chiefly comprised of three trainings, and they are included in the Six Perfections. So if one takes those as one's vows, they are: "Generosity, ethical discipline, patience, enthusiasm, meditative stabilization, and wisdom—those six comprise the training of the spirit of venturing towards awakening."

According to the Cittamātra tradition there are four defeatlike actions and forty-four secondary faults. According to the Madhyamaka tradition, for those of sharp faculties there are eighteen vows for kings, ministers, and so on. For those of middling faculties there are four vows, and for those of dull faculties, there is one vow. *The Advice to a King Sūtra* states:

> Great King, you [542] have so many activities and so much work, you may not be able at all times and in all ways to practice the perfections from generosity to wisdom. Therefore, great King, whether you are walking, getting up, sitting, lying down, waking up, or eating, constantly bear in mind and cultivate the aspiration, faith, yearning, and longing for genuine, perfect enlightenment. Take delight in the virtues of others. Having done so, make offerings to all the *buddhas, bodhisattvas, śrāvakas,* and *pratyekabuddhas*. Having done so, treat all sentient beings in the same way. Then, so that all sentient beings may be complete in all the qualities of the Buddha, dedicate this each day to supreme enlightenment.
>
> Great King, if you do that, you may also rule your kingdom, and your royal duties will not fall into decline. The collections towards enlightenment will also be perfected.

– This is advice to a king who is trying both to rule his kingdom and to apply himself to spiritual practice. One of the great kings of ancient Tibet, Songtsen Gampo, did both. In the present, His Holiness the Dalai Lama not only leads the Tibetan government-in-exile, but is utterly dedicated to spiritual practice. Due to dedicating their lives to altruistic service, both King Songtsen Gampo and His Holiness the Dalai Lama are free of hatred and attachment. –

Therefore, it is [543] important for those of you who are educated to practice those *bodhisattva* trainings. Uneducated people find it difficult to understand them, and that is the basic reason why *geshes*[34] travel to the monastic universities in central and western Tibet and spend their lives studying Madhyamaka and the perfection of wisdom. Those topics are difficult to understand, and the explanation of them is very elaborate. Nevertheless, this does not mean you may discard them, for this is the root of the Mahāyāna Dharma. Without this, no matter how good your practice is, you succumb to the pitfall of the Hīnayāna *śrāvakas* and *pratyekabuddhas*. Without this, it is as if you were farming without planting any seeds, so you will not obtain the fruition of spiritual awakening.

– In order to practice *bodhisattva* trainings first you must study and practice the Four Immeasurables—love, compassion, empathetic joy, and equanimity—as well as the Six Perfections. The first five of the Six Perfections—generosity through meditative stabilization—serve as the cause for the sixth, which is the perfection of wisdom. Actually wisdom is there from the beginning. Understanding what is to be avoided and what is to be followed is an expression of wisdom. But the first five Perfections act as the basis for the realization of emptiness, or ultimate truth.

In Tibet there have been many uneducated, illiterate people. Here in the West almost everyone is literate, and so people not only know how to recite the *sādhanas*, but have the potential to understand them as well. Over the years, many books on Buddhism have been translated into English and are readily accessible. I encourage you to study them and apply what you learn, rather than wasting your time with other kinds of books that are of no benefit at all.

"Geshe" literally means "spiritual friend," but it's also the title of a person who has earned a degree in Buddhist monastic education. There have been many such highly educated people in Buddhist history, some from India, such as the great Atiśa, and in Tibet there have been many from each of the four spiritual orders of Nyingma, Kagyü, Geluk, and Sakya. The strategy that each followed was to first seek out a genuine spiritual mentor. Those who engaged in the formal monastic training commonly spent years in debate. Many of you probably have seen films or witnessed such debate for yourselves, with much hand clapping, jumping around, and shouting to critique and defend positions. That isn't for exercise, but rather serves to gain an understanding of the Six Perfections. First by studying and then by debating each point, a thorough and critical understanding is gained.

There are many advantages in such an approach. People in monastic universities spend years casting off all mundane concerns and activities, while applying themselves single-pointedly many hours a day to such education. They saturate their minds with these elements of Dharma—discussing and trying to gain understanding. There are many advantages to this—especially if you have a long life, because this education takes many years to complete. This conceptual, theoretical training must be followed by single-pointed practice. It's not enough, of course, simply to gain intellectual understanding. First, you gain theoretical understanding and then you must apply it in practice. This is the method that leads to enlightenment, not intellectual understanding alone.

For centuries, in the Tibetan tradition, there have been two types of Dharma settings. One is monastic colleges, where theoretical study and debate take place—the first two of the three stages of hearing, thinking, and meditation. The other is meditation centers, which were originally set up for those who had completed their theoretical training and were now ready to devote themselves to single-pointed practice.

If you haven't first heard and pondered the teachings, what do you have to meditate on? Such training centers have been reestablished in India by the Tibetan refugees. In Tibet this tradition for those *lamas* and monks who have survived is beginning once again to flourish. This simply shows that the qualities that are developed in such practice cannot be destroyed physically. The material of the buildings can be destroyed, but the qualities developed in the heart and mind cannot be destroyed, so the Dharma still flourishes. –

If the benefits of this were present as form, the sky would not hold it. Even when you are sitting doing nothing, your merit continues to grow. Since you have become a child of the *buddhas*, you become an object of homage for the world's gods and humans. *The Questions of Śūradatta Sūtra* states:

> If the merit of the spirit of awakening were to take on form, [544]
> it would fill the whole of space, and extend even beyond that.

A Guide to the Bodhisattva Way of Life states:

> When the spirit of awakening has arisen, in an instant a wretch who is bound in the prison of the cycle of existence is called a child of the *sugatas* and becomes worthy of reverence in the worlds of gods and humans.[35]
>
> From that moment on, an uninterrupted stream of merit, equal to the sky, constantly arises even when one is asleep or distracted.[36]

The training of this boils down to one point: Consider, "Whatever virtue I commit, be it great or small, I shall do so not for my own sake alone but for the sake of all sentient beings. And in the future, in order to serve all sentient beings, I shall manifestly become a *buddha*. In order to become enlightened swiftly and without troubles and obstacles, by means of the roots of virtue accomplished today, as soon as I pass away from this life may I be born in the pure realm of Sukhāvatī."

[545] If you know it, recite *The Sukhāvatī Prayer* and dedication and so on. Even if you do not know it, every night say, "May I be reborn in Sukhāvatī." All the practices are included in that.

On the contrary, if you perform virtue just for your own sake, this is incompatible with the vows of the spirit of awakening, so this is a great fault. As it is said:

> Upon making such a promise, if I do not put it into action, then having deceived those sentient beings, what destiny shall I have?[37]

– If you make the promise that you will attain enlightenment for the benefit of all sentient beings and then do nothing about it, you are tricking all sentient beings and deceiving all the *buddhas*. This is a great big lie. So then, what kind of future life will you have? –

Moreover, to take birth in Sukhāvatī, this development of the spirit of awakening is important. *The Splendor of Amitābha Sūtra, The Splendor of Sukhāvatī Sūtra*, and so on state that upon developing the spirit of awakening and making prayers of supplication, one will be born in that pure realm; but they do not say that one will be born there without prayer. The focus of this meditation is solely that of love, compassion, "sending and receiving."

– The practice of "sending and receiving," called "tonglen" in Tibetan, includes the cultivation of the Four Immeasurables: love, compassion, empathetic joy, and equanimity –

Upon receiving the vows of refuge and the spirit of awakening in this way, your practice of refuge and the spirit of awakening will always be complete, [546] and all practices of the stages of generation and completion and all recitation of *mantras* will be like towers erected on a firm foundation; and they will lead you further on the path. Without this, they may merely protect you from dangers, but they will not lead you on the path to enlightenment; so this is important.

– Without refuge and the spirit of awakening, you can perform rituals or ask others to perform various rituals, *mantra* recitations and so forth, to help with various obstacles you may be having. Indeed, this might help you, but these tantric practices will not lead to enlightenment. They will just counteract certain temporary problems. For this reason, refuge and the spirit of awakening are crucial.

Right after giving teachings on refuge and the spirit of awakening, the *lama* often consoles students by saying, "If you can, develop a genuine the spirit of awakening. If you can't, at least develop a kind heart." In response many people think, "Oh, good, I already have that." What makes you think so? Just because you are nice to your children? Dogs are nice to their pups. Lions, tigers, and rattlesnakes care for their young. So that's not so special, is it? In fact, many people are nice to just a few people, but not to everyone. That is basically an expression of attachment. A kind heart must extend to all sentient beings. That is what is meant by altruism: you wish that all sentient beings may be well. –

This concludes the teachings on the vows of refuge and the spirit of awakening.

CHAPTER TWO

Narratives of Actions and Their Consequences

Homage to Avalokiteśvara!

[548] These profound practical instructions of Avalokiteśvara on causal actions and their effects are a method for abandoning the sufferings of the miserable states of existence. In these narratives, I shall give concise explanations of the meaning of the expositions in the *sūtras*, for they can be understood easily by ordinary people.

Long ago in the city of Khamgya there lived a wealthy merchant who every year killed many of his cattle to make sacrificial offerings of them. When he was on the verge of death, as his last testament he instructed his son to do likewise; and his son did so year after year. On one occasion, as a cow was being led to the slaughter, it let out a great bellow. An *arhat*[38] witnessed this with a sense of sadness and wonder. [549] "What is it?" someone asked him, and the *arhat* replied quietly, "That cow that is to be slaughtered was previously the wealthy merchant who every year slaughtered cattle for sacrificial offerings and whose final wish was that this practice be continued. He was reborn as a cow belonging to his own family. Now is the seventh time he is to be slaughtered as such."

The monk spoke to the beast, saying, "The basis for this is something you initiated yourself. The sacrificial offering was something you performed yourself, thereby killing many cattle. So now what's the point of your loud bellowing?" Having slaughtered many cows, he was born as cows belonging to his own family, [550] where he was slaughtered over and over again.

– This chapter consists of a series of concise accounts pertaining to *karma,* actions and and their ethical consequences, drawing from a number of narratives in the *sūtras.* Because the narratives are very straightforward, they don't really need any commentary; by just reading them, you will understand them.

These stories were narrated by Karma Chagmé Rinpoche, but each one can be traced back to the Buddha's speech. Many people in the past have accepted them as being valid and have been guided in virtue on the basis of them. They're here for our use.

Even in these times, some people think that certain types of killing can be virtuous and actually a part of spiritual practice. In Buddhism, the act of killing is said to be negative. Although killing is generally a harmful deed, out of compassion and wisdom a highly realized *bodhisattva* may see that other people will be protected by killing a particular person. Over and above being of benefit to others, it will also benefit the person being killed because this great *bodhisattva* may have the ability to direct the consciousness of the killed person to a pure land, where he will experience great bliss and spiritual unfolding.

When a great *bodhisattva* kills someone, of course, that person will experience pain and suffering. However through this experience, he will be able to purify unwholesome *karma* that has been accumulated. Then, by offering one's own flesh, bone and so forth, the dying person is able to accrue merit. With that purification and merit, the *bodhisattva* is able to send that individual's consciousness to a pure land where he experiences great well-being.

Having said that, for people like ourselves, who are still subject to the mental afflictions, including the three poisons, killing is unquestionably unwholesome. If we kill others, people like us will go down to the miserable states of existence as a result of our deed. This cycle can be perpetuated for many eons.

What allows great *bodhisattvas* to kill? One factor is that they are not killing either from anger or attachment; they have only one motivation for engaging in killing: compassion. Today, some doctors engage in euthanasia, killing people whom they believe have terminal diseases. This raises a number of questions. Is the motivation of these physicians pure compassion? I really can't judge, on the one hand, but this kind of killing is very suspect. Only a *buddha* can size up another person with confidence.

A great *bodhisattva* may take the life of another through a ritual meditation involving a *phurba.*[39] When this is done, the adept then purifies the mind-stream of the being who is about to be killed by the ray of light that issues forth from the *phurba.* For ourselves, if we think another person needs to be put out of his or her misery, we would need to ask ourselves: Do we have this implement and the ability to use it? Can we actually transmute the person's body into the five fleshes and the five ambrosias, as is to be done in this practice?

One might think that suicide doesn't harm anybody else so it should be okay. But the problem is that in committing suicide you've destroyed your own precious human life of leisure and endowment. Moreover, you set up a pattern that once initiated tends to repeat itself for up to 500 lifetimes. Then lifetime, after lifetime, after lifetime, you will fall into this same tendency to commit suicide. –

The effects of an action may ripen in other lifetimes following this life. For example, long ago, when people could live for countless years, there was a son of a ship's captain, named Yajña, who set out on a voyage to find jewels. His mother, however, objected and would not let him go. Kicking her in the head, he went anyway. Fearing that he would not be able avoid problems resulting from his deed, he took the eight lay precepts, and he set out to sea with five hundred companions. But they were shipwrecked and the others perished. The captain's son clung to a copper globe and drifted over the sea. Eventually he arrived at a city, like an abode of gods, with a golden wall, where he was taken in hand by four goddesses. Here he experienced happiness and delight for many hundreds and thousands of years.

Eventually he left, and in a city with a silver wall he was cared for by eight goddesses and experienced happiness and delight for hundreds and thousands of years. Again he departed, and in a city with a lapis lazuli wall he was cared for by sixteen goddesses and experienced happiness and delight for hundreds and thousands of years. Again he went on his way, and in a city with a crystal wall he was looked after by thirty-two goddesses [551] and experienced happiness and delight for many hundreds and thousands of years. Upon departing from there he came to a forest of thorn trees with an iron wall. There he found a man whose head was being gashed by a revolving wheel of swords. This man asked him, "This is a minor hell. What did you do that made you arrive here?" When he had told his story, it appeared that they had both engaged in similar conduct. His experience of happiness and delight on the way to this hell was due to his keeping the eight lay precepts, while his being gashed on the head by swords was a penalty for kicking his mother in the head. "As soon as I heard the sound of you, my sin was exhausted. You come to my bed and listen," he said, and he passed away. Then the captain's son was afraid, and he meditated on love and compassion with the visualization of "sending and receiving." He paid homage to his father and mother and prayed that in all his lifetimes he would honor his parents. His mother also performed virtuous deeds and dedicated them to her son. As a result, he remained in that minor hell for a bit less than sixty years, with the wheel revolving just above his head. [552] Then he passed away, and even though the wheel did not touch his head, occasionally he would have headaches. It is said that this captain's son later became the Teacher Śākyamuni himself.

Thus, honoring the Three Jewels, parents, and teachers is said to be very important. The Lord said, "There should be no difference between the way you treat me and the ways you treat your parents, abbots, and teachers. The consequences of your behavior do not diminish in this or later lifetimes."

If you make a gift and later regret it, even if you are reborn into affluence you will later become impoverished. Long ago there was a youth named Drakpa who offered a calf to the Buddha Lokpa Detsel and his Saṅgha, then later felt regret for doing so. In all his rebirths he was first rich and later became poor. Eventually he took birth in Rājagṛha, and as soon as he was born, his mother died. People said he was born under an evil star, and he was taken out and left with corpses in a cemetery. [553] As a result of his offering the calf, milk flowed from the breasts of one of the corpses and he did not die. Later on, he took monastic ordination with Buddha Śākyamuni and achieved liberation.

Even when one's life is over, one's *karma* is not. Even if one passes from one life to another among the six states of existence, one is born again where one had lived previously. In Śrāvastī there was a poor householder who died with attachment for his household. He took rebirth as a worm on a hump-backed bull belonging to that household, and as soon as he was born, a crow ate him. He took rebirth and was eaten in that way seven times.

While going for alms in Magadha, Maudgalyāyana came upon a householder holding a child on his lap, eating a fish, and throwing the remains to a black female dog. "I don't have any alms to give you," he said. The fish was the householder's father in his previous life. Due to being a fisherman, his father was reborn many times as a fish and was killed and eaten. The female dog was his mother, who neither engaged in acts of generosity nor kept her precepts. Clinging onto her wealth and family lineage, she died with attachment [554] and was born again and again as the watchdog of that household, where she watched over and guarded the house. His child had previously been his enemy, who killed his father for the sake of his wife. Due to his attachment to that woman, he took birth in her womb. That is the account told by Maudgalyāyana illustrating how the cycle of existence is devoid of essence.

Long ago there was a magistrate in the court of a king, who acted as an official witness for loan transactions in that region.[40] The son [of the magistrate's brother] made a large loan to someone, who gave a bribe to the magistrate's wife [so that he could avoid repaying the loan]. The wife, in turn, persuaded the official to allow this. The two people involved in the loan met with the magistrate, and he lied, saying there was no need to repay the loan, and he did not make him pay it back. As a consequence of that, the magistrate was first born in hell, then for five hundred lifetimes he was born as a hulk of flesh with no eyes, ears, or other sense faculties.

In Śrāvastī there was a wealthy householder whose possessions [upon his death] were about to go to the king, but he had a son born with male genitals, [555] but with no sense organs, just empty sockets and a mouth. The boy lived, so the king did not get the householder's possessions. The Lord was asked how that happened, and he said it was due to circumstances in a previous life. That official liked to be generous, so he always was born into affluence, but due to telling a lie, he was born with incomplete sense faculties.

Long ago, thirty-two people stole a bull and took it to an old woman's house. The bull knew it was to be killed, and it prayed, "May you be killed!" The bull was slaughtered, and together with the old woman, those people ate it. Later on, the old woman bought some incense, mixed it with butter, and with her thirty-two companions anointed a *stūpa* with it. They prayed that in all their rebirths they would be born as mother and sons, with long lives, high standing, and wealth. That virtue and sin ripened individually. In all their lifetimes they were born just as they prayed, but five hundred times the being that had been the bull killed them all simultaneously. [556]

Once in Śrāvastī there was a king named Prasenajit who had a minister by the name of Kuraṅga. The youngest of the seven sons of the minister had a wife named Anurādhā, an intelligent woman who also found favor with the king. She gave birth to thirty-two eggs which turned into thirty-two strong and valiant sons. Another minister maliciously started a rumor that they were going to assassinate the king, so the king sent out some powerful men who murdered them all at the same time. From the Lord Anurādhā took full ordination as a nun. It is said that the king was a reincarnation of the bull, the mother was the old woman, and the thirty-two sons were the thieves. Such are the consequences of killing one bull.

Long ago there was a wealthy man who had no son, so he took a second wife who bore him one. His first wife stabbed the boy with a needle and killed him. She denied murdering him, and took a false oath to that effect.[41] [557] On another occasion she made an offering to a *pratyekabuddha,* and upon seeing him fly in the sky, she felt reverence and devotion. She prayed, "May I become like you!"

Having murdered the boy, she was reborn in miserable states of existence and experienced tremendous suffering. Later, she took birth as a fine woman in Śrāvastī who married and had two sons. Her husband was killed by a poisonous snake, one of her sons was swept away by a river, and the other was eaten by a wolf. Her parents' household went up in flames, and all her relatives were consumed in the fire. Eventually she took up with another man and had a son. That husband became intoxicated, killed his son, and forced his wife to eat his flesh. Grief-stricken, she ran away, and met another man whose wife had died. She took up with him, but he died. According to the custom of that region, she was buried in the cemetery together with her husband's corpse. A thief dug up her grave, took her away, and made her his wife, [558] but the law caught up with him, and he was executed by the king. Again she was buried in the cemetery with his corpse. This time a wolf dug up her grave, but she escaped, met the Lord and took ordination. Even after she attained the state of an *arhat,* she suffered pain as if a burning iron spoon were piercing her from the crown of her head to the soles of her feet; and she continually complained loudly of the pain. That was the residual *karma* of stabbing the boy with a needle, and the fact that she was widowed so many times was due to her evil, false oath. Her attainment of the state of an *arhat* was due to her worship of the *pratyekabuddha,* and each of these actions ripened in one life.

Long ago, during the time of the Buddha Vipaśyin, ten thousand monks attained the fruition of the path.[42] While they were living in the wilderness, some merchants offered them a jewel, turning it over to a monk who served the monastic community. Later on, when food became scarce, they considered selling the jewel, but the monk who received it countered, "This was given to me, not to all of us!" When he was told the truth of the matter, he insisted, "This is mine. You eat shit!"

As soon as he passed away, he was reborn in a great hell, [559] and for ninety-one eons he took birth into sewage, and he was repeatedly reborn into sewage during the times of many *buddhas* of the past. Then he took birth in a small lake as a large creature, similar to a snake, but with four limbs and a human mouth and eyes. This lake was putrid, for all the people in the adjacent city, which was in the region of Vulture's Peak, disposed of their sewage into it. There he was bitten by many small insects, which attacked him as they darted above and beneath him in the lake. As they moved about, the stench of human filth spread. For many tens of thousands of years he died and was reborn there. It is said that he must remain there until all the one thousand *buddhas* [of the present cycle of *buddhas*] have come and gone. That is in the "Chapter on the Monk Kyunte."[43]

Countless eons ago, in the region of Vārāṇasī, a man exchanged all his possessions for gold, which he hid in seven pots.[44] Eventually, when he was on the verge of death, he could not get his mind off his treasure, and he was reborn as a snake who protected that gold. After many years, the city fell into ruins and became a wasteland, but he still repeatedly took birth as a snake. [560] Once when a man approached, the snake called out to him, "I have gold. Use it to make a feast for the Saṅgha! On the day that you do so, invite me, too. If you fail to do so, I'll make you sorry!" The man took one golden pot with him and sold it. On the day that he made a feast for the Saṅgha, he took a reed basket to bring the snake along. The Saṅgha taught Dharma to the snake, and it offered the other six pots of gold, and he still took birth as a snake. It is said that the snake eventually became Śāriputra and that man who offered the gold for him became the Teacher (Śākyamuni).

During the time of the Buddha Kāśyapa, there was an old monk *arhat* with an ugly voice and a youth with a pleasant voice who were practicing chanting together. The youth complained, "Your chanting is like the barking of a dog." "Don't say that," the old monk replied, "I am an *arhat*." The youth regretted his words and confessed, but he still took rebirth five hundred times as a dog. Eventually he was born as a dog in Śrāvastī, where a merchant's son broke its leg and abandoned it in an isolated place. [561] Śāriputra gave the dog food and taught it Dharma; and after it passed away, it took birth as a brahmin's son who took the novice monastic ordination from Śāriputra and became an *arhat*.

The preceding have been narratives concerning the disadvantages of nonvirtue. I shall now synthesize the meaning of *The Sūtra of the Wise and the Foolish* concerning the advantages of virtue.

– The point of these narratives is that we should not disregard even the smallest of nonvirtues, but instead do our best to abstain from any negative action whatsoever. After we have attained enlightenment, we will have the freedom to serve sentient beings in whatever way we find necessary. Until then, we are the sentient beings who need to be led to enlightenment. We need to avoid nonvirtue because it not only produces suffering, but obstructs our own path to enlightenment. Bear in mind that a single nonvirtue, even a small one, can give rise to long-lasting and severe results, as we've seen in these narratives. Such deeds are like a single match which can reduce an entire forest to ashes. Likewise, even a single burst of anger can destroy the virtue of many lifetimes. So be careful!

Just as any type of nonvirtue of the body, speech, or mind—great or small—can lead to dire consequences, so can even small virtues lead to great results. Therefore, do not ignore even the most insignificant of virtues. –

Long ago, at the end of the era of the Buddha Kāśyapa, there were two brahmins who undertook an *upavāsa* fast. One of them prayed to be reborn as a king, and his prayer was fulfilled. The other prayed to be reborn as a god, but that evening his wife persuaded him to have dinner, and he was reborn as a *nāga*. That king had a watchman who guarded the fence around his orchard. On one occasion the watchman discovered an enormous, sweet fruit that emerged from a spring, and he turned it over to the king's guardsman, who presented it to the queen, and she then offered it to the king. The king inquired about it and demanded, "Let the person who found this bring me many more like it! If he does not, [562] he shall be executed!" The man wept and waited by the spring, so the *nāga* magically appeared as a human and asked what was wrong. Once the story was told, the *nāga* brought a tub-full of fruit and sent this message to the king: "O King, you and I were friends. You purely maintained your *upavāsa* fast, so you took birth as a king, while my fast was blemished, so I took birth as a *nāga*. Give me a copy of the eightfold *upavāsa* fast. If you don't, I will turn this region into a lake and wipe it out."

"As the Buddhist doctrine has fallen into decline, such a copy is not to be found," replied the king, but he commanded his ministers, "Look for it. If you don't find one, you will be executed!" A minister asked an old man, who replied, "There is a pillar of a certain house that constantly emits light, so look there." The pillar was split open, and *The Sūtra on Dependent Origination* and a copy of the eight one-day precepts was found inside. The king put them inside a small golden box and sent it to the *nāga*. The *nāga* was delighted and offered the king many jewels. [563] The *nāga* and the king kept the *upavāsa* fast and also encouraged others to do so, as a result of which they were both reborn as gods. Upon coming to meet Śākyamuni, they listened to the Dharma and thus attained the fruition of stream-entry. Never again did they fall to any of the miserable states of existence, and they experienced the joy and happiness of gods and humans. It was prophesied that finally they will attain liberation. That is from the third chapter entitled "The Mendicant Keeps the Precepts."[45]

Countless eons ago, King Brahmadatta and his retinue went to a pleasure grove, and behind its enclosure a man was singing in a loud voice. Enraged, the king had him imprisoned and prepared to execute him. One of his ministers, however, encouraged the king not to execute the man, but rather make him his servant. Eventually he took monastic ordination and became a *pratyekabuddha*. The minister made devotions to him and prayed, as a result of which in all his rebirths he was invariably born into a prestigious and wealthy family, or as a long-lived god, or was born with an exceptionally fine human body. Eventually he [564] was reborn as the son of a wealthy, but childless, merchant and his wife. His father would not let him take monastic ordination. So the boy thought, "If I were to take rebirth into a low class of society, I would be allowed to become a monk," and threw himself off a high boulder. But he landed unscathed. He then jumped into a river, but he did not drown; and he took a deadly poison, but without effect. Since he had broken the king's law, three times the king had arrows shot at him, but they fell to the ground.

The king told him, "You must be a god or a demon!" When the boy explained why he wanted to die, the king gave him permission to become a monk. He then took monastic ordination in the presence of Buddha Śākyamuni and became an *arhat*. Thus, due to saving a life, wherever that minister was born, nothing could shorten his life; and finally he attained the state of an *arhat*.

Ninety-one eons ago, a poor man sold some wood for two gold coins, which he offered to Buddha Kanakamuni and his Saṅgha. As a result, for ninety-one eons he was born as a human being, and [565] wherever he took birth, he was born with gold coins in his hands. He was always wealthy and his prosperity was unending. Eventually he took birth in Rājagṛha as the son of a woman householder. The infant was astonishingly beautiful, and he was born with his fists clenched. Upon opening his fists, it was found that he was holding two gold coins, and even when they were removed, more gold coins continually reappeared so that they filled a storeroom. Later on, he took monastic ordination in the presence of the Buddha, became an *arhat*, and came to be known as the monk Golden Ornament.

Long ago, during the era of Buddha Kanakamuni, there was a poor man who served as a janitor for the Saṅgha due to his faith. Gathering flowers from a meadow, he cast them towards the Saṅgha and offered prayers. As a result, for ninety-one eons, wherever he was born, he had a fine and beautiful form, and he enjoyed excellent food, drink, and material possessions. Eventually he was born in Śrāvastī as the son of a great and prestigious householder. His form was extraordinarily attractive [566], and as soon as he was born, a shower of celestial flowers fell from the sky. So he was named Kusumadeva.[46] Later on, the son invited Śākyamuni and his retinue and worshiped them. In his home, jeweled cushions and food all manifested simply by his thinking of them. Then he became a monk and attained the state of an *arhat*. Thus it is said that one should not disregard even a small gift, thinking there is no merit in it.

Long ago, during the era of Buddha Kanakamuni, there was a householder who made devotions to each member of the Saṅgha. Rejoicing in this, a poor man took a handful of white pebbles, imagining them to be jewels, and cast them towards the Saṅgha while offering a prayer. As a result, for ninety-one eons he spontaneously acquired jewels, food, clothing, and possessions. Then he took birth in Śrāvastī as the son of a householder, and as soon as he was born, a shower of the seven precious substances fell from the sky, filling his house. Thus the boy was named Devaratna. Eventually he became a monk and attained the state of an *arhat* in the presence of Śākyamuni. [567]

Long ago, when the Buddha called Protector of Merit[47] was alive, there was a Buddhist monk who traveled everywhere encouraging people to practice virtue.[48] At that time there was a woman named

Daniśka who was extremely poor and destitute. Her husband and she had but one piece of cloth to wear for the two of them. They would alternate wearing it so that whenever one went outside, he or she would wear it, leaving the other one naked. While in such circumstances, the monk spoke to the woman of the benefits of generosity, and with the agreement of her husband, they offered their cloth; and the two of them remained naked in hiding. The monk offered the cloth to the Buddha, who, taking the smelly cloth in hand, declared, "This is the only utterly pure act of generosity." The king and queen removed their own clothing and ornaments from their bodies and sent them to the poor couple. The man and his wife came and listened to the Dharma from the Buddha. Then for ninety-one eons wherever they took birth, they were born with clothing and were very prosperous. Eventually she took birth in Śrāvasti as an extraordinarily beautiful daughter of a woman householder. [568] Since she was born wearing a lovely white cloth, she was named Śuci. As the girl grew up, her clothing also increased in size, and she wore no other garment. Eventually she took ordination as a nun in the presence of Śākyamuni, and her cloth turned into all the garments of a Buddhist nun. Eventually she attained the state of an *arhat*.

Long ago in the land of Apadeva there lived a very prosperous householder who was avaricious and merciless.[49] He had an old woman servant who worked her whole life but lacked clothing to cover her body, and she never had enough food to eat. Once when she was carrying water, she cried out loud as she thought, "Now I have no food or clothing. I am so old, but still I must work, and I can't die!" On that occasion Ārya Katyāyāna came along and asked, "Will you sell me your poverty and your misery?"

"How can I do that?" she asked.

"Wash yourself, and offer me a bowl full of water," he replied, and she did so. [569] He made a prayer of dedication for this offering, gave her a single instruction on spiritual practice, and told her to recite the name of the Buddha.

Eventually she passed away and took birth as a goddess in the Heaven of the Thirty-three. Then that goddess together with a retinue of five hundred made offerings at the burial site of the old woman. The people of that region witnessed this and asked why it was being done. They were then told the old woman's story. Those celestial beings received Dharma teachings from Katyāyāna, and each one of them attained fruition.

Long ago, following the *nirvāṇa* of the Buddha Vipaśyin, some householders were making devotions to many Buddhist monks.[50] A poor man and his wife wept for they had nothing to offer. The woman said, "Let's look around in [your parents'] storeroom, and if there is the tiniest thing there, let's offer it." Upon searching around, they found a single gold coin, which they put inside a pot. They then filled the pot with clean water, covered it with a mirror, and offered it. Due to that virtue, they both took birth as gods in the Heaven of the Thirty-three [570]; and for ninety-one eons, wherever they were born, they were golden in color and endowed with extraordinary beauty; and they were wonderfully prosperous. Eventually one took birth in Śrāvastī as a golden-colored son of a wealthy householder, and the other as a similarly beautiful girl in the region of Campa. As soon as they were born, springs began to flow in their homes; and upon scooping up the water, it turned into jewels, food, and clothing according to their heart's desire. Eventually the two married, invited the Buddha as their guest, and listened to the Dharma from him. Both then took monastic ordination and became *arhats*. He was the monk Suvarṇadeva [and she was the nun Suvarṇaprabhā]. Such was the merit of the small act of generosity of those poor people.

– *The Sūtra of the Wise and the Foolish* mentions in more detail that the mirror was one of the wife's few possessions, so, this together with the gold coin was offered to the Saṅgha. As a monk, he was named Suvarṇadeva, literally the God of Gold, and she was the nun Suvarṇaprabhā, meaning Golden Light.

From these narratives and other sources, we can see that long ago, there were various regions in this world which were extraordinarily prosperous. They were filled with bounty, great happiness, prosperity and felicity, and some of these places still exist, though it seems they are becoming fewer and fewer. It also seems that there were other regions that were utterly miserable, where people were surrounded by enemies, famine, drought, war, and plague. We may well ask, together with the people living in such circumstances, Why do they have to suffer so much? Are they being punished for something they've done in the past?

What creates such circumstances of felicity and adversity, whether for individuals or whole societies? The answer is *karma*. It is our own actions either in this or in previous lifetimes. It is *karma* that creates nations. It's *karma*—our actions, our behavior—that creates national situations, environmental situations, as well as personal situations.

You may regard these teachings on *karma* as alien or foreign, but this is a mistake. In fact, the teachings on *karma* pertain to all honorable and dishonorable actions, to virtue and nonvirtue, and the truth of these assertions is not simply contingent upon one society as opposed to another.

In this present phase of history many countries have deemed it acceptable for mothers and fathers to kill their unborn children. What *karma* is involved there? The aborted fetus is experiencing the result of its own actions of killing in some previous lifetime, and this *karma* has not yet been exhausted. Therefore, they still must experience the consequences of their having killed.

When hearing of abortions or other people being killed for any reason, one may complacently conclude that this is simply their *karma*, so they are getting their just rewards. While it is true that such death comes as a consequence of their own actions, probably in previous lives, if we are the ones doing the killing, there is no way we can justify our acts.

If we kill others, we will then experience the consequences of our actions. Therefore, there's no way to justify our killing on the grounds that it's the other's *karma*. In some countries people tend to eat just about anything—bugs, reptiles, mammals, and anything else that moves. This attitude—"If it moves, kill it and eat."—leads only to rebirth as the very creatures that are killed and devoured. Such people will be among their own victims as they experience the consequences of their actions.

In many countries where hunting animals as a sport is accepted, people kill deer with high-powered rifles and then boast about having "bagged" a certain number of their victims, even showing pictures of themselves standing by their prey, as if they had done something extraordinarily heroic. But what courage does this take?

The precept of not killing, which is included among the *upāsaka* vows, or lay precepts, refers to the intentional killing of living beings, including humans and those who are in the process of becoming human; so it includes killing an embryo or fetus. Therefore, especially if one has taken these precepts, one should be extremely cautious about killing a human being, either born or unborn.

The second of the three physical nonvirtues is taking that which is not given, or stealing. Engaging in this nonvirtue entails taking something which has not been given to you and which has an owner. You can do it by trickery or deceit. You can do it by just quietly filching something, or you can do it by robbing someone at gunpoint. There are various ways of doing this, but they all boil down to taking that which is not given, or stealing. The karmic consequence of such an action is poverty and generally meeting with no success. Or, even if one has a little success, it will fade away.

When people have this experience, they feel that they have done everything needed to succeed, but regardless of how hard they strive, success eludes them; and they wonder how could this be happening to them. They think, "I have done everything right and I'm still not succeeding." There's no need to be confused. Poverty and failure come as a result of one's previous actions. Now, one is simply experiencing the consequences of one's own deeds.

The third of the three physical nonvirtues is sexual misconduct. This refers primarily to adultery, or engaging in sexual intercourse with someone else's spouse. But it also includes engaging in sexual intercourse in the presence of representations of the Buddha, such as a shrine room or temple, or in the presence of one's spiritual mentor. It is considered sexual misconduct to have sexual intercourse with a woman who is ill. If you're wondering about the consequences of sexual misconduct, just look around. Modern Western society reveals many of the consequences of sexual misconduct, such as the high percentage of marriages ending in divorce. When couples try to explain why they are breaking up, each spouse always thinks it's the other's fault, but in reality it is often the consequence of their own sexual misconduct, either in this or previous lives.

Although Buddhism has a lot to say about ethics, we should primarily focus on avoiding the ten nonvirtues of killing, stealing, sexual misconduct, lying, abuse, slander, idle gossip, avarice, malice, and holding to false views. It is also best to avoid taking alcohol or any intoxicating substance including drugs that can alter the mind. By becoming intoxicated, you can easily break your precepts or engage in other nonvirtues; so for that reason, anything that dulls or confuses the mind is to be avoided.

There is the famous story of a woman who became infatuated with a monk. After he refused to yield to her amorous advances, she came to him leading a goat and holding a pot of beer and told him, "You have to make a choice. You can either drink this beer or have sexual intercourse with me. If you refuse, I will kill the goat." She seemed pretty desperate.

Taking a moment, he thought, "I can't have sexual intercourse with her, because that breaks one of my primary vows, and I shouldn't drink the beer, because that, too, would be breaking one of my precepts. But I don't want her to kill the goat either, and then have to bear the blame for that. So, given these three options, maybe taking the alcohol is the least of these evils." He then agreed to drink the big jug of beer. As a result, he became totally drunk, and then proceeded to have sex with her and killed the goat. So as it turned out, he was not able to avoid any of the nonvirtues.

Not only should we abstain from nonvirtues, we should also engage in their opposing virtues. The opposite of killing, for example, is not simply not killing, but rather protecting and saving the lives of others. The karmic consequences of such actions are a long life span, freedom from illness, and felicity. The opposite of stealing is generosity, which leads to prosperity. The opposite of sexual misconduct is following pure ethical discipline, resulting in favorable rebirth and establishing a firm basis for progress along the spiritual path. –

During the era of the Buddha Vipaśyin, there was a householder who offered a gold coin to the Buddha, received three verses of practical instructions, and abstained from such nonvirtuous acts as killing.[51] As a result, for ninety-two eons he was very prosperous and enjoyed long life. Eventually he was born in Śrāvastī as the son of the wife of a wealthy householder. [571] One day as an infant he fell from his mother's lap into a river and was swallowed by a large fish. The fish was killed by a fisherman in a town downstream, and the infant was retrieved still alive from the belly of the fish. He was then adopted by a rich merchant who had no son. The previous householder heard of this and told him, "That is my son. Return him to me!"

The other merchant replied, "I made offerings to the gods, and the gods granted the boy to me when he emerged from the belly of a fish." They could not come to a settlement, so they met with the king, who told them, "Let the boy be shared by the two of you." Both men were wealthy, so the boy grew up in the lap of luxury. When he had grown to adulthood, he told his two fathers that he wanted to become a monk. Both fathers loved the boy so much that they could not refuse him, so he took monastic ordination in the presence of Śākyamuni. He became an *arhat* as the monk named Two Families. Due to offering the gold, in all his lifetimes he was prosperous; and due to abstaining from killing, even though he fell into a river and was swallowed by a fish, he did not die. It is said that due to receiving the vows of refuge, he became an *arhat*. [572]

Long ago, following the *nirvāṇa* of Buddha Kāśyapa, there was a householder who erected a *stūpa*, built an assembly hall for the Saṅgha, and provided sustenance for them for a long time.[52] Eventually the *stūpa* and assembly hall fell in ruins and the supply of food for the Saṅgha was cut off. That householder had a son who became a monk, and he restored what had fallen into ruin and provided for the Saṅgha as had been done before. As a result of his prayers, he was later born as King Mahākāpina in the Golden Land. In his domain there were eighty-four thousand fiefdoms under his reign, and he was extremely powerful. As he was preparing to subdue King Prasenajit of central India, the Lord manifested himself as a *cakravartin* and conquered him. That king then took monastic ordination and became an *arhat*. Thus, as a result of the merit of his restoration, he was born as a powerful king and attained fruition.

Long ago, a man came to honor the *stūpa* of Buddha Kāśyapa, in which there was a small statue of an elephant which had been the mount of the Bodhisattva when he came down from Tuṣita [to enter his mother's womb].[53] The man repaired the [broken statue of] the elephant, painted it, and anointed it. As a result [573], in all his lives that man enjoyed long life, nobility, and inexhaustible prosperity. Eventually he took birth in Śrāvastī as the son of a householder, and as soon as he was born, a golden baby elephant spontaneously appeared in the man's storeroom. As the boy grew up, so did the elephant, and its urine and feces were of gold. The young man always rode the elephant, and even when King Ajātaśatru stole it, it would not stay with the king but returned to the young man. Eventually the youth took monastic ordination from the Lord and was known as the monk Elephant Helper. As there were many people who came to look at the elephant, it was not allowed to remain with him. So he told it three times, "You are no longer needed," and it disappeared into the earth.

Long ago, at the end of the era of the Buddha Vipaśyin, five hundred monks were devoting themselves to solitude while investigating the reflectionlike nature of phenomena. At that time, one monk provided for them by going out for alms. Among them, four monks attained fruition, and they offered fine prayers on behalf of the person who provided food for them during their retreat. [574] For sixty-one eons, the one who went for alms took birth into the prosperous realms of gods and humans. Eventually he was born to a householder in Kosala, and even there he had a seven-storied house of the seven kinds of precious substances; so he had prosperity like that of the gods, for he had a retinue of many gods and goddesses. Later he took monastic ordination from the Lord and became an *arhat*.

Countless eons ago, there lived two thousand *ṛṣis* upon a mountain.[54] Hearing that it would not rain for twelve years, a wealthy householder promised to be their patron for that duration. He appointed five hundred men to provide for them, but they tired of it and complained, "This continual nuisance is for the sake of those beggars." At that time there was a man who called the *ṛṣis* to their meal, and who had a dog that followed him. One day he forgot to call them, but his dog went and barked, and the *ṛṣis* came.

After twelve years had passed, they said, "Rain will fall, so plant your crops," and he prepared his fields. [575] Only the jujube trees grew, and they were so filled with fruit that they filled all his storehouses. Then the five hundred men grew in faith, and they confessed their earlier harsh words. Because they called them beggars, they were born five hundred times as beggars. Eventually they became five hundred beggars in Śrāvastī, where they took monastic ordination and became *arhats*. That was the benefit of their confession.

A king and his ministers invited Śākyamuni and his retinue to be their guests, but they said, "Don't invite the monks who were beggars." So at Śākyamuni's command, each of [the beggars] took an almsbowl full of the fruit of the unplanted harvest of [the northern continent of] Kurava. They had their meal together with Śākyamuni, and everyone was filled with faith. Thereafter, they were all invited together.

That householder was the Lord, the treasurer was Prince Victorious, the man who called [the *ṛṣis*] was King Upana, and the dog became a householder named Fine Voice, who had a beautiful voice in all his lifetimes.

In Śrāvastī there lived a woman named Nyen-gamo [576] who was poor and destitute.[55] By begging she obtained a little oil, made of it a small oil-lamp, and offered it to the Lord. The next morning the wick of the lamp had not burned down, and Maudgalyāyana,[56] thinking that the oil-lamp was not needed during the daytime tried to put it out, but he could not. Then the Lord prophesied that after two countless eons this woman would become the Buddha named Light of the Lamp.

Long ago, the Buddha Kāśyapa and his retinue were simultaneously invited to be the guests of a wealthy woman and a poor woman, and they first went to the poor woman. With a sense of superiority and the arrogance of affluence, the wealthy woman complained, "You didn't come to me first, but to that beggar-woman!" As a result, she took birth five hundred times as a beggar woman. The next day, with faith and devotion she met the Buddha and received his prophecy concerning her enlightenment, and everyone offered innumerable oil-lamps to the Lord.

– In Tibet, some time ago, there was an extremely wealthy patron who made vast offerings to all the monastic communities of Lhasa. Extensive offerings were made to the three monastic universities, which housed twenty-five thousand monks. But in extending his generosity in this way, he came to think of himself as a great philanthropist, and his arrogance grew.

Meanwhile, an old beggar woman, who saw that he was a benefactor for these monasteries, sincerely rejoiced in his generosity. Having much faith she rejoiced in his merit and virtue, but because she was so impoverished she could afford to make only one butter lamp by placing a little animal fat in a horse's hoof. This she offered together with the thousands of butter lamps offered by the wealthy patron. As they were burning, a wind rose and blew out all the lamps except hers.

A *siddha* who witnessed this commented that even though the philanthropist had spent a great deal of money on his offerings, his motivation was contaminated by his own conceit. On the other hand, the old woman, who could make only a modest offering, had done so with pure faith and humility.

In making any offering, the motivation must be one of pure faith and of compassion, without thinking about what you will get in return. Then your act of generosity is truly a virtue and will have fine consequences. But if an act of generosity is motivated by conceit, little good will come of it. –

Long ago, [577] a monk named Āryamitra decided to beg in order to offer oil lamps for three months to the Buddha Rinchen Tsukpü. A daughter of a king gave him a great quantity of oil, so without needing to beg, he obtained oil-lamps to offer for three months. For a countless eon, the two of them enjoyed the joy and happiness of gods and humans, and their bodies were extraordinarily beautiful. Finally, that monk became the Buddha Dīpaṃkara, and the girl became Śākyamuni. It is said that even after they became *buddhas* many people offered them oil-lamps.

During the era of Buddha Kāśyapa, a new monk mocked another monk who was jumping over a gully, saying, "You jump like a monkey!"[57] The monk replied, "I am an *arhat*, so do not engage in idle gossip." Although the monk confessed, he took birth five hundred times as a monkey. Due to his subsequent confession, [as a monkey] he met with Śākyamuni and offered him honey. He passed away, and as soon as he took birth as a human, his house was filled with honey. Eventually he took monastic ordination, [578] and became an *arhat* as the monk Excellent Honey. Thus, it is said that it is important to guard against idle gossip.

Long ago, one of many *stūpas* of Buddha Viśvabhūj fell into ruin, and an old woman found ten people to help her restore it.[58] As a result of their prayers, for ninety-one eons they took rebirth together as gods and humans, with fine, attractive bodies, and honored by everyone, without ever falling into hell. Eventually she became Sumana, the young daughter of the householder Anāthapiṇḍika. Beautiful as she was, a prince took her for his bride, and she gave birth to ten eggs that turned into ten sons. Her sons later took monastic ordination and became *arhats*. That old woman became the daughter, and the ten men became ten *arhats*.

Once when the Lord was teaching Dharma, five hundred swans flew by and heard him.[59] Delighted, they wanted to descend, but a hunter snared them [579] and killed them. Immediately they were reborn in the Heaven of the Thirty-three. Recalling their previous lives, they came to meet the Lord and attained the state of stream-entry. Thus, the Buddha exhorted others to apply themselves diligently to the Dharma that he revealed.

It is said that to generate a malicious attitude towards monks wearing the saffron garb is to generate a malicious attitude towards all the *āryas* of the three times; so this is an immeasurable sin; whereas if one generates faith, there is great merit. It is said that a lion named Firm Mind showed respect for a hunter wearing saffron-colored clothes, and as a result for a hundred thousand eons it became a *cakravartin*; and finally it became a *buddha*.[60]

The above are narratives from the *sūtras*, so they are to be believed. This concludes the supplementary chapter on actions and their consequences.

– The preceding narratives demonstrate that many motivations stemming from a variety of mental states may influence our actions, and different beings may perceive a single object in different ways. *Devas* see water as ambrosia, humans see it as water, animals as simply something to drink, *pretas* see it as mucous or urine, and hell beings see it as lava. This one object is seen from the perspective of each type of sentient being as something quite different due to their differing *karma*.

In terms of the variety of ways reality can be viewed, take the example of His Holiness the Dalai Lama. Many people regard him as the very embodiment of Avalokiteśvara. Some people think he is extremely good, while other people think he is bad. A variety people can have very different perceptions of just one person. In this world much gossip is spread, and all of it stems from people's *karma*—from their own actions and the ensuing consequences—with the root source being their minds.

We can see how easily the mind shifts. Some people may have very pleasant experiences during the daytime, but when they fall asleep, they have nightmares with great sadness and misery. Upon waking, they are happy again. For other people just the opposite occurs. They're miserable during the daytime, but when they fall asleep, they have sweet dreams. Again, all of these changes are simply due to the mind.

Using myself for an example, some people say I'm good, while others say I have a sharp tongue. Some people say I'm honest and others dishonest. People say all kinds of things. On the one hand when they gossip about me, it would be easy to view them with anger and irritation, but more realistically such people are to be viewed with compassion. In the meantime, just because people say I'm good, it doesn't make me good. If they say I'm bad, it doesn't make me bad. It doesn't make me anything. All of these viewpoints are impermanent and are fundamentally just appearances of the mind. So, don't make a big deal of them. The big deal is your own mind!

Within the tradition of the Great Perfection, the *Guhyagarbhatantra* says that the rootless essence of everything is the mind. On the one hand, the mind is the foundation, or root, of all phenomena, but the mind itself is without root, or essence. When it's said that the whole of *saṃsāra* and *nirvāṇa* has the mind as its root, we can ask, "Whose mind is it? Is it the mind of a single individual?" The answer is no; it is the mind of all sentient beings. The relationship of *saṃsāra* and *nirvāṇa* to the mind of the

Buddha is not to the mind of one *buddha* but to all the *buddhas*. Innumerable conceptual elaborations of the mind develop, and by following after these, we perpetuate our existence in the six states of existence of *saṃsāra*, while also perpetuating the three poisons of the mind. Essentially, we perpetuate our own *saṃsāra* by grasping onto that which is nonexistent as being existent. For this reason, the Buddha taught the Four Noble Truths, the two types of identitylessness, namely personal and phenomenal identitylessness, and the view of emptiness.

Due to this tendency of grasping onto that which is nonexistent as being truly existent, we grasp onto phenomena as being enduring and permanent, which is an eternalistic extreme. Looking at the various *kāyas*, or bodies of the *buddhas*, the *dharmakāya* is the very nature of the mind. The four types of *sambhogakāya* activities—peaceful, expansive, powerful, and ferocious—are simply displays of the mind. Next is the *nirmāṇakāya* level, including all of the pure realms, the palaces, the displays of primordial wisdom, and all qualities of the *buddhas*, which are simply of the nature of the mind. Then we can look at the desire, form and formless realms of *saṃsāra*. All of these, together with the interrelationships of actions and their consequences, stem from the mind. All of the happiness and sorrow one experiences stems only from the mind.

Sometimes people say, "Oh, what that person said is exactly right." Or another person may say, "Oh, but that's not true." Bear in mind the ten analogies that the Buddha gave regarding all phenomena, declaring them to be like echoes, reflections, mirages, and so forth. People simply grasp onto that which is not real as if it were real. Bear these ten analogies in mind; they are really very suitable objects for meditation. But in the meantime, it's important that we don't develop an attitude of being special. None of us is special. If you want to become special, then recognize the nature of your own awareness. If you want to be special, get out of this web of *saṃsāra*. If you haven't done this, you're not special.

As I speak of the unreality of our experience, you may think that perhaps *karma* doesn't really have any truth to it, but this is a false conclusion. Look to the great masters of the past from the Kagyü lineage. They often recited a prayer which states: "May I realize the subtleties of actions and their consequences." It is only when one gains a very high realization known as "the one taste of all phenomena" that one can really penetrate into these subtle relationships, these subtle interconnections of actions and their consequences. To have this full realization of the subtleties of *karma* means you have gained the two types of knowledge: ontological and phenomenological. Ontological wisdom is the realization of emptiness, which is the nature of all phenomena. The phenomenological wisdom of a Buddha is the knowledge that penetrates the full range of phenomena, especially regarding actions and their consequences. These relationships are inconceivably subtle. Ontological and phenomenological knowledge can be likened to the trunk of a tree, and the fruit is the eighty-four thousand collections of the Buddha's teachings. So, don't think that the teachings on *karma* are somehow left behind or become inconsequential once one has gained very high realization. –

CHAPTER THREE

Actions and Their Consequences

Homage to Avalokiteśvara!

[582] A rough explanation of actions and their consequences has been presented in the preliminaries to the instructions on the profound practical teachings of Avalokiteśvara, but it is difficult to gain from that more than a partial understanding. Precise comprehension of actions and their consequences is not achieved until one has accomplished great single-pointedness. Until there arises the realization of the "one taste appearing in numerous ways," the subtlety of actions and their consequences is not discerned. Thus, the Kagyü masters of the past prayed, "Bless me that I may discern the subtlety of actions and their consequences." For us, all felicity and adversity and all joys and sorrows of birth and death and so forth are dominated by our *karma.*

– "Great single-pointedness" is the state of *samādhi* that arises due to investigating the nature of awareness, *rigpa.* The "one taste appearing in numerous ways" is a specific realization which is also called the "realization of the sole *bindu.*" What is this one taste that appears in numerous ways? It is the single nature of all of *saṃsāra* and *nirvāṇa*. It is seeing all phenomena simultaneously as being of one taste and one nature.

Spiritual success and mundane success all really stem from the merit you have accumulated in the past due to virtuous activity. Without merit, even if you give tens of millions of dollars towards a particular end, you won't have the success you are aiming for. It really comes down to your own previous actions. So it's important not to blame our lack of success on someone else when we experience failure or disappointment. Rather we must recognize that if we want to have success, we need to plant the seeds of virtue. If we want to avoid misfortune, then we need to avoid the source, which is nonvirtue. In the meantime, instead of blaming others for our failures, we must identify our own limitations and shortcomings and dispel them. –

The Chapter on the Cycle of Existence of Birth and Death states: [583]

> Wherever one is born in the three realms,
> That birth is dominated by *karma*.
> *Karma*, too, is something committed in the past.
> Death as well is dominated by *karma*.
> When the time comes for birth and death,
> The gods gradually fall from the heavens.
> Despite their great miraculous powers, they are powerless to remain.

– You can't give someone else either good *karma* or bad *karma*, any more than you can give them virtue or nonvirtue. These are things that we accumulate and commit for ourselves. Whether we die in the womb, have a short life or a long life, these are a result of our *karma*.

Even great gods, such as Indra and Brahmā, with their extraordinary powers, are powerless when the *karma* that propelled them into their present existence is exhausted. The reason for the precept not to take refuge in mundane gods such as these is that they, like ourselves, are still entrapped in this cycle of existence. Since they have not liberated themselves, it would be difficult for them to liberate anyone else, so they are not suitable objects of ultimate refuge. Moreover, if you take refuge in, or absolutely entrust yourself to, other beings who are subject to the five poisons, you really have a problem, because they can't release you from something they are not free of themselves. So this precept is truly for your own sake.

Some mundane gods may actually be great *bodhisattvas*, or even emanations of the *buddhas* appearing in the form of Indra, Brahmā, and so forth. Nevertheless, it is generally good counsel not to take ultimate refuge in any of them, for it is difficult to discern which ones are actually *bodhisattvas* or emanations of *buddhas*. In a way, we don't really need to worry about this. We don't have much, if any, direct contact with such gods anyway. –

To make this easy to understand, I shall explain this with no formal outline. Definite action is discussed in the collection of *sūtras* in *An Analysis of Actions*:

> What action definitely gives rise to rebirth? Upon performing any virtuous action, one makes a definite dedication saying, "Due

> to this, may I take such and such a rebirth." And engaging in the five deeds of immediate retribution [584] leads to rebirth.

– Whenever you engage with pure motivation in powerful virtuous deeds and then dedicate the merit of those actions, that prayer will lead to the rebirth to which you dedicate it. So this prayer is said to have the greatest importance. Wherever you wish your consciousness to go after death, pray towards that end. Do so frequently—whether you pray to be reborn in the presence of a certain spiritual mentor or in the pure realm of Sukhāvatī or anywhere else. Frequently pray and bring to mind your wish to be reborn in that realm.

When you or someone whom you know is on the verge of death, don't just wonder what you should do. Dedicate your virtue and make prayers that you or they may be born in Sukhāvatī, and engage in virtue and dedicate that virtue towards that end. That is what can be done.

As a result of any great virtue such as gaining a realization of emptiness, in the very next life you will ascend to a more lofty realm of existence. On the other hand, if you commit some horrendous nonvirtue, such as one of the acts of immediate retribution, you will go straight down to a miserable realm of existence. Have no doubt about this. –

If you strive in virtuous conduct and constantly pray to be reborn optimally in Sukhāvatī, as a middling option on the Glorious Copper-Colored Mountain, or at least in a human region that has Dharma, you will definitely be born there; so this is important. If any of the five deeds of immediate retribution or a major infraction of *samaya* occurs, and you die without confessing it, you will definitely be reborn in a miserable state of existence; so confession is important.

Even though roots of virtue have been accumulated, if no prayers are made concerning the time of their maturation, there is no certainty as to the manner in which they will ripen. *An Analysis of Actions* states:

> What action does not definitely give rise to rebirth?—when there is no dedication whatever after one performs any virtuous deed.

There are four possibilities concerning definite and indefinite actions. If you engage in any intense virtue or sin, it is even possible for it to ripen right now in this life. In the words of Gongchik Dorje, "The consequences of your present actions may ripen even now." [585] It may also happen that a virtuous or nonvirtuous action does not ripen in this region in this life, but ripens when you have gone elsewhere. This is like the worldly aphorism, "One goes in search of the fruits of one's generosity." *An Analysis of Actions* states that virtuous and nonvirtuous action may ripen after one has gone to another region, as in the case of the merchant Maitrakanyaka. This action may ripen in another land.

– The merchant Maitrakanyaka kicked his mother in the head, and then went to sea, traveling from one very strange land to another. That narration describes how an action committed in one place may ripen in that same lifetime, but in another land. –

Thus, I shall concisely explain the points that are taught extensively in *An Analysis of Actions* in the collection of the *sūtras*. Once you have committed a sinful, nonvirtuous action, if you disclose and confess it with great remorse and restrain from doing it again in the future, that *karma* is enacted but then not accumulated. If you fully engage in any virtue or sin with your mind but not your body nor with your speech, it is accumulated but not enacted. If you carry out a sinful deed without shunning it, and due to a lack of remorse, [586] do not confess it; and if you do not disengage or restrain from it in the future, that deed is performed and accumulated. If you do not intentionally engage in any virtue or sin, it is neither enacted nor accumulated. So with respect to enacting a deed, there are four possibilities as to whether or not it is accumulated.

Upon enacting and accumulating *karma* that leads to birth in hell, if you do not confess it, do not regret it, and do not restrain from it in the future, that is *karma* for being reborn in hell without deliverance until your life span [there] is exhausted. Upon performing an action that leads to birth in hell, if you slightly avoid it, confess it, and restrain from it, you will be freed from hell after half your life span in hell has gone by. After performing and accumulating *karma* that leads to birth in hell, if you intensely regret it, greatly confess it, and utterly restrain from it in the future, you will be freed from hell as soon as you are reborn there. For example, this occurred in the case of King Ajātaśatru, who killed his father.

– Middling people in the above case still have to spend half a life span in a hell realm, because although they recognize that they did something unwholesome and confess it, they then only restrain from doing it halfheartedly, not completely applying the four remedial powers. Therefore, such people do not completely purify that *karma*. You can find many examples of this. Alcoholics can recognize that their drinking is unwholesome and may even regret it, but they often just slip back into the same patterns. This applies to a wide variety of nonvirtues.

We are vivid examples of this. We know what is virtuous and what is nonvirtuous. But even as we apply ourselves to the Dharma, we tend to fall back into our old habits. We know that nonvirtue leads to misery and that virtue leads to happiness and flourishing; yet we still tend to fall back. So this is a case of recognizing something is wrong, but due to the power of our habitual propensities, we return to our old habits. We continue to perpetuate the nonvirtuous tendencies we've accumulated in the past and come up with all kinds of excuses why each time it was a special, extraordinary circumstance: "I had to do it," or, "Even though it's unwholesome, it's for the sake of the Dharma," or " I have to do this for the sake of sentient beings," or, "I have to do this for my family." These are simply clever excuses stemming from our habitual propensities. This is what is so hard to change, and why we keep falling back.

During the time of the Buddha, as a prince, King Ajātaśatru killed his father so that he could become king. Later, he felt intense remorse for this action and confessed it. It is said that even though he was born in hell, his experience there was like an arrow just touching the ground. As soon as he arrived there, he was instantaneously released. –

As it is said,

> In the case of engaging in unspeakable deeds,
> By reprimanding oneself, thorough confession,
> And restraint, those deeds diminish,
> But it is not said that they are utterly eliminated.

[587] In that way there are four possibilities in terms of whether one remains for the full extent of one's life span.

If you first delight in generosity and make gifts and offerings, then later regret it due to avarice, you will be reborn as the child of a wealthy and prosperous person; then in the early part of your life you will have great happiness and prosperity, but in your later years you will be impoverished and miserable. If at first you dislike generosity, offering, and so on and are disrespectfully irritated by it, but then when it is done you are pleased and free of regret, you will be born as the child of a poor person; then after you have matured in body and mind, you will obtain wealth by seeking for it with great hardship. It will then increase and flourish, and in your later years you will be affluent and happy. If at first you are delighted with generosity, offering, and so on and faithfully engage in that, and later do not succumb to regret due to avarice, you will be reborn into affluence, your prosperity will increase and flourish, and you will be wealthy and happy for your whole life. In the case of those who have no spiritual vision at all [588] and never perform even a single act of generosity or offering, if they keep a small vow such as a one-day fast, they will be reborn into a poor household, and for their entire life they will be miserable due to hunger and poverty. That is a simple explanation of four possibilities in terms of actions and their consequences for joy and sorrow.

Upon making great gifts and offerings to pure objects, after becoming wealthy, you will have little avarice and you will be able to dedicate your wealth to the Dharma. By making few offerings and gifts to fine people, even if you become wealthy, due to great avarice you will not be able to dedicate your wealth to the Dharma. By making many offerings and gifts to impure objects, you will be without great prosperity, and whatever you have you will be able to dedicate it to the Dharma, but it will run out and you will be impoverished. If you maintain a little ethical discipline, such as a one-day fast, engage in no sinful deeds, and make no offerings or gifts, you will be reborn as a very poor and destitute person; and even if you acquire food and clothing with great difficulty, [589] due to great avarice you will be unable to dedicate the slightest bit of it to the Dharma. Those are the four possibilities in terms of the extent of one's ability to give, as taught in *An Analysis of Actions* in the *sūtras*.

– To differentiate between gifts and offerings: gifts are given to our peers, whereas offerings are made to the objects of refuge. The usual consequence of making gifts and offerings is that we establish tendencies for generosity in our mind-stream, which continue into future lifetimes. While this karmic repercussion is internal, it manifests externally as prosperity, which also follows into future lives. Beyond that, just as practicing generosity suppresses whatever predisposition for avarice you may have in this lifetime, so too, it will be suppressed in future lifetimes, and you will be able to dedicate not only your wealth but everything to Dharma without any limitations or reservations. All of this assumes that the generosity is performed in a spirit of gladness and with pure motivation.

To imbue even more meaning to a gift or an offering, why not dedicate the virtue of that deed to the attainment of enlightenment for both yourself and others? If you do that, then you are following in the footsteps of the *buddhas* of the past. By so doing you are dedicating it to something that is of benefit in this lifetime and in future lifetimes both for yourself and others. So why not dedicate your gifts to something truly sublime and transformative instead of simply perpetuating your existence in this cycle of existence?

Even if you have been born as a *cakravartin*, you still remain in *saṃsāra*, so you have not been liberated from the cycle of existence. Whether you are a king or a queen of the world, whether you are rich or have immense power, you are still within the domain of suffering; you still are not liberated. So why would you aspire to such a state when it's simply just more of the same—suffering? Moreover, we tend to be proud of our various qualities—wealth, power, intelligence and good looks. What really is the basis for this pride when conceited and arrogant people remain in the midst of suffering? If these mundane qualities were truly beneficial, we would expect people who have them to have become *buddhas* by now. Instead these people are just coming closer to death.

In our world, many people are infatuated with celebrities. We are especially thrilled to see them in the flesh if they are rich, powerful, or famous, but what is so amazing about having accomplished fame or power or wealth? After these people die, their bodies begin to rot, and we want to get as far away from them as possible. Human skin is human skin whether it is on a corpse or a living body. Physically it's the same. Likewise, when you peel off the layers of skin to reach the flesh, it is the same flesh whether it is from a fresh corpse or a fresh living body. This is the same for the bones, the intestines and vital organs. What is there to be proud of? Why do we get so excited about seeing someone else's skin even if it is a celebrity's?

In fact, we feel disgust when we see a toilet, but when we see a human body walking around filled with the same stuff inside, we think it's wonderful. All this fascination with other people's bodies and the pride that we generate in ourselves is simply a display of delusion. That's nothing to be proud about.

The Hīnayāna tradition follows the method of meditating on impurity by looking throughout the components of the body. When you do this starting with the skin and further analyzing the flesh, bones, intestines and so on, you find there is really nothing that's truly attractive. This is not a contrived meditation because, in fact, it is focusing on precisely what the body is comprised of. So again I ask, what are the grounds of arrogance? Why are we so proud of our appearance when the body is composed of these impure and disgusting substances?

What is the basis for our arrogance? Many people who are clever, rich, famous or powerful still don't know what behavior is to be avoided or what needs to be adopted to find genuine happiness. What grounds do we have for pride and conceit when, having some understanding, we don't put it into practice? Many brilliant people who are great leaders of the world are clever at perpetuating nonvirtue, but they are ignorant when they fail to recognize what is virtuous. In the meantime, we grasp onto that which is nonexistent as being existent; we grasp onto that which is impermanent as permanent, reliable and abiding. In order to cut through these delusional ways of viewing reality, the Buddha taught the ten analogies which describe the nature of reality. There have been limitless *buddhas* who have come in the past and yet here we still remain—acting in the opposite way, puffed up with our own qualities. Truly we are the objects worthy of compassion.

If you are a genuine practitioner, you are in the process of transmuting your five poisons into the five types of primordial wisdom. Once that transformation is complete, you've become a *buddha*. Upon attaining this, is there anything to be proud of? Having transmuted even the mental affliction of pride into primordial wisdom, there is absolutely no ground for the quality of pride or conceit. If you are not yet a *buddha*, there is no basis either, and if you are in between, there is no ground for pride. So really there is no ground for arrogance or conceit in any stage whether you are a sentient being or a *buddha*.

We have the opportunity to recognize our own faults and limitations in terms of our physical, verbal, and mental behavior. Right now we have the chance to recognize what needs to be avoided and what needs to be adopted. Insofar as we can recognize the unwholesome deeds we have committed, now is the time to disclose them and apply the remedial powers so that they can be completely purified. There is no reason why you should feel helpless and not know what to do. Rather you need to embrace your present situation and take advantage of it. Now is the time! When you have done a virtuous deed, recognize it. Now is the time to confess; now is the time to take precepts; now is the time to develop compassion. Now is the time to turn away from *saṃsāra*. Genuinely practice Dharma if you are fed up with the cycle of existence.

It is the quality of knowing what is to be avoided and what is to be followed that provides the essence of compassion. It is for this reason that compassion arises towards all sentient beings. This same reason is the basis for cultivating the Four Immeasurables. Of the four, equanimity is worthy of great praise. We know how to say, "I love you" to our spouses and children. That's easy. But it's also mixed with a mind of partiality because we love our relatives and not strangers, whereas equanimity creates a level field.

We may easily understand giving gifts to our friends and relatives, but what about the implications of giving street people money? We may want to help them out by giving them a dollar, but by and large we don't follow them to see if they go buy drugs, liquor, and cigarettes or food. So is this a pure act of generosity? Are these people impure or pure objects? Your own *karma* depends entirely on your motivation. If you give with the idea that the person is going to buy some alcohol or cigarettes, then your giving is an impure act of generosity, regardless of what the person does with it. If you give this gift with a pure motivation, then whatever the person does with it is that person's responsibility. For you, the act is already finished and it's made so by your motivation.

You may feel drawn to give a gift, but if you give it disrespectfully, maybe with anger, and later look back with satisfaction, the karmic repercussion from this is rebirth into poverty. But in your later years, once again, you will become affluent, although it will be through great difficulty.

Motivated by our own jealousy, we may discourage other people from giving gifts or making offerings by telling them, "You shouldn't give that to so and so," or, "That gift is unworthy." This is a great nonvirtue. It has detrimental consequences for you and induces regret on the part of the person who has engaged in those acts of generosity. There are some types of giving which are impure from the outset. For example, spraying pesticides on fields and orchards is clearly an impure act. You are actually using a substance that causes death. Or, if you manufacture weapons or supply any component to make a weapon, that would entail an impure motivation because they are used to kill sentient beings; the whole act is impure. So once again the crucial issue is your motivation. –

Ordinary individuals who have accumulated great collections [of knowledge and merit] will be reborn as great kings, such as world monarchs, who will be well in body but mentally unhappy. Those who become *arhats* without accumulating merit, as is said of the Elder

Likunchika, have in fact achieved superior realization, but they are chronically ill. They are unwell in body, but mentally joyful. *Arhats* who have accumulated merit, as is said of the Elder Balanantin, such that they have previously accumulated collections [of knowledge and merit] and have not achieved superior realization, are endowed with both physical and mental well-being. Those who have neither accumulated those collections in the past nor achieved realization in the present are unwell in both body and mind. Those are four possibilities in terms of the joys and sorrows of actions and their consequences.

– Even if you have a great store of merit and knowledge, practice Dharma, and take birth as a king, there is nothing so amazing about this if you do not really know how *saṃsāra* functions and do not recognize the genuine causes of joy and suffering. Without such knowledge, your body may be healthy, but your mind will be afflicted. Becoming an *arhat* without accumulating merit also leads to physical illness, because the body still exists together with the residue carried over from previous *karma*. Unwholesome *karma* that has not been purified will still manifest, for example as chronic illness, after you become an *arhat*.

If you have completely and irrevocably freed your mind from all mental afflictions of ignorance, hatred and attachment, you will remain in a state of happiness, but you may still be subject to physical illness. In his final life, an *arhat* who is not accumulating more *karma* causing him to be propelled back into the cycle of existence may have lingering physical ill health. In contrast, once his life is over, a king who does not recognize the causes of suffering and joy simply takes birth again among the six realms of existence, perpetuating his *saṃsāra*. For this reason, it's very important to dedicate whatever virtue you accumulate to the attainment of perfect and complete enlightenment.

Over the course of many centuries in Tibet there have been many *tertöns*, or "treasure revealers," and it goes without saying that *tertöns* must have purified their obscurations. However, among *tertöns*, there are varying degrees of merit. In the case of the *tertön* Ratna Lingpa, he had cleared out obstructions and also accumulated great merit, so he encountered few if any obstacles in discovering *termas*, or hidden treasure texts. Furthermore, the *termas* he found were great and numerous, and he had all that was needed to preserve and maintain them. That was a consequence of his accumulation of past merit.

But there are other *tertöns* who have purified their obstructions, but have not accumulated great merit and knowledge. In this case they encounter obstacles in the process of discovering *termas* and their discoveries tend to be few in number. Once such *tertöns* discover them, they may need to resort to writing them down on tree bark because they can't even obtain paper on which to write them down. If this is true for *tertöns*, surely it goes without saying that it goes for us as well. –

For all the six states of existence alike, [590] if you must take birth in the same place even after death, your life span was exhausted but not your *karma*. If at first you are happy, but in your later years you are miserable, or if in the early part of your life you are poor, destitute, and miserable, but in your later life you are happy and prosperous, your *karma* was exhausted but not your life span. For all the six states of existence alike, if you are not reborn where you died but are born elsewhere among the six states, both your life span and *karma* are exhausted. Those who become *arhats* or *pratyekabuddhas* due to the power of meditation do not exhaust their life span or their *karma*, but their mental afflictions are extinguished. Those are the four possibilities in terms of the exhaustion of one's life span and *karma*.

– In the case of the death of a young child who had an excellent disposition and very good behavior, it may well be that his or her life span was exhausted but not his or her *karma*. So with these virtuous tendencies it is very possible that this child will come right back once again taking a fortunate rebirth. –

Those who are born in a miserable state of existence such as that of an animal but are beautiful and attractive have maintained ethical discipline out of a motivation of hatred. Those who are born in a miserable state of existence such as that of an animal and are ugly and repulsive are experiencing the consequences of the *karma* of improper ethical discipline motivated by hatred. [591] Those who are born in a miserable state of existence such as that of an animal and then are smelly, with unclear and dull faculties, are experiencing the consequences of the *karma* of improper ethical discipline motivated by delusion. Those are four possibilities in terms of one's appearance in a miserable state of existence.

In the case of performing an apparently virtuous deed with the intent to harm someone else, for that virtuous deed there is *karma* that yields a consequence of suffering. In the case of performing a nonvirtue, such as the four primary downfalls, with the motivation of the spirit of awakening, for that nonvirtuous deed there is *karma* that yields a consequence of joy. For example, such practices as "union and liberation" in Secret Mantra are committed with this in mind. In the case of engaging in sin with a sinful intention, for that misdeed the consequence is just suffering. In the case of performing virtue with the motivation of the spirit of awakening, joy arises as the result of virtuous *karma*. That is a simple explanation of the four possibilities in terms of one's motivation as taught in the collection of *bodhisattva sūtras*.

– You may think you are doing something virtuous and yet have an intention to do harm. For this ostensibly virtuous deed the result of such *karma* is in fact the experience of suffering. One example of this type of action is the ritual sacrifice of animals. People who perform such an act may be motivated to commit a virtuous deed as they offer the sacrificed animal to their objects of devotion, but the actual deed is one of inflicting harm. For this reason the consequence of their action is suffering.

Nowadays, we grapple with the question of mercy killing. If a horse breaks a leg, people say, "Oh, I love my horse so much that I feel I must 'put him down.'" Likewise, when our pets become old and ill, people often choose to "put them to sleep." It's interesting that we use such euphemisms for killing our animals. Our motivation may be to help our pet, but it is questionable whether the deed is virtuous or not. How can we justify it being genuinely virtuous?

If you really deeply consider the types of behavior people engage in—physical, verbal, and mental behavior—you will become nauseated with cyclic existence. But you must think about it very deeply; otherwise, you will come away with a sense that *saṃsāra* is good.

There are examples among the great *mahāsiddhas* of India, such as Tilopa, who seemed to engage in acts of killing. From an ordinary point of view, it seemed that Tilopa killed animals and then cooked and ate their flesh. In actuality, he liberated the consciousness of these creatures so that they went directly to a pure realm. It was also said that Tilopa went to the palace and had sexual union with a princess. Eventually they had a son, and the irate king decided to execute Tilopa. At the moment the king came to kill Tilopa, he found him drinking alcohol and holding the princess' hand. With his other hand, he held his son's hand. Immediately upon seeing the king, he transformed his son into a *vajra* and his consort, the princess, into a bell. The alcohol became a flood which engulfed the kingdom. *Mahāsiddhas* can perform these extraordinary acts, but without their level of realization, I doubt that such deeds could be virtuous. –

If you behave sinfully with a virtuous intention, [592] even though you are reborn in a favorable state of existence, you become poor and destitute, with the hardships of joys and sorrows, and suffering due to illness and so forth. That is *karma* in which the propulsion is by virtue, and the completion is by sin. If you behave virtuously with a sinful intention, even though you are reborn in a miserable state of existence, you prosper, as in the case of the *nāga* kings and *pretas* who fly through the sky. Even though they are physically animals and *pretas*, they have long life and prosperity. That is *karma* in which the propulsion is by sin, and the completion is by virtue. If you accumulate sin with a sinful intention and you are born in a miserable state of existence, you will experience intense suffering. That is *karma* in which both the propulsion and the completion are by sin. If you behave virtuously with a virtuous intention and are born in a favorable state of existence, you will always experience joy and prosperity. That is *karma* in which both the propulsion and the completion are by virtue. That is a simple explanation of the meaning in the *sūtras* concerning the four possibilities in terms of propulsion and completion. [593]

– Propulsive *karma* literally propels you into another existence, so it is responsible for determining your next rebirth. The qualities of your life while you are in that existence are enacted by the completed *karma*. –

If, with an evil intention, you harm or commit even a small nonvirtue towards a pure object, as the consequence you must experience great suffering; and if you commit a small virtue, such as honoring a pure object with a faithful, reverent intention, great happiness will occur as a result. That is *karma* in which a small deed ripens into a great effect.

– The fact that a small deed towards a pure object has so much weight is due to the nature of the object or person with whom you are interacting. So, please be careful in terms of the Three Jewels, the Buddha, Dharma, and Saṅgha. Be very cautious in terms of your behavior of body, speech, and mind, because even a small nonvirtue can give rise to a very large consequence. But remember that, conversely, even a small virtue can give rise to a very powerful and very happy effect. This situation is not created by Buddhism; it is simply the nature of actions and their consequences; that is just the way the world works. –

Once sinful *karma* is accumulated, unless you can utterly purify it by regretting it and intensely confessing it, eventually you must definitely, infallibly experience [its consequences]. *The Treatise on Discipline* states:

> Even over hundreds of eons
> Actions do not dissipate,
> And when the conditions and time are ripe,
> The consequences happen to sentient beings.

– Whether your behavior is virtuous or nonvirtuous, if the *karma* is not counteracted and purified, when the causes and conditions come together, it will inevitably ripen. When I lived in Tibet, there was an elderly woman whose teacher was also my primary spiritual mentor, the embodiment of the enlightened activity of Dudjom Rinpoche. After performing a divination, he told her that there would be major obstacles for both herself and her family. To avert the problems that might arise, he advised her to request that certain ritual Dharma practices be performed.

Upon hearing this, her husband and her father agreed, but then she reconsidered and said, "Oh, why bother? Many people don't sponsor any kind of Dharma practices, and they're fine, so why should we spend our money that way?" So due to her shortsighted perspective, she didn't have the practices done on behalf of her family. Right now you may be experiencing the results of virtue as prosperity and felicity, but when that runs out, you will experience the fruits of nonvirtue. While you are experiencing the fruits of virtue, if you are not sowing seeds of further virtue, then your virtue will become exhausted, leaving you with only the dregs. This woman's children and her other relatives were all killed by the Chinese. –

If a sin is not confessed after committing it, with the passing of each day it grows; so even a small sin becomes great. If it is confessed, even if it is not utterly purified, [594] it is not compounded. A *sūtra* states:

> If no antidote is applied to utterly counteract
> Virtuous and sinful deeds,
> They increase and remain,
> And even after eons [their consequences] occur.

That is an explanation of the non-dissipation of actions and their consequences.

Now since there are many cases of behavior that are mixtures of virtue and sin, which of those ripens first? The more powerful one ripens first. If the power of virtue and the power of sin are equal, the one with which you are more habituated ripens first. If they are equal in that regard, whichever one is clearer in the mind at the time of death ripens first. If they are equal in that regard, the one that was committed first ripens first. Ārya Rāhulabhadra says,

> In terms of the consequences of actions,
> Whatever is heavier, more serious, more habitual,
> And whatever was committed earlier
> Has consequences that occur first.

That is a concise explanation from the *sūtras* concerning which deeds give rise to their consequences first. [595]

Ordinary people might think, "It's not true that happiness results from performing virtuous deeds and suffering results from committing nonvirtue. Those who devote their whole lives to Dharma and virtue have short lives, many illnesses, poverty, and various sorts of suffering; while murderers, hunters, soldiers, robbers, and thieves do just fine." For sinful people who are happy, the consequences of virtue they have committed in previous lives are ripening in this life; and all their merit is getting used up in this life. In the future they are bound for inescapable regions, so that is their final virtuous *karma*.

Due to committing sins in this life, the consequences of immense suffering will occur following this life. As an analogy, due to eating food mixed with poison, for a little while it is sweet and one is satiated; but later on, one dies in agony. *The Set of Aphorisms* states: [596]

> As long as sin does not ripen,
> Foolish people think it is sweet.
> When sin ripens,
> Then they burn.
>
> As long as sin does not ripen,
> It is seen as acceptable.
> When sin ripens,
> Then suffering is experienced.

A Letter to a Friend states:

> Even though one engages in sinful deeds,
> One is not immediately cut as if with a weapon.
> But when the time of death comes,
> The consequences of sinful deeds become apparent.

When suffering occurs in this life due to practicing Dharma and virtue, this is a case of experiencing in this life the consequences of sins that have been committed in previous lifetimes. The effects of practicing virtue and Dharma in this life will occur in future lifetimes as sublime, immense joy. *The Set of Aphorisms* states:

> As long as the good does not ripen,
> Virtue is seen as inferior.
> When virtue ripens,
> Then it is seen as joy. [597]

Some people practice Dharma single-pointedly or establish powerful roots of virtue, as a result of which in this life they take on all vices, sins, and obscurations from previous lifetimes. Then everything that would result in immense suffering in miserable states of existence in other lifetimes is purified simply by suffering from illness in this life. It is said that in the next life and thereafter they will achieve the glory of proceeding from one joy to another. *The Perfection of Wisdom Sūtra* states:

> Subhūti, any son or daughter of good family who takes the words of a *sūtra* such as this, memorizes them, chants them, comprehends them, and earnestly meditates on them will experience pain and torment. Why? It is like this: by suffering in

> this life, those sentient beings purify the nonvirtuous deeds of previous lifetimes, deeds that would give rise to rebirth in miserable states of existence; and they will achieve the enlightenment of the Buddha.

[598] *The Great Nirvāṇa Sūtra* states:

> Simply by having a headache, catching a contagious disease, being struck with illness, or being despised by others, sons or daughters of good family who yearn for the sublime Dharma swiftly achieve unsurpassable enlightenment.

By single-pointedly practicing the sublime Dharma in this life, all the karmic obscurations of previous lifetimes swiftly ripen, just as a great deal of smoke is produced before flames rise up. The occurrence of illness and suffering is called "the arousal of *karma*," for it is a sign of the swift achievement of the supreme *siddhi*. Orgyen Rinpoche speaks at length on the manner in which many adversities, such as illness and suffering, arise due to engaging in the profound practices of the Mantrayāna. Just as cleansing a vessel causes filth to emerge, so is this the arousal of *karma* due to purifying obscurations. This is like the cases of Gyarey, Götsangwa, Lorey, and so forth, [599] who, just before they achieved *siddhis*, had near-death illnesses of edema, a disease brought on by lice, and a disease caused by *nāgas*, due to engaging in single-pointed practice.

– A more recent example of this is the last incarnation of Karmapa. As many of you know, he died from cancer in Chicago, though he had a myriad of diseases. People would come into his room asking how he was feeling and he would reply, "Not sick." Dudjom Rinpoche also died from illness as did Kalu Rinpoche. Many spiritual mentors die from serious illnesses. There are various ways of understanding how this takes place. Their experience of illness may be partially due to the fact that they are taking on the infractions of *samayas* by their own disciples. That is one possibility. Or they may be experiencing the fruits of the residual karmic obscurations from their own past. Or their illness may be simply a manifestation for the sake of others—to show others the nature of actions and their consequences and the nature of *saṃsāra*: birth, sickness, aging, and death. This is simply the nature of reality, and people should be aware of this. This was certainly the case in the life of Buddha Śākyamuni. He passed away to demonstrate the truth of impermanence. –

There are others who spend their whole lives single-pointedly practicing Severance, and even great beings who dwell on the *bodhisattva* grounds and have fine, experiential realization are purified, just before they die, by great, sustained suffering due to illness. That occurrence of fierce, unbearable pain purifies all the residual karmic obscurations at the time of death; and this is a sign that they will attain spiritual awakening in the *dharmakāya* of death or else take birth in a pure realm. When the noble Milarepa experienced excruciating pain from some offering, the old woman who arranged for this offering said she would help by taking on his pain. He then transferred it to her for just an instant, and she screamed in anguish, saying "Take it back!" He then transferred it to a rock, and it cracked apart. He said this was a purification of residual karmic obscurations, and he took it upon himself. Lord Phakdrup, Dromtönpa and so forth also [600] say that their affliction by leprosy was a purification of remaining karmic obscurations, and they died with their minds dwelling in joy.

– The single-pointed practice of Severance does not mean simply performing all the rituals with precision, but rather single-pointedly applying your mind to the cultivation of the stages of generation and completion as you engage in the outer rituals. What are you severing, or cutting through? You are cutting through to the two types of identitylessness, namely personal and phenomenal identitylessness. This is the real core of this practice. People who are not aware of this and focus on how to ring the bell or sound the *ḍāmaru* are really just going through a charade as if they were playing a role in a Halloween party.

Just as we prepare ourselves before a meal by washing our hands, this fierce unbearable pain is a preparation, a final purification, before the "meal" of death. This may be an opportunity for great spiritual realization. –

With such points in mind the master Dezhin Shekpa says,

> The inexhaustible three miserable states of existence are the
> cycle of existence.
> Rather than being reborn in worlds without leisure,[61]
> May [my *karma*] ripen in this very life,
> And may I not experience it on other occasions.

By making this prayer, it may be fulfilled, as in the case of Neudzok Nakpa, who knowingly accepted an invitation [by people who intended to murder him].

Thus, even if bad things happen to pure Dharma practitioners when they are on the verge of death, it is not certain that this is bad. For example, the Bodhisattva Supuṣpacandra was executed even though he was blameless,[62] and the King of Kalingka declared, "Even though my major and minor limbs were amputated, I did not experience thoughts of hatred."

– I witnessed a more recent example of this type of generosity by my own root spiritual mentor, Tulku Natsok Rangdröl. In 1958, I consulted with him about whether I and others should flee from the Chinese Communists who had invaded Tibet. He told me, "You don't have the *karma* to have to suffer under the subjugation of the Communists; so there is no reason for you to stay. But I will not be going with you, because even though you don't have this *karma*, I do. On the one hand, I have *karma* that needs to be purified, and on the other hand, I will remain for the sake of sentient beings. I know what will happen to me. I will be tortured and murdered. I see very clearly this will take place, but I'm going to stay anyway."

My companions and I fled into exile, and later I learned that he was caught by the Chinese Communists, imprisoned, and tortured for years in a concentration camp. Finally, they dragged him behind a running horse until his body literally fell apart. That is how he met his death. I heard reports about the years he was held in the concentration camp. Whether he was ridiculed, abused, or physically tortured, he simply peacefully smiled at his captors saying, "Whatever you wish to do, feel free to do it; you have my permission. The more you hurt me, the more I will pray that I can be of benefit to you." –

In terms of actions that give rise to visible experiences, due to committing intense virtue or sin in your preceding life and the one before that, it may be necessary for it to ripen in this lifetime. [601] If so, when previous *karma* ripens in this life as long life and good health, even if a thousand extremists and Bön *ṛṣis* were to curse you, they could not harm you. When *karma* ripens for great prosperity and power, even if enemies should rise up from the four directions, they would be unable to rob you of your power. When *karma* ripens as a short life and a multitude of illnesses, a thousand *ṛṣis* who have accomplished "words of truth" might try to protect you, and Kumārajīvaka himself might be called as your physician; but they could not help you. When *karma* ripens for losing your prosperity and power, all your food, possessions, and prosperity will vanish like water poured into sand, and your dearly beloved relatives and servants will join with your enemies and come after you. In that case, not even the compassion of the Three Jewels can protect you, let alone anyone else.

For example, when Virūḍhaka, the king of an outlying region, was waging war, Maudgalyāyana asked whether he might cover the city of Kapila with a single almsbowl so that it would not be seen; [602] but he was told that he should let the *karma* be purified. Then five hundred members of the Śākya clan were killed, and five hundred Śākya girls had their legs amputated at the knees. Apart from describing the manner in which this was due to their past actions, Śākyamuni, though present, could not protect them. Moreover, all the benefits of the names of the *buddhas, dhāraṇis,* and *mantras* are effective except when previous *karma* is coming to fruition. That is *karma* that gives rise to visible experiences.

– The term "extremist" refers to those who hold to extreme views or practices, such as animal sacrifices and so forth, and in general the word refers to Indian non-Buddhists. Due to virtuous *karma* ripening in this lifetime, if such extremists or Bön *ṛṣis* were to practice black magic, even they could not harm you. When one accomplishes the state of contemplative realization known as "words of truth," in the moment that one makes a prayer, it is immediately fulfilled; but even that cannot help you when your *karma* ripens. Even Kumārajīvaka, an emanation of the Medicine Buddha, who had such extraordinary healing powers that with one touch of his hand he could make an illness vanish—even he cannot help you when your *karma* is ripening.

The point of speaking about the inevitability of *karma* is not to make us feel that we are helpless victims. Rather, it is to point to the importance of confessing negative actions and purifying them by the four remedial powers. If you purify unwholesome *karma* by such means, you can avoid the results. What a thousand *ṛṣis* and Kumārajīvaka can't do for you, you can do for yourself. Similarly, without merit nothing good can come, even mundane prosperity. If you have no merit, even if someone were to give you millions of dollars, it would just vanish or you might simply die. Either way, you would be incapable of benefiting from that gift.

Remember that you were naked when you emerged from your mother's womb. Did you have anything in your pockets when you were born? Only with the accumulation of merit and the purification of nonvirtuous deeds can wisdom arise. How can this be of benefit? The accumulation of merit and the purification of nonvirtuous deeds is of benefit in the future. But it is a mistake to think that this is only a particular cultural tradition—someone else's tradition. Bear in mind that right now you are in a fortunate situation because you have the opportunity to be able to purify unwholesome *karma* from the past and to accumulate beneficial *karma* that can give rise to good fortune in the future. If you procrastinate, this opportunity will eventually be lost. So we can act like the toddler who instead of drinking a cup of milk knocks it off the highchair without ever getting the chance to take a sip. We can do the same thing with Dharma if we wish. But now we have the good fortune to have the opportunity to be able to put it into practice.

These comments about the nature of *karma* and the significance of merit, confession, and purification are true for everyone—whether you're an ordinary sentient being or a *bodhisattva* dwelling on one of highest *bodhisattva* grounds. No one can ever simply establish us on a *bodhisattva* ground or grant us merit. The accumulation of merit, the purification of nonvirtuous deeds, the attainment of realization—all of these come from within. It's never given by one person to another. So, if you long for an enduring state of well-being, this is the path to follow.

In my own monastery of Dhomang, there was an abbot who led a very simple life, even though his family was very wealthy. When the Chinese were occupying Tibet and battles were raging, people responded in various ways. Some did ritual practices while others stockpiled weapons and ammunition. The only response this abbot gave was, "Look, people, this is *karma* ripening. If you want to respond, recite *Oṃ maṇi padme hūṃ*, perform devotions, and purify yourselves. This will help, but nothing else will, because this is *karma* ripening."

When people heard him, many would smile condescendingly and think he was a fool. As it turned out many of his companions were killed, but he's still at Dhomang Monastery today.

To give another example, when Mao Tse Tung died, His Holiness the Dalai Lama not only wept with compassion for him because he knew what a terrible rebirth he faced, but he requested that monks and *lamas* perform religious devotions on his behalf. –

Heavy sins such as the five deeds of immediate retribution and powerful virtues definitely ripen in the very next life without any other lives coming first. It is possible that any minor virtue or vice may be catalyzed by conditions and ripen in this life; and if conditions are not encountered, they may also remain for a hundred eons. But without dissipating, [603] eventually they must definitely ripen. That is *karma* that gives rise to experiences in other lifetimes.

– For any one of these five deeds of immediate retribution, the immediate result is a terrible rebirth in a miserable state of existence, whereas powerful virtue may give rise to the attainment of enlightenment immediately following this life—even in the *bardo* prior to the next life. If you wonder whether a minor vice or virtue can just vanish over the course of many lifetimes, the answer is no. It is preserved indefinitely. –

When bad *karma*, such as a short life span and a multitude of illnesses, is catalyzed by spirits and ripens in this lifetime, it is possible that religious services and medical treatment may be able to counteract this and postpone it. This is like postponing a lawsuit. If you have no previous bad *karma* at all, it is impossible for spirits to harm you, and illness will not arise. By worshiping and actualizing mundane gods, the *karma* of long life, good health, and great prosperity may be drawn in and ripen in this life. This is like taking your wages for next year and the year after and using them up them this year. The *siddhis* of the deities of primordial wisdom are not like that, for they arise due to the previous prayers and power of compassion of those deities.

It is said that an example of *karma* that is not necessarily experienced is the *karma* in the mind-stream of an *arhat*. For instance, before

Śākymuni became a *buddha*, it would have been necessary for him to take birth five hundred times as a *cakravartin*; but he attained spiritual awakening before that could happen. [604] So he dedicated that merit to provide the physical necessities of his disciples. Thus, he said, "Even in times when one cannot get a handful of rice for a handful of pearls, my disciples will not be wanting in terms of their physical necessities." This is the reason why, if we monks purely keep our vows and *samaya*, we will not be destitute in order to practice Dharma.

The virtue of the desire realm is non-meritorious *karma*, and the virtue of the form and formless realms is immutable *karma*. Moreover, the virtue of the higher realms is solely positive *karma*, the nonvirtue of the desire realm is solely negative *karma*, and the virtue of the desire realm is mixed *karma*. Uncontaminated virtue is *karma* that extinguishes the ripening [of *karma*]; the consequence of positive *karma* is joy, the consequence of negative *karma* is suffering, and that of mixed *karma* is a mixture of joy and suffering. Uncontaminated *karma* extinguishes those *karmas*. [605] For example, in order to save the lives of five hundred people, a greatly compassionate ship's captain killed a demonic, evil man with a short spear; and for the sake of the Teachings, Lhalung Palgyi Dorje assassinated King Langdarma. Those were deeds in which the intention was positive and the enactment was negative. An act such as making a gift in order to kill someone entails a negative intention and a positive enactment. Making a gift with a pure intention, for example, is *karma* with a positive intention and a positive enactment. An action such as killing in order to eat meat entails a negative intention and a negative enactment.

– Wholesome deeds performed in the desire realm, in which we live at present, are virtuous, but they are tainted by the eight mundane concerns. Even though they are virtuous, they are said to be non-meritorious *karma*. The virtue of the desire realm is a mixture of negative and positive *karma*, while the virtue of the form and formless realms is solely positive.

What is uncontaminated *karma*? It is the *karma* of one who has gained a direct, unmediated, nonconceptual realization of emptiness. This uncontaminated *karma* purifies all the contaminated deeds. There is nothing better for purifying nonvirtuous *karma* than the realization of emptiness. It is also the principal feature of the stage of generation and the stage of completion. It is the greatest means of purification.

In terms of virtuous and nonvirtuous actions, when you see other people who seem to be progressing very well in their practice and experiencing good fortune, how should you respond? I suggest that you remember they are experiencing the fruition of their own previous actions. Rejoice in that! Take heart and be glad for them! In fact, if you can rejoice in their prosperity and progress, your very rejoicing is of benefit to you. On the other hand, if you're jealous of their good fortune, the result will be unfortunate for yourself.

There are people who experience all types of ups and downs. At one moment they're doing really well, and then the bottom falls out. They experience the worst obstacles both worldly and spiritual, being abused and rejected by others. When these people come to your attention, they should be objects of your compassion, not objects of your own abuse and rejection. Whether they are your friend or your enemy, it should make no difference. When you see people who are having a rough time, pray for their well-being, regardless of whether they are your friend or enemy. It's a disgrace to hear a Buddhist say that certain people really deserve their misfortune. When we have this kind of judgmental response, we break our own *samaya*, leading to our downfall. Focusing on and drawing people's attention to others' faults is really a great fault on our own part. This is especially true for Buddhists because we are trying to escape from this cycle of existence. Our fixation on the faults of others is an enormous obstacle to achieving our own liberation from *saṃsāra*. So be careful regarding others. And be especially careful with your Dharma brothers and sisters.

When we are abused, slandered, and rejected by others, this actually serves to purify our own negative *karma*, while those who treat us in this way are the ones who are actually harmed. In fact, the one who is receiving the abuse may be receiving benefit in the process.

Some Buddhists lament when they hear others abuse Buddhism or think of the Chinese Communists destroying Buddhism. My response is that there is a certain duration for the Buddha's teachings, and once that has passed, they will vanish. At that time, no matter how much effort is given to restore and revitalize them, it will be pointless. But until that time has come—and it has not come yet—there's nothing that anyone can do to actually destroy it—not the Chinese or anyone else. Until its time is finished, the Dharma will remain. People say that the Dharma was destroyed in Tibet and certainly there is some truth to that statement, but there are places in Tibet where it is flourishing now more than ever. Even if everyone in the world ganged up to destroy the Buddhadharma, they would be unable to do it. If the whole world rallied together to abuse and destroy a certain teacher, they couldn't if his time hadn't come. But if a Buddhist teacher's time is finished, even if the whole world rose up and tried to prolong his life, it would be of no help.

This is like the blooming of flowers in the spring and summer; it is simply the course of things. Conversely, fall and winter are the time when flowers die. No matter what you do, no matter how much you tend them, they will die in the fall and winter. But in the spring new flowers blossom once again. This is the nature of *karma*. It's very difficult to counteract or try to avert *karma*. This is the nature of things; when it ripens, there's no turning it back.

Does this pertain only to Buddhism? No, this is true for all types of Dharma as well as the mundane world. This is simply the nature of *saṃsāra*. This is the nature of the impermanent reality we're experiencing.

Please take note that the ship's captain was himself an emanation of Śākyamuni, and Lhalung Palgyi Dorje had attained the *bodhisattva* grounds. In order to engage in those actions, you must have the qualities of a highly realized being. Without that, you'd better not consider them. –

The virtuous *karma* from the desire realm up to the third meditative stabilization gives rise to the experience of joy, while the nonvirtue of the desire realm is *karma* that gives rise to the experience of suffering. The virtue of the third meditative stabilization on up is *karma* that gives rise to the experience of meditative stabilization.

– Virtuous *karma* from the desire realm up to the third meditative stabilization, which are stages of meditative development in the form realm, is *karma* that gives rise to the experience of joy. There are four stabilizations which we can experience with the human body, but they are also states of existence in the form realm within which various *devas* dwell. This experience of joy from the virtuous *karma* of the desire realm up to the third meditative stabilization is temporary; it is not the joy of liberation or of enlightenment. "The third meditative stabilization on up" includes the fourth stabilization, which is also in the form realm, and the formless realm having four states of meditative absorption. –

The ten contaminated and uncontaminated virtues are virtuous *karma*, the ten nonvirtues are nonvirtuous *karma*; liberating *nirvāṇa* entails ethically neutral *karma*. Afflictive *karma* of the higher realms is obstructive, ethically neutral *karma*. Carpentry, for instance, constitutes non-obstructive, ethically neutral *karma*.

– The passage referring to the ten contaminated and uncontaminated virtues and ethically neutral *karma* seems to either have a section missing from the text, or there may be a scribal error.

The afflictive *karma* of the higher realms is obstructive, ethically neutral *karma*, because the form and formless realms are devoid of nonvirtue, but the mental afflictions are still operative. Therefore, that *karma* is said to be "obstructive, ethically neutral *karma*." Mundane activities such as carpentry or drinking a glass of water and so forth are called non-obstructive, ethically neutral *karma*. –

The *karma* that creates the inanimate universe is *karma* that is common to sentient beings in general, while the *karma* that creates the sentient beings in the universe is individual *karma*.

– Common, or collective, *karma*, consists of actions that sentient beings have committed together. They experience the maturation of that *karma* together as their inanimate environment, while our own existence as individual sentient beings is the result of our own actions, not that of communal action. –

Thus, to synthesize all positive and negative *karma,* all nonvirtues are included among harms inflicted for one's own sake against the Three Jewels and against sentient beings. All virtues are included among actions one performs in order to serve the Three Jewels and sentient beings. *A Guide to the Bodhisattva Way of Life* states:

> All the joy in the world
> Comes from the desire for others' happiness,
> And all the suffering in the world
> Comes from the desire for one's own happiness.
>
> Enough of much talk!
> Note the difference between the fool,
> Who seeks his own benefit,
> And the sage, who works for the benefit of others.[63]

The same text also states that all that is included in abandoning sin and performing virtue, and that is included in subduing one's own mind. *The Sūtra of Individual Liberation* states:

> Commit no sins whatsoever,
> Perform bountiful virtues,
> Completely subdue your own mind—
> This is the teaching of the Buddha.

The three collections of the Buddha's teachings are synthesized in that. The text *Questions to Chen-ngawa* states:

> While making prostrations, the master said, "I have no other practice but to abstain from the ten nonvirtues." Potowa said, "You may be able to understand emptiness with your awareness, but earnestly consider the profundity of actions and their consequences."

– The three collections of the Buddha's teachings are the *vinaya,* the *sūtras,* and *abhidharma.* After being asked about the nature of ethical discipline, Milarepa replied, "I don't know anything about *vinaya,* but I do know how to subdue my own mind." So what is the *vinaya*? It simply means to subdue your own mind. –

Consider, "Since all suffering originates from nonvirtue, I must avoid even small nonvirtues, which are causes of suffering; and since all happiness arises from virtue, I must accumulate virtues from the smallest to the greatest." Day and night continually confess and abandon your sins, and earnestly perform virtues. [608] This concludes the supplementary chapter on causal actions and their consequences.

CHAPTER FOUR

An Introduction to Parables and Their Meanings

Homage to Avalokiteśvara!

[610] These are the profound practical instructions of Avalokiteśvara. This is an introduction to parables in conjunction with their meanings for the purpose of identifying your own mind-itself as the *dharmakāya*.

While giving the complete, combined empowerments and teachings on all the secret peaceful and wrathful deities, Orgyan Rinpoche taught the following: It is said that long ago in Go Phodrang Phardey in the land of India, in the center of the region of Orgyan, there was a structure built of precious substances, with five doors and inexhaustible wealth, a palace wherein dwelled King Ākāśagarbha. With 84,000 districts, he ruled over many subjects. His queen was named Vimalaprabhinimanojñā and his son, Prince Kiraṇa, had not come into his strength and was foolish. [611] His wise minister was named Sūryānaśim. In short, he possessed a splendid entourage, realm, subjects, and wealth.

Once near the King's palace there was a great festival held in a marketplace, and Prince Kiraṇa, together with his entourage, went to see the show. The prince went to watch the various spectacles displayed by an illusionist, and he was carried away by them. After getting separated from his companions, he became confused about the way back to the palace and lost his way. The prince wandered by foot in lands of people of more than one race and became a vagrant. He forgot his homeland and wandered from the gates of one city to another, eating beggars' food [612] and wearing beggars' rags. Living in the company of foolish derelicts, he found nowhere to sleep but on doorsteps and experienced great misery.

Many months and years went by, and the kingdom, having lost its princely heir, was on the verge of collapse; and there was fear that the royal line of King Ākāśagarbha had come to an end. At that time, the young beggar-prince, in roving about among all the city-states, happened to arrive at the door of the wise minister Sūryānaśim. The minister, recognizing him as the prince, exclaimed, "Oh, our prince who was previously lost has returned! You need not beg. Come to the palace!" and he began to lead him there.

The beggar-prince replied, "I'm no prince. When I search my memory, I recall being only a vagrant. You may bring me to the palace, but I'm not fit to be king. So I shall not go."

The minister replied, "As a young, foolish prince, not come into your strength, you went to watch an illusionist's show in the marketplace. Getting caught up in the spectacle, you left the domain of the palace and went wandering. Now, even though you live as a vagabond, you [613] are indeed the prince. So you will be given the seat of royalty. If you persist in your doubts about being the prince, I ask you: What was your original homeland? What was the palace? What was the city? What was your home? What was your class? Who was your father? Who was your mother? Who were your companions? What was your occupation?"

The beggar found he had nothing to say, and he was stunned. "Well then," he requested, "Tell me in detail about all these things and grant them to me."

The minister gave names to the realities and pointed out his homeland; and he likewise told the prince everything about his district, palace, city, home, sleeping quarters, family, and parents. The wise *brahmin* then bathed the prince, took him outside, placed him on the throne, and established him in the palace. There he was crowned, with the diadem placed upon his head, and clothed in royal garb. All at once he was offered the wealth of his domain, a coronation ceremony was held, and he was given the kingdom and the royal palace. He became like his father. In an instant, even though he did not discard his identity as a beggar, he no longer lived in the manner of a beggar.

The misery of being a vagrant disappeared by itself, and the kingdom and [614] all his subjects without exception came under his rule. And they lived in great joy and happiness.[64]

Here is a brief explanation of the meaning of that parable:

"Long ago in Go Phodrang Phardey in the land of India": With realization there is spiritual awakening,[65] but without realization, there is the cycle of existence. What was before then no one knows.

"in the center of the region of Orgyan" signifies an absence of size and dimensions.

"there was a structure built of precious substances" refers to the empty essence of everything.[66]

"with five doors": unimpeded openness.

"and inexhaustible wealth": without decline due to faults and without increase due to excellent qualities.

"a palace": the all-pervasive essence of the ground.

"King Ākāśagarbha": not falling to the extremes of *saṃsāra* or *nirvāna*.[67]

"With 84,000 districts": mastery over all types of realization, and mastery over the 84,000 gateways to the Dharma.

"he ruled over many subjects": invulnerable to all mental afflictions.

[615] "His queen was named Vimalaprabhinimanojñā": dwelling together with the appearances of the displays of your own luminosity.

" and his son, Prince Kiraṇa": neither realizing nor being confused by the momentarily arising expressions of your own creative power [of awareness].

"had not come into his strength": realization had not manifested.

" and was foolish": spontaneous and ineffable.

"His wise minister": This is the spiritual mentor in whom realization has manifested.

"was named Sūryānaśim": knowing how to manifest out of compassion.

"In short, he possessed a splendid entourage, realm, subjects, and wealth": The revelation of the bountiful perfection of all the phenomena of the cycle of existence and liberation from the expanse of the total-ground.

"Once": when there is an attraction to confusion.

"near the king's palace": the proximity of the total-ground with the cycle of existence.

"in a marketplace": [616] the locus of distraction, namely the five sense-fields, which are your own appearances.

"there was a great festival": the arising of the various objective appearances of the six fields of experience.[68]

"Prince": conceptual confusion, namely, momentarily arising conceptual dispersions.

"Kiraṇa": numerous thoughts and analyses.

"together with his entourage, went to see the show": together with ideation concerning the five senses.

"illusion": the arising of various appearances.

"the various spectacles displayed by an illusionist": all kinds of appearances of yourself and confusion.

"the prince went to watch, and he was carried away by them": the creative power [of awareness] reveals itself by way of the momentarily arising five senses.

"getting separated from his companions": wandering off to the six fields of experience.

"he became confused about the way back to the palace": not ascertaining the ground.

"lost his way": not having found the path to enlightenment, which is the locus of the appearance of primordial wisdom, [617] you enter the suffering of activity due to reifying apprehended objects.

"in lands of people of more than one race": differentiating between the cycle of existence and liberation.

"the prince wandered by foot": you circle around in the three realms and the six types of sentient existence, and the fruits of confusion ripen.

"became a vagrant": like a vagrant, you do not dwell in the ground, but circle around among the gates of the cities of the wombs of deceptive appearances.

"He forgot his homeland": forgetting the ground of the original nature of existence.

"wandered from the gates of one city to another": One becomes conceptually confused about activities and thoughts occurring due to dynamic, karmic, vital energies; and you are activated by grasping onto apprehended objects. One experiences the individual sufferings of the six types of sentient existence, and becomes confused in the midst of dispersing thoughts and cravings.

"eating beggars' food:" experiencing various kinds of suffering.

"wearing beggars' rags": entering into, or dwelling [618] among dualistic attachments and hatred and the five poisons.

"Living in the company of foolish derelicts": living in the company of confusion due to the deceptive appearances of the six types of objects.

"he found nowhere to sleep but on doorsteps": sleeping amidst the five poisons and external appearances due to habitual propensities.

"and experienced great misery": wandering in the cycle of existence while experiencing actions and their consequences.

"Many months and years went by": with the separation from the total-ground of great bliss, you are afflicted with immeasurable suffering for eons.

"the kingdom, having lost its princely heir, was on the verge of collapse": you stray from the *buddha*-nature.

"there was fear that the royal line of King Ākāśagarbha had come to an end": there is fear that the noble[69] line of the speech or the family of the Buddha has come to an end.

"At that time, the young beggar-prince": the experience of momentarily arising thoughts, which is the very locus of confusion.

"in roving about": [619] continuing in the suffering of all the six types of sentient existence.

"among all the city-states": traveling to all favorable and miserable types of rebirth.

"happened to arrive at the door of the wise minister Sūryānaśim": this indicates finally awakening from your karmic excursions, and meeting with a realized spiritual mentor who carries the practical teachings.

"The minister": the spiritual mentor, who heals the confused mind of the student.

"recognizing him as": recognizing our own mind as the Buddha.

"the prince": momentary awareness.

"exclaimed, 'Oh, our prince who was previously lost has returned!'": although the wandering total-ground is the *buddha*-nature, it wanders in the cycle of existence.

"You need not beg": indicates that you need not wander in the cycle of existence.

"'Come to the palace!' and he began to lead him there": leading you by identifying your own environment as a *buddha*-field.

"The beggar-prince replied": [620] not believing in yourself, you think, "I am not a *buddha*."

"I am no prince": you are without the fruits of joy.

"When I search my memory, I recall being only a vagrant": having forgotten your basic mode of existence, you recall your habitual propensities pertaining to the cycle of existence, which only cause you to wander on.

"You may bring me to the palace, but I am not fit to be king": you think that your mind is not fit to be a *buddha*.

"So I shall not go": your mind does not enter into reality-itself, but remains obsessed with inferior behavior.

"The minister replied": the spiritual mentor.

"As a young prince": indicates the vagrant wandering of the total-ground, and the momentary arising of the creative power of the disciple.

"foolish and not come into your strength": indicates that realization had not yet become manifest.

"you went to watch an illusionist's show in the marketplace": not knowing yourself, you behave due to deceptive vital energies.

[621] "Getting caught up in the spectacle": getting caught up in the objects of the six fields of experience.

"you left the domain of the palace and went wandering": the ground wanders in the cycle of existence due to grasping onto dispersing thoughts and to attachment and hatred.

"Now, even though you live as a vagabond, you are indeed the prince": the essence of the total-ground is the *buddha*-nature.

"So you will be given the seat of royalty": you are brought to the ground.

"If you persist in your doubts about being the prince": thinking that your mind is not a *buddha*.

"What was your original homeland?": indicates that you are not born from the total-ground, and that dispersing thoughts are momentary arisings.

"What was the palace?": on what foundation do you exist?

"What was the city?": what is the locus of your dispersing thoughts?

"What was your home?": where was the abode of your momentarily arising thoughts created?

[622] "What was your class?": what kind of momentarily arising events are the dispersions of the mind?

"Who was your father?": the cause.

"Who was your mother?": the contributing condition.

"Who were your companions?": the accompanying events.

"What was your occupation?": determining with certainty.[70]

"I ask": this indicates seeking out the master of the psycho-physical aggregates by inquiring about the agent of behavior, of hopes and fears, and of ego-grasping.

"The beggar found he had nothing to say": upon the collapse of dispersing thoughts and obsessions, there is realization of the essential reality-itself, which is not established as any essence.

"he was stunned": this means that you do not know how to articulate it.

"Well then, tell me in detail about all these things": when you imagine the spiritual mentor on the crown of your head, you feel it is possible that even you might be a *buddha*.

"grant them to me": this means that with confidence you ask your spiritual mentor to reveal these things.

"The minister": [623] a spiritual mentor who has genuine realization.

"gave names to the realities": this means that these are practical teachings that present a parable together with its meaning.

Accordingly, just as the prince did not know he was a prince and became a beggar, you fail to recognize your own mind-itself as the *dharmakāya*, and you wander in the cycle of existence. Just as the minister recognized the prince and brought him to the seat of royalty, the spiritual mentor identifies your mind-itself as the *dharmakāya*; and upon becoming freed from the suffering of the cycle of existence, you achieve the excellent qualities of a *buddha*.

AN INTRODUCTION TO A PARABLE AND ITS MEANING TAUGHT BY SIDDHA ORGYAN

It is said that in the land of India there was once a captain who owned a precious [wish-fulfilling] jewel from the outer ocean. All his needs and desires were produced by this gem, and his household was very wealthy, prosperous, and luxurious. Eventually this captain passed away, and when his wife and children found all their wealth exhausted, they became [624] very poor and destitute, and they went begging. Upon meeting with a friend of the captain, they told him what had happened to them, and the friend replied, "It's impossible for you to be destitute! What kinds of things do you have at home?"

"We have nothing at all except a smooth stone stashed between the folds of a cotton quilt," they replied. The friend took them back home, and after a careful search, the dirt-encrusted jewel was found beneath a pillow. Then the friend rinsed it with scented water, fastened it to the crest of a victory banner, and made immeasurable offerings, praises, and requests to it. It is said that as a result, all their needs and desires were bountifully fulfilled. Moreover, if it were not for the friend, the jewel would have been left beneath the pillow, and the mother and children would have starved to death.

As in this parable, the mind-itself, the inborn *dharmakāya*, is primordially present in you, but it is like the jewel left beneath the pillow. [625] As a result of not realizing the existence of the *dharmakāya* in yourself, you wander in the cycle of existence. Just as the friend recognized the jewel, then made offerings, here, due to an introduction by a holy spiritual mentor, you realize your own mind-itself as the *dharmakāya*, then your own and others' welfare is bountifully accomplished.

– The question isn't whether we have the *dharmakāya*, but whether we recognize it. You do not have a you. Where are you? Are you in your head, in your torso, in your feet? Is your whole body you? Where are you to be found? When you are unable to find this you, the basic assumption of your own existence is undermined. It is the task of the spiritual mentor to point out your own nature to you. You are the *dharmakāya*. Your very identity is that of the *dharmakāya*. Once you recognize this, you may wonder why you have searched and searched years for the truth, when the truth you seek has always been within you. As an analogy, when astronauts go into space, they go around and around the planet, but finally they land back on earth. Similarly, we wander around looking for the truth, looking for liberation, when, in fact, our own identity is the fulfillment of this yearning! –

Once in the land of India there was a great king who passed away, leaving behind an orphaned son. A minister abducted the child and abandoned him to a band of idiots. The orphan became utterly destitute in terms of his clothing, food, and lodging, and he became indistinguishable from the idiots' children. Eventually a *brahmin* examined his features and recognized that he was endowed with the fine characteristics of the royal class. He bathed the child with scented water, burned fine incense, clothed him with fine garments, adorned him with fine ornaments, placed him on a high throne, and appointed him as the sovereign of the kingdom. Thus, in an instant he arose in the royal family of the entire region, [626] and all his subjects experienced joy and happiness.

Likewise, your own mind-itself has been primordially present as the spontaneous *dharmakāya*, but it has been obscured by adventitious contaminations; and without recognizing it, you have wandered in the cycle of existence. Upon receiving the blessings of a holy spiritual mentor, you are introduced to it; and, upon identifying your mind as primordially present as the *dharmakāya,* you are liberated from the sufferings of wandering in the cycle of existence.

– In the past, out of their great compassion, great teachers such as His Holiness the Dalai Lama, His Holiness Dudjom Rinpoche, and His Holiness Gyalwa Karmapa have offered empowerments, oral transmissions, and teachings. All these have been offered by these great *lamas,* but when these *lamas* appear like the sun rising in the east, it is as if we turn our faces toward the west. Think deeply about the above parable and its meaning.

In the past our minds have been obscured by delusion and ignorance. As a result of these obscurations, we have failed to recognize its nature as the *dharmakāya.* This is none other than failing to recognize our own identity. With the help of a spiritual mentor we are introduced to the nature of our own minds, which enables us to identify the nature of our own minds as the *dharmakāya.* By so doing, we are liberated from *saṃsāra.* Once you recognize the nature of your own mind as that which can neither be benefited or harmed, you will know that even if a thousand *buddhas* come to see you, they will not benefit your mind, and even if a thousand *māras* turn upon you, they cannot harm your mind. This is the nature of the *dharmakāya.* Ponder this deeply. –

THE PARABLE OF THE OLD MAN LOSING HIS CORD

In one region there once lived an old man and woman. At the bottom of a valley a great spectacle was taking place, and the old woman encouraged her husband to go see it. "I might mistake myself for someone else," he replied, "so I'm not going."

"You won't make that mistake if you fasten an identification sign on yourself, so go!" she retorted. Tying a purple cord on his leg, she sent him on his way.

Getting carried away by the spectacle, he let the cord on his leg be cut off. Then, mistaking himself for someone else, [627] he went around asking other people, "Hey, who am I? Who am I?"

These other people replied, "You moron! You are yourself!" But he did not recognize himself. Eventually he ran into his wife and complained to her, "This morning I told you I would go and mistake myself for someone else, but you didn't listen. It's your fault that I didn't recognize myself!" And he was on the verge of beating the old woman.

"The deity will show you your nature. Make homage to the deity," she said, and she made him bow many times to the deity. After awhile he became exhausted and fell asleep, and while he was sound asleep she fastened another purple cord on his leg and left it there. He woke up, and said, "Now here I am!" and so he recognized himself. Even when the old man did not recognize himself after the cord was cut off, there was no reason for his confusion. While he was present in his own identity, [628] he became confused about something about which there was no reason to be confused.

To explain the parable: just as the old man initially became confused about something about which there was no reason to be confused, while your own mind-itself is primordially present as the *dharmakāya*, you wander in the cycle of existence due to not recognizing it. Just as the old man recognized himself once a cord was tied to his leg, so you see your own face of the *dharmakāya* due to being introduced to it by means of the oral instructions of a spiritual mentor; and this eradicates the basis for wandering in the cycle of existence.

– The point of this parable is that the old man was himself whether or not the old woman tied a cord to his leg, so there is no reason why he should mistake himself for someone else or forget who, in fact, he was. In a similar way, our primordial nature is *buddha*-nature, but due to grasping onto appearances as being truly existent, we fail to recognize our own nature. We fail to recognize who we are. We should find this embarrassing, but instead we take it quite in stride. When a spiritual mentor points out to us the nature of our mind as the *dharmakāya*, he is introducing us to the very nature of our own being, and through this recognition we will no longer wander in the cycle of existence.

Last night you were dreaming that you were someone, but who were your father and mother in the dream? When were you born? Where did you live? Who created you? When you woke up this morning, what happened to the individual in that dream? Did that person die? Either way, where did that person go? We tend to say, "Oh, that was different. That was just a dream and was fictitious, whereas what I am experiencing now is the truth, not fiction." Isn't this how we feel?

From a Buddhist perspective what is real is that your own nature is that of a *buddha*. What is fictitious is your identity as a sentient being. So with this in mind, ask yourself again, "Where did I, as the person in last night's dream, go? During the daytime you may feel that you have awakened as if you were already a *buddha*, recognizing that your identity, circumstances, and so forth in the dream are fictitious. If so, at night are you as deluded as if you were an ordinary sentient being? What will happen when you fall asleep tonight? What will happen to this "*buddha*like person" that you are right now? Where will your excellent qualities, your virtues go when you once again fall asleep? Please, dwell on these things. –

THE ANALOGY OF SEEING A ROPE AS A SNAKE

A man once mistook a multicolored rope moving back and forth within a thicket of bushes for a poisonous snake. Concerned that it would bite him and he would be injected with the snake's poison, he became terribly frightened. This was not a case of visual distortion, for his eyes saw only a multicolored rope, without discerning the blood, [629] mouth, or eyes and so on of a snake. So how did he get confused? He became confused by mentally imputing the multicolored, wriggling rope as a snake, even as a poisonous snake, with its harmful qualities and so on. Then someone else pointed out to him, "This is not a snake. It's a rope," and took him by the hand and showed him. In this way he was freed from his fears about a poisonous snake.

To explain the analogy: At the outset there was no reason to confuse the rope for a snake. Likewise, while the mind-itself is present as the *dharmakāya*, you fail to recognize yourself. In that light, you are carried away by the waves of the cycle of existence and experience suffering. Just as he was freed from his fears about a poisonous snake as a result of someone else identifying the rope for him, when a spiritual mentor shows you the nature of the mind, your own face as the *dharmakāya* is revealed; and you achieve certain freedom from wandering in the cycle of existence. That case of being confused about something for which there is no reason to be confused [630] is said to be due to "adventitious contaminations." On the contrary, thinking that the mind-stream turns bad and experiences suffering—while ignoring the agent that causes you to wander in the cycle of existence, namely the "adventitious contaminations"—constitutes a failure to determine the nature of existence of the mind. You should earnestly seek out the meaning of this, and with the three parables and their meanings determine for yourself the manner in which the mind becomes confused.

– From the outset, there was no reason for him to think that the rope was a snake because the rope was never a snake; it had always been a rope. That is just its nature. To think your mind-stream is the problem, rather than the adventitious contaminations that distort and pollute it, is simply a result of failing to determine the actual nature of the mind. In each analogy this failure is found: one does not recognize the nature of the mind, and from this lack of recognition all attachment and hatred arise. Moreover, such mental afflictions arise due to the apprehension of something unreal. Thoroughly examine these points.

We may think that we are practitioners of Dzogchen, but in the meantime, we think that other people are the ones with the problems. The point of this practice is to turn inward and recognize our own nature. Even when we become highly realized, we may have the sense that there are some external beings who are supportive, such as *devas* and *ḍākinīs*, and others, such as *māras*, who are out to destroy us. On the very morning of his enlightenment, even Buddha Śākyamuni, with *devas* and so forth in attendance, seemed to be assailed by a host of *māras*, but all of this was created by his mind.

We create all of our mental afflictions. As soon as we start faulting others, and as soon as we designate others as our enemies and our friends, we are deluded. These thoughts arise because we have failed to recognize our own nature. All of the harping on how sensitive, pure, and good we are, as opposed to how bad others are, is pure fiction. Such delusion is our problem, and when these aversions and attachments are applied to different spiritual traditions, sectarianism and prejudice arise, which is also our problem. It is not the problem of the different religious orders or traditions themselves.

Once again, the crucial point is that all the attachment and hatred that arises in our own mind is our own problem. It is like losing the cord. We are responsible for it. Whatever mind state we get into, whether it is good or bad, all of this is like the old man who lost his cord. It is all taking place in a fictitious setting where we have forgotten our own identity. Once you have realized the two types of identitylessness—personal and phenomenal—then your mind is analogous to an empty house. There is simply no door for attachment, hostility, craving, and so forth to enter. It is a totally clear place. Once you have recognized your own nature, it is like venturing into a land where everything is made of gold—not even a single pebble is ordinary. Similarly, when we recognize our own nature, there is no place for a thought or perception of impurity—no objects of attachment or hostility. When we enter into a mind state that has aversion for the other side and attachment for our own, it really is an embarrassment because we are simply engaging in fiction.

Sometimes, we fail to recognize our own faults and become obsessed with dwelling on the faults of others. Or we act as if we have the qualities of a thousand *buddhas*. We may even act as if we are speaking from an utterly sublime state of pure vision. We praise some people, talking at length about their excellent qualities; then from our lofty position we turn to those whom we hold in contempt and express our disdain for them, speaking at length about their horrible faults. We do this as if we were being totally objective. This is ridiculous, because we do not have the qualities of a *buddha*. Rather, when we enter into this mind state, we don't even have the virtue of an intestinal parasite.

To review the last sentence of the parable, check out your own experience. Are you confused or not? Are you involved in this type of fiction or not? You have created all your friends and enemies, the objects of your attachments and aversions. They are your own fictions. The objects of your aversion and attachments are not something that exist in reality. They are fictions that you create for yourself and to whom you have emotional responses. You need to determine for yourself, in terms of your own experience, whether or not you are confused in this regard, whether or not you are deceived by these fictions. If you find that you are confused, then determine if it is positive or negative. Specifically, examine the objects of your own attachment, anger, and hatred. Determine for yourself if they are truly existent or not. Are they real or are they not? If you recognize that they are primordially unestablished, ungrounded, then they do not have their own intrinsic existence. So you do not need to elaborate any further. Then, just leave it and observe the nature of your own mind. –

Once in the land of India there was a king who was devoted to Dharma but had a son who was uninterested in spiritual practice. The king summoned an illusionist and commanded him, "Create an illusion as a means of causing this son of mine to be drawn to Dharma."

The illusionist asked, "What is the prince attracted to?"

"He likes horses," the King replied.

The next morning the illusionist brought a fine horse adorned with a saddle and bridle and asked the prince whether he wanted to buy it. [631] The prince admired it and replied, "I do want to buy it, but first I shall put it through its paces," and he mounted the horse. Not being able to control the horse, he rode far away over hill and dale. After coming to a desert region on the shore of the ocean, the horse threw him, then swam into the ocean. There was no way the prince could get back to his homeland, and there was not a single person nearby. When he had fallen into fear and dejection, an old, wild-haired woman came along and told him that this region was totally uninhabited. "Where did you originally come from?" she asked, and he told her his story.

"This is the shore of the ocean, and there are no dwellings or inhabitants here," she told him. "But I have a daughter. Would you like to stay with her?"

Reflecting that even though he was a prince, he had no other option, he moved in with the daughter. After quite some time, the couple had a son and a daughter. Eventually the old woman died, and when they were carrying her corpse into the hills, his wife became overcome with misery at her mother's death and leapt into a river. While trying to save her mother, [632] the little daughter also fell into the river and was swept away by the current. While the prince was thinking how to save her, his young son was carried away by a wolf while he was sleeping. Overcome with grief, the prince wept, beat his chest, and pulled out his hair. In time he grew old, and his hair turned completely white.

Then the illusionist dispersed the illusion. The prince then summoned his ministers from every corner of his domain and told them he had an account to tell of his felicities and adversities. His ministers retorted, "No felicities or adversities have happened to you. You haven't moved from your throne! The food that was put before you hasn't even gotten cold." Despite their response, the prince wouldn't listen, and insisted on telling his story in detail. When he had finished, he said, "There is no point in any of this," and he relinquished his kingdom and entered the gateway of Dharma.

In this parable, while the prince did not move from his throne, the illusionist confused him by the power of *mantras* and physical substances, and for a long time he experienced suffering. Likewise, while the mind-itself of our minds is the [633] *sugatagarbha,* which does not move away from the nature of the *dharmakāya,* we fail to recognize our own nature; and by the power of the various sins and obscurations we accumulate, we wander in the cycle of existence and experience suffering for a long time. Just as the prince did not move from his throne even while he was entranced by the illusion, even while we wander in the cycle of existence, the causal *sugatagarbha* does not enter into evil.

– In this context the "causal" *sugatagarbha* refers to the *sugatagarbha* that is the cause, or ground, of the path, and yet it is also the path itself, as well as the fruition of the path. If it were not for the *sugatagarbha,* we would have no Dharma practice or anything else at all. –

Take the analogy of uncontaminated, pure gold. If a goldsmith were to sweep it into a dogdish or grime and it was covered with dirt, it would become filthy. But after melting it down, it could be made into beautiful ornaments such as a golden-adorned saddle, earrings, bracelets, or rings. Or melting them down, it could be molded into a statue of the Buddha, and when that is consecrated, it could become an object of homage and worship for everyone. Although there are these three things that can be done to it, the essence of gold is immutable. [634] Likewise, all the time that we wander in the cycle of existence, achieve the *bodhisattva* grounds and paths, and ultimately attain spiritual awakening, the essence of the mind is immutable.

Just as an ordinary stone does not turn into silver even if it is melted down, if the essence of spiritual awakening were not present in the causal mind-stream, the fruition of spiritual awakening would not be accomplished even with the practice of Dharma. It is said,

"All phenomena arise from causes." Since silver is present in silver ore, when it is melted down, it first becomes partially refined, then more refined, and finally it turns into pure silver. Likewise, since the *sugatagarbha* is present in the mind-stream, once we know this and enter into practice, first experiential realization arises, then we gradually progress along the *bodhisattva* grounds and paths, and finally we attain spiritual awakening.

– The first experiential realization is the recognition of the nature of the mind. The strategy for progressing along the grounds and paths is first to engage in the preliminary practices, thereby establishing a suitable foundation. Next, one should perform the deity practices of the stages of generation and completion, and finally we are able to enter into the practice of Dzogchen. In this way, we circle around and recognize our own nature. –

The Profound Inner Meaning states:

> The stainless essence of the *jinas* is sequentially impure, partially impure and partially pure, and utterly pure. Likewise, it is said that it is sequentially present as sentient beings and as *tathāgatas*. So realize this meaning.

[635] Thus, this mind-itself is primordially present as the essence of the *dharmakāya*. So identify and recognize it with certainty; and without modifying or adulterating it with any hopes or fears, it is enough simply to attend to the essence of whatever appears. As an analogy, after forming sugar into various divine forms, demonic forms, and human forms, when they are eaten one after the other, even though their forms are different, they all have the same sweet taste of sugar. Similarly, whatever virtuous and nonvirtuous thoughts arise in the mind, by observing their essence, they arise as Mahāmudrā, just as all the different forms of sugar have the same sweet taste.

This concludes the supplementary introduction to parables.

– It is necessary to identify with certainty your own mind-itself as the *dharmakāya*. However, this is not a push-button procedure. It is not something that you simply decide to do, push a button, then find it is completed. As long as we remain in the midst of uncertainty, it is a gradual procedure.

In order to gain that kind of recognition, or the identification of the nature of your own mind, the first step is to find a genuine teacher, from whom you must receive teachings. Then in the process, you should be able to rid yourself of your uncertainties and doubts. The way you do this is by hearing the teachings and learning. Without entering into the first phase of the threefold process of hearing, thinking, and meditation, what will you have to meditate on? How can you meditate if you have not heard any teachings? In fact, some people do try to do this. They sit very still with their eyes glazed over as if they were in meditation. But since they have not learned any Dharma, they don't know what to meditate on. Instead, they just sit there. Maybe they are thinking about the big breakfast they had this morning or they are planning a delicious dinner. Without having learned how to meditate, it is doubtful that anything more significant is taking place.

In Tibet, it was customary for the disciple and teacher to check each other over for a period of three years. The disciple would decide if the teacher in question was genuine, and the teacher would see if the disciple was one to whom he wanted to entrust his training. This process is difficult in the West, where people seem to have no time. Everything is hurry, hurry. Nevertheless, you can find a good spiritual mentor. When you do, don't be fickle, flying from one mentor to another, dabbling in this and in that; for if you do, you will accomplish nothing at all. There are many fine spiritual mentors available. The kind of spiritual mentor from whom it is worth receiving guidance is one who, out of a pure motivation of compassion, teaches the nature of actions and their consequences, causes and effects.

First, hear the teachings. But the mere acquisition of knowledge alone will not suffice. It will not purify or transform your mind. The next phase is to contemplate the teachings. But while pondering the teachings may give rise to a theoretical understanding, that, too, cannot truly transform the mind and eradicate the source of suffering. Once you have eliminated your doubts and uncertainties and developed sound understanding, it is time to practice. This is like planting an apple tree. It isn't enough just to have the seed, you must plant it. Once you have put it in the ground, you can't just walk away. You need to fertilize and water the seed to make sure that it germinates into a sprout and then into a sapling. You need to cultivate it so that it reaches maturity as a tree. Then you can watch the apples grow and ripen. Finally, at the culmination of this process once the fruit is ripe, you are ready to reap the harvest.

Similarly, as a result of the three phases of hearing, thinking, and meditation, we can accomplish our own goals as well as those of others. Right now our highest priority is our own goals, most of which we pursue by means of the three poisons of attachment, aversion, and delusion. In that way we can't accomplish our own or others' deepest aims. For this, the path of Dharma alone is effective. –

CHAPTER FIVE

A Prose Identification

Homage to Avalokiteśvara!

[638] These are the profound practical instructions of Avalokiteśvara. The purpose of receiving this instruction on the union of Mahāmudrā and Atiyoga is to know the essential nature of the mind. This is important. Although this has already been treated in the main presentation on identification,[71] I suspect that those who are new to this may not yet have identified the nature of the mind; and even for those who have, I shall present an easily understood prose introduction so that their ascertainment may increase.

This knowledge of the essential nature of the mind is the best way to purify obscurations, as *The King of Dharma Sūtra* states:

> If one knows the mind as non-unitary and nondual, this is comparable to removing with the swipe of a cloth dust that has accumulated on the surface of a mirror for a thousand years. [639] By holding up a single oil-lamp, one dispels the darkness in an empty house that has lingered for a thousand years. Likewise, simply by knowing the real truth that the mind has no dual nature, sins that have been accumulated for countless eons are purified in a single instant.

– Solely due to the fact that we fail to recognize the essential nature of our own minds, we dualistically grasp onto appearances and reify them, thereby perpetuating our existence in *saṃsāra*. To counteract this grasping and reification, we must recognize the essential nature of our own minds.

Should you be satisfied once you know the essential nature of your own mind? No. As in the case of a child, it's not enough simply to be born: The child must be taken care of until it is able to survive on its own. Moreover, it is not sufficient to attend to the child's physical needs alone. The child must receive an education and develop excellent qualities. Then once children have reached a level of maturity and have developed understanding and knowledge, they are ready to survive on their own. Similarly, in terms of spiritual practice, it's not enough to know the essential nature of the mind, for then you must maintain it. This is done initially by ascertaining the essential nature of the mind, but if this certain knowledge begins to fade or is lost entirely, then you must restore it. This is the way you maintain such certainty and insight.

Within the Buddhist tradition, some declare that all sentient beings have the *capacity* to attain enlightenment, even though they are not yet enlightened. In particular, the Nyingma and Kagyü orders, on the other hand, maintain that the *buddha*-nature, or *tathāgatagarbha,* is a present reality, and not just a potential, that must be recognized; and that recognition needs to be maintained in order for spiritual maturation to take place. By so doing, you transform the fruition of perfect enlightenment into the path to awakening. –

If you can constantly sustain the awareness of the essential nature of the mind, you may not even need to devote yourself to retreats and solitude. *The Lamp of the Moon Sūtra* states:

> If one knows the nature of the mind, even if one's body remains in the marketplace, one's mind dwells in the wilderness. In the wilderness of the body dwells the Buddha of the mind. [640]

– If you maintain awareness of the essential nature of the mind, you don't really need to go into retreat, because you are sustaining that meditative state wherever you are. For instance, wherever His Holiness Dudjom Rinpoche went, whatever activities he engaged in, he constantly maintained that level of realization. With that perspective, all activities and events are perceived as creative expressions of awareness. –

What analogies are presented for realizing the essential nature of the mind? *The Essence of the Tathāgata Sūtra* states:

> As an analogy, a maid wraps a statue of the Tathāgata composed of precious substances in a smelly cloth and places it inside her blouse. Then the maid's master retrieves it from her blouse and removes the smelly cloth, so that the precious statue becomes an object of worship for himself and a basis for others to accumulate merit. Similarly, the *tathāgatagarbha,* the luminous mind-itself, concealed by the defilements of the mental afflictions, dwells in the bodies of all sentient beings in the cycle of existence; but it

> is not known. In reliance upon a spiritual friend, who is like the master in that analogy, one is helped to realize the *tathāgatagarbha,* the luminous mind-itself. Then one is liberated from the cycle of existence oneself, and one frees others as well.

– When I am in retreat, thoughts of the three times arise naturally. But these thoughts aren't stored in a mental bank account. They arise naturally, and they vanish naturally. If this weren't true, where could there be a bank large enough to hold them all? Now, the mere fact that thoughts arise is not an obstacle if, during the arising and vanishing of these thoughts, you are able to focus on the natural luminosity of the thoughts themselves. However, as the thoughts arise, if your judging mind grasps onto them and becomes unhappy with their sheer number and their content, that may be a problem. But the simple arising and passing of thoughts itself should not be seen as a problem.

What can you do when you find yourself judging the thoughts? First, abandon the idea that you can get immediate results from your practice, and don't even wish for such instant realization. It happens slowly, slowly, step by step. Can you gain realization by such gradual means? There is no reason why not, because right now you have all the necessary causes and conditions to accomplish enlightenment. You have the teachings and practices of the nine *yānas,* all of which are designed to bring enlightenment in this very lifetime. Furthermore, there are many examples of people who have accomplished liberation in the past. Looking at the lineage *gurus* of the past, from generation to generation, we are reminded of great spiritual mentors who have accomplished enlightenment. So why can't you achieve the same result? See if there are any real differences between those adepts from the past and yourself.

If you have the desire to put the teachings into practice, there is no reason they should not yield the result. On the other hand, if you have no desire, then of course there will be no result. Likewise, without practice there can be no result either. It's not something anyone else can do for you, any more than they can satiate your hunger by eating your dinner for you. If you're too busy to take your medicine, then you cannot be healed. Perhaps you can sponsor someone else to practice Dharma, which can have blessings and merit, but there is no way that this other person can transfer his or her realization and spiritual maturation to you. –

The Immaculate Thought Sūtra states:

> Mañjuśrī asked, [641] "Lord, what is the experience of a monk who cultivates the *samādhi* of engaging in contemplation?"
>
> [The Buddha] replied, "As an analogy, if one extinguishes a fire [in a house] by whatever means, smoke stops coming out the windows. Likewise, upon recognizing the mind as empty awareness, one experiences the empty appearances of visual forms, empty sounds, empty smells, empty tastes, and empty

tactile objects. If water is not stirred up, it is limpid; if the sky is not obscured, it is clear; if the mind is not modified, it is blissful. In that regard it is said:

> A contemplative who knows the essential nature of the mind
> Dwells in the nature of meditation
> And in primordial reality,
> Regardless of what he does.

That is said to be the experience of *samādhi*.

– How amazing to assert that when the mind is not modified, it abides in a state of bliss! Everything we do to the mind—adopting certain types of conduct and avoiding others—entails modifications of the mind. What does it mean for the mind to be blissful? Does it mean you are so happy, you are tingling with bliss? No, because that is just one more expression of grasping. Rather this is bliss that totally transcends conventional reality. In its natural state, the mind is blissful and is liberated. Just as water that is not stirred up is limpid and clear, so is this true of the mind. Everything that we adopt and reject entails modifications that stir up the mind, inducing dualistic grasping. So, in this phase of the practice you stop all of that and let the mind remain in an unmodified state.

Various types of ideation naturally arise, and they are self-arisen and self-ceasing. They naturally vanish. In the course of their natural arising and vanishing, they neither inflict harm nor bestow any benefit. In this quality of awareness you are totally beyond the domain of either harming or benefiting the mind. In this context, in fact, the thoughts that arise are not different from the nature of the mind-itself, just as the waves that arise on the surface of the ocean are not different from the ocean. –

The Questions of King Miyowa Sūtra states:

> When appearances are naturally clear, without any clinging or grasping, they are pure in their own state. Do not think otherwise.

The Questions of Brahmā Sūtra states:

> Do not think, "These are memories and thoughts [642] and these are feelings." Clearly settle in the non-abandonment of the inconceivable mind of primordial wisdom. Otherwise, there will be no success.

The Questions of Ngangpa Giryin Sūtra states:

> Know that if there is no distraction, this is the contemplation of the natural luminosity of reality-itself.

The Questions of Maitreya Sūtra states:

> Nonconceptually rest in the steady vision of appearances. That alone is the best of meditations.

– Without concepts, leave your awareness, just as it is, in the steady vision of appearances. If you can do so, that is indeed the best of meditations. In terms of recognizing the nature of awareness, the spiritual mentors of the past, including His Holiness Dudjom Rinpoche, stated that it could be ascertained in the interval following the cessation of one thought and prior to the arising of the next thought. In that interval there is an emptiness. How long is this interval? It's a mistake to think it is short in duration. Rather, it is the very nature of both *saṃsāra* and *nirvāṇa*. In the very steady vision of appearances, right in the instant, in the instantaneous vision of the instantaneous moment of appearances, you can recognize the essential nature of the mind. It is said that all the *buddhas* can be found in a single atom, which indicates the single nature of the whole of *saṃsāra* and *nirvāṇa*. –

The Questions of Dewa Lodrö Sūtra states:

> Not thinking of anything is said to be great meditation.

The Questions of Śrīmatībrāhmaṇī Sūtra states:

> The "natural clear light of all phenomena" refers to primordial awareness that is free of laxity and excitation. Why? Because awareness is unborn, unceasing, and primordial.

The Sūtra on Possessing the Roots of Virtue states:

> One's own primordial wisdom is clear, blissful consciousness that does not conceptualize about anything, [643] and that is apprehended as the *dharmakāya*.

It is said, "Not experiencing objects as external to the mind, and not thinking of them as within the mind is the best of meditative stabilizations."

The Questions of King Katsal Sūtra states:

> The "view" is not analyzing one's mind; it is the best of experiences of reality.

– "Not analyzing one's mind" entails being disengaged from all acceptance and rejection, or all preferences. But be aware that this practice is not just being spaced out or falling into a stupor. Remember that until you ascertain the nature of the mind, you do need to continue in the practices of abandoning that which is nonvirtuous and adopting that which is virtuous. –

The Questions of Brāhman Tsangpa Sūtra states:

> Consciousness of the unity of meditation and the view is dwelling continually in clarity and nonconceptuality. That is equivalent to the mind of the Buddha.

– In terms of the meditation and the view, you first need to gain some understanding of the view, then you may enter the practice of meditation. To have only theoretical understanding of the view is not enough; you must meditate. Conversely, it's not enough to meditate without understanding the view. But there is a deeper state: through meditation, you dwell in the view, and that is the fruition of the path. This is in effect transforming the fruition into the path. What is the fruition? It is the view and the view becomes the path. This is a very important point: the view is the fruition, the path is the fruition, the meditation is the fruition. Simultaneously they are the fruition. –

The Questions of the Girl Regöma Sūtra states:

> With one's own mind dwelling in its own reality, without accumulating any merit, obscurations are purified; and without taking rebirth, one will doubtlessly reach the state of spiritual awakening in this very life.

The Questions of King Dewa Sūtra states:

> One who knows how to observe the mind with the mind is the best of contemplatives. [644]

The Perfection of Wisdom Sūtra states:

> When the continuum of awareness is unceasing, with the mind not reified, reality-itself is known well.

The Questions of King Dejin Sūtra states:

> Not withdrawing one's mind, but leaving it in its own nature, is the best of meditations.

The Questions of Brahmā Sūtra states:

> Settling the mind evenly in the mind, the mind is not objectified by the mind.

– In this practice, you rest the mind in the mind, but the mind is not an object of concentration. So how do we accomplish this? Düdjom Lingpa commented, "Never disengage from space." That is, always leave your visual gaze resting in the midst of space. –

The King of Tantras Equal to Space states:

> When the mind becomes conjoined with an ordinary body, the person who realizes his own mind as the *dharmakāya* becomes a *buddha* in that very lifetime. Why? Because the root of ignorance is cut.

Tilopa asked a primordial wisdom *ḍākinī*, "What is Buddha like?" The primordial wisdom *ḍākinī* replied, "Tilopa, if the mind observes the mind, [645] that which is doing the observing is your own mind, and that which is being observed is also your own mind. Thus, when the mind is observed, just as space is not to be seen, both the observer and the observed are purified. Then when that luminosity is realized, that is the spontaneously present Buddha; it is the Buddha that enters the path; and it is also the Buddha of manifest realization. When that is realized, the mind is unborn and undying, so the *māra* of the Lord of Death is conquered. The mind is ascertained as primordial wisdom devoid of inherent existence, so the *māra* of the *deva* child[72] is conquered. The mind has no location among the psycho-physical aggregates, so the *māra* of the aggregates is conquered. The mind has no mental afflictions, so the *māra* of the afflictions is conquered. In that way, when the four *māras* are conquered, all the myriad thoughts concerning objective appearances are ascertained as your own mind; and when they are ascertained as the mind, the mind is called the unborn and undying *dharmakāya*. Tilopa, know this!" [646]

– When the observer and the observed are purified, they are not cleansed, but rather they disappear, for they are both primordially ungrounded. In the earlier examination of the mind, one ascertains that the mind has no color, no shape, and no substance, and is therefore like space.[73] Moreover, it is primordially ungrounded because although it appears, it has no inherent existence, so it is not truly existent. Thus, the nature of the mind is beyond the three times of past, present and future, and it is beyond birth, abiding, and cessation.

Are the myriad thoughts purely subjective, or are they both subjective and objective? Thoughts create both the subject and the object, and if you recognize the nature of thoughts, you will see them to be of the very nature of awareness. All phenomena are both designated by thought and are creative expressions of awareness. –

This unstructured consciousness of the present, the instant that is free of mental engagement, is called Mahāmudrā. As it is unblemished by contaminations, even though it appears, it is untainted within the three times. This instantaneous consciousness is without resistance to evil and without affirmation of good; it has no path on which to proceed; and it has no mental afflictions or antidotes for overcoming them. Since it does not exist, it is not found even if it is sought. Everything is included in this instantaneous consciousness of the present, so this is called the embodiment of all the *buddhas*; and once you come to this conclusion, there can be no disputing it. This consciousness of the present is the basic ground of all excellent qualities, so there is no inconsistency in regarding it as the ground. This consciousness of the present is not created by anyone, so there is no inconsistency in saying it is spontaneously present. If you say, "In reality it is like this...," it does not act as an object of any mind, nor is it any substance, [647] so it is nondual. This consciousness of the present is free of any basis of superimposition or mistaken denial, for it is the absolute space of phenomena, free of birth, cessation, and remaining, and it is present as the great *dharmakāya*.

– The uncreated consciousness of the present is free of afflictions, because it is uncontaminated by any afflictions, and within it there is no path on which to proceed. In this awareness there is no judgment. There are no bad thoughts. There are no good thoughts. There is no wanting to get rid of this or wanting to cultivate that. If we look for mental afflictions, they are certainly easy to find; they are right before us. But if you seek the mind, it cannot be found, because it is primordially ungrounded; although it appears, it has no inherent existence. If it were grounded, it would really have mental afflictions, and there would be remedies for them. But because the mind-itself is primordially ungrounded, it has no afflictions or antidotes to overcome afflictions. Everything is present in this instantaneous consciousness of the present.

The nature of the mind-itself is beyond the scope of any conventional mind, so if you try to describe it with the conventional mind, you've already missed the point. It cannot be described; it is not conceivable by the relative mind, for it is nondual. –

If you investigate that very reality, what birth and abiding is there? What inherent nature is there? What aspect is there? What form is there? What consciousness is there? What appearance is there? What emptiness is there? What existence is there? What nonexistence is there? What *buddha* is there? What sentient being is there? What awareness is there? What ignorance is there? If you observe carefully, no observable object is seen by any subject in any aspect. Such vision as that is the great vision, for it is the vision of thatness. It is not a vision of something existent. Thus *The Tantra of Non-abiding* states:

> This is Mahāmudrā: it is unblemished by contaminations, it is without negation or affirmation, [648] and no path or antidotes are to be found. This is the embodiment of all the *buddhas*. This is the basis of all excellent qualities. This is spontaneously present. It mentally engages with nothing and is without duality of any kind. This is free of superimpositions and mistaken denial, present as the great *dharmakāya*. If birth, abiding, nature, and cessation are observed, in this none are to be seen. This is the great vision of thatness.

Such a *tantra* is received only with the purity of one's own mind-stream and the power of one's spiritual mentor. The same treatise states, "By means of blessings, this is received from one's spiritual mentor."

– How can the purity of your own mind-stream be experienced? Through practices such as meditation on Vajrasattva. How can you receive the power of your spiritual mentor? By the blessings of your spiritual mentor. For example, as you receive an initiation, you should see the *vajra* master as the *buddha* from whom you are directly receiving the initiation. Therefore, to receive the above *tantra*, a student must have faith and pure vision of the spiritual mentor.

It is then the spiritual mentor's task to give the empowerment, oral transmission, and explanation. By the confluence of these two—what the spiritual mentor brings to the relationship and what you as a student bring to it—you are able to receive what you already have, that is, you recognize what is already your own. –

In one verse *The Tantra that Liberates the Whole World: A Commentary on the Meaning of Great Compassion* teaches:

> Sever the root of the three times.
> Without contrivance, release the three doors and concentrate.
> That primordial reality, free of the three bases,
> Sustains quiescence and insight.

– "Primordial reality" refers to awareness, free of the three bases. What are the three bases? They may be understood in either of two ways: as the three times, the past, present and future; or as the three doors of the body, speech, and mind. –

[649] From what does your own mind arise? Where does it remain now? Where will it finally go? You may look, but everything is empty, utterly ungrounded. While in that experience, rest without moving your body, without speaking, and without modifying your mind. As an analogy, if an elephant herder is too strict, the elephant will charge him in anger; and if he does not watch the elephant, it will escape. Thus, he relaxes and concentrates, and watches from afar. Likewise, if your own mind is too tight, it will become exhausted, and thoughts will proliferate; and if you do not meditate, your habitual tendencies will carry on automatically. So relax and concentrate. With the sentry of introspection recognize awareness. When you leave it as it is, without modification, among thoughts of the past, thoughts of the future, thoughts of the present, and the unmodified ground, you are freed

from the first three. [650] Without clinging, sustain quiescence that remains without modification, and insight that freshly arises as experiential, uncontaminated, primordial wisdom.

– The origination of the mind is empty; and its present location and eventual destination are empty and ungrounded, so it has no root or basis in reality. With the sentry of your attention, conjoined with conscientiousness and introspection, recognize awareness. Note the qualities of meditation Karma Chagmé emphasizes: following a middle way without too little or too much tension, while cultivating mindfulness, introspection, and conscientiousness. All of these are facets of the path that we need to cultivate. Other passages of this text state there should be no meditation, no meditator, and nothing to meditate on. Are these two statements inconsistent? No, they are not incompatible. The very nature of Dzogchen, the Great Perfection, is that there is no meditation, no meditator, and no object of meditation. But as long as we are bound up in dualistic grasping, we do need to apply ourselves to the path, and that is why this is pointed out by the author.

When you relax and concentrate with introspection and without modification, you are free from thoughts of the past, present, and future, as well as the unmodified ground. When you are free of thoughts—not following after or grasping onto thoughts of the past, present, and future—where are you going? There is no place to go, so you remain in the unmodified ground. This abiding mind, without modification, is quiescence, and this insight into emptiness is nonconceptual. These two states are to be sustained: quiescence that remains without modification, and sustained insight which freshly arises as experiential, uncontaminated, primordial wisdom. When this insight arises, if a sense of clinging arises towards it, it is no longer insight. Insight can be sustained only if there is an absence of clinging. This is analogous to letting your gaze rest in the space in front of you—not on a visual object, but in the intervening space itself, with nothing on which to grasp, nothing to which to cling. –

Likewise, *A Treatise of Instruction of the Greatly Compassionate Supreme Light* states:

> Recognize ideation as your own mind; it arises from the mind, and is released as the mind. Recognizing that it is created by the mind, know it as the mind; and whatever appears, recognize it as your own mind, without negation or affirmation. That is the dawning of the unknown *nirmāṇakāya* of awareness, a state of subtle, immaculate bliss, empty, and homogeneous. It is the primordially present nature of being: undistracted, unmodified, ordinary consciousness. While emptiness cannot be grasped as a thing, it is self-illuminating, and is experienced without grasping; so that is the experience of perfect enjoyment of the primordial wisdom of awareness.

Realize all external ideation as your own mind. Realize the internal mind-itself as being empty of substantiality. Realize the intermediate experience as great bliss. The undifferentiated occurrence of the external, internal, and intermediate is released as a unity. Then [651] that unity is free of the extremes of unity and nonunity, the external and the internal; it is without categories and is all-pervasive. This vivid, unsubstantial, naturally clear, unmediated, groundless, essential nature of awareness that is invariably without illumination or obscuration is the *dharmakāya*.

– The "dawning of the unknown *nirmāṇakāya* of awareness" is said to be unknown because previously it has not been recognized. Therefore, at the moment one recognizes it for the first time, that which was unknown becomes known. It is not adventitious or temporary, but it is primordially present. In this section, the *nirmāṇakāya* is referred to explicitly, while the *sambhogakāya*, the embodiment of perfect enjoyment, is only implied.

I believe "external ideation" refers to the entire outer environment composed of the elements and so forth. This is referred to as ideation because the outer environment is fabricated by thoughts, so you should realize that this outer environment is your own mind. Bear in mind the ten analogies of all phenomena being like reflections and so on, and finally realize the intermediate experience as great bliss. This undifferentiated occurrence of the external, internal, and intermediate is analogous to the essential nature, the nature, and all-pervasive compassion of awareness, which refer to the *dharmakāya*, *sambhogakāya*, and *nirmāṇakāya*. These three are realized at once. This is like a single medicine that can simultaneously cure a hundred illnesses in a single instant, or a single word of practical advice that is like a key that opens a myriad doors of understanding. It is also likened to the well-known expression: If you know one point, all is liberated. This is naked awareness, fresh and unadulterated. It is beyond benefit or harm. It is not illuminated by anything, nor can anything obscure it.

As you become familiar with this awareness, you will be in a position to ask questions. This prose presentation is like a map, so as you read this section, many questions are bound to arise. And that is fine, but it is most important to come up with reasonable questions to ask realized practitioners. Attend closely to the teachings and do not forget or simply discard them after reading them once. You need to put these teachings into practice because that is the only way that you will have worthwhile questions to pose to others. –

King Trisong Deutsen asked Orgyen Rinpoche Padmasambhava, "Great master, in order for causal sentient beings[74] to accomplish the result of Buddhahood, at the very beginning the view of realization is crucial. So who is endowed with the view of realization?"

– Various views have been discussed within this text. The first is the view of meditation; second is the view of realization; and third is the view of the fruition. Initially, you receive practical instructions from a spiritual mentor; you then gain some understanding, and upon that foundation you meditate. As a result of meditation, eventually realization arises, and that is the view of realization. As you sustain and cultivate such realization, you finally achieve the view of the fruition. At that point you are completely beyond any doubts or questions; your ascertainment is utterly complete. You are so absolutely confident in your realization that even if all the *buddhas* and *bodhisattvas* were to tell you that you are wrong, you would be totally unmoved. –

The master answered, "The pinnacle of all views consists of essential, practical instructions for enlightenment. All galaxies, all the *sugatas* of the three times and the ten directions, and all the sentient beings of the three realms are one reality: they are included in the essential mind of the spirit of awakening. That which is called 'mind' is uncreated and manifests in various ways."

– No one else creates or destroys this ideation for us. Ideation spontaneously arises, it is spontaneously present, and it spontaneously disappears. –

"Well then, what is the difference between *buddhas* and sentient beings?"

"Nothing apart from their realization and nonrealization of the mind. [652] Unknown to you, Buddha is present within you. Due to failing to recognize the essential nature of the mind, you wander among the six states of existence."

– We wander among the six states of existence due to grasping onto that which is nonexistent as if it were existent, onto that which is not real as being real. This grasping establishes the causes for further rebirth among these six states of existence. Just as a waterwheel revolves around and around, we accumulate the causes for the six types of rebirth. –

"Well then, what method is there to fathom the mind?"

"For that, the practical instructions of a spiritual mentor are needed.

"The so-called mind exists as an experience of mindfulness and knowing. Do not observe the mind externally but internally. Seek out the mind with the mind. Establish the mind-itself with the mind. Observe: whence does the mind initially arise, where is it located now, and where does it go in the end? In that regard, by observing for yourself this mind of yours, no place of origin, no location, and no destination are found.

There is no way to indicate its essential nature by saying, 'It's like this....' Thus, having no exterior or interior and no observer and observed, the mind is great primordial wisdom, free of a center or periphery, great, empty, primordial wisdom, originally free and all-pervasive. Primordial wisdom, which is naturally present in its own mode of being, is not something created. The recognition of the presence of primordial wisdom in yourself [653] is the view. Strive to fathom it!

"The ground and that which has the ground is like space, primordially, spontaneously present. It is like the sun, having no basis for the darkness of ignorance. It is like a lotus, unblemished by flaws. It is like gold, not changing from the nature of reality-itself. It is like the ocean, without movement. It is like a river, without interruption. It is like a presence, without meeting or parting. It is like Mount Meru, without moving or changing. It is said that upon fathoming such a reality, one is endowed with realization from the time of gaining confidence."

– In the essential nature of awareness there is no ground, so it is like space, primordially, spontaneously present. Like the sun, the nature of awareness is simply one of illumination free from all mental afflictions and never obscured by any conventional reality. Nor is it contaminated by faults. One's psycho-physical aggregates, one's body and mind, which have arisen by the force of previous *karma*, neither harm nor help awareness. It is even impervious to the five poisons; so to the minds of those who have realized the essential nature of awareness these poisons cannot be harmful. On the contrary, as they arise, such contemplatives simply recognize their arising and perceive them as primordial wisdom. Therefore, they have no power to hinder, harm, or obscure.

The nature of awareness does not change. Just as gold is initially concealed by earth, so too, without being harmed by *saṃsāra* or benefited by *nirvāṇa*, the nature of awareness is concealed as we wander through the six states of existence. It isn't here today and gone tomorrow. It has no center, no periphery, and no measurable depth; it is boundless. This essential nature of awareness is the essential nature of both *saṃsāra* and *nirvāṇa*. It is the essential nature of all *buddhas* and is present in all sentient beings. It neither comes nor goes; it neither comes together nor falls apart; it is just present. There are no lapses in it, so for those in the hell realms, just as for those in the state of Buddhahood, awareness is continuously present. In the past, present, and future one is not separated from it.

When you realize the essential nature of your own awareness, you are realizing the nature of all the *buddhas*. You are encountering all the *buddhas*. You are realizing the essential nature of all of your spiritual mentors. You are receiving all the empowerments. You are receiving all the blessings. You are receiving the realization of both the stages of generation and completion.

This is the realization of Mahāmudrā, the realization of Dzogchen, and the realization of the union of Mahāmudrā and Dzogchen. –

Orgyen Rinpoche introduced [awareness] to his disciples, including the king and his subjects. This is his advice to the Lady [Yeshe Tsogyal]: "Faithful one, listen! The mind has no essential nature, so leave it in its natural, unmodified, spontaneously present state, without meditating. By dwelling in that state, the mind-itself will be naturally liberated, and you will become a *buddha*." [654] Thus, Tsogyal was liberated right there.

– Awareness, like the ocean, is a spontaneously present state, without meditating. You need not do something special; you need not adopt a special posture; you need not bring something to mind as the object of your meditation. Just rest your mind, without disturbing it. Just as water naturally flows downstream, you need not do anything to it. Just as bubbles naturally arise and dissipate within the water, you need not do anything; they self-arise and self-release. Just as silt builds up, it naturally subsides if you leave the water alone. Similarly, if various thoughts arise in the mind, you need not do anything to them. Just let the mind rest in its natural state and the silt of the mind will subside by itself. Just as clouds arise and vanish naturally in the sky, so too will the mind-itself be naturally liberated, naturally released.

How many times have you heard the phrase, "Let your mind be in an unmodified, unfabricated, uncontrived state"? Meanwhile, we do just the opposite by putting our minds in all kinds of contrived, constructed states. Why? Because we are not satisfied with simply letting the mind rest in its own nature. Why? Because we run in a hundred different directions trying to find something new, trying to find satisfaction. But we end up getting nothing. In this way people run the risk of developing misconceptions about Buddhism. They build up expectations, dabble in a bit of everything, and yet practice only a little. With the resulting disappointment, they may become disillusioned and adopt mistaken notions about the Dharma. This happened fairly frequently in Tibet. When such people died, they were actually worse off than those who had no spiritual practice at all. The remedy for this situation is to practice according to your own abilities. Simply see what you can do and then do it. Right now, you and all other sentient beings are endowed with the essential causes for spiritual awakening, and you have the contributing conditions of a spiritual mentor and the Dharma. So you do not need much else.

Why do we not meet with success? Because we have an insufficient realization of the Four Thoughts that Turn the Mind! On the one hand, we want to attain *nirvāṇa*, yet we burrow deeper and deeper into *saṃsāra*. Such scurrying in many directions comes from an insufficient realization of the Four Thoughts that Turn the Mind. We have not yet fathomed the significance of refuge. We have not really applied ourselves purely to serving others. We say "I love you" so easily, but genuine service is much more difficult for us because we have not cultivated the Four Immeasurables. Because we fail to actually get down to practice, when the time comes for our own death, we will have nothing that is of benefit. Then even if a great king were to come to our aid, we would be beyond help.

I witnessed this many times in Tibet. People would go from one *lama* to the next, hoping that the *lama* would say something nice, hoping to be acknowledged as a *tulku*. If a *lama* does this, does it make you any better than you already were? It really doesn't make you better or worse, does it? In fact, people with no past faith in a particular *lama* would suddenly develop great faith in that same person if he said that they were a *tulku*. Now they would proclaim his teachings to be very profound, whereas before they had no regard for him at all. In contrast, if they met with a very honest and direct *lama*, they would respond by having less and less faith in him. They wouldn't want to hear his teachings; they wouldn't even want to be near him. If you really want to be happy, that is not the way. Rather take in the Dharma and digest it. In the meantime, do not deceive yourself; do not puff yourself up. Just apply yourself to the Dharma, and like a sprout, day by day your Dharma practice will slowly, slowly rise up with the light of the sun and flourish.

I have been called a *tulku*, but I see no change because of that. What change has occurred is solely due to the kindness of my *lamas* who, right from the beginning, taught me the alphabet. That brought about some change. Although I received benefit from initiations, I could not receive great benefit from them alone. To get real benefit I had to put them into practice. If you don't, you are simply inflating yourself full of the gas of pomposity, but in the meantime, everything inside turns into smelly garbage. People who do this with no understanding of the Dharma should really be viewed with compassion. However, those who do this while knowing what is virtuous and what is nonvirtuous are just accumulating causes for lower rebirth. Again, I am saying this to emphasize the importance of practice.

Actually, the vital essence of receiving an empowerment is the maintenance of the *samayas*, just as the essence of being a monk is the keeping of the precepts. Similarly, the very vital core of the *bodhisattva* path is the cultivation of the spirit of awakening, the cultivation of the Four Immeasurables, and the Six Perfections. All of these stem from turning the mind away from the cycle of existence. If you do that, these others arise naturally. It is only our attachments to *saṃsāra* that give rise to the feeling that we have no leisure, no understanding, no attainment, and no satisfaction, while in the meantime we just pile up a mountain of pride and conceit. –

His advice to Lang Palgyi Sengge: "Son of good family, listen! All phenomena are the mind-itself, and there is nothing that arises from anything else. The mind has no inherent nature, so it is beyond expression and thought. Rest lucidly in the unmodified state that is without the distinctions of good and bad, acceptance and rejection, negation and affirmation, or outside and inside. In that state the body and mind are blissful, and unborn, unceasing consciousness is experienced. Those are the indications of the warmth of realization, so at that time you will have reached the realization of the Buddha." Thus, Lang Palgyi Sengge was also liberated.

His advice to Vairocana: "Son of good family, listen! All phenomena arise from the mind. The mind is not something that is to be apprehended; it is without a periphery or a center, without convergence or dispersion. Rest undistractedly in the unmodified state of great equality. By meditating in that way, ideation will arise as primordial wisdom, and that itself is spiritual awakening." Thus, Vairocana was liberated. [655]

– The term "great equality" is akin to the theme of equanimity that figures so prominently in Buddhism. Bear in mind that equality in this sense is considerably beyond the commonly discussed human rights issues of equality for all, in the sense of all people being created equal. This is a very deep state of equality. Within the context of Buddhism as you cultivate the spirit of aspiring for awakening, a crucial facet of this practice is the development of a sense of equality between self and others, such that you cherish others just as much as you cherish yourself. This is a total even-mindedness, or equality. Yet, that is not the type of equality referred to here. This great equality refers to the indivisibility of *saṃsāra* and *nirvāṇa*. You now perceive all thoughts as arising as primordial wisdom, including the three poisons of the mind: attachment, hatred, and delusion. These three manifest specifically as the three *kāyas* and as primordial wisdom. Sublimated attachment manifests as the *nirmāṇakāya*, hatred as the *sambhogakāya*, and delusion as the *dharmakāya*. Moreover, through the sublimation that occurs by discovering the essential nature of each of these, attachment manifests as the primordial wisdom of discernment; hatred manifests as mirrorlike primordial wisdom; and delusion manifests as the primordial wisdom of the absolute space of phenomena.

When the essential nature of these poisons is not understood and they are not sublimated, delusion is the source of all nonvirtue, all suffering, and the perpetuation of the cycle of existence. Although we aspire for happiness, owing to delusion we cultivate the causes of our own grief and destroy the causes of our happiness. When attachment is not sublimated, it generally gives rise to rebirth as a *preta*, and when hatred is not understood, it leads to rebirth in the hell realms.

These afflictions of the mind are very powerful, for they lie at the root of all the misery and disgrace that befall us. In Tibet sometimes people would proudly say, "I was so angry!" as if their hatred was a sign of their courage and virility, rather than a mere disgrace. This is true for people in the West as well. There is nothing that cannot act as an object of attachment. Tenaciously holding onto our viewpoint as being the one true perspective is merely an expression of delusion. At the moment you find any one of these afflictions beginning to arise in your mind-stream, that is the time to be most attentive; because once the mind has been absorbed into the mental affliction, it is very difficult to extricate yourself from it. This is true not only for ordinary beings, but even for those who are advanced along the path. Great *lamas* and heads of state are all in the same situation, so remember from the very beginning that it is important to recognize the affliction and to be very careful. –

His advice to Nup Namkhey Nyingpo: "Namkhey Nyingpo, listen! The mind is free of conceptual elaborations. Rest in the unmodified, unadulterated state that is without an "I" or a self, that is self-arisen and self-pacified. By dwelling in that state, indications of the warmth of realization will automatically occur; and that itself is spiritual awakening." Thus, Namkhey Nyingpo was liberated.

His advice to Kumāra: "Jñāna, listen! The mind is not initially produced by causes, and in the end it is not destroyed by conditions. Remain in the unborn state that is free of activity and effort, without articulation. In that state, you will find the fruition without seeking it. Spiritual awakening is nowhere else than that." Thus, Kumāra was liberated.

His advice to Ngenlam Gyalwa Chog-yang: "Gyalwa Chog-yang, listen! The spirit of awakening of awareness cannot be cultivated in meditation, nor can it be conceived. Rest without dispersion or contraction, letting your senses be, and with ideation calming itself. [656] In that state, self-calming mindfulness will arise in the mind, and spiritual awakening will be achieved right there." Thus, Gyalwa Chog-yang was liberated right then.

His advice to Nanam Dorje Düdjom: Dorje Düdjom, listen! The spirit of awakening of awareness is primordially self-arisen, primordially self-present, without a periphery or a center. Rest in unmodified, self-arisen, natural luminosity, which is ungrounded in any basis. Rest like that, and you are freed of the fluctuations of the mind, and just that is spiritual awakening." Thus, Dorje Düdjom was liberated and attained *siddhi*.

His advice to Pal Yeshe Yang: "Yeshe Yang, listen! There is no subject/object duality in the mind, so it is without fluctuation or movement, without action or effort. Rest in the unmodified state that is without hope or fear, with no dispersion or contraction. Not being distracted from that reality is Buddhahood." Thus, he was liberated.

His advice to Sogpo Lha Palgyi Yeshe: [657] "Lha Palgyi Yeshe, listen! The spirit of awakening is without activity, so, without seeking it, it is self-arisen. It is without effort or accomplishment, so rest in the unmodified state of natural luminosity. In that state the continuum of fluctuation and movement will cease. At that time, know that you are a Buddha." Thus, Palgyi Yeshe was liberated.

His advice to Yeshe Dey: "Yeshe Dey, listen! This mind is without negation or affirmation, without agent or action, without subject or object, without modification or effort. Rest without acceptance or rejection. If you rest in that state without distraction, that is spiritual awakening itself." Thus, Yeshe Dey was liberated.

His advice to Kharchen Palgyi Wangchuk: "Palgyi Wangchuk, listen! The mind is primordially insubstantial, without anything on which to meditate. To the intellect it is ungrounded and unmodified. Let it be self-arisen and self-displaying. Dwelling in that state, you become a *buddha* without rejecting the cycle of existence." [658] Thus, Palgyi Wangchug was liberated.

His advice to Dram Gyalwey Lodrö: "This mind is inconceivable and nonobjectifiable, transcending existence and nonexistence, substantialism and nihilism. Let it be with no meditator or object of meditation. If there is no vacillation or shift away from that state, that is called the '*dharmakāya*.'" Thus, he was liberated.

His advice to Ö Palgyi Chungwa: "With respect to the mind there is no knowledge or knower, no apprehension or apprehender. Rest in a clear state devoid of an inherent nature. There, if nonconceptual consciousness does not change, that is called 'Buddha.'" Thus, he was liberated.

His advice to Drenpa Namkha: "This mind appears, but has no inherent nature; it is clear, but is without conceptualization; it is inconceivable and inexpressible. Let your experiential realization be free of the movements of the mind. Dwelling in that reality, although your body is human, your mind is called the 'Buddha.'" Thus, Drenpa Namkha achieved *siddhi.* [659]

His advice to Ödren Palgyi Wangchuk: "The spirit of awakening appears but is empty; it is empty, clear light; and it is without anything to modify or cultivate. Rest in the state of self-arisen, great, primordial wisdom. Not shifting away from that is called spiritual awakening.'" Thus, he was liberated.

His advice to Ma Rinchen Chok: "The mind is not any essential nature at all. There is nothing to place nor anything on which to meditate.

It is unmodified, self-arisen, and fresh.[75] Rest in the state of primordial, spontaneous presence, and meditate lucidly. In that state the mind is freed of movement, and there is no fruition other than that." Thus, he achieved *siddhi.*

His advice to Nup Sang-gye Yeshe: "The spirit of awakening appears but is empty. Rest in the state of indivisible appearance and emptiness, in the state of indivisible awareness and emptiness. Without vacillation, rest in the inconceivable state. Dwelling in that state is called the '*dharmakāya.*'" Thus Sang-gye Yeshe was liberated. [660]

His advice to Langdro Könchok Jungney: "The mind-itself is insubstantial and originally pristine. It is empty of inherent nature and is without modification. Rest in the state without an object of meditation or a meditator. From that alone, the result of spiritual awakening is achieved." Thus, he was liberated.

His advice to Lasum Gyalwa Jangchup: "The mind-itself is unborn and unceasing, free of substance and signs. Empty of inherent nature, it is clear and unceasing. If there is no wavering from the reality of just that, this is called 'spiritual awakening.' That is the realization of the *dharmakāya.*" Thus, Gyalwa Jangchup was liberated.

Orgyen Rinpoche's *The Stages of the Path of Secret Mantra* states:

> There are three crucial aspects of settling the mind: (1) Do not vacillate as usual; (2) do not be dispersed by conceptualization, (3) but without any mental fabrications, evenly leave consciousness in its own state. By so doing, meditation will come by itself. If there is vacillation and dispersion, the meditative state will not arise. [661]
>
> Secondly, this is the essential nature of the meditative state that arises: by leaving it like that in its own state, all coarse and subtle ideation remains dormant right where it is. Once it is calmed, the mind will lucidly remain in its own state. That is called "quiescence." With no cessation of the luster of that, there comes a lucid, unmediated, objectless, natural luminosity. That is called "insight." Those two will also steadfastly remain in the essential nature of a single, indivisible moment of consciousness. That itself is called "quiescence and insight." If one dwells upon an object, this is a meditative experience. If one dwells without an object, this is understanding. If one is steadfastly present in the essential nature of that consciousness, this is realization. That is called the realization of the *buddhas* of the three times. That is not created just by the practical instructions of one's spiritual mentor, nor does it arise from the great wisdom of the disciple. It is called reaching the nature of being or the character [of awareness].

The Four Syllables of Mahāmudrā states:

> Position your body in the posture of Vairocana, with its seven characteristics. [662] Like a great *garuḍa* soaring in the sky, rest in an unmodified, primordial state, without effort or accomplishment. Like an ocean free of waves, rest without fluctuation or movement. Like the sun free of clouds, rest with an all-illuminating luster. Rest in the knowledge that all feelings, like ripples in water, are the mind. Like a small child gazing at a shrine, rest with unceasing clarity and without grasping. Like a bird flying through the sky, rest without leaving any trace.

The Mahāmudrā Precipitance states:

> Position your body in the posture of Vairocana, with its seven characteristics. With your body and mind inwardly relaxed, bring nothing to mind from the three times of the past, future, or present. By leaving the mind in an unmodified state, the previous mind has passed, the future mind is not yet arisen; and this very consciousness of the present remains like space, clear, empty, and free of elaboration. That itself is called "undeluded consciousness," [663] "the clear light of the mind-itself," "primordial, innate bliss," and "the great bliss of the *dharmakāya*." All at once rest in the state of recognizing just that, without modification, free of effort or accomplishment.
>
> Resting in the observation of deluded consciousness entails steadily observing with the eyes of wisdom whatever virtuous, nonvirtuous, and ethically neutral ideation arises. After all the observed ideation has been calmed, the mind is not nonexistent; rather, the empty, clear, limpid, immaculate, and vivid essential nature of the mind is the nonduality of the absolute space and primordial wisdom. Whatever essential nature is seen, the mind is seen. If one realizes the mind, one is a *buddha*. How is it seen? One sees that without beginning, it has no convergence or dissolution; it pervades all phenomena; it transcends the fields of experience of the six senses; and it is utterly ungrounded in color, shape, and so on.
>
> The nondual identification of delusion and non-delusion: [664] By steadily observing with the eyes of wisdom any thoughts that arise, there is nothing to be recognized at all. Ideation disperses and is empty. Moreover, that empty dispersion emerges from the empty state of the mind-itself; it abides in the empty state of the mind-itself; and it is calmed in the empty state of the mind-itself. Separate from the empty state of the

mind-itself, there are no bad thoughts to be rejected. Like the ocean and its waves, there is no distinction between deluded and non-deluded consciousness. Thus, whatever ideation arises, immediately and steadily observe it, and unwaveringly, precipitately remain in that state.

The Wish-fulfilling Gem Instruction on the Mind states:

> Do not waver and do not meditate. Release ambition and rest.
>
> "Not wavering" entails not engaging in distractions concerning the past, not engaging in distractions concerning the future, and not engaging in distractions concerning the present. "Not meditating" entails [665] not engaging with any object of recognition. The reference to "ambition" means to proceed by getting rid of all mental exertion. From the state of non-wavering and non-meditation, thoughts suddenly emerge; then, without following after the thoughts, apply unwavering mindfulness to whatever thoughts arise.

Gyalsey Thogmé says:

> If you observe the essential nature of brilliance in the nonconceptual state of the mind, you dwell in sheer emptiness that is ungrounded in anything. That is called clear, empty awareness without grasping. From the outset it is obscured by dualistic ideation concerning existence and nonexistence with regard to everything; so it is not recognized. You are seeing its essential nature by the power of your practice, so observe the empty, essential nature of the mind while carefully excising any superimpositions. In this way, excellent qualities arise more and more fully, and this is the path that serves as the cause of the supreme *siddhi*. So rejoice in this and practice! [666]

Gyatönpa Chökyi Zangpo says:

> By settling your body, speech, and mind effortlessly and loosely, between the cessation of past consciousness and the arising of future thoughts, luminous, nonconceptual consciousness is the ground. By fixing your gaze luminously and unwaveringly on that, with no object of observation or observer, if you experience clear emptiness, free of conceptual elaboration and devoid of all recognition, that is the identification [of awareness]. If that does not arise, there is no identification. By resting like that, if dualistic thoughts suddenly emerge, that is the cycle of existence; and the entire phenomenal world is nothing other than apparitions of ideation. If ideation is purified, *nirvāṇa* is not to be sought

elsewhere; for the clear light of your own mind is Buddha. By observing whatever thoughts arise, clear emptiness without a trace becomes distinct, and that is *nirvāṇa*. The whole of *nirvāṇa* is none other than the arising of ideation as primordial wisdom.

What is practice? Ideation is superimposed by the intellect. Its prior nonarising, [667] its intervening arising, and its final release are all three without an inherent nature. Upon leaving it without modification in its own state, if it remains, observe the essential nature of its remaining. If it disperses, there is nothing to do but observe the essential nature of its dispersion. The luminosity of simply not wavering from the state of bliss and luminosity is the core of the practice. By resting in that state, excellent qualities will gradually arise, so that must be sustained, whether or not there are pitfalls.

You must practice by releasing your mind, with no gladness or disappointment with regard to any good or bad experiences. In general, have no yearning for meditation that assembles good things; rather, it seems that the mind must be merged and sustained with whatever occurs. Whatever joys and sorrows, illnesses and obstacles occur, steadily observe them. Arouse your awareness and watch. Whether you are ready or not, constantly watch, and after awhile the mind will become soothed. With that as an indication, merge in that way with whatever uncontrolled thoughts that occur, [668] and there will be progress.

– Whenever any good experiences happen, we tend to become happy, but that happiness is just one more form of ideation. If we become disappointed when a bad experience arises, that, too, is just one more form of ideation. While reading this material, a hundred million questions may arise, but all those questions are further expressions of ideation, and even if there were time to seek answers to all those questions, the answers themselves would be expressions of ideation. As a result of this practice, your mind will become soothed, flexible, peaceful, and relaxed. If you practice in an uptight fashion, it just makes the mind more uptight, or it may even make you go crazy. –

The Tantra Synthesizing the Quintessence of Great Compassion states:

> Transform self-releasing memories and thoughts into the enlightened mind.

Whatever thoughts you recall of the past, future, and present, the remembered object and the rememberer are self-appearing, and mindfulness is sustained. They are empty and are released with no inherent nature. That is the mind of the Sugata, and that empty recollection of phenomena is the transformation into the path of the enlightened mind. That concludes the teaching of the prose identification of the mind.

– We must be very cautious when it comes to transforming thoughts into enlightened awareness. This does not mean you can do whatever you like—that any thought that comes up is fine and you can carry it through. That is not transforming thoughts into primordial wisdom, nor is it the perception of thoughts appearing as enlightened mind. It's just having a chaotic mind. Once when Düdjom Lingpa was giving teachings on Atiyoga, someone overheard only a part of the teachings and afterward thought he was beyond good and evil. Singling out a nice fat sheep that was ready for slaughter, he decided to apply his understanding of Dzogchen to this situation, thinking, "In reality, no sheep will be killed, and no person will kill it, so it is okay." This was a total misconstrual of the practice of Dzogchen. To gain proper understanding, you need to go stage by stage, first hearing, then thinking, and finally meditating.

Nowadays many people express an interest in understanding Dzogchen simply because they like it. Not only is that not good enough, it is pointless. There must be a much deeper motivation for penetrating to the meaning of Dzogchen, and this stems initially from a disillusionment with *saṃsāra*. From this disillusionment, you bring forth a yearning for a lasting state of joy, which leads you to entrusting yourself to the objects of refuge: the Buddha, Dharma and Saṅgha. Given these as your motivation, if you then seek an understanding of Dzogchen, it will be meaningful.

First cultivate the Four Thoughts that Turn the Mind, thereby turning your mind away from the cycle of existence. If you engage in the preliminary practices, your mind will naturally turn away from attachment to this cycle of existence, and naturally a deep yearning for liberation will arise. First, however, become familiar with the qualities of *nirvāṇa*. Once you understand them, you will have some incentive to seek liberation.

Please bear in mind that within the Mahāyāna, there are many avenues of practice and by following the Mahāyāna alone, liberation will take many eons. Within the Mantrayāna are the outer and inner *tantras*, culminating in the inner *tantra* practice of Atiyoga, Dzogchen, through which it is guaranteed that one can achieve perfect enlightenment with one body and in one lifetime. Such swiftness of attainment is amazing, but it is guaranteed only through your own understanding—through hearing, thinking, and meditation. With that understanding faith naturally arises in the practice, as well as such great delight and enthusiasm that even if everyone told you to abandon the practice, you would shrug them off. With that kind of understanding, you have a genuine reason to engage in the practice of Atiyoga.

You could enter into Dzogchen practice because some *lama* said to you, "Meditate! This is Dzogchen. This is a great practice, just do it!" But you would be practicing without knowing the qualities of the Three Jewels, and without any real sense of the difference between Hīnayāna and Mahāyāna. So with this approach, even if you entered into Dzogchen practice, how could you meditate? If you have obstacles in your practice, they stem from trying to skip over what needs to be practiced stage by stage, gradually and sequentially. We must engage in practice with our eyes and ears wide open, with our senses fully clear. Americans take notes on everything wherever they travel. Japanese and Chinese tourists take their cameras and snap photos everywhere. We should bring that kind of interest and vivid awareness on our own travels on the path to enlightenment. –

CHAPTER SIX

The Identification of Mahāmudrā

Homage to Avalokiteśvara!

[670] These are the profound practical instructions of Avalokiteśvara. The teachings of the *sūtras*, *tantras*, and *siddhas* on identifying one's mind-itself and this awareness as Mahāmudrā are like counsel given in secret; so gain certain knowledge [of this point].

– The essential nature of your own mind is the *sugatagarbha*. A *sugata* is one who has gone to bliss, and *garbha* is an embryo, womb, or essence. Where is this essential nature present? You can say it is present within yourself, but it is more accurate to say simply that it is you. By identifying your own nature, you cut through all conceptual elaborations and simply settle in the nature of your own awareness. This essential nature has no shape or color. It's not adventitious, nor does it occur at some later time; rather, it is originally, perfectly free by its own nature, naked and fresh.

By gradually becoming familiar with this nature, actual insight is gained, which culminates in gaining confidence. Once this confidence is attained, you simply remain in that state and sustain that confidence without further elaboration. This subtle nature is not sullied by the faults of *saṃsāra*, so do not mix it with anything else. Do not try to find something else to do; simply dwell in the confidence that has been attained. Persistently remain in this state and be satisfied with that recognition.

To gain such a naked realization, it's vital that the disciple be spiritually ripe through preparation. Once you see your own spiritual mentor as a *buddha*, feel genuine compassion for others, and have faith in the Buddha and the Dharma, you may be introduced to the nature of awareness, and that may give rise to the genuine view and allow certain insights to arise.

As a byproduct of being on the path and gaining genuine insight, disciples may gain paranormal abilities such as clairvoyance. If used with an improper motivation, you may simply confuse yourself and others so much that both are defeated, for this is like putting on handcuffs. Therefore, these paranormal displays are regarded as the temptations of *māra*. Although many have attained *siddhis*, such as flying through the sky or passing through the earth, they are thought of as potential dangers until one reaches the state of "extinction into reality-itself," which is the final phase of the Leap-over stage of Dzogchen practice. Until then, one must have a view as vast as space, but one's actions must be extremely precise and conscientious. –

The Mound of Jewels Sūtra states:

> The secret reality of all the *buddhas*
> Cuts off conceptual elaboration and is devoid of substantiality.
> It has no inherent nature and is immutable.
> This is to be known by contemplatives.

– The *buddhas* don't hold this "secret reality" only to themselves; rather, it is a secret to us, because even though we are the very ones who have it, we don't yet realize it. This secret reality is without substantiality, so it is unborn and unceasing, utterly immutable. It is neither unattainable nor is it hidden for a future time. Rather, it is for you to recognize your own present nature.

Let's pursue this point—the nature of our own minds—by way of an analogy: All the teachings—the *sūtras*, *tantras*, stage of generation and completion practices, and so forth—can be likened to various parts of a tree: the roots, trunk, branches, leaves, and flowers. Insofar as we are caught up in conceptual elaborations, even if we realize the many parts, we will fail to understand the actual fruit yielded by the tree. These teachings enable us to recognize the actual nature of the fruit—our own self-nature. Do not ask whether *saṃsāra* or *nirvāṇa* exist. Ask yourself, "Do I actually exist?"

Take yourself as the object of inquiry and ask yourself, "If I exist, where do I exist?" Next, investigate your body, to see if this "I" can be found. The most effective progression to follow in this regard is to begin with the preliminary practices, move on to quiescence, then proceed to this point of examining the nature of your own existence, asking yourself whether or not you truly exist. By following this sequence, you will see that it is untenable to conclude that you do exist; but it seems equally implausible that you don't exist! –

The Great Synthesis Sūtra states:

> Everything is included in the state of reality-itself,
> So it is the Great Perfection.

The Questions of Nairātmya Sūtra states:

> Phenomena are free of all conceptual elaborations. [671]
> That is the sole *bindu*.

– The sole *bindu* is the unitary nature of the whole of *saṃsāra* and *nirvāṇa*. The *bindu* is symbolically represented as spherical in shape, because it is without a center or a periphery. That is also true of *saṃsāra* and *nirvāṇa*, which are without a center or periphery. This *bindu* is of the nature of the three *kāyas* of the Buddha and indeed, of all the *buddhas*.

Is it true then that all sentient beings are in reality *buddhas* since everything is of the same nature? Yes. The only difference is that the *buddhas* have recognized their self-nature, whereas we have not yet realized our own nature. Therefore, sentient beings remain as unmanifest *buddhas*.

The Mound of Jewels Sūtra also states that the nature of all the *buddhas* is the sole *bindu*. This is the point of the secret teachings of the *buddhas* and of the great *siddhas* of the past. What is the nature of this sole *bindu*? It is you, yourself. If you recognize your own nature, then you will see it is this sole *bindu*. Because of the reality of this sole *bindu*, an inherently separate, independent "I" and "you" and so forth must be nonexistent. –

The Splendid Assemblage Sūtra states:

> It was not initially created by scholars;
> Its nature is not modified by things;
> When it is realized, it is Mahāmudrā.

The Glorious Bhairava Tantra states:

> If your own mind-itself, the root of all phenomena,
> Is not realized,
> Even if you train well in hearing, thinking, and meditating,
> The result will not be achieved.
> You will be like a blind man without a guide.
> So realize your own mind.

– This recognition of the nature of your own mind-itself is like a single medicine that cures a hundred diseases or the one key that opens a hundred doors. Without that realization, even if you have heard many teachings, studied logic and debate, and even meditated extensively, the result cannot be achieved.

Nowadays, many Tibetans place a high priority on hearing and pondering the teachings, perhaps even too much. On the other hand, if you haven't heard or thought about them, and haven't gained clear understanding, meditation is like trying to scale a high, sheer cliff without hands. Hearing and thinking are indispensable, but relying on them alone is not enough. Please bear this in mind: Even if you were to apply yourself for a thousand years, you wouldn't be able to understand the entire body of teachings in the *sūtras*, the *tantras*, and so forth. Even memorizing them would not give rise to realization or liberation. Although there would be a blessing, it would not radically transform your mind. With hearing and thinking as an essential foundation, venture into practice. This crucial point of recognizing your own nature is the fruition of hearing and thinking. This is the one key, the one medicine. –

The Tantra of the Two Bindus states:

> If you lack the actual realization of the mind-itself,
> You will not become a buddha even if you draw every single *maṇḍala*. [672]

The Vajra Pavilion Tantra states:

> This contemplation is the supreme realization of the mind.
> Without reliance on this, [such realization] will not occur;
> So whatever subtle *samādhis* of the lower [*yānas*] are considered,
> Mahāmudrā will not be fathomed.
> If the root of ignorance is not cut,
> All one's hearing, thinking, and meditation
> Remain only verbal designations associated with one's habitual propensities;
> But one's own essence is not realized.
> Therefore, penetrate it from the beginning to the end.

The Questions of King Dewa Lodrö Sūtra states:

> One who meditates on emptiness and luminosity[76]
> Surpasses others.
> This is the mode of being of a great meditator,
> So due to this very realization of the mind,
> Spiritual awakening definitely occurs.

The Tantra of Entering into the Renunciate Life states:

> The characteristic of your own mind
> Is perfect spiritual awakening—the great mystery.
> It is unknown to all intellectuals,
> So I shall explain everything to you.

– An intellectual is defined here as someone who searches externally for knowledge. Such people may have mastered hundreds of different disciplines, but they remain as ordinary people, with the great mystery of their own minds still hidden from them. –

The Tantra of the Sole Bindu states: [673]

> There is a reason for applying yourself to the mind: do not cling to anything at all! Do this uninterruptedly at all times.

– This simple piece of guidance about thoughts that arise in the mind is often taught by *lamas*: Whatever comes, just let it come; whatever goes, let it go. Without acceptance and without rejection, whatever comes to the mind, let it be.

From the perspective of this particular practice, the sheer presence of thoughts arising is not a problem. Thoughts continue to arise in the mind until we are *buddhas*, so don't expect them to go away soon! We, who are on the path, need to nurture ourselves, as if we were tiny infants, by cultivating mindfulness, introspection, and conscientiousness, so that we spiritually mature. So we must practice sequentially, step by step.

People with a very high degree of spiritual maturity due to many lifetimes of practice may come into their present life ready to enter directly into Mahāmudrā and Dzogchen practice. Such a person is like a *garuḍa* chick that flies immediately after emerging from its egg. Those who enter this life on the verge of enlightenment may enter directly into these practices and at the point of death, they may gain liberation.

Hearing these teachings on Mahāmudrā, some novices may be so drawn to them that they immediately adopt this as their primary practice. However, if we enter directly into this practice, it is imperative that we do other practices as well—no matter how much we may wish to focus on this alone. Instead of just letting the thoughts be, there is a great likelihood that we will follow after and be carried away by them, and that's not the practice at all.

To gain real progress, follow the sequence of hearing, thinking, and meditation, cultivate quiescence followed by insight, then on the basis of that foundation, you will genuinely be able to enter into the practice of Dzogchen and see all phenomena as displays, or creative expressions, of awareness. From that point in your practice, let ideation simply be. In terms of awareness and its displays, all that appears to the mind is like water and moisture, like fire and heat. The latter are simply expressions of the former. You will no longer see *saṃsāra* as problematic, nor will you see the qualities of the Buddha as extraordinary. They will be of one taste. But beware of entering this practice prematurely, without a proper foundation, and winding up chasing after every thought that arises without any discrimination.

For the purpose of guiding sentient beings to liberation, two great Dzogchen masters, Longchen Rabjampa and Jigmé Lingpa, showed the eight signs of realization. The essence of their practice was thorough disillusionment with the cycle of existence. From that perspective, it was clear to them that sentient beings didn't know what to avoid or what to follow; they didn't understand the root of their own suffering. In response, they cultivated the Four Immeasurables, particularly great loving-kindness and compassion for all sentient beings. With this foundation, they entered into the practice, not following their own ideas, but relying on the essence of the *sūtras* and *tantras* and applying that in practice. Longchen Rabjampa and Jigmé Lingpa followed this progression as have all of the *siddhas* from the Mahāmudrā and Dzogchen traditions.

Through proper practice one eventually gains realization, but that by itself does not suffice. It's indispensable to cultivate, to sustain, and deepen such insight, without letting your behavior deteriorate. Don't think that you can do whatever you feel like doing. Your realization must be balanced with proper conduct. On the other hand, don't get bound up with rules either, so that you are too tight and your conduct obscures your realization. It's really simple: bear these both in mind and keep them both in balance. –

The Tantra of the Full Enlightenment of Vajrasattva states:

> The root of the phenomena of *saṃsāra* and *nirvāṇa*
> Is your own mind.
> Whatever memories and thoughts appear to the mind,
> Like haze in the sky,
> They are not grounded in any substance.
> They have no color and no shape,
> And even the eyes of primordial wisdom of the Buddha
> Do not see them as even a particle of matter.

– Whatever appears to the mind—memories, thoughts, and so on—be they positive or negative, are not grounded or rooted in any reality. From the ultimate vantage point, the perspective of a *buddha's* primordial wisdom, they are not seen as having any substance, any reality—not even one atom of reality.

Coming back to the theme that your own mind is the root of *saṃsāra* and *nirvāṇa*, ask yourself: Are you good? Of course, you are. Are you bad? Yes. In both cases, you are still the same person. When you recognize the nature of your own mind and become a *buddha*, is that still you? Yes. Are you the person who is wandering around in *saṃsāra*? The answer, again, is yes. It is you. It is this one phenomenon, your own mind, that is the root of the whole of *saṃsāra* and *nirvāṇa*, but your experience of it differs according to whether or not you've realized your own nature. –

The Tantra of the Full Enlightenment of Vairocana states:

> Because it has left off with all discernments of existence and nonexistence,
> And because it cannot articulate itself,
> The actuality of primordial wisdom itself
> Is called the Tathāgata.

The Tantra of the Exposition of Meditative Stabilization states:

> The essential reality of your own mind
> Is not grounded as a substance, and it transcends signs.
> Apart from the continuity of awareness,
> The *vajra* mind-itself is undemonstrable.

– The essential reality of your own mind transcends signs, which are objects of conceptual grasping. Is the *vajra* mind-itself nonexistent? No, because it is of the nature of the whole of *saṃsāra* and *nirvāṇa*. Does that mean it is existent? No, because it has not been seen by any of the *buddhas* of the three times. Therefore, it is said to be undemonstrable. –

The Tantra of Identifying Self-arisen Awareness states: [674]

> In terms of the view, observe your own mind.
> It is the clear *dharmakāya*, outside of which there are no objects.
> If you constantly remain unseparated from that,
> In reality there is not even a speck of change.

The Tantra of the Black Skull of Yama states:

> It is originally nondual, like the essential nature of space;
> It is divorced from articulation and conventions, and without modification;
> Primordially present, it does not need to be sought elsewhere.

The Cultivation of the Spirit of Awakening states:

> The mind and reality-itself are primordially nondual.
> Although you may seek the nature of the mind, it is not found.
> It cannot be indicated to others by saying, "It's like this...."

The Tantra Equal to Space states:

> Before there were any *buddhas*,
> There was not even the word "sentient being."
> The essence of the Dharma is I, myself.
> When that is realized, it is the *dharmakāya*.
> If you bow to me, this is manifest spiritual awakening.[77]

The Tantra of Self-arisen Bliss states:

> To acquire the view by which you ascertain your own awareness,
> Without distraction, observe with your mind.
> It does not possess an object. [675]
> Observing itself, the mind is clear.

The Tantra of All Views states:

> The spirit of awakening is the reality of awareness.
> What is past consists of just habitual propensities;
> What arises later consists of mental afflictions;
> Thoughts arise as the five doors [of perception];
> Without succumbing to those three, there is the primordial nature.
> With nothing to apprehend with the eyes, it is naturally clear;
> It is unobstructed primordial wisdom itself.
> Your own essential nature is the *dharmakāya*.
> It is without substance and is ascertained as consciousness.
> Your own mind is unmodified.
> Your own mind does not originate from anything else.

– The spirit of awakening is the essential nature of awareness. Without grasping onto whatever arises as the past or the future, or onto thoughts that arise as the five doors of perception, there is the primordial nature, the ultimate mode of being. When this realization dawns for those who are on the path, it's as if the sun has illuminated everything. Clarity arises. On the other hand, for those dwelling in reality, there is no sense that something arises or that anything is illuminated. This is simply the nature of reality. –

The Glorious Tantra of Vajra Delight states:

> Great primordial wisdom dwells in the body.
> It is utterly free of all conceptualization,
> And it pervades and knows all things.

The Tantra of the Supreme Class of Kīla states:

> Everything that appears as phenomena
> Is the *kīla*[78] of your own primordial wisdom.
> The nature of the mind is unapprehendable.
> The nature of space is insubstantial.

The Essence of the Tantras states:

> The luminosity of the phenomenal world is the essence.
> The luminosity of consciousness is the *dharmakāya*. [676]
> Without grasping, it is spontaneously present.

The Tantra of the Sole Bindu states:

> Know that even the Three Jewels imbued with signs
> Are actually devoid of signs.
> Realize your own mind, without signs, as the *dharmakāya*.
> Therefore, the Three Jewels are complete in yourself.

The Tantra of Great Space states:

> Resting without modification in reality-itself,
> Without appearances, is meditation.

The Tantra Equal to Space states:

> Whatever signs of ideation occur,
> They are the great unimpeded, the self-arisen, and the self-pacifying.
> Unmodified and uncreated, they are naturally luminous.
> If you rest in the unmodified state of great equanimity,
> As a mere convention that is called "meditation."

The Tantra Free of Contention states:

> Undistracted mindfulness is the recitation.
> [Acting] accordingly is the accomplishment.

– In the stage of generation, *sādhanas* are chanted and *mantras* recited, but in this stage of practice, simple, undistracted mindfulness fulfills the purpose of these recitations, and acting accordingly is the accomplishment of the fruition. This undistracted mindfulness entails not simply having a calm mind, but actually recognizing the nature of your own awareness. By so doing, the purpose of all the recitations is fulfilled. –

The Tantra of the Synthesis of Awareness states:

> The ground is emptiness, the *dharmakāya*.
> If the wise do not forget this reality, [677]
> Great *samādhi* will flow uninterruptedly.
> The mind is the real ground.
> Just as there are no bird-tracks in the sky,
> There is no inherent nature in this.
> That is called mindfulness of the constant fluctuations
> Of the moments of the mind.

The Essence of the Self-arisen View states:

> The recognition of your self-cognizing primordial wisdom
> Is the reality of the self-arisen nature of everything.
> Pure like the sky, luminous like the sun,
> It is just unflagging luminosity.
> It is just pervasiveness, without substance.
> It is not nonexistent, for it is conscious and knowing.
> It is just awareness, empty by nature.

– The assertion that primordial wisdom is pure like space and luminous like the sun negates any notion of its being a mere vacuity. The assertion that "it is not nonexistent, for it is conscious and knowing" refutes the misconception that primordial wisdom is simply nonexistent. It is not nonexistent, for it is the cause of the whole of *saṃsāra* and *nirvāṇa;* nor is it existent, because it has never been and will never be perceived by any *buddha* of the three times, or anyone else at all. In reality, it transcends our concepts of both existence and nonexistence. –

The Tantra of Self-arisen Bliss states:

> By identifying your own mind as the *dharmakāya,*
> It is seen to be naturally luminous, with no apprehension of an object.
> Primordially present, it is without increase or decrease,
> And it is divorced from the activities of the body and mind.

The same treatise states:

> The self-cognizing sentry is insubstantial and free.
> Unmistaken mindfulness has no going or coming.
> Whatever memories and knowledge occur,
> They are insubstantial at the very moment of their arising. [678]

The Tantra of the Vast Expanse of Space states:

> The pure, profound *dharmakāya*
> Is unborn and unceasing.
> The signs of ideation are purified from the basis,
> And it is free of the nature of mental afflictions.

– Since the pure, profound *dharmakāya* is unborn, it is unceasing. Signs of ideation are purified in the sense that they are released, or cleared out. Monks in the monasteries of Tibet undergo extensive training programs in the *sūtras* and the study of logic, but the fundamental goal of this education is to realize the nature of the mind as the *dharmakāya.* Where is the *dharmakāya* located? It's often said your own awareness is located in your heart—but is it really? There are good reasons for believing that is not the case. When you analyze the body, beginning with the outer covering of skin and continuing inward, can you find the *dharmakāya*? Where do you see the mind? You probably won't find it, but it is sometimes said that awareness dwells in the heart.

The *dharmakāya* is free of the mental affliction of grasping onto the "I" because there are no mental afflictions in the essential nature of the *dharmakāya.* However, what is the relationship between the *dharmakāya* and mental afflictions? Rather than viewing mental afflictions as impurities to be rejected and the *dharmakāya* as a purity to be realized, you should ascertain that the nature of your mental afflictions is none other than the *dharmakāya.* If you don't realize the essential nature of your mental afflictions, you are once again caught up in dualistic thinking. But as long as you are involved in such thinking, the mental afflictions are certainly to be abandoned. –

The Tantra of Supreme Meditative Stabilization states:

> Consciousness in its own mode is fresh.
> Without being distracted to anything else, observe the mind.
> Upon observation, consciousness is seen to be insubstantial and luminous.
> Do just that continuously, without distraction,
> For meditation is not to be sought elsewhere.

The Sūtra of Liberated Primordial Wisdom states:

> The mind-itself is clear light.
> Whatever appearances of objects arise from it,
> They are revealed as the reality of the unborn.
> Being mindful of the unborn
> Is called dwelling constantly in the *dharmakāya*.

The Tantra of the Gathering of Mysteries on Non-mental-engagement states:

> If you realize the superb reality of the mind,
> There will be accomplishment within one lifetime.

– If the superb fundamental nature of the mind is realized, there will be spiritual accomplishment within this lifetime. In fact, realizing the essential nature of even one thought sheds light on the nature of all mental events. If you are liberated from one mental event, you're liberated from them all. To realize the nature of one mental event is like realizing the nature of one bubble. But that's not enough. You must realize that the essential nature of the ocean is no different than the essential nature of that one bubble. By recognizing the relationship between the bubble and the ocean, you will no longer see the one bubble as an isolated event separate from the ocean, but instead will realize the nature of the entire ocean.

Applying this process to a mental event, you will understand it is no different from the essential nature of the mind-itself, which is analogous to the ocean. By realizing the essential nature of this one thought, all thoughts will be liberated. It is not that one thought is good and another bad, or one is liberated, another not. As you practice, you need to continue to release thoughts again and again. Don't think it's enough to do it just once. –

The Tantra of Inconceivable Mysteries states:

> The pinnacle of all phenomena [679]
> Is the absolute space that is without inherent presence.
> A mind that has no view
> Observes Mahāmudrā.
> Everything is of the nature of my mind.

The Tantra Equal to Space states:

> Confusion and nonconfusion are of the same nature.
> A being does not have two mind-streams—
> It is this very clear light awareness.
> Let your unmodified awareness be.

– Both deluded and undeluded states of consciousness are primordially the nature of the *sugatagarbha*, the *buddha*-nature. A person doesn't have one good and one bad mind-stream. You're not a *buddha* in one moment and a sentient being in the next. The nature of your mind-stream is this clear light awareness. If you penetrate to the essential nature of one thought, you penetrate all thoughts. Just let your unmodified nature be. That is the practice.

There are four types of "letting be." The first is letting your view be, like a mountain. When you let it be, you become like a mountain, unmoving. Recall that people who are ready for this practice can enter this state like the *garuḍa* that flies immediately upon emerging from its shell, but most people must follow a more gradual route.

Second is letting meditation be, which is like letting the ocean be. Without the view, the meditation cannot follow. In this letting be, the body remains completely unmoving, completely still. The speech, like the strings of a lute which have been cut, is completely silent. The gaze remains fixed and steady with no target, or object of focus. Like the ocean, the mind is unmoving, the body is unmoving, the speech is unmoving, and the gaze is fixed and unblinking.

Third is letting appearances be. Let all appearances to the six doors of perception—positive or negative, virtuous or nonvirtuous—just arise. Whatever arises to the mind, let it arise. Don't follow after it, don't grasp onto it, don't impede it, and don't respond with either hope or fear. These appearances are like waves that drift along the surface of the ocean, while their nature is no different than the ocean. They are also likened to rays of sunlight, which are no different than the sun. That is the practice of letting appearances be.

Fourth is letting the fruition be, which is letting awareness be. This entails being free from the sense of there being anything to be attained or anyone to attain it. You are free of any hope—even the hope for spiritual awakening. You are free of any anxiety—even the anxiety of not attaining spiritual awakening. This is because through letting awareness be, you have ascertained the very nature of your own awareness, and you know the nature of that awareness is Buddha. A *buddha* doesn't hope to become a *buddha,* nor does a *buddha* fear that he will not become a *buddha.* When you realize the essential nature of your own awareness, you will know there is nothing to be attained. You will know there is no Buddhahood to be found elsewhere. There is nothing to be feared in terms of nonattainment, nor is there anything to be hoped for in terms of attainment.

What is it like to have gained success in these practices of letting be? When you become experienced in letting be like a mountain, it's like climbing to the highest peak in a mountain range. From that lofty point you can look out over the entire range. Similarly, once you have gained realization of this authentic view, everything else can be seen. In this state there is no difference between meditative equipoise and post-meditative experience. There is complete homogeneity, unlike our present state when it's difficult for us to enter into proper meditative equipoise. In this advanced state not only do you have genuine meditative equipoise, but no experiential distinction exists between the actual meditative state and the post-meditative state.

Once you have gained the experience of letting be like an ocean, you completely transcend the threefold distinction of meditator, object of meditation, and meditation. All phenomena within *saṃsāra* and *nirvāṇa* appear to the mind with utter limpidity, as if you were looking out on a vast ocean in which the water is completely transparent and luminous. It is like looking at images in an utterly clear mirror. In this state, in contrast to our present state there is an all-knowing quality to your awareness. You are imbued with both types of knowledge: ontological and phenomenal. Moreover, you have confidence. All phenomena to which you direct your awareness become clear, and you have the confidence of a *garuḍa* in flight, without any trepidation of falling to the ground. Similarly, you attain the confidence of complete freedom. Moreover, all positive and negative events appear as self-displays, or creative expressions, of awareness, just as waves arise from the ocean.

Closely related to this realization is seeing the sole *bindu*, which is the fundamental unity of the whole of *saṃsāra* and *nirvāṇa*, seeing for yourself the one taste of reality of *saṃsāra* and *nirvāṇa*. To elaborate further: The three embodiments, namely the *dharmakāya*, *sambhogakāya*, and the *nirmāṇakāya*, correspond to the essence, the nature, and the all-pervading compassion of awareness. The *sambhogakāya* emerges as a creative display of the *dharmakāya*, and the *nirmāṇakāya* is a creative display of the *sambhogakāya*. This relates to the assertion that if one recognizes the nature of one thought, this sheds light on the nature of all ideation. For instance, if it's raining and you decide to test one drop of water to see for yourself if rain is wet, that one test gives you insight into the nature of the other drops of water. By knowing the nature of one thought, you know the nature of all thoughts.

The state of letting appearances be, which is also called "letting your conduct be," and letting awareness be are both utterly transcendent states that cannot be expressed in words. In practice we reach these four stages of realization gradually, by first cultivating a spirit of emergence and by being very conscientious with regard to our behavior and its ethical consequences. –

The Tantra of Nonconceptuality states:

> The innate mind, originally ungrounded,
> Is the Mahāmudrā, which conceives of nothing.
> Untouched by all phenomena,
> Rest in that unmodified state.

The Tantra of Non-dwelling states:

> In the pure wood of all ideation
> The great fire of clear light
> Blazes forth as Mahāmudrā.
> That is the supreme deed of equality.
>
> Enlightened from the very beginning,
> Primordial wisdom abides in your own mind-stream.
> In terms of the three Dharmas for training the mind, [680]
> There is no certainty that what you desire will occur.
>
> Only with the continuum of undistracted mindfulness
> Will the essence occur at this very time.
> With the growth and perfection of inconceivable compassion,
> There is the Mahāyāna.
>
> Without meditative equipoise or the post-meditative state,
> There is no interruption in this mind-stream.
> Great contemplatives who cultivate this
> Do not become fragmented.

– The thoughts, images, and so forth that arise in our minds are like an endless forest. Shall we try to cut down each tree, one by one? If we were to cut one down, another would immediately grow up, so that would be an endless and futile task. Rather, let them all be consumed in the great fire of the clear light of Mahāmudrā.

The term *the three Dharmas* refers to the variety of methods for training the mind. You may apply yourself to these methods, but there is no guarantee you will achieve the exact result you have in mind. As a result of their meditation, some people experience primarily a sense of bliss, others a sense of clarity, and still others a sense of nonconceptuality. Clinging to the experience of bliss leads to rebirth in the desire realm, clinging to clarity leads to rebirth in the form realm, and clinging to nonconceptuality leads to rebirth in the formless realm. By not clinging to any of them, you are in the position to realize their essential nature as being the three *kāyas* of the Buddha. Thus, the actual nature of the bliss that arises is the *nirmāṇakāya*. The essential nature of the clarity is the *sambhogakāya*, and the essential nature of nonconceptuality is the *dharmakāya*. In this practice, the *kāyas* are not accomplished one by one, but simultaneously. The minds of the great contemplatives who cultivate this do not become fragmented. As various types of ideation arise, their minds don't become fragmented and thus they may achieve liberation in this lifetime, in the dying process, or in the *bardo*. –

The Tantra of Inconceivability states:

> The mind is the *dharmakāya*, so it is nothing at all.

> The body is the *sambhogakāya,* with its signs.
> Because it can illuminate phenomena, it is the *nirmāṇakāya.*
> Always worship the *maṇḍala* of the three embodiments.
> Because it manifests the results of signs,
> This is called the inconceivable, superior view.
> With a single voice of the speech of all the *buddhas,*
> This is proclaimed as the great, unsurpassable *tantra.*

The Tantra of Saṃbhuṭa states:

> Turning away from oneself,
> And seeking everywhere in the realms of the universe,
> No *buddha* is found elsewhere. [681]

The Tantra of Inconceivable Mysteries states:

> The pinnacle of all phenomena
> Is the absolute space that is without inherent presence.
> A mind that has no view
> Observes Mahāmudrā.[79]

The Vajra Pavilion Tantra states:

> Outside of the jewel mind,
> There are no *buddhas* and no sentient beings.

The Glorious Tantra of Secret Activity states:

> All phenomena are of the nature of the mind,
> And the mind is of the nature of emptiness.
> Everything is empty, of one taste.
> This is the absolute space, in which there is no rejection or acceptance.

The Secret Vajra Ḍāka Tantra states:

> Due to realizing one's own mind for oneself,
> Sentient beings are originally *buddhas.*

The Tantra of Saṃbhuṭa states:

> Due to the obscuration by the darkness of ignorance,
> The Buddha is said to be other than the body.

The Five Stages states:

> Thus, the three primordial wisdoms
> Arise from the pure, clear light,
> Bearing thirty-two signs,
> And endowed with eighty fine symbols. [682]
> The Omniscient One, endowed with all supreme aspects,
> Arises from that.

The Glorious Tantra of Secret Activity states:

> The apprehended and the apprehender
> Illuminate all objects.
> Since the mind-itself is inconceivable,
> Do not conceive of anything.

– Other practices, such as the stage of generation and certain practices within the stage of completion entail the use of thought and conceptual grasping. But the point of this citation is that since the very nature of the mind is both nonconceptual as well as inconceivable, do the most simple practice: don't conceive of anything. Go beyond all the objectifying and grasping entailed in the various practices of the generation and completion stages. –

The Guhyasamāja Tantra states:

> In terms of ultimate reality,
> Meditate on the things of the three worlds as insubstantial.
> The actual meditation on insubstantiality
> Is meditation having nothing on which to meditate.
> Therefore, meditation on substances and non-substances
> Is without an object.

The Primary Tantra states:

> The cultivation of single-pointed contemplation
> Entails thinking of nothing whatever.

The Glorious Tantra of Royal Ambrosia states:

> By meditating on the clear light, whose nature is empty,
> It is not found,
> Nor is it found by not meditating.
> Meditation itself is conceptualization,
> And not meditating is also conceptualization.
> Without having a speck of anything on which to meditate,
> Do not be distracted for an instant. [683]

– On the one hand, you may try very hard to meditate, but the meditative state doesn't arise. Consequently, you may give up meditating, and the meditative state still doesn't arise. On the other hand, if you actually recognize the clear light nature of your own mind, there is no need to meditate...and there's no need not to meditate. –

The Questions of Madröpa Sūtra states:

> One sees by looking with the eyes of wisdom.
> Seeing without seeing is seeing reality.

Seeing the immutable with the eyes of wisdom
Is seeing the Buddha.

– To see beyond conventional reality is to see with the vision of the Buddha. This practice is like pointing everywhere while asking, "Where am I? Where am I?" Eventually your finger comes around, points to your own nose, and you recognize your own nature. –

The Ornament for Higher Realization states:

The object of this is insubstantial.
The agent is said to be mindfulness.

The King Doha states:

Without being mindful of conventional truth,
The mind becomes no mind.
The transformation is the best of the best.
Know that this is the ultimate, the supreme.
The mind is unified in *samādhi* without mindfulness,
And that is the complete purification of mental afflictions.
Just as a mud-born lotus is not polluted by mud,
One is not tainted by the ocean of faults arising from cyclic existence.

– A *doha* is a spontaneous song of realization. In the state of realization referred to here, awareness has gone beyond any object of mindfulness, and so the mind becomes no mind, which is to say that there is no substantial existence, no intrinsic nature, to the mind-itself. This is the best of the best. Bear in mind that the *buddha*-nature is primordially pure. If the essential nature of your own mind is in fact pure, then why do sentient beings suffer? Conversely, if we have arisen from *saṃsāra* and dwell in *saṃsāra,* how can our *buddha*-nature be completely pure? Just as a lotus rooted in mud remains unpolluted, sentient beings born into the swamp of *saṃsāra* arise from it with our own awareness untainted by its faults. Similarly, the *buddha*-nature cannot be polluted by the faults arising from cyclic existence. This is like the sun, which remains unsullied by a cloud cover.

This brings us back to the familiar theme that all of the *buddhas* of the past are *buddhas* only because they have recognized their own nature, while we sentient beings remain in cyclic existence subject to suffering simply due to not yet realizing our own nature. –

The Doha Treasury Treatise in One Hundred and Ten Verses states:

The mind that looks neither outside nor inside
Thinks of nothing and intends nothing. [684]
The mind that is distracted in conceptual elaborations concerning configurations of composites

Demonstrates the nature that is without transference or engagement.
Meditate on the ordinary essence of the mind.
This mind which is like that of a crazy person is dissociated from action.
Meditate on primordial wisdom, which is untainted by extremes.
O contemplatives who do not close your eyes and do not meditate,
Who sit on a cushion in solitude, with no homeland,
Meditate on the essential nature of the mind,
The reality that is devoid of the stains of attachment and hatred.
This indivisibility of cause and effect is the essential mind.
There is no need to effortfully strive to experience that.

– If you look for the mind outside or inside, it will not arise as an object of thought or intention. Composite phenomena throughout the phenomenal world capture and distract the mind in innumerable conceptual elaborations. However, this distracted mind indicates a deeper nature that transcends any transference of consciousness, as in taking rebirth. It indicates a mind that is free of action. So meditate on the natural essence of the mind.

Meditate with your eyes neither wide open nor closed. This will help to cut down on distractions. For those of you on the path it is preferable to simplify your lives in terms of your possessions and so forth. For those meditating on the essential nature of the mind, it's very helpful to live in solitude possessing only a cushion. This solitude need not necessarily be a solitary place, for it can be the inner solitude of Milarepa, Yeshe Tsogyal, and Longchen Rabjampa. Each dwelled in solitude, isolated from delusion, anger, attachment, pride, jealousy and doubt. In further examining their lifestyles, you will see that they lived in utter simplicity, leaving no relics behind. In the case of Longchenpa, it is said that throughout the winter and summer he carried only one yak-hair sack that held all his belongings. Each of these great beings displayed outer simplicity and inner freedom.

Like these great beings of the past, should we give all of our possessions away and reduce ourselves to poverty as the first step to engaging in spiritual practice? If so, shall we assume that the millions of homeless people have gained some spiritual insight? Obviously not. Poverty alone is not the solution. First abandon the five inner possessions of the mind, namely the five poisons; the outer simplicity will then take place as a matter of course. Giving up your outer possessions without releasing your inner afflictions will have no benefit. Think of refugees who leave their countries with only their clothes on their backs. Their enforced poverty does not lead to spiritual awakening. In fact, due to the tremendous stress and hardships they endure, some even become crazy. The transformation that needs to take place is the inner transformation of the five poisons into the five primordial wisdoms. We need to recognize that our real enemies are these inner afflictions of delusion, attachment, anger, pride, and jealousy, not what we own. –

The One Hundred and Sixty Verses of the Public Doha states:

> O foolish ones, upon realizing the mind of the mind,
> All detrimental views will naturally be released.
> Due to the power of great, supreme bliss,
> If you dwell in that, the ultimate *siddhi* will be experienced.

– Upon realizing your own essential nature, all views, all opinions, beliefs, and perspectives will naturally be released. More accurately, it is not so much that views and so on are wrong or misleading; rather, it is the grasping onto them that makes them detrimental. Upon realizing your own essential nature, grasping onto views, together with the habitual tendencies to do so, is naturally released. –

The Treasury Treatise of the Secret Embodiment states:

> Mahāmudrā does not rely upon anything else,
> So the object of meditation is yourself, and the meditator is
> your own mind. [685]
> In the state beyond the intellect there is freedom from objectivity.
> Since that is the fruition, there is no reliance on anything else.
> Meditation, accomplishment, and *mantra* recitation are your
> own mind.
> Your chosen deity is also your own mind,
> So the prophecies of *ḍākinīs* and so forth are your own mind.
> In the state beyond the intellect there is freedom from objectivity.

– The meditator, the object of the meditation, and the meditation are your own nature. In the state beyond intellect, you are disengaged from all objective referents. You grasp onto nothing with your awareness. Even your chosen deity is your own mind, whether it is male or female, peaceful or wrathful. This holds true, also, for the pure realms.

Even the prophecies of *ḍākinīs* are simply of the nature of your own mind. In Tibet, among men and women practitioners, it was more often men who went crazy, but in the West, it seems that women more commonly go crazy, and when they do, they often claim to be *ḍākinīs*, declaring that whatever comes out of their mouths is a wondrous revelation. There's nothing so amazing about a prophecy being channeled through your awareness. If you are not amazed that the nature of your own mind is the *sugatagarbha*, then how can you be amazed at these so-called revelations? –

The Treasury of Secret Speech states:

> Oh, how then will the cycle of existence be left behind?
> Having no causes or contributing conditions, the thatness of the mind,
> Which is not an object of thought, remains as Mahāmudrā.
> Due to the power of thatness, one is freed of signs,
> And in one lifetime Mahāmudrā is realized.

– How can you be freed from *saṃsāra*? If you truly recognize the nature of *saṃsāra*, you will see that this phenomenal world, which has no ground in reality, doesn't need to be either abandoned or rejected. You need only realize its actual nature. Bear in mind once again that the essential nature of *saṃsāra* and *nirvāṇa* is your own mind. The magnificence of *nirvāṇa*'s nature is your own mind; the terrible qualities of *saṃsāra*'s lowest realms are the nature of your own mind. The relation between *saṃsāra* and *nirvāṇa* and your own mind is like that of the sun and the rays of light from the sun, like fire and the heat of the fire. If you recognize the essential nature of *saṃsāra* and *nirvāṇa* as your own mind, then in one lifetime, Mahāmudrā will be realized. –

The Treasury of Secret Mind states:

> With the revelation of the characteristics of Mahāmudrā,
> Free of an apprehender and an apprehended, faults and so forth are incinerated.
> If it is observed single-pointedly, this is the foremost excellence.
> Doing so single-pointedly, there is no cultivation of excellent qualities.
> Thoughts are self-illuminating, and they are calmed in the taintless state. [686]
> Without mindfulness and without appearances, they are like reflections in a mirror.

– One of the characteristics of Mahāmudrā is that it's free from any type of dualistic grasping of subject and object. Being free of an apprehender and an apprehended, all faults and so forth are incinerated. Flaws exist as flaws only if you do not recognize their actual nature. If you do recognize their nature, you see them to be of the nature of Mahāmudrā. Simply to observe this single-pointedly is the most excellent cultivation, and no other is necessary. These thoughts and other phenomena are self-illuminating—they naturally appear, yet they are ungrounded and without substantial existence like reflections in a mirror. –

The Non-mental-engagement of the Three Embodiments states:

> Where there is no disengagement from this,

> In an instant there is freedom from the objects of mindfulness
> and grasping.
> It is difficult to investigate the *vajra* mind.
> The vision of the mind as the mind has an equal taste,
> And it is revealed by the pinnacle of outer and inner meditative stabilization.
> The contemplation that dwells in the innate reality
> Is perfected in the mysterious, absolute space of primordial wisdom.

– The equal taste may be interpreted in several ways: One sees the three embodiments of the *dharmakāya, sambhogakāya,* and *nirmāṇakāya* as being of one taste, or one nature. Another interpretation relates to the spirit of awakening, in which one regards others equally, with no sense of some beings as more dear than others. Finally there is the one taste of *saṃsāra* and *nirvāṇa*. The contemplation that dwells in the innate reality, natural purity, is perfected in the absolute space of primordial wisdom. That is Dzogchen, the Great Perfection; that is the Great Seal, Mahāmudrā. –

The *Doha* of the glorious recluse Saraha states:

> Oh, let the mind observe itself without distraction!
> If you realize your own thatness,
> Even the distracted mind will arise as Mahāmudrā.
> This is the state of great bliss, in which signs are self-releasing.

– Do nothing else, attend to nothing external, simply be aware of your own mind. By realizing your own essential nature, even the distracted mind arises as Mahāmudrā. This state of great bliss is free of all faults, including the fault of ignorance, so it is equivalent to the omniscient state of spiritual awakening. This is closely related to the assertion that by liberating one thought all are liberated; by gaining insight into one thought there is insight into all. Insofar as one dwells in that state of awareness, there are no thoughts, no discrimination. Through realizing the nature of your own mind, you realize the one taste of *saṃsāra* and *nirvāṇa*. –

The *Doha* of Virupa states:

> The expanse of the reality-itself of the mind does not exist as "this is it."
> Thus, in that there is no duality of meditation and the object of meditation.
> Rest without distraction in the state in which there are no thoughts of existence or nonexistence.

The *Doha* of Tilopa states: [687]

> I, Tilopa, have nothing to reveal.

My abode is neither isolated nor non-isolated.
My eyes are neither open nor closed.
My mind is neither structured nor unstructured.
Know that the innate cannot be brought to mind.

The *Doha* of Nagpopa states:

When you are free of striving on the path, that is the innate state.
There is no way to calculate suchness by means of concepts.
When you see the definitive meaning that is incalculable and unmistaken,
There is no dualistic grasping onto "empty" or "not empty."
Proceed to the culmination of the extinction of phenomena and the extinction of the intellect.

– Imagine that you have to cross a river, which unfortunately has no bridge, so you have only one option: to jump in and swim. Once in, you see all types of filth, as well as carnivorous creatures just waiting for the perfect prey. With great effort, you finally reach the other side and collapse on the sun-warmed sand, which is covered with scented, beautiful flowers. At that moment, you realize you are completely exhausted. That is like the state of being free from striving on the path. That is the innate state. This state cannot be calculated. When you see the true import of the teachings, it is unmistaken; there is no longer any dualistic grasping onto the notions of empty or not empty. –

The *Doha* of Maitrīpa states:

If you know your mind to be unified with the enlightened mind, that is the chosen deity.
Do not withdraw your consciousness, but gradually eliminate thoughts.
If ideation occurs in the mind, the contemplative
Lets it be relaxed and unstructured, like a cotton puff.
Eliminate activity and let your own mind observe itself.

The Mahāmudrā Gaṅgāma states:

The mind, like the essence of space, transcends the objects of mentation. [688]
Relax it in that state, without directing it or placing it.
When the mind has no intentional object, that is Mahāmudrā.
If you familiarize and acquaint yourself with that, unsurpassable enlightenment will be achieved.

The Synthesis of Naropa's View states:

It is said that the mind dwells [like] space,

And self-awareness itself, free of conceptual elaboration,
Appears and is empty, is empty and appears.
Thus, it is indivisibly appearing and empty.

The Synthesis of Maitrīpa's Words on Mahāmudrā states:

Rest in the unstructured nature.
The unthinkable is the *dharmakāya*.
Resting without modification is meditation;
Seeking and meditating involves the deceptive intellect.

The Nine Seeds of Precious Practical Advice of Paṇchen Śākyaśrī states:

Whatever appears, if you leave it where it is, is spontaneous presence free of activity.
If you apprehend whatever arises, awareness is liberated right where it is.
If you sever the dispersive quest, all thoughts vanish into the absolute space.
These three are the nature of being of your own mind, so cultivate them as the main practice. [689]

The Zhijepa Tradition of Phadampa states:

Your own mind free of grasping,
Without mental consciousness being scattered
To the appearances of the five senses,
Is the great method of placing the mind.

The Disclosure of the Secrets of Songtsen Gampo states:

By looking, there is no object to be seen,
But by resting without looking, reality-itself is seen.
By resting without achievement, the mind-itself is actualized.
Without grasping and without relaxing, [the mind] is liberated right where it is.
Rest without grasping onto anything at all.
When there is recognition, [the mind] is liberated in its own state.

In the Great Perfection many distinctions between the mind and awareness are discussed, but they come down to one point. *The Tantra of the Blazing Clear Expanse of the Ḍākinīs* states:

That which is called "awareness, awareness"
Is awareness due to being cognizant and clear.
Previous ideation is liberated right where it is;
Future grasping does not arise;
In that interval there is freedom from the structuring and contamination of antidotes.

This interval and division, free of taints,
Is to be recognized as awareness. [690]
Its essence is empty, and its nature is clear,
And its compassion is able to appear to all.
That is the nature of being of awareness.

Dechen Lingpa's Letter states:

Primordially existent awareness, this *dharmakāya*,
Is self-arisen, self-appearing, without knowing its own essential nature.
Thus, one revolves about in the sequence of the cycle of existence.
Right from today know your own essential nature!
You are all manner of things;
Likewise, if you reject or affirm that which is to be abandoned, you are shackled.
In reality phenomena are ungrounded;
Being nonexistent, deceptive appearances are not obtained by grasping.
This which is naturally settled, unstructured, fresh, and loose
Is primordially the original Buddha.
Without engaging in modification, contamination, investigation or analysis of good and evil,
Constantly post the sentry of mindfulness free of distraction.
In terms of the great, pervasive homogeneity of the equal taste of the cycle of existence and liberation,
Why do you call this "the nonarising of ignorance"?
Dispensing with the thought of diligent striving in Dharma,
Dwell in the state of inactivity, free of exertion. [691]
This fresh consciousness of the present moment
Is Mahāmudrā, the contemplation of the *jinas*.
Rest with no craving for meditative equipoise, post-meditative achievement,
Experiential realization, primordial wisdom, and so on.
Even if you have achieved spiritual awakening, you are awareness.
In the cycle of existence and the miserable states of existence, you are confused.
Therefore, apart from just your own awareness,
Do not foster hope or fear, acceptance or rejection, negation or affirmation.

Rendawa Zhönnu Lodrö says:

> In this way observe the absolute space of the innate mind:
> This is the indivisibility of skillful means and wisdom and the Mahāmudrā of one taste.
> It is the original mind that is free of illumination and obscuration, laxity and excitation.
> Rest in your own state, without contaminating it with the thought of wishing to meditate.
> Rest at ease, and post the sentry of mindfulness.
> Like a bird that flies from a ship in the expanse of the ocean,
> Circles around and comes back to rest on the ship,
> However much the masses of thoughts flow out,
> In the end, they come to rest in their own abode, the absolute space of phenomena. [692]
> Thus, there is no need to make a point of stopping ideation.
> Release in openness, and post the sentry of mindfulness.
> Like applying a *mantra* to poison,
> Thoughts and mental afflictions arise as great primordial wisdom.
> Do not think this is to be accomplished by means of striving.
> The darkness of obscurations is dispelled by self-arisen clear light.
> Thus, o contemplatives, if you want to experience the self-arisen clear light,
> Do not accomplish it by means of nonconceptualization.
> If you wish to calm waves,
> When you try to make this happen, they arise all the more.
> Likewise, even if you apply antidotes to stop ideation,
> The waves of thoughts will flow out again.
> When you just leave them alone,
> After awhile the waves of water will subside.
> Likewise, if you know how to practice at ease, without exertion,
> The waves of ideation will naturally be calmed.
> The release of ideation into the absolute space is quiescence;
> Upon cutting off conceptual superimpositions, there is insight;
> And when appearances and the mind are indivisibly merged, that is union. [693]
> Like a crystal vessel filled with water,
> In the originally pristine, spontaneously present, absolute space

There are no tainted, habitual tendencies of mental afflictions to be eliminated,
Nor do you modify your mind with antidotes to achieve nonconceptuality;
So upon what shall you meditate with what antidote?
When your own unborn mind dwells in the absolute space,
Without seeing signs of problems and antidotes or acceptance and rejection,
And when there is neither anything on which to meditate nor any meditator,
Problems are self-liberating, and remedies are self-appearing.
At first, the road to travel is like a stream rushing down a gorge;
In the middle, the *ārya* path is like the current of the Ganges;
At the end, like the expanse of the ocean,
It is immovable by anything, and that is the path of omniscience.

Kyemé Zhang Rinpoche says:

To meditate on Mahāmudrā,
Without binding yourself to a set discipline,
You certainly do not need to calculate according to the stages
Of the preliminaries, the main practice, and the conclusion.
There is no need to calculate periods of times or the lunar date. [694]
Whenever you remember to do so, rest in the expanse.
There is no beginning, middle, or end.
The continuum of your unborn mind never ceases.
With regard to the pollution brought up in the waves of water,
It will become pure if it is left alone without doing anything to it.
If the shroud of obscurations of your own thoughts
Is left alone without modification, it is purified as the *dharmakāya*.
Without altering anything, rest in the expanse.
Do not withdraw your consciousness, but let it go free.
Do not crave anything, but rest in openness.
Do not focus on an object, but rest in openness.
Do not engage in many tasks, but rest in being present.
Without trying to direct the mind,
Let it be without a ground, like the intervening space.
Without thinking of the past, future, or present,
Let your consciousness be fresh.

Whether or not thoughts flow out,
Do not make a point of meditating, but rest at ease.
In short, without meditating on anything,
Let your consciousness roam freely.
There is no need to be anxious about anything.
Be vividly present in the experience of the *dharmakāya*.

The Four Dharmas for Subduing the Borderlands taught by Serlingpa states: [695]

Cast it far and set it free;
Let it loose and let it be.

– You don't really throw your mind, just completely release it, just let it go. Imagine a heavy sheaf of wheat tied to your shoulders. Now visualize cutting the cord with a knife. Suddenly it's off of your shoulders—you completely let it loose. It's as loose as a comb going through silken hair; there is no resistance. Let it be gentle, let it be loose, and let it be. –

The glorious Sakyapa Dragpa Gyaltsen says:

Observe the mind of the mind that is mindless.
If there is something to see, it is not the mind-itself.
Seeing the unseen is the vision of the mind.
Rest without distraction in the unseen mind.

The Eight Verses by Sakya Paṇḍita says:

If it is sent far, it does not go;
If it is closely bound, it does not stay;
If it is well examined, it is ungrounded;
So what is its nature?
Insofar as you crave it a little,
You will be fettered.
If you know its nature,
You will be released from all fetters.

The Collected Teachings of the Lady Labdrön states:

Therefore, rest in a state of no-thinking.
Do not follow the tracks of feelings and thoughts.
Like the natural illumination of a flash of lightning in the sky,
Whatever thoughts arise, leave them as they are.

And: [696]

Likewise, if you recognize your own mind,
There is no need to accomplish spiritual awakening elsewhere.

According to the teachings of Gyalsey Thogmé, who appeared later:

> These appearances, just as they are, are your own mind.
> The mind-itself is originally free of the extremes of conceptual elaborations.
> If that is known, the signs of the apprehended and the apprehender
> Are not brought to mind—that is a practice of the children of the *jinas*.

And:

> Freely release bodily activity,
> Like a bale of straw whose string has been cut.
> Freely release verbal activity,
> Like a lute whose three strings have been severed.
> Freely release mental activity,
> Like a cord that remains cut.

Lord Marpa Lotsawa says:

> The dualistic dispersions of the mind
> Dissolve into the absolute space of phenomena, free of conceptual elaborations.
> This illusory mechanism of external appearances
> Is realized as great, unborn pervasiveness.
> The essential nature of the mind, the internal apprehender,
> Is like meeting someone with whom you are already acquainted.

And:

> This appearing object of the mind, which is apprehended externally, [697]
> Is unceasing as a great pervasiveness,
> And it is realized as the unborn *dharmakāya*.

Lord Milarepa says:

> Both the sentient beings of the three realms of the cycle of existence
> And the *buddhas* in *nirvāṇa*
> Are encompassed within the body of reality.

And:

> Both the objective phenomena that appear to the six collections [of consciousness]
> And your own unborn mind
> Nondually arise together.

Lord Rechungpa says:

> Amazing! The wondrous and magnificent phenomena
> Of forms are nondual appearances and emptiness;
> Sounds are ineffable, empty noise.
> This realization is the union of bliss and emptiness.

And:

> From the nature of the appearing *dharmakāya*
> Is the realization of the indivisible object of observation and the observer.

Lord Gampopa says:

> Now know this empty, clear, essential nature of appearances and awareness
> To be the *dharmakāya*.

And:

> By knowing appearances and sound as the mind,
> There is a continuous stream of joy and delight.
> The crucial point of great bliss is discovered.

Düsum Khyenpa says:

> Buddha is found in your own mind. [698]
> Be free of the attitude of wishing to achieve *siddhis*.
> By knowing one thing, you know the realization that is all-liberating.
> Be free of the attitude of engaging in hearing and thinking.
> Realize the reality of the nonduality of cyclic existence and quietude.
> Be free of the attitude of anticipating the time of spiritual awakening.

The Protector of the World Rechenpa says:

> To float in naked awareness,
> Do not wear the clothing of the signs of ideation.
> In the natural abode of the innate essence
> There is no point in considering bondage and liberation.

Tromdragpa says:

> With the clear recognition of self-arisen awareness,
> Your contemplation is not distracted for an instant.
> Like shining a lamp in the darkness,
> There are no errors or obscurations—amazing!

Karma Pakṣi says:

> Without accomplishing the three embodiments,
> This Mahāmudrā, your own mind, is spontaneously discovered as the ground;
> So there is no need to seek it.

And:

> This awareness, your own unmodified, innate mind,
> Is recognized for yourself, and it is left in whatever appears.

And: [699]

> Free of the intellect and without mental engagement,
> Is the practice during the time of meditative equipoise.
> And doing this with the potency of luminosity and awareness
> Is the practical advice for avoiding pitfalls.
> Train in seeing all that appears as illusory,
> And train in seeing everything as the unceasing displays of awareness.
> That is the practice during the post-meditative period.

Orgyenpa says:

> Ordinary awareness recognizes itself.
> Meditating on the nature of the cycle of existence,
> There is no need to achieve liberation.
> Meditating on the variety of appearances,
> There is no need for meditative equipoise.
> In the Mahāmudrā of mindfulness of appearances
> There is no need to stop appearances.
> In the meeting of the mother and child experiential clear light
> There is no need to hold onto anything with mindfulness.

Rangjung Dorje says:

> In general, when you say "the view, the view,"
> For the view, observe your own mind.
> If there is nothing to be seen upon looking,
> Just that is the sovereign vision.
> Look again! Look again! Observe the mind!
> In the palace of the unborn mind [700]
> Dwells the *dharmakāya* of immutable bliss.
> When the mind sees its own essential nature of awareness,
> How could it be found by seeking anywhere else?

Rölpey Dorje says:

> Know this original, ordinary consciousness
> To be the *dharmakāya*.
> Know these thoughts of all sorts of things
> To be primordial wisdom.

Khachö Wangpo says:

> However you grasp onto the textual doctrines,
> You err in terms of the reality of the mode of being.
> For those who see with an intellectually fabricated view
> The state of realization remains dormant.

And:

> If you recognize your own mind for yourself, you are a *buddha*.
> What is to be done with a lot of hearing and thinking about conventions?
> Let the conceptual designs of the textual doctrine disappear.
> This natural liberation of whatever is seen is the path of enlightenment.

– No matter how knowledgeable you are of the doctrine, as long as you still grasp onto these texts, you miss the mark when it comes to recognizing the actual nature of being of reality. The proper sequence is hearing, thinking, and meditation, but if you are still grasping, you are in error. It is as if you are hibernating and are closed in on yourself. Let the conceptual designs of the doctrine go! Just let go of your grasping! –

The teachings of Drungkyi Kün-ga Namgyal state:

> Achieving the warmth of experience that is a portent of realization,
> The mind achieves serviceability in terms of bliss, clarity, and nonconceptuality.
> That freedom from the errors of pitfalls is called *single-pointedness*. [701]
> Having purified the clinging onto experiences, there is no object;
> And you realize for yourself the absolute space and awareness as empty.
> In meditative equipoise you are freed of the five aggregates, and in the post-meditative state you experience [phenomena as] illusions.

See the essential nature that is free of debilitating taints.
The path of seeing, free of conceptual elaborations, is called *nonconceptual, primordial wisdom.*
All phenomena included within the array of the cycle of existence and liberation
Are realized as characteristics of the mind of union.
Free of exertion and with the dominion of self-appearances,
The realization of profound and vast wisdom is called *the one taste.*
Due to this there is liberation, and the grasping of the day and night is purified.
The self-appearing, pristine, innate kingdom is revealed.
The absolute space and awareness are unified, and the mother and child clear light are joined.
The spontaneous accomplishment of the three embodiments is called *no-meditation.*

Such teachings gradually become evident. This concludes the identification.

– With bliss, clarity, and nonconceptuality the mind becomes serviceable. In this passage the term "single-pointed" refers to the recognition of reality. Clinging ceases, resulting in there being no object. It is very difficult to achieve this state of realization in which we neither affirm nor negate, so that we can view phenomena and thoughts as the play of the mind, and gain decisive insight free of all grasping. Hopefully, we will practice and lead our lives so that we can die without remorse, and without having broken any of our precepts or allowed our *samayas* to degenerate. Since novices are easily disturbed, we are generally encouraged to live simply and in relative solitude without distractions. In that simplified environment we can practice stage by stage.

Which key Dharma practice really opens the door to the path? It is meditating on impermanence—the reality of death and the general truth of impermanence. Strive diligently to realize these truths, because they give insight into the genuine practice of Dharma. Meditating on death and impermanence should not result in feelings of anxiety, but rather should motivate you to disengage from the eight mundane concerns and to apply yourself to meditation. If you don't know how to meditate, find an authentic spiritual mentor, one well versed in the *sūtras* and *tantras* and motivated by a genuine spirit of awakening. Under the guidance of such a spiritual mentor, you can be prepared to set out on the path of the Great Perfection, doing so for the sake of yourself and all others. –

CHAPTER SEVEN

How to Follow the Path of the Leap-over

Homage to Avalokiteśvara!

– Only by garnering a thorough understanding of both Mahāmudrā and Dzogchen can you lay a sound foundation for this stage of teachings. Without a proper basis, the Leap-over phase of practice will not be fruitful and meaningful. For the practice of both Mahāmudrā and the Breakthrough stage of the Great Perfection, the cultivation of quiescence and insight are indispensable foundations. For the cultivation of quiescence and insight the preliminary practices, including the stages of generation and completion, are essential. This is the traditional sequence of practices for this training.

Without a suitable foundation, you run the risk of turning out like a *lama* in Tibet who was asked by one of his students, "Lama, what are you meditating on?" The *lama* answered, "I am meditating on patience." Sometime later the boy returned and asked, "Lama, now what are you meditating on?" Very righteously, the *lama* replied, "Patience." Returning a third time, the boy asked, "Lama, what are you meditating on?" Again the spiritual mentor said, "I am meditating on patience." The boy said, "O Lama, go eat shit!" Immediately the *lama* yelled, "Me eat shit? You eat shit!"

The practice of quiescence is included in the Hīnayāna, Mahāyāna, and Vajrayāna. In fact, it is present throughout the entire path up to and including spiritual awakening. Actually, all the *yānas* and types of practice are imbued with insight as well as quiescence. To emphasize this point: quiescence and insight are significant for everyone, not solely for Buddhists, until each sentient being has achieved liberation from cyclic existence; for without that quiescence and insight, we remain subject to mental afflictions. –

[704] These are the profound practical instructions of Avalokiteśvara. Having already presented introductions to both the Breakthrough and Leap-over stages of the Great Perfection, the reason why the union of those two is needed is stated in *The Secret Tantra of the Sun of the Blazing Clear Expanse of the Ḍākinīs*:

> With no Breakthrough, there is no Leap-over.
> With no Leap-over, there is no Breakthrough.

The Tantra of the Compendium of the Contemplations of Samantabhadra states:

> If the meaning of this Breakthrough is not realized,
> Even if the Leap-over is experienced, it will be dualistic.
> Confusing the meaning with non-experiential gibberish
> Is like throwing gold nuggets back into a stream.

[705] Thus, the union of the twofold vision of the ground—namely, attending to the essential nature of the Breakthrough, Mahāmudrā—and the path—namely, the clear light of the Leap-over—is the pinnacle of the nine *yānas*. Moreover, it is prophesied that in degenerate times in this snowy land [of Tibet] this will flourish and spiritual fruition will be attained. *The Tantra of the Great Perfection Inquiry into Deceptive Appearances* states:

> When many years have gone by
> After I have passed into *nirvāṇa*,
> The supreme fruition will be attained
> By countless beings in the northland.

The Tantra of Treasures states:

> After five hundred [years], the Secret Mantra[yāna] will flourish in the regions to the north. [706] From that time on, this fruitional Dharma of the Secret Mantra[yāna] will be experienced by some individuals. They will attain states of fruition that will not be meager.

When Orgyen Rinpoche was about to leave for the Land of the Cannibals, he said:

> In the future, fortunate people will gradually appear, and if they practice single-pointedly, results will occur before long, even though it is a degenerate era; and there will be many who attain *siddhis*.

Therefore, the clear light Leap-over should be practiced. In this regard there are four topics: (A) first of all striking the critical points in terms of the body, speech, and mind; (B) on the basis of the three critical points, letting direct perception come to you; (C) teachings on the way the four visions appear if you practice; and (D) concluding advice.

A. Striking the Critical Points

Here there are three topics: (1) the critical points of the body, (2) the critical points of the speech, and (3) the critical points of the mind. [707]

1. Striking the Critical Points of the Body

In this regard there are three topics: (a) the *nirmāṇakāya* posture like a squatting *ṛṣi*, (b) the *sambhogakāya* posture like a reclining elephant, and (c) the *dharmakāya* posture like a lion sitting in the position of a dog. *The Primary Tantra on the Penetration of Sound* states:

> In the *dharmakāya* posture of a lion, one is free of all confusing fears and sees with *vajra*-eyes. In the *sambhogakāya* posture of reclining like an elephant, one experiences reality-itself and sees with lotus-eyes. In the *nirmāṇakāya* posture of a squatting *ṛṣi*, one is emanated in the aspect of reality-itself and sees with Dharma-eyes.

The Pearl Garland states:

> There are three kinds of bodily tasks: remaining in the manner of a lion, an elephant, and a squatting *ṛṣi*.[708]

If there are many seeking guidance, the *nirmāṇakāya* posture is sufficient.[80] *Avalokiteśvara's White Instructions on the Supreme Light of Daytime Contemplation* states:

> On occasion, practice the *nirmāṇakāya* posture of a squatting *ṛṣi*.

If there are few disciples and this is not a public teaching, let there be no more than seven disciples. When the sky is clear and windless, lead your disciples to a solitary place.

a. The Dharmakāya Posture of a Lion Sitting in the Position of a Dog

Position your body in the posture of a dog: rest both soles of your feet on the ground; clench your hands in *vajra*-fists; plant both your big toes on the ground; like a lion, stretch the upper part of your body upwards; extend yourself powerfully towards the ground; and direct your [visual] faculty to its object.

– Rest the soles of your feet flat on the ground. Plant your big toes on the ground and like a lion stretch your chest upwards. To make a *vajra*-fist, tuck your thumbs inside your palms, touching the base of your ring fingers; and curl the remaining fingers around the thumbs. Without bending your wrists hold your arms straight between your knees, which lean out to the sides, and forcefully extend yourself to the ground, suggesting a strong, powerful posture. In some traditions, people place their fists on the ground in front of their feet; others a little back. Raise the chin and your eyes slightly, and direct your eyes to their object, namely empty space. –

b. The Sambhogakāya Posture Like a Reclining Elephant

Lie facing down like an elephant; press both knees against your chest; let your toes point outwards; plant both elbows on the ground; [709] and raise your chin slightly upwards.

– In this posture your eyes are directed neither upwards nor downwards, but gaze straight ahead (horizontal to the ground) or to the left or right. Among the three postures this is considered to be the easiest. Kneel with your chest facing the ground, allowing your toes to naturally point outward so that you are somewhat on your belly, raise the upper part of your chest, and rest your chin in the palm of your hands. –

c. The Nirmāṇakāya Posture Like a Squatting Ṛṣi

Sit upright with your ankles next to each other; rest the soles of your feet on the ground; let your body be erect; press your knees against your chest; cross your forearms while hugging your knees; and let your spine be straight and erect.

– Resting the soles of your feet flat on the ground, sit with your knees bent and your ankles next to each other. Press your knees against your chest, rest your elbows on your knees, cross your arms, with the right arm crossed over the left, and rest your hands on your shoulders. Hold your torso erect, keeping your spine straight. –

By striking the three critical points of the body in those ways, the primordial wisdom of awareness that is present in your body will manifestly arise. As an analogy, although a snake has limbs, if it is not squeezed, they are not evident.

2. The Critical Points of the Speech

Here there are three topics: (a) revealing the speech, (b) stilling the speech, and (c) stabilizing the speech. In terms of revealing the speech, over the course of three or four days let your speech subside to the point of silence. In terms of stilling the speech, completely silence your speech, without letting it be mixed with words to anyone else. [710] In terms of stabilizing the speech, stabilize by not saying anything, as if you were mute.

– Completely silence your speech like the silence of the broken strings of a lute. Through this phase of practice, you enter into an inconceivable and ineffable state. Arising from this deep experience and merging into an experience of emptiness, you completely silence your speech. To cease speaking is part and parcel of this ineffable and inconceivable experience, but that experience is very different from making an intentional decision not to talk for awhile, which is really nothing special. –

3. The Critical Points of the Mind

Do not let your awareness be distracted elsewhere. Do not let it disengage from the focused target.

– Although the text uses the word "target," it pertains to all three postures. In terms of the *dharmakāya,* the gaze is directed upwards into space, so that is your target. It is very important that you do not allow your gaze or attention to wander from that. Keep it right on the target. In the *sambhogakāya* posture, the gaze is horizontal, so whatever appears in that field is your target. In the *nirmāṇakāya* posture direct the gaze downwards, several finger-widths beyond the tip of your nose, without allowing either your gaze or your attention to wander off. It is crucial to find a middle path in terms of your posture not being too tight or too loose. If it is too sloppy the whole significance is lost. On the other hand, it shouldn't be absolutely rigid. Try to aim for something in between. –

B. On the Basis of the Three Critical Points, Letting Direct Perception Come to You

Here there are three topics: (1) the critical points of the apertures, (2) the critical points of the object, and (3) the critical points of the vital energy.

– The apertures refer to the eyes; the object is space, and the critical points of the breath pertain to the vital energies. –

1. The Critical Points of the Apertures

The critical points of the apertures are the eyes, as stated in *The Primary Tantra on the Penetration of Sound*:

> In terms of the apertures, gaze with the eyes [in accordance with] the three embodiments.

No Letters states:

> Gaze with the eyes into the domain of space.

The Pearl Garland states:

> In terms of the apertures, do not move from thatness.[81]

Nirvāṇa Traces states:

> In terms of the apertures, look up, down, and to the side.[82]

Here there are three topics: (a) with the *dharmakāya* gaze you look up in order to stop delusive appearances at once; (b) [711] with the *sambhogakāya* gaze you look horizontally in order to see the essential nature nakedly; and (c) with the *nirmāṇakāya* gaze you look downward in order to gain control over the vital energies and mind. Do not disengage from those three types of gazes.

2. *The Critical Points of the Object*

This involves the outer absolute space and the inner absolute space. *The Primary Tantra on the Penetration of Sound* states:

> The absolute space is outer and inner: the outer is apprehended as a cloudless sky, and the inner as a lamp-lit path.

– This cloudless sky has not even a trace of haze. The inner lamp-lit path is the channel of awareness running from the heart to the eyes and then out into your visual field. Implicit within this is the aspect of emptiness, so once you gain experience, the distinction between inner and outer dissolves, and the nonduality of outer and inner is realized. By gazing outwardly into space, you actually cultivate, purify, and make more manifest what is inner, namely, awareness. Through the outer, the inner becomes manifest. –

The Blazing Lamp states:

> By resting your awareness in the outer absolute space, self-awareness is purified and illumined in its own state.

The Tantra of Naturally Arising Awareness states:

> The nature of the absolute space is a halo.

– The relationship between the outer and the inner can be understood with the metaphor of pouring a cup of water into the ocean, at which point it is no longer distinguishable from the ocean. Similarly, if you cup your palms together, space is enclosed between your palms, but when you open them, it is indistinguishable from the space all around. –

Nirvāṇa Traces states:

> The critical point of the object is the sky, free of conditions. The inner absolute space is the pristine lamp. Moreover, there is no

object of attachment in empty space, [712] so by focusing on the critical point of the object, namely the absolute space, primordial wisdom rests at ease.

3. *The Critical Points of the Vital Energies*

There are three critical points of the vital energies: (a) retention, (b) expulsion, and (c) slowness and stability. *The Primary Tantra on the Penetration of Sound* states:

> The critical point of] the vital energies comes from firmly restraining them and fully expelling them.

Nirvāṇa Traces states:

> The critical point of the vital energies is revealed in their being very slow.

First retain the breath gently, then expel it far outwards as if you were shooting an arrow. Afterwards, let the breath be very slow as it naturally settles. In terms of the critical point of awareness, imprison the strands.[83] *No Letters* states:

> The essential nature emerges like strands, minute, glittering, and darting about.

– Let the breath, which is of the same nature as the vital energies, be natural, without altering it in any way. The crucial points of the practice are the gaze of the eyes, the posture, and letting the breath be natural. Imprison the shimmering *vajra*-strands of awareness by confining them with your attention.

In terms of practice, as you direct your gaze in front of you, these *vajra*-strands of awareness will appear in the space in front of you. If these strings of *bindus* start to move, do not jerk your eyes around or try to hold onto to them by moving to the left or right. Rather, "imprison" these strands by keeping your gaze very steady, and then gradually these *vajra*-strands will become stabilized, and excellent qualities and realizations will emerge from that. In contrast, if you apply to such an experience your ordinary, neurotic mind, no stabilization or excellent qualities can result. –

The Tantra of Naturally Arising Awareness states:

> The embodiments of light, imbued with the five primordial
> wisdoms,
> Manifest vividly as strands.
> They come and go,
> Waver and spread out.

The Fulfillment of the Power of Primordial Wisdom states: [713]

> The self-appearing lord of awareness
> Dwells as strands of primordial wisdom.

Nirvāṇa Traces states:

> Hold the strands in the prison of awareness.

In that way, let your awareness, never separated from the three locations, observe the strands. At first have many, short sessions, then gradually increase the duration of the sessions. Then practice at specific times during the day and night, as a result of which you will be trained in one and a half months.

C. How the Four Visions Appear

The manner in which [visions] arise as a result of such practice is taught in *Avalokiteśvara's White Instructions on the Meaning of Daytime Contemplation*. The perceptual vision of reality-itself, called "the *vajra* strand of awareness," is like a crystal rosary. Without wavering, forcefully focus on that vision, which is free of the extremes of appearances and emptiness, at the point between your eyebrows.[84] By so doing, there will arise visions due to dynamic vital energies being extinguished externally, and the vital energy of primordial wisdom being inserted into the central channel; and they are called "the six daytime signs." *The Perfect Expression of the Names of Mañjuśrī* states: [714]

> The great bonfire of wisdom and primordial awareness
> Arises from space and arises from itself.

Due to the insertion of the vital energy of the posterior channels into the central channel, there is said to be a shining redness like a blazing fire, called "the illumination of the great light." Due to the convergence of the vital energy of the anterior channels into the central channel, there is said to be a flash like lightning, called "the shining appearance of primordial wisdom." Due to the convergence of the vital energy on the left, there is a shimmering whiteness like the moon, called "the fire of the world." Due to the convergence of the karmic energies on the right, there is a shimmering redness like the sun, called "the lamp of primordial wisdom." Due to the convergence of the upper vital energy, there is a shimmering blackness like Rāhu, called "the great, glorious clear light." Due to the convergence of the vital energy in the central channel, it is said that there appears a minute, dark *bindu* of rainbow light.

– The above are references to the types of visions that one may experience in this practice. These are actually visual perceptions, not conceptual images, not of *buddhas* or other divine beings, but of your own awareness. Insofar as you have a direct vision of your own awareness, you are a *buddha*. Sometimes when people have a vision, they think they have received an amazing transmission or a mystical revelation, and they immediately tell other people. When doing this, people should be embarrassed. By gaining a genuine realization of the nature of our own awareness, we transmute the mental afflictions of the five poisons into the five primordial wisdoms. That is the reason we practice. As genuine realization arises, there is no need to tell other people that we've had certain visions. Those who actually have genuine experiences don't feel the need to talk about them! –

Ratna Lingpa's *Wish-fulfilling Gem: Instructions on the Quintessence of the Clear Expanse* states:

> By meditating in that way, at first, [715] at the point between the eyebrows there appears something like rainbow light, called "the pristine lamp of the absolute space." Inside that is "the *bindu* of the empty lamp," which is like concentric circles from casting a stone [into a pool]. Inside that, which is like a circular plate of armor, appears a *bindu* the size of a mustard seed or a pea. Inside that are "the *vajra*-strands of awareness," which are minute like knots in a hair of a horse's tail, like pearls strung on a thread, like iron chains, like garlands of flowers rustled by a breeze, and so on. They all appear in sets of two, three, and so forth. They are your own awareness, called "the *vajra*-strand," and "the sole *bindu*."
>
> The absolute space and awareness are present without uniting or separating, like the sun and its light rays. The mark of the absolute space is a halo, the mark of primordial wisdom is a *bindu*, [716] and the marks of the embodiments are the strands. In terms of their location, while residing inside the *citta*, the *bindu* mark of primordial wisdom and the strand marks of the embodiments perceptually appear in the pathway of the senses. That dispels views entailing the grasping of speculation, analytical views of the intelligence that are constructed by words, the intellect, and so forth.

– In this phase of the practice, the most common posture is that of a squatting *ṛṣi*, but it is also possible to practice in the ordinary cross-legged posture. In terms of location, the actual *bindus* reside in the *citta*, which is the heart, but they appear in the pathway of the senses—the eyes. Inside the circular plate of armor appears a *bindu*, the size of a pea. However, some see a *bindu* of a different size, and some don't see a *bindu* at all. The *vajra*-

strand is composed of minute *bindus*, strung in a sequence. Two, three or more of these *vajra*-strands of awareness appear within each *bindu*, and the *vajra*-strands themselves are composed of *bindus*, like pearls on a silken thread. There may be two, three or a hundred of these pearls on each *vajra*-strand. Therefore, the number of *vajra*-strands within each *bindu* and the quantity of *bindus* for each *vajra*-strand may vary greatly.

Just as the sun sinks below the horizon, visions and realizations from this phase of practice dispel all intellectual, conceptual views cultivated in the past. These visions do not arise due to your intelligence or learning. They appear by devoting yourself to a genuine spiritual teacher and practicing the correct postures and gazes. Then gradually, stage by stage, your own internal qualities manifest externally as these visions. On the other hand, if you jump into this practice without the guidance of a genuine spiritual mentor and without following the proper sequence of practice, obstacles will arise. Whether you ascend or fall through this practice is your own affair.

What happens if you practice Mahāmudrā and Dzogchen? What can you expect? Some Tibetan intellectuals have declared that you become a nihilist, saying that this view perfunctorily dismisses the "skillful means" aspect of the practice, as well as cause and effect—*karma*. Moreover, these intellectuals conclude that this is a practice devoid of mindfulness, in which the clarity of mind is blocked, with only nonconceptuality no different than deep sleep remaining. They equate this mindless, nonconceptual state, devoid of clarity, to Dzogchen meditation.

In fact, the authentic practice of Mahāmudrā and Dzogchen entails a union of luminosity and emptiness, not a blockage of clarity. It is said that the practice of Dzogchen transcends thought and the conventional mind, and that within the practice of Mahāmudrā there is no mental engagement. In actuality, the transcendence of thought and the lack of mental engagement entail a disengagement from the conventional mind that takes conventional reality as the object. Therefore, the actual meaning of this practice is that you transcend the conventional mind and fathom ultimate reality.

Throughout the nine *yānas*—including the Hīnayāna, Mahāyāna, and the outer and inner Vajrayāna—indivisible skillful means and wisdom are indispensable. Moreover, for each *yāna*, the infallible law of cause and effect is crucial. Through the culmination of Mahāmudrā, or the four visions of the Leap-over practice, the reality of cause and effect remains. It seems that what critics of Mahāmudrā and Dzogchen are really condemning is nihilism, but genuine practice of these teachings does not succumb to this pitfall—entering into a mindless state with no regard to *karma*, with no skillful means.

As we delve into these practices of the Leap-over stage of Dzogchen practice, it is as if we are coming down from the top floor—down from the highest stage of practice. The four visions of the Leap-over stage are called visions because they appear to you directly. The first is the direct vision of reality-itself. This entails a direct vision of the ultimate mode of existence of all phenomena. It is direct, in that it is an utterly unmediated perceptual insight, rather than an experience of conceptual constructs, language, and so forth. This occurs only after one has identified the view in terms of one's own experience. All the myriad teachings in the Hīnayāna, Mahāyāna, and Vajrayāna eventually lead disciples to this direct experience of the ultimate nature of reality.

Once you have gained such a vision, you must become thoroughly familiar with this realization through practice, so it doesn't grow vague and fade out of your consciousness. This sequence of experience entails the vision of progress in meditative experience, which further develops the initial insight you have gained. As a result, you enter into the third of the four visions—the vision of reaching consummate awareness. Your practice has now come to perfection, like a fully ripened peach, like a well-trained child whose excellent qualities have been brought to perfection, or like Buddha Śākyamuni. But even that is not the final vision. The final state is the vision of the extinction of all phenomena into reality-itself. That is the point at which you no longer rely on teachings or practices; you have achieved the spiritual awakening of a *buddha*.

Among the four visions, the first vision corresponds to penetrating into the nature of phenomena as they are—the ontological knowledge of a *buddha*. The third is analogous to the phenomenological knowledge of a *buddha*—seeing the full range of phenomena. The indivisible arising of these two types of knowledge corresponds to the fourth of these visions, which is the culmination of the previous three. –

A Mound of Jewels: Instructions on the Quintessence of the Ḍākinīs states:

> The direct vision of reality-itself directly appears as subtle and pure, clear and lustrous, naturally brilliant, and wondrous. The lamp of the pristine absolute space directly appears, imbued with the five colors of a rainbow, vertically and horizontally, like the tips of arrows and spears, like fish-eyes, like pinpoints of light, like holes in a fine-meshed net, like blazing jewels, and like a *stūpa* all covered with *bindus* and minute *bindus*. Inside all of them clearly appear [717] *vajra*-strands of the nature of awareness. Recognize them, and practice without wavering or uncertainty.

– There is no certainty that each of these images will appear to you. For some people one or two types arise, while for others more may appear. However, the only way they do occur is by practicing with enthusiasm and perseverance in the correct posture and with the appropriate gazes, applying your body, speech, and mind to the training. –

Karma Lingpa's *The Natural Liberation of Seeing: Experiential Instructions on the Transitional Process of Reality-Itself* states:

> First, in terms of the direct vision of reality-itself, the spiritual mentor teaches, "Perform the critical point of the body like this, perform the critical point of the speech like this, and for the critical

point of the mind, focus on this." By students practicing like that, without relying on superimpositions due to imagination and words, they directly see as their object the vision of the awareness of reality-itself in empty space, without its being contaminated by any compulsive ideation. So that is called the "direct vision of reality-itself."

Thus, by practicing in accordance with the critical points, between your eyebrows there is the "lamp of the pristine absolute space." It appears like the colors of a rainbow [718] or the eye of a peacock feather. Inside it is the so-called "lamp of the empty *bindus*," and it is like the concentric circles of ripples when you throw a stone into a pond. Inside a form like the round plates of a shield there appears a *bindu* about the size of a mustard seed or a pea. Inside that are the so-called "*vajra*-strands of awareness," which are fine like knots tied in a strand of a horse's tail, like a string of pearls, like an iron chain, like a lattice of flowers moving with the breeze, and so on. All those appear in combinations of two, of three, and so on, and they are called the "sole *bindu* of the strand of your own awareness."

The absolute space and awareness are neither joined nor separated, but are present in the manner of the sun and its rays. The mark of the absolute space is a halo, the indication of primordial wisdom is the *bindus*, and the mark of awareness and the embodiments is the strands. In terms of their location, they are present in the center of the *citta*, [719] and in terms of their pathway, they directly appear to the eyes.

– When this lamp arises, it is clear and firm and appears in various colors. It does not arise automatically or very quickly, but comes gradually as a result of practice. Inside a form like the round plates of a shield, there appears a *bindu* which is like a bubble—it appears, yet lacks any substantial, or inherent, nature. These *bindus*, like pearls, knots, and flowers, are all interconnected in strings of two, three, and so on. Although they are called the sole *bindu*, it is not to say that you see only one *bindu* in this phase of practice, but rather this refers to the one essential nature of all phenomena.

The six "lamps" are: the *citta* lamp of the flesh, located in the heart; the lamp of the hollow crystal *kati* channel, which is a pale, delicate channel connecting the heart to the eyes; the fluid lasso lamp, referring to the eyes, which are like a lasso; the lamp of the pristine absolute space; the lamp of the empty *bindus*; and the lamp of self-arisen wisdom. –

The Primary Tantra on the Penetration of Sound states:

The direct vision of reality-itself

> Certainly emerges at the gate of the senses
> In the pure, clear, cloudless sky.

It is said:

> Views of grasping onto speculation, intelligence that is formed by words and the intellect, and analytical views vanish.

Nirvāṇa Traces states:

> With the direct vision of reality-itself, speculative views vanish.

The Clear Expanse states:

> Identified by forcefully gazing at the pure sky, free of conditions, a lamp appears to the gateway of the senses, beautiful like the eye of a peacock feather, with the *bindus* joined together in strands, moving about as they dart to and fro.

The Tantra of Naturally Arising Awareness states:

> Embodiments of light imbued with the five primordial wisdoms are illuminated as strands. They come and go, moving and spreading out. [720]

The Perfection of the Lion's Might states:

> This essential nature of self-appearing awareness
> Manifests as strands of primordial wisdom.

The Jewel Inlay states:

> From the fluid lasso lamp the fully perfect Buddha manifests in the aspect of embodiments of strands of awareness.

– The eye is fluid in nature; like a lasso, it reaches out to things far away; and like a lamp, it illuminates. Therefore, it is called the fluid lasso lamp. From this the Buddha manifests in the aspect of the *vajra*-strands of awareness. –

The Clear Expanse states:

> In the originally pure, essential nature
> The nature of spontaneity is present,
> Pervading all the Compassionate Ones,
> Appearing from the channels stemming from the pure *citta*.
> Its essential nature appears to the gateway of the senses,
> And it is called the direct perception of awareness,
> Which is free of intellectual analyses.

– Unlike the view that the mind is at first contaminated and then gradually, through practice, becomes pure, in this context the essential nature of the mind is originally pure, and it corresponds to the *dharmakāya*. The nature of spontaneity, which is already present, is the *sambhogakāya*, and the Compassionate Ones who manifest from that are called *nirmāṇakāyas*. –

Nirvāṇa Traces states:

> Whoever sees this critical point of direct perception
> Does not return to the three realms.

Now due to gazing [721] at the *bindus* of rainbow light, when the three rainbow light rays appear in the intermediate state, you will be liberated upon identifying the five primordial wisdoms as yourself.

– By familiarizing yourself with this practice during your lifetime, after your death when you enter the intermediate state, you will be prepared when the various rainbow light rays appear. These light rays are so brilliant you can hardly gaze at them; but through your previous practice, when they do appear, you will recognize them as your own nature, and you will be liberated. This is likened to a child recognizing its mother. –

Avalokiteśvara's Tantra Identifying the Secret Path of the Supreme Light of Primordial Wisdom states:

> Son of good family, the cessation of your breath and the pristine domain of the Buddha, which is like the sun appearing on the surface of a mirror, appear simultaneously. At that time, when a dark blue light is seen, consider this to be the empty nature of your own awareness as the primordial wisdom of the absolute space of phenomena; and you will realize the self-arisen Vajrasattva with his consort and entourage.
>
> When a yellow light is seen, consider this to be the empty nature your own awareness as the primordial wisdom of equality; and you will realize the self-arisen Ratnasambhava with his consort and entourage.
>
> When a red light is seen, consider this to be the empty nature of your own awareness as the primordial wisdom of discernment; and you will realize the self-arisen Amitābha [722] with his consort and entourage.
>
> When a green light is seen, consider this to be the empty nature of your own awareness as the primordial wisdom of accomplishment; and you will realize the self-arisen Amoghasiddhi with his consort and entourage.
>
> When a white light is seen, consider this to be the empty nature of your own awareness as mirrorlike primordial wisdom; and you will realize the self-arisen Vairocana with his consort and entourage.

> When a pure vision of the Lord of Mysteries arises, spiritual awakening will be achieved by recognizing and attending to this as the five primordial wisdoms.

– These various lights appear during the intermediate state following death, and if you recognize them, you will realize they are the five types of primordial wisdom. By failing to recognize them, due to insufficient preparation, fear and terror will arise, and having no time to think about them, you will fall into bewilderment. –

Thus, it is said that by continually gazing at these *bindus* and minute *bindus* of rainbow light, you will not return to the cycle of existence. A *tantra* states:

> The nature of the strands is the pristine, primordially pure, nondeceptive Buddha.

By practicing in that way, on the basis of the direct vision of reality-itself there arises the visions of progress in meditative experience. [723] Inside the *bindus* arise single embodiments, half embodiments, forms of deities and their consorts, and strands present wherever you look. That constitutes progress in meditative experience. In terms of further practice, the Vidyādhara Kumāraja says that exceptional clarity ensues from gazing while your eyes are covered with a woolen cloth or a yak-tail fan and so on.

– Within each *bindu* there may appear a single form of a chosen deity without consort, or perhaps just a portion of the deity, such as its head or hand implement. As you progress during the second phase of the practice, deities in union with their consorts may arise, and *vajra*-strands of awareness will appear wherever you look. At this point the *vajra*-strands of awareness are seen everywhere and are very stable. Please bear in mind that this is a more advanced state in the Leap-over practice. Don't expect this to happen at the beginning, but only after you have entered into the second phase of progress.

In this practice some people gaze at the sun by covering their face with a scarf, but doing so can damage the eyes, so rather gaze with the sun to your side so that it shines through the cloth at an angle. –

The Natural Liberation of Seeing: Experiential Instructions on the Transitional Process of Reality-Itself taught by Orgyen Rinpoche states:

> Second, in terms of the visions of progress in meditative experience, among visionary experiences and cognitive experiences, cognitive experiences arise in various ways such as a sense of bliss, a sense of clarity, and a sense of emptiness. Unstable and

transient, they are common to the various *yānas*, and they are not especially important. Furthermore, such traditions as Mahāmudrā also say that cognitive experiences are like mist, and one should not place credence in the value of such experiences. Rather, one should place the strongest emphasis on the value and so on of realizations. [724] Here, the criteria for the value of realizations are determined by way of visionary experiences; and since visionary experiences are not transient, they should be most strongly emphasized. Thus, as a result of cultivating visionary experiences, at times the absolute space and awareness become clear and at times they do not.

By continuing to practice, the absolute space and awareness are separated from the point between the eyebrows [they become separated from sensory phenomena[85]], and the lamp of the empty *bindus* effortlessly arises and approaches. The *bindus* turn into the size of peas, and awareness proceeds like a bird that is just able to fly.

By continuing to practice, visions of the five lights transform so that they appear in a fragmented fashion, vertically, horizontally, like spear-points, similar in aspect to [holes in] a black yak-hair tent, and like the squares of a chess board; and those lights pervade everything in front of you. Moreover, the *bindus* also transform so that they are like a mirror, and awareness appears in the manner of a running deer.

By continuing to practice, visions of the absolute space appear in the aspects of a jewel lattice, [725] lattices and half-lattices of light, checkered, radiant, like spear-points, and a multi-layered *stūpa*, a thousand-petaled lotus, a halo, the sun and moon, a castle, a sword, [a *vajra*,][86] a wheel, and like the shape of a fish-eye. Moreover, that light fills the environment in which you live. The *bindus* become like brass bowls, and your awareness becomes like a bee hovering over nectar.

By continuing to practice, the light saturates the environment, the *bindus* become like rhinoceros-skin shields, the light pervades everywhere you look, and the absolute space and awareness constantly appear day and night. A single body of a deity appears in each of the *bindus*, and individual, subtle divine embodiments arise in the midst of awareness. Awareness remains motionlessly.

When such appearances arise, the appearances of the intermediate state are determined in that way, [726] so there is no later intermediate state. Thus, the practice of the transitional process of reality-itself is just this main practice.

– If you become attached to a sense of bliss, this will lead to rebirth in the desire realm; attachment to a sense of clarity leads to rebirth in the form realm; and becoming attached to a sense of nonconceptuality gives rise to rebirth in the formless realm. Sometimes as these experiences arise, people become excited thinking, "This is great!" Conversely, if they don't have them, they become depressed. Therefore, it is better to emphasize actual realization, as opposed to cognitive experiences of their being good, bad or nonexistent. For those engaged in the practice of Severance, a variety of visionary experiences may arise as signs of success in the practice. However, if you grasp onto them, this leaves you more vulnerable to harmful spirits. So progress itself, if misconstrued, actually becomes detrimental. On the other hand, if you don't grasp onto the visions, no harm will come and you can continue in your practice. The crucial point is not whether you have visions, but whether you identify with and grasp onto them. If you don't, they are considered part of the path.

Similarly, while engaging in the cultivation of meditative quiescence, gross thoughts and compulsive ideation naturally arise in your mind. You may respond by wondering, "How can I possibly have such disgusting thoughts?" You may even think you are crazy, but this is only detrimental. In fact, you are seeing aspects of your own mind, and it is good for them to manifest. In fact, simply recognizing their nature and releasing them is a sign of progress in the cultivation of quiescence. As with the previous example, it is the grasping that is detrimental.

With dreams, too, it doesn't matter so much whether you have a prophetic dream or a nightmare, it is the grasping onto the idea that the dream is good or bad that is detrimental, not the mere appearance of the dream itself. Throughout the waking consciousness and in the dream state, problems arise from grasping onto visions, imagery, and thoughts that arise to the mind's eye. If you truly want to see if these are significant, check them out empirically. You will see for yourself that they are not firm; they have no essence, no inner profound significance to them. Moreover, responding to them with self-grasping as they arise only ignites more attachment and anger, which then gives rise to a great deal of nonvirtue. Please check this out for yourself.

It is said by many *lamas* that the effortlessly appearing *bindus* appear not only when your eyes are open but also when closed. By continuing to practice, they can appear like round pinpoints of light shining through a black yak-hair tent. Due to the nature of your practice in this lifetime, when you come to the point where light pervades everywhere and the absolute space and awareness constantly appear day and night, you will no longer be subject to the intermediate state. –

Avalokiteśvara's White Instructions on the Meaning of Daytime Contemplation states:

> To bring about progress in the *nirmāṇakāya* posture, in that posture practice the *caṇṭalī prāṇāyāma* entailing ignition and descent.

> By not being separated from the direct vision of the awareness of reality-itself, you will see radiantly clear black *bindus* as visions of light about the size of mustard seeds presenting themselves as objects of your mind at unpredictable times during the day and night. They are not imagined but appear perceptually. They are not existent, and they have no external existence whatsoever. Under the influence of the vital energies, they increase and decrease; but in reality they are without increase or decrease, for they arise as the five lights that are the natural luster of primordial wisdom. Those five-colored lights occur vertically, horizontally, as [holes in] a black yak-hair tent, and as squares on a chessboard; and your environment and so on arise variously in the forms [727] of *stūpas*, thousand-petalled lotuses, pavilions, checkered squares, temples, pinpoints of light, lattices and half-lattices, and so on.

The Primary Tantra on the Penetration of Sound states:

> In the visions of progress in meditative experience,
> The colors and shapes of primordial wisdom arise
> Vertically and horizontally.
> Various *bindus* and two embodiments
> Manifest as objects appearing to awareness.

Nirvāṇa Traces states:

> Due to the visions of progress in meditative experience,
> In the intermediate state primordial wisdom becomes
> manifest.

What is an analogy for the lamp at the time of the intermediate state? It is said that this is like encountering someone with whom you were previously acquainted. Like that analogy, upon thoroughly familiarizing yourself with the perception of the clear light of reality-itself, experiential visions progress; and you reach consummate awareness. Later on in the intermediate state, there is confidence, for primordial wisdom becomes manifest; in self-appearing *buddha*-fields you become a *buddha* [728] from the state of the clear light; and you serve the needs of beings in the ways in which they need to be trained.

A Mound of Jewels: Instructions on the Quintessence of the Ḍākinīs states:

> Then as a result of practicing, the visions of consummate awareness arise. Inside each *bindu* is a complete set of *buddhas* of the five families with their consorts, all the galaxies are filled with radiantly glowing strands, and you gain mastery over the arising of self-appearing awareness.

The Natural Liberation of Seeing: Experiential Instructions on the Transitional Process of Reality-Itself states:

> Thirdly, as for the vision of consummate awareness, by continuing to practice, five divine embodiments with consorts appear inside each of the previous *bindus*. They are innumerable and immutable, and they reach a consummate amount, as if by the handful and by the pound. Then you may even stop meditating. At that time, your body is liberated into clear light, its elements proceed into their natural purity; the aggregates of your material body are liberated in their own state; [729] appearing and yet not inherently existent, you are naturally liberated as a *sambhogakāya*; and as the *sambhogakāya* is nakedly recognized, grasping onto the embodiment is released in its own state.

– At this point the *bindus* and *vajra*-strands of awareness appearing to the mind's eye are innumerable and immutable. As if heaped on a scale by the handful and the pound, they mound up until coming to complete fullness, reaching a consummate amount. In the cultivation of the spirit of awakening, when it arises naturally all the time, even when you are sleeping or playing, it develops without effort. Likewise, in this phase of practice, the meditation develops effortlessly and naturally.

At this time the elements of the body proceed into their natural purity, and the material body is actually liberated in its own state. To the degree that there may still be the appearances of impurities—of the contaminated aggregates, of flesh, bone, and so forth—these are transformed into clear light. You are now free of all conceptual grasping; even grasping onto your own form as the *sambhogakāya* is naturally released into its own state. There are no concepts. You no longer think, "This is the *sambhogakāya*, this is the *nirmāṇakāya*, this is a spiritual mentor, this is a monk wearing robes." This state is nakedly realized without any meditation, completely free of any type of conceptual constructs. –

Avalokiteśvara's White Instructions on the Meaning of Daytime Contemplation states:

> To bring about the consummation of the *sambhogakāya* posture, in that posture, practice in reliance upon a *karmamudrā*, a *mudrā* of light, or a primordial wisdom *mudrā*. If you practice without being separated from the field of progress, the karmic vital energies are transformed into the vital energies of primordial wisdom, they are brought into the central channel, and all the apertures of the channels of delusion, which are the pathways for the movements of conceptualization, are filled with *bindus* of *bodhicitta*. As a result, you gain mastery over the qualities and blessings of *mantras*, you obtain divine vision, extrasensory perception, and

> supreme and common *siddhis;* galaxies become clear, and you enjoy the six sensory fields of experience. The five embodiments of the primordial wisdom of awareness appear inside each of the *bindus* that fill the phenomenal world. [730]

– A *karmamudrā* is a physical consort, a *mudrā* of light is a consort visualized when generating oneself as one's chosen deity; and the primordial wisdom *mudrā* is the nature of your own awareness. Karmic energies are so called because they propel us into *saṃsāra* in dependence upon the mental afflictions with which they have been accumulated. At this point the vital energies are still impure, but they are transformed into the vital energies of primordial wisdom by bringing them into the central channel. The channels through which conceptualization takes place are filled with *bindus* of red and white *bodhicitta.* The impure *bodhicitta* is naturally released and now only pure *bindus* of *bodhicitta* fill these channels. –

The Primary Tantra on the Penetration of Sound states:

> The vision of consummate awareness
> Is the vision of the signs and symbols of the *sambhogakāya*:
> From the indeterminate colors of the rainbow
> Appear the *buddhas* and their consorts of the five families.
> Then these fivefold pairs are connected to luminous *bindus*
> Bearing the appearance of the divine male and female embodiments.
> Upon the extinction of delusive appearances, there is spiritual awakening.

Nirvāṇa Traces states:

> With the vision of consummate awareness
> The *sambhogakāya* is recognized.

It is said that if this is realized, there will be no intermediate state. *Avalokiteśvara's Tantra Identifying the Secret Path of the Supreme Light of Primordial Wisdom* states:

> When the breath goes out at the verge of death, after you finally exhale and there is no inhalation, there is an *opening of primordial wisdom* in the space in front of you; and brilliant lights of five colors appear to you. By recognizing them—like applying an alchemical elixir to metal, or like holding up a lamp in a dark room—[731] you are instantly liberated upwards without impediment. Son of good family, until you are parted from your breath, that is the called *the cord of Vajrasattva* and *the cord of the current of compassion.* Cords of five-colored lights stretch out in the space in front of your eyes, or they may appear like a stair-

> way. At that time, direct your awareness to your eyes, and focus your eyes on the unbroken cord of compassion. By so doing, you will be liberated upwards without impediment. Or, when that cord of compassion extends out as the five colors, by recognizing them as primordial wisdom, you will attain the *maṇḍala* imbued with the five primordial wisdoms, and with no breath you will become a *buddha*. Lord of Mysteries, the complete outer, inner, and secret empowerments are revealed.

The Mound of Jewels of the Great Perfection states:

> Then the vision of the extinction into reality-itself appears. Upon the extinction of the progressions of experiences, grasping onto the three embodiments [732] disappears right where it is; awareness distinctly comes to its ground; grasping onto an object of meditation and a meditator is released in its own state; the deception of ignorance is utterly purified; and you reach the originally pure contemplation of Samantabhadra.

– It is very likely when the three embodiments—the *dharmakāya, sambhogakāya,* and *nirmāṇakāya*—first appear, some subtle grasping will still remain. In this phase of the practice, even that previous subtle form of grasping has vanished, and you no longer identify or label these embodiments because you are of one nature with them. Prior to this point, awareness appeared in various visions of the *bindus* of the *vajra*-strands, but now awareness radiantly, vividly, nakedly comes to its own ground and recognizes its own nature. The object of meditation and the meditator are of one nature, ignorance is forever dispelled from its root, and you reach the culmination of this path. –

Avalokiteśvara's White Instructions on the Meaning of Daytime Contemplation states:

> For the vision of the extinction of phenomena, practice whichever of the three postures you like, and practice in the unstructured state that transcends the intellect, without the intrusion of grasping onto the divine embodiments and the *bindus* as yourself or others. Then, by realizing the experience of never having been deluded, there is no fear of the cycle of existence. Spiritual awakening is present within you, so there is no hope or anticipation regarding enlightenment. The three embodiments are complete in yourself, and in the state free of extremes, with no duality of self and other, all the qualities of the Buddha are perfected. The habitual propensities of the elements of the body are extinguished. The vital essences vanish into the five lights. Verbal articulation and words are extinguished and vanish into a state that is inconceivable and

> ineffable. The intellect is extinguished, and phenomena [733] are extinguished, vanishing into the originally pure state that transcends the intellect. In that you are awakened as the *dharmakāya*.

– If it is true that our actual nature has never been deluded, how can we account for the fact that we act the way that we do? It is simply because we have not yet recognized our own nature. I'll illustrate this with a dream I had last night. I dreamed of a very large, aggressive, powerful, yellow-green, poisonous snake. Next to me stood a friend, who cautioned that it could strike at any moment. Then this friend reached out and grabbed the snake by its head. At that moment I recognized that dream as a dream. I recognized not only how real this extremely threatening poisonous snake appeared, but it seemed as if my friend were truly standing next to me. Everything seemed completely real, and yet upon recognizing the dream as a dream, I realized that everything in the dream had no basis in reality. Next, I wondered: how is it that we arrive in *saṃsāra* and how is it that we wander in cyclic existence?

As we look around in this dreamlike waking state, everything seems to be real, but it is no more substantial than the events of a dream. How can we be deceived when a deceived being doesn't even exist in reality? In reality, we have never been deluded. To be sure, I am not speaking of nihilism because these phenomena do appear, but they have no basis in reality.

At this point in practice grasping onto a subject and object—an I and a you—no longer occurs. When the visions of the *bindus* of the *vajra*-strands of awareness arise, there is no sense of thinking, "Oh, I see them." There is no sense of duality; there is no anticipation of the future course of your spiritual development. All of that has passed. You leave everything in its natural state. There is no more practice. –

The Natural Liberation of Seeing: Experiential Instructions on the Transitional Process of Reality-Itself states:

> Fourthly, in the vision of the extinction into reality-itself, the progression of the preceding visions comes to an end, and in those experiences of visions there is no nature of grasping onto appearance or non-appearance. At that time there occurs what is called *the vision of extinction into reality-itself*. Experiences are extinguished, the material body is extinguished, the grasping of the sense faculties is extinguished, the assemblage of deluded thoughts is extinguished, all philosophical tenets and delusive appearances are extinguished, and then your contaminated body disappears and you become a *buddha*. That is called *extinction into reality-itself*, for it entails the extinction of activity, delusive appearances, and the visions of progress in meditative experience. It is called *the extinction into reality-itself*, but it is not nonexistence as in the case of nihilism, in which there is an extinction

into nothing. Rather, inexpressible primordial wisdom of knowledge and excellent qualities become manifest. In short, the power of the qualities of the three embodiments [734] is brought to perfection.

The Primary Tantra on the Penetration of Sound states:

> The vision of the extinction into reality-itself
> Is empty of experiential visions,
> So the body is extinguished, and the objects of the senses are extinguished.
> Once the deluded assemblies of thoughts are naturally released,
> One is separated from words, which are the basis of expression.

And:

> Thus, upon the cessation of the continuum of the body, the contaminated aggregates disappear, and to the mind one manifestly becomes a *buddha*.

Nirvāṇa Traces states:

> Due to the vision of the extinction into reality-itself,
> The fruition of the Great Pefection, free of activity, is attained.
> Upon reaching the culmination of the ground and the path in this way,
> *Nirvāṇa* is to be sought nowhere else.

– The phrase "the fruition of the Great Perfection, free of activity" refers to freedom from conventional or mundane activity. One is free even of the activities of progress in meditative experience. Now you may ask, Are *buddhas* more active than sentient beings like ourselves? Of course, a *buddha* is immeasurably more active than we are. However, a *buddha's* actions are not mundane. Just as the rays of light from the sun are of the same nature of the sun, so, too, are a *buddha's* actions of the same nature as a *buddha*. A *buddha's* activities are natural, spontaneous, all-pervasive displays of a *buddha's* awareness. –

D. Concluding Advice

It is best to attain the *great transference body*, free of birth and death, or immortality, like Orgyen and Vimalamitra; or one's contaminated aggregates may vanish into a mass of light, like Garab Dorje and Śrī Siṃha. *Avalokiteśvara's White Instructions on the Meaning of Daytime Contemplation* states:

> The perfect Buddha is Awakened with no residual aggregates. [735]

It is middling to reach the ten grounds in this lifetime. *The Tantra of Naturally Arising Awareness* states:

> The "grounds" do not exist separately. In an individual who sees the truth, the grounds are completely present.

After extensively explaining the ways in which the ten grounds are attained, it states:

> A person who sees the truth reaches this without casting off this shell. People who do cast off the shell reach the grounds in this way.[87]

The ways to reach the sixteen grounds are then discussed at length. Among them, the names of the first ten grounds accord with the general explanations, while the others are taught in a somewhat altered order. Thus, although there seem to be many dissimilarities, the eleventh is *the total light*; the twelfth is *dispassionate lotus-eyes*; the thirteenth is *the vajradhara*; the fourteenth is *the great assembly of wheels*; the fifteenth is *perfect splendor*; for the sixteenth *unexcelled primordial wisdom*, Devakuśa, Sukhāvatī, and the City of Great Liberation have the same meaning; the seventeenth is *bearing the vajradhara name*; [736] the eighteenth is Aṭakāvatī; the nineteenth is the *unsurpassed*, or *unexcelled, perfection*; the twentieth is *the perfection of the nature of the three worlds*; and the twenty-first is the *dual quest*, or *the ground of the effortless bindu*, which is the culmination.

– The Mahāyāna tradition in general teaches that one reaches the ten *bodhisattva* grounds that culminate in Buddhahood. Of the sixteen grounds referred to in this text, ten are common to other treatises, while the eleventh to the twenty-first grounds of Dzogchen that follow vary in order and name according to specific texts. –

Orgyen Rinpoche says:

> The Great Perfection is the culminating path. Then no Dharma that transcends misery is to be sought elsewhere, for this is the ultimate. Even if the final paths of the lower *yānas* are reached, if the opening of the qualities of the Mantra[yāna] is not seen, then one should enter into the Mantra[yāna], and one must train in hearing and thinking. Even if one comes to the culmination of the Sūtra[yāna], one has not come to the culmination of the Mantra[yāna], for this is the culmination of all paths. There is nothing superior to that, so in it the grounds are complete and

> the paths are complete. There is nothing greater than that, so it is given the name "the Great Perfection."

– When you have reached the fourth vision, the vision of extinction into reality-itself, you need not seek out any other Dharma. Once you have come to the culmination of the lower *yānas,* you should enter into the Vajrayāna, which is the culmination of all paths, and train from the beginning in hearing, thinking, and meditation. The reason for this progression is that within the culmination of the Mantrayāna is the implicit culmination of the Sūtrayāna. The culmination of the Sūtrayāna does not subsume the culmination of the Vajrayāna, so you must not stop training after reaching the culmination of the Sūtrayāna. –

Ratna's *Wish-fulfilling Gem: Instructions on the Quintessence of the Clear Expanse* states: [737]

> The best is that the contaminated aggregates are liberated into the clear light. Middling is to attain spiritual awakening in the transitional process of reality-itself. The least is to be born instantly in the five *nirmāṇakāya* pure lands and then to attain spiritual awakening without any intermediate state.

Avalokiteśvara's White Instructions on the Meaning of Daytime Contemplation states:

> In manifestly perfect spiritual awakening, one becomes a *buddha* with the clear manifestation of a pristine sky, rainbows, showers of flowers, earthquakes, sounds, delicious aromas, sacred relics, naturally arising [representations of a *buddha's*] body, speech, and mind, granular relics, and so on.

– The above description is of the external signs such as rainbows, showers of flowers, and earthquakes that may appear when one attains Buddhahood. "Granular relics" are fine, crystalline, white powder left after the cremation of a great being. In Tibet in the twelfth Tibetan month of 1958, both the *nirmāṇakāya* speech and body emanations of Düdjom Lingpa passed away in the region of Golok. They lived about one hour's walk away from each other, and they passed away at the same time. Although it was mid-winter and very cold, flowers fell from the sky. There was unseasonal thunder and a type of frozen precipitation that is very fine and smaller than hail. This I witnessed for myself, so I pass this on to you so you will know that when great holy beings pass away, they manifest such signs of their spiritual awakening. –

The meaning of those [passages] is stated in *Nirvāṇa Traces*:

> Due to the direct vision of reality-itself,
> One transcends words of grasping onto speculation.

> Due to progress in meditative experience,
> The primordial wisdom of the intermediate state is made manifest.
> Due to the vision of consummate awareness,
> One recognizes the *sambhogakāya*.
> Due to the vision of the extinction into reality-itself,
> One attains the fruition of the Great Perfection, free of activity.
> Upon coming to the culmination of the ground and path in this way,
> There is no doubt that one achieves *nirvāṇa*. [738]

The Primary Tantra on the Penetration of Sound states:

> From that come the four visions.
> Due to the direct vision of reality-itself,
> One transcends words of grasping onto speculation.
> Due to the vision of progress in meditative experience,
> Delusive appearances pass away.
> Due to the vision of consummate awareness,
> The three embodiments transcend the visions of the conceptual path.
> Due to the vision of the extinction into reality-itself,
> The ongoing path of the three realms of *saṃsāra* is broken off.

The best achievement is to attain spiritual awakening with no residual aggregates or to attain spiritual awakening together with the residual aggregates. The middling achievement is to attain spiritual awakening in the intermediate state and to reach sixteen grounds. The least achievement is to be born in the *nirmāṇakāya* pure lands, and after remaining in the five pure lands for one hundred and twenty years, one receives empowerments, blessings, and prophesies from the five families of *jinas*. Then after five hundred years, one ascends to the pure land of the flaming volcanos, and as soon as one sees the face of the supreme Heruka, one becomes a *buddha* in the youthful vase form, indivisible from Samantabhadra. [739] That is the ground of the synthesis *bindu*,[88] or the effortless *bindu*, and it is said that in reality it is the sole *dharmakāya*.

That is a complete synthesis of the way to proceed along the Great Perfection path of the Leap-over. If you desire extensive knowledge, look to the seventeen *tantras*, *The Seven Treasures*, and so forth.

CHAPTER EIGHT

Guidance on the Path of Transference

Homage to Avalokiteśvara!

[742] These are the profound practical instructions of Avalokiteśvara. If you die without having come to the culmination of practicing by means of this meditation, bring this escort on the path of transference. This is of benefit even if you have no practice, for the Palmo Tradition, the Dawa Gyaltsen Tradition, and the Tshombu Tradition of *The Essential Instructions of Avalokiteśvara* call this "the advice for transference to enlightenment without meditating."

– If through hearing, thinking, and meditation you have not yet arrived at the culmination of this practice, at the time of death you should certainly implement the teachings on the transference of consciousness. Generally speaking, it is very rare to receive Dharma teachings in the West, and equally rare to find people who actually put the teachings into practice. Even more rare are those who practice according to the traditional path. If you practice these teachings on transference, this will lead to rebirth in a *buddha*-field. Even though these teachings are called transference to enlightenment without meditation, this practice does nevertheless entail meditation. There is still no push-button way to enlightenment! –

The Tantra of the Compendium of the Contemplations of Samantabhadra states:

> If this is applied when the indications of death have not
> occurred,

> You will incur the great misdeed of killing a deity.
> This obstructs [the attainment] of human life for five hundred rebirths. [743]

– Divinations, dreams, and doctors' prognoses are some of the tests used to determine when death is imminent. If so, it is your responsibility to apply any means available to turn death away, by taking medicine, engaging in religious rituals, and so forth. Only when these methods fail is it appropriate to fully engage in the practice of transference. To do so prematurely leads to the great misdeed of killing a deity—the peaceful deities dwelling in your heart and the wrathful deities residing inside of your head. Furthermore, your channels are of the nature of *vīras*, and the vital energies that flow through the channels are the nature of *ḍākinīs*. Therefore, if you practice the stage of generation and apply the transference teachings prematurely, it is equivalent to killing the deity that is the core of your practice. If you follow an ordinary practice and apply transference before it is appropriate, the result is the transgression of killing a human being. In either case you have committed a terrible misdeed. –

[The indications of death are] unfavorable prognostications drawn from divinations, astrological calculations, and dreams, alterations of one's previous personality traits, the movement of the breath through just the right or left [nostril] for as long as a fortnight, the absence of a life-form in the space in front of you,[89] a sense of being upside down, triangular in shape, or being like a wrapped-up corpse, and the absence of a white luminosity of the eyes and the inner roar in the ears.[90] These can be checked out in more detail elsewhere. Even if you do not know them, if your doctor finds your pulse and urine to be unfavorable, you are suffering from a chronic disease, your body is wasting away, and so on, practice three times whatever means you know for cheating death. Even if you do not know any, apply yourself to whatever religious rituals you can. If even that does not help, [744] and death is certain, the transference is be practiced if you doubt whether you will maintain your spiritual practice, or you do maintain it, but there is no one to attend to your corpse.

Whether you practice transference or some other spiritual discipline, it is important that it be free of attachment and craving. The Great Perfection *tantras* state:

> Alas! At this time when the transitional process of dying is appearing to me,
> I shall abandon attachment, craving, and grasping onto anything.
> Without wavering, I shall enter the experience of the clear, practical instructions.

I shall transfer my own unborn awareness to the absolute
space of space.
I am about to be separated from the composite of my body of
flesh and blood.
Know that it is impermanent and illusory![91]

– At this point, it is most important that you be free of attachment and craving and recognize that the mind has always been primordially free of grasping. All grasping that appears to arise, be it virtuous or nonvirtuous, is purely adventitious, fleeting, and superficial. –

In the space in front of you imagine all your spiritual mentors and chosen deities as you do when you go for refuge. Gather together into a single *maṇḍala* all the objects of your attachment and craving, including your body, possessions, tent, house, land, livestock, and relatives; and earnestly visualize offering these three times to your spiritual mentor and the Three Jewels. Recite the verse of offering the [*maṇḍala*] three times. [745] Then, like a benefactor who has finished making an offering, have the conviction that whoever takes them and whoever does anything to them, those things have no owner.

– In Tibet, when an unmarried landowner was on the verge of death, he would commonly offer all his belongings to his spiritual mentor and his local monastery. Those who lived in the monastery offered all their possessions to the other meditators. Spouses who were close to death and who could not give everything away would mentally offer their personal and joint possessions.

I recall a monk named Yeshe Rabsel who was in retreat in northern India for thirty years or more. Three or four times a year he would leave retreat, and except for the clothes he was wearing, he would offer everything he had to His Holiness Dudjom Rinpoche. One abbot named Akyong Khenpo offered everything in his monastery three or four times a year to the monastic college. In fact, some of the monks in his monastery would hide their favorite possessions, so they wouldn't be given away, but everything else was offered. This I witnessed for myself, and there are many other similar accounts.

Practitioners do this in preparation for their death. On the one hand, we have no absolute certainty as to the moment of our death. On the other hand, we are all subject to grasping, and our grasping acts as the cause that perpetuates our existence in *saṃsāra*. It isn't our possessions that harm us, but rather our grasping onto them. At a glance it may seem that high-profile *lamas*, such as the Dalai Lama, Gyalwa Karmapa, and Sakya Trizin Rinpoche, don't give away their possessions. But what does the Dalai Lama really own? Not much more than a bowl for his tea; everything else belongs to the Tibetan people and the Tibetan government in exile. Similarly, what may seem to be the belongings of Gyalwa Karmapa and Sakya Trizin Rinpoche are actually possessions of their monasteries.

Wealthy people find this practice very difficult, because it's hard to give away things that seem on the surface to be the cause of our happiness. If we are suffering, it's much easier to give away our possessions, because we all want to be free of suffering. That's why it's said that felicity is more difficult than adversity.

Although it says that one should recite the traditional offering of the *maṇḍala* three times, any form of offering will do. Most importantly, offer your possessions without expecting to receive a show of gratitude, without boasting, and without wondering how your money or possessions will be used. Drop all expectations, whether you have offered hundreds of thousands of dollars or just one penny. It shouldn't matter if the recipient gives your gift to a dog or to the Three Jewels. It should no longer concern you. The act of generosity is finished, and you need only to rejoice in having engaged in virtue. –

Then focus your awareness on the transference or your other spiritual practice. *The Vajra Stanza of Avalokiteśvara* states:

> One who is knowledgeable and skilled in the meaning of transference
> Will be transferred by way of the enlightened body, speech, and mind,
> After familiarizing himself with the indications of death,
> The [white] vision, the [red] expansion, the [dark] attainment, and the inborn clear light.

The Tantra of the Ḍākinī Realizations states:

> If consciousness, mounted upon the vital energy,
> Is transferred through a lower passage,
> Even a person who is familiar with Dharma
> Will be reborn in a miserable state of existence,
> Just as a man who has set out on a journey
> Is influenced by his companions.
>
> If consciousness, mounted upon the vital energy,
> Is transferred through an upper passage,
> Even a person who is habituated to sin
> Will be reborn in a favorable state of existence,
> Just as a man who has set out on a journey
> Is influenced by his companions. [746]

– Due to karmic influences, even if you have engaged in virtue, without developing some habitual propensities for directing your awareness in an upward direction, your consciousness may exit through a lower passageway at death, and you will be reborn temporarily in a miserable state of existence. Although one may begin a journey with the intention of going in one direction, when influenced by friends, one may go in the opposite direction. Thus, the practice of transference is said to be like an escort on a journey who helps you reach your chosen destination. The above theme relates to the vows of refuge, which include disassociating oneself from people who are antagonistic to Dharma. Does that imply that we should not have compassion and loving kindness for such people or for those who have no spiritual practice? Not at all. Rather this vow is for the protection of Dharma practitioners. We can easily fall under the domination of other people when our Dharma practice is weak, and if our companions' lifestyle is incompatible with the Dharma, we may fall under their sway and find ourselves in trouble. –

The Tantra of the Compendium of the Contemplations of Samantabhadra states:

> By transferring like that, there is no return,
> There will be no fear in the intermediate state,
> And you will manifestly achieve perfect spiritual awakening.

There are numerous extensive explanations of transference and there are many differing sequences of visualization; but this transference is renowned and known by everyone, so there is no need to explain it in detail. This is the synthesis of the Tshombu Tradition, the Dawa Gyaltsen Tradition, and the Palmo Tradition of *The Essential Instructions of Avalokiteśvara*, which was taught by Buddha Amitābha to Ācārya Padmasambhava. *The Transference of the Primordial Wisdom of Great Bliss: Instructions on Emptying the Cycle of Existence* is a specialty of the Mahāsiddha Karmapakṣi. Karmapakṣi says that whenever we give public Dharma teachings, we give these instructions. Even if you practice others' Dharma for the dying process, if this is chanted in a loud voice by everyone and the transference is enacted, you will be enlightened in an instant. For everyone, this transference [747], he says, has an enormous blessing.

Imagine yourself as Avalokiteśvara, white in color, with one face and four arms, with the interior of your body immaculately empty. Imagine that your lower orifices, genitals, mouth, navel, both nostrils, both ears, the point between your eyebrows, and the mark of Brahmā are each blocked with a red syllable *Hrīḥ*. In the center of your body is the central channel, white on the outside and red on the inside. Its upper end at the crown of the head is open like the mouth of a trumpet. Its lower end at the threefold junction beneath the navel is blocked with a *Phaṭ* such that the opening is swollen shut. On a lotus and moon seat at your heart, of the nature of your vital energy, mind, and consciousness, is Avalokiteśvara, white in color, with one face and four arms. As tall as your first thumb-joint, this small form has all the qualities of Avalokiteśvara, and imagine that it is imbued with radiance and splendor. One handspan above the crown of your head imagine a red lotus with a thousand petals [748] and a disc of a full moon. Upon it, of the nature of all the primary and lineage spiritual mentors, chosen deities, *buddhas,* and *bodhisattvas,* is Buddha Amitābha, ruby-red in color, with one face and two arms. In his hands in the *mudrā* of meditative equipoise he holds an almsbowl filled with ambrosia. His head is marked with an *uṣṇīṣa,* his feet are marked with wheels, and he is adorned with the signs and symbols of enlightenment. Imagine that he is wearing the three types of monastic robes and is sitting in the *vajrāsana.*

Mentally invite all those in whom you place your hopes and your trust, including Amitābha in Sukhāvatī, and all the spiritual mentors, chosen deities, *buddhas,* and *bodhisattvas* in the *buddha*-fields in the ten directions. They dissolve into [the visualized being]. With the conviction that all the objects of refuge are embodied there, recite three times: "Homage to Buddha Amitābha." Then by uttering the syllable *Oṃ,* imagine your own mind, as Avalokiteśvara, ascending to the crown of your head; and imagine the upper portion of his radiant white body emerging at your crown. With the utterance of *maṇi padme hūṃ,* [749] imagine your own mind, as Avalokiteśvara, descending to your heart and remaining there. It is good to practice the preceding several times.

When you are on the verge of death, have the people present with you melodiously chant the six-syllables in a loud voice. With the forceful utterance of *Oṃ,* your own consciousness is sent through the central channel of Avalokiteśvara up to the crown of your head; and it dissolves into the heart of Amitābha. Again visualize Avalokiteśvara at your heart, and he ascends again and again. Meditate like that until your breath is gone.

As signs of success in the transference there is a convergence of warmth at the crown of the head, steam and swelling on the crown, and rainbows and granular relics will appear at that time, or after three, five, seven or more days. Moreover, if you are well acquainted with the Great Perfection in this life, and if you constantly see the divine embodiments of the Leap-over, [750] there is nothing more for you to practice.

– The mark of Brahmā is located at the top of the head, where a baby has a soft spot. In other teachings, the eyes are included among the apertures to be blocked, but in this case they are not. Below the navel, the two side channels curve inside to join the lower end of the central channel forming a threefold junction, which is blocked completely with the syllable *Phaṭ.*

At the point when you recite "Homage to Buddha Amitābha" three times, you may recite *mantras* invoking the names of other *buddhas.* With the utterance of *Oṃ,* the form of Avalokiteśvara at your heart ascends halfway through the crown of your head. With the utterance of *maṇi padme hūṃ,* he descends again and rests at your heart. By practicing in this way during the course of your life, you can easily implement this training at the time of your death.

When you are actually on the verge of death, visualize yourself as Avalokiteśvara, with Amitābha in the space above your head. Then send the Avalokiteśvara in your heart up through the crown of your head, dissolving into the heart of Amitābha. Unlike the practice sessions that you will have engaged in during your lifetime, at this point, Avalokiteśvara does not descend down the central channel. Again visualize Avalokiteśvara at your heart and send him up through your crown to Amitābha's heart. Repeat this over and over as long as you are still conscious.

The signs of success in transference can occur only through previous training, so if you wish to have such signs at the time of your own death, put these teachings into practice now. If today you are too busy pursuing mundane activities, at the time of your death there will be no such signs. At the time of death, if you have achieved the vision of progress in meditative experience in the practice of the Leap-over, in which you constantly see divine embodiments, there is no need to maintain your spiritual practice as mentioned above. –

An Introduction to the Quintessence of the Clear Expanse states:

> When a person is struck down with an illness, when the indications of death are complete, especially when the [power of the] elements is withdrawing, when the exhalation is long and inhalation is difficult, when the white and red visions arise and your consciousness becomes muddled, the "secret path of Vajrasattva" appears in the space in front of you, like an extended white cord of light from your *cakṣu,*[92] like an upright spear, or like a ladder, continually appearing to penetrate the sky. It may also occur in five colors. At that time, focus your own awareness on your [visual] faculty, and focus your [visual] faculty on the cord of light. By so doing, your awareness will dissolve into the light, and at that very time you will doubtlessly become manifestly, perfectly enlightened.
>
> It is enough to see the cord leading to the upward openness of the pure lands, called the "path of the contemplation of the four primordial wisdoms." [751] That path is devoid of virtue and sin and good and bad actions. This is the crucial point of the forceful method of enlightenment for great sinners.

This was stated by the Great Orgyen.

– If you are truly on that stage of the Leap-over, you simply focus on this secret path of Vajrasattva, this cord of light, and you will become a *buddha.* If you are not at that level of visionary experience but are adept in the Breakthrough stage of Dzogchen, you simply attend to the nature of your own awareness through the dying process. The inner and outer space are seen to be indivisibly of the same nature. Know that your own nature is the nature of the whole of *saṃsāra* and *nirvāṇa*. This originally pure awareness is the mind of all of the *buddhas.*

The path of the contemplation of the four primordial wisdoms completely transcends the demarcations of actions that are virtuous, nonvirtuous, good or bad. Imagine two people, one of whom has spent most of his life devoted to virtue as well as the practice of the Breakthrough and the Leap-over. The other has accumulated many nonvirtuous actions, but later devoted himself to the practice of the Breakthrough and the Leap-over. When on the verge of death, both will be have the same exceptional opportunity to attain enlightenment. Practically speaking, the mind needs to be transformed through engaging in the preliminary practices, which are the foundation for both the Breakthrough and the Leap-over. On the whole, our minds have not turned away from *saṃsāra*. Why? Because the preliminary practices have not been fully understood. As a result of engaging in the preliminary practices, the mind actually turns away from cyclic existence, which lays the foundation for proceeding on to further practices. There are many examples in the history of Tibetan Buddhism of great *lamas,* who in the early part of their life committed very negative deeds, then their minds turned away from *saṃsāra,* and in that very lifetime they attained Buddhahood. –

A person who has realized *non-meditation* does not remain in spiritual practice, for such a person has already become enlightened in this lifetime. Remaining in spiritual practice is for those who still have to make some progress in terms of cultivating the path. People who have realized *the one taste* do not remain more than three, five, or seven days, for they become enlightened as the *dharmakāya* at death. People who have realized *freedom from conceptual elaboration* have great control over how long they remain. Those with *great single-pointedness* remain long and firmly; but if they have attachment and craving for the experiences of bliss, clarity, and nonconceptuality, they will mistakenly stray off to the three realms of the gods. Whether or not they will stray [at death] depends on whether or not they stray while they are alive. Those with *middling single-pointedness* will be able to maintain their spiritual practice if their fatal illness is gentle and they have an aide; but if they are bewildered at death and have no aide, they will not maintain their practice. [752] The former proceed according to their resolution to remain for a given number of days, for on the verge of death they have the power of the mind. Those with a *small degree of single-pointedness* will not maintain their practice. Those comments are passed down from the teachings of Drungchen Kün-ga Namgyal.

– Of the four stages of Mahāmudrā, the highest is the stage of *non-meditation*. During the dying process those who have realized this state are already enlightened, so there is nothing more they need to do. Those who have realized the third stage of *the one taste* remain for three, five or seven days and then attain enlightenment as the *dharmakāya* at death. In this context, "remaining in spiritual practice" means you are able to sustain the clear light of death during the ultimate stage of the dying process. Those who have accomplished the second stage of *freedom from conceptual elaboration* have great control over how long they remain. The first stage of *single-pointedness* is divided into great, medium, and small phases. If those who have achieved great single-pointedness are attached to the experiences of bliss, clarity, and nonconceptuality while they are alive, they will experience such attachment when they die. Those with middling single-pointedness, who have a gentle fatal illness, who are not bewildered, and who have someone to help them through the dying process can remain for as long as they intend in the realization of the clear light of death. Those with small single-pointedness will not be able to remain in that state at death. –

The Tantra of the Blood-drinking Manifestation states:

> The *siddhi* of the time of death[93]
> Is taught in terms of the dying process.

The meaning of that is explained in Lord Chökyi Wangchuk's *Treatise on the Six Dharmas*:

> When a contemplative fathoms the experience of death for himself, he should consider thus: "It is impossible for genuinely true phenomena to perish. When perceiving death and fear, this is not grounded in truth, so death appears even though it is not grounded in reality." By reflecting in that way, you will maintain an attitude of indifference towards death. Then you offer your material goods and provisions to the [Three] Jewels. You abandon the causes that disturb your *samādhi*, such as the grief of your relatives. [753] If you can, sit in the physical posture as you would for the practice of *tummo*,[94] but if you cannot, then remain in the posture of a sleeping lion. Bring to mind your spiritual mentor, the [Three] Jewels, and your chosen deity, generate heartfelt faith, and go for special refuge. Recognize the real nature of your death as the ultimate reality of the clear light. Repeatedly bring forth the aspiration and the firm resolution for the sake of all sentient beings to actualize the state of the Mahāmudrā of union in the transitional process of becoming.

Then when you are dying, visual appearances dissolve, so forms are not clear; auditory appearances dissolve, so sounds are not heard; olfactory appearances dissolve, so odors are not sensed; gustatory appearances dissolve, so tastes are not experienced; and tactile appearances dissolve, so feelings are covered over. Due to earth dissolving into water, you have no physical strength; due to water dissolving into fire, the mouth and nose become dry; due to fire dissolving into wind, the warmth of the body withdraws; due to wind dissolving into consciousness, [754] your external breath ceases, while your internal breath does not quite cease.

During that period, at the time of the visions [signifying] the first phase, the internal sign is like smoke, and the external sign is like the moon rising. Secondly, at the time of the increase, the internal sign is like fireflies, and the external sign is like the sun rising. Thirdly, at the time of the attainment, the internal sign is like an oil-lamp, and the external sign is like darkness. Then in the fourth phase the attainment dissolves into the clear light, and the external sign is like the appearance of dawn, while the inner sign is of consciousness like a cloudless sky. The nonconceptual, intellect-transcending clear light arises, without a center or periphery. At that time, the clear light on which you are meditating now and the natural clear light are both present in the manner of a child meeting its mother. As a result, the eighty conceptual natures cease, and the nonconceptual, natural illumination of the *dharmakāya* becomes manifest.

– When a meditator knows beyond a doubt that death is very near, he should recognize all appearances as being purely delusive in nature. This means that even the event of death itself is ungrounded in reality; it's simply an appearance that you can then face with complete fearlessness. This is known as gaining confidence. It is not pretending that death isn't coming, as if we were covering our eyes to avoid seeing something awful. This is realizing its nature with a warrior's attitude.

You view your possessions, your friends, and relatives as dreamlike, lacking true existence. You go for special refuge, not simply the outer and inner Vajrayāna mode of taking refuge, or the outer and inner Sūtrayāna mode, but the refuge that is unique to Dzogchen. This entails taking refuge in terms of the essence, the nature, and compassion of awareness: the *dharmakāya, sambhogakāya* and *nirmāṇakāya*. You take refuge in the nature of your own awareness as the three *kāyas*. You take refuge in all appearances as being the body of the Buddha, all sounds as the speech of the Buddha, and all thoughts as the mind of the Buddha.

At the time when the eighty conceptual natures cease, discursive thought ceases, the conceptual mind is completely dormant, and the nonconceptual, natural illumination of the *dharmakāya* manifests. –

The Natural Liberation of Seeing, an introduction taught by Orgyen Rinpoche, states: [755]

> When you are dying, earth dissolves into water, water dissolves into fire, fire dissolves into air, air dissolves into consciousness, and consciousness dissolves into the clear light. Then at the conclusion of the appearances of the visions of the white path, the red path, and the black path, the ground clear light, the great, originally pure, primeval Buddha, the real Samantabhadra, is encountered. When awareness dwells in its own state, in its own ground, the cessation of the breath and the appearance of the clear light of the naturally luminous *maṇḍala* of the *dharmakāya* occur simultaneously. This is like the simultaneous setting of the sun and rising of the full moon, with no intervening darkness.[95]

– In the best of cases, those who have trained well experience no death or intermediate state, because the cessation of this life is simultaneous with their attainment of Buddhahood. Those on a lower stage of practice may go to a *buddha*-field, but in either case there is no experience of the intermediate state and no continuation in the cycle of existence. –

The Primary Tantra on the Penetration of Sound states:

> Here the transitional process of reality-itself is explained.
> When you arrive at death,
> Consciousness dissolves into space.
> When space dissolves into the clear light,
> All gross and subtle appearances cease...
>
> Upon the cessation of the four external elements, [756]
> The internal elements are released into the clear light.

Avalokiteśvara's White Instructions on the Meaning of Daytime Contemplation states:

> O son of good family, at the time of death unwaveringly take this advice to heart. Do not be attached to the impure appearances of this world. Do not crave them. Focus your consciousness at the crown of your head and do not let your mind become scattered. In the first transitional process, the appearance of integration of the absolute space and awareness is like pristine space. You will experience a unified sense of bliss, clarity, and nonconceptuality, in which your mind is limpid, clear, and free of thoughts. This is common to all sentient beings, and it is an indication of the vital energy and mind converging in the central channel. Therefore, at that time recognize that as the *dharmakāya*,

> which is nondual with your previous meditative experience. By so doing, you will be enlightened in the first transitional process.

– As you go through the process of dying, it is most important that you do not allow your awareness to become distracted. Hopefully, someone attending to your needs will remind you that you are dying. Then, having caught your attention, the attendant can warn you that now is not the time to have any attachment to your possessions, friends, or relatives. –

Avalokiteśvara's Instructions on the Natural Liberation from the Miserable States of Existence states:

> Then your breath stops as a result of exhaling [757] and not being able to inhale. At that time you will experience a great, medium, or small degree of suffering as a result of great, medium, or small virtue and sin. Then if you are a self-purified contemplative with mastery over yourself, since the mind is not subject to death, it merges with the clear light, like a child meeting its mother. Or "the integration of the absolute space and awareness" may occur at that time, so you become enlightened in the state of Amitābha, the originally pure nature of the Great Perfection.

Avalokiteśvara's Instructions of the Peaceful and Wrathful Lotus states:

> Then when the outer breath is about to cease, lie down on your right side in the [sleeping] lion posture, which constricts the fluctuations [of vital energy]. Press down firmly on the pulsation of the two throat arteries. That prevents the vital energy from leaving the central channel, and it guarantees that it leaves through the passage of the aperture of Brahmā. Identify awareness at this time.

– If you are an experienced practitioner, now is the time for your spiritual mentor or someone else to point out the nature of your awareness to you. If no one is available who can do this, simply engage in the practice of transference. –

To sustain your spiritual practice it is very important to press down slightly with your fingers on your throat arteries. [758]

If you doubt that you will maintain your spiritual practice, or even if you can, if you are concerned that such creatures as a cat or a weasel may be nearby, or there may be a clamor, engage in the union of your spiritual practice and the *dharmakāya* transference: First of all, imagine your body in the form of your chosen deity, such as Avalokiteśvara.

Block the eight orifices with the syllable *Hrīḥ*. Visualize your central channel, and imagine Buddha Amitābha at the crown of your head. Many times send your consciousness, as a white *bindu* marked with *Hrīḥ* at your heart, up to the heart of Amitābha at your crown. Then let your practice be the cultivation of the essential nature of the mind, by focusing your awareness at your heart without imagining anything. Whatever appears, such as the visions of the white pathway and the red pathway, observe the essential nature of the appearances.

When the external breath ceases, the body is to be covered and handled with care. Press down slightly with your fingers on [the dying person's] throat arteries. If you know how to visualize [this person's] spiritual practice, do what you can. If you do not know how, call the person by name [759] and say three times, "Do not be distracted from your spiritual practice." As a result, the person may first remember the earlier identifying instructions by his spiritual mentor; secondly, he may identify his own naked awareness as the clear light; thirdly, with this recognition, it is certain that he will be liberated as the *dharmakāya*, with no union or separation. It is said that such a person is liberated by identifying the first clear light.

– The term "spiritual practice," refers here to the specific practice performed during and following the dying process. If you doubt that you can maintain your spiritual practice during and following the dying process, or you think external interferences, such as dangerous creatures or loud noises, may disturb your *samādhi*, then engage in the union of your spiritual practice and the *dharmakāya* transference.

Do not block your central channel as you perform this visualization. Further, I feel that it may be better to alter the above technique for practitioners like ourselves: Allow your awareness to rest in its own nature, focusing not at your heart, but at the crown of your head, imagining your own mind to be indivisible with the mind of Amitābha. Whatever appears, such as the white, red or black vision, do not focus on the specific characteristics of the vision, simply attend to the nature of awareness. –

The omniscient Dölpupa says:

> Although many good and bad things appear, [in reality] there is nothing good or bad.
> Everything is the dance of the *dharmakāya*.
> Thus, simply observe whatever appears
> With no hope or fear, rejection or acceptance, negation or affirmation.
> Rest in the state of equality, free of conceptual elaborations.

> Since someone is with you, if there is no interval in which you
> are distracted,
> After the external breath has ceased and before the internal
> breath stops,
> You will remain in the state of the clear light, as if in a coma,
> For three, four, five, six, or more days.
> If you have previously well identified the essential nature and
> are thoroughly familiar with it,
> You will dissolve into the state of the clear light of awareness.
> Even if you do not dissolve, [760] this is superior
> To other arduous meditation for months and years on end.

– An experienced practitioner whose corpse is not disturbed may remain in the state following the cessation of the outer breath, but prior to the cessation of the inner breath, for more than six days. Practice may continue, and due to ascertaining the essential nature of awareness, such a person may rest in the clear light of awareness in the dying process. With some prior experience, during the dying process one can realize in just a few moments that which could take months or years of practice during the course of a life. This presents a very precious opportunity for practice. However, if you have no prior experience, when you enter the final stage of the dying process it is as if you become comatose. –

It is the responsibility of the attendant to the dying to attend to the position of the dying person's body. The body may be in the posture of a sleeping lion; the eyes should be half-open, and the mouth should be as if smiling. If [the dying person] meditates on the essential nature of the mind, and if fine, experiential realizations arise, that is sound practice. For those who are attached to the experiences of bliss, clarity, and nonconceptuality of quiescence, their [body] will take on a fine luster and so on. Those who are firmly established in the stage of generation will strengthen their spiritual practice by letting their awareness remain in the seed syllable at their heart. If they repeatedly engage in the cultivation of insight, they will proceed on the path without going astray. In *The Great Exposition of the Six Dharmas* it is said that instances of people remaining as if they were in spiritual practice even though they had no practice and had not even received instructions are due to their being possessed by *gandharvas* and obstructive, malevolent entities. [761]

If the clear light is not recognized, as soon as awareness and matter are separated, the second clear light appears. It is said that at that time, if [the attendant] again says, "Do not be distracted from your spiritual practice," it is possible for [the dying person] to recognize the practice and not be confused even after awareness and matter have completely separated. The Great Perfection gives an extensive explanation of the way one is liberated following the appearances of the eight modes of dissolution. The way in which the transitional process of reality-itself appears is not explained in texts of the New Translation School, such as *The Six Dharmas,* so some people doubt its authenticity. However, in Lord Atīśa's treatise *The Kadam Volume* and Machig's text *An Explanation of Severance* there are concise accounts of how sounds, light, and rays appear as the assembly of peaceful and wrathful deities. So it is not true that the New Translation School has no record of this.

Even if the spiritual practice is not sustained, one's consciousness remains without mindfulness in the body. Very sinful people and those bearing bad character traits will proceed to a hell realm by way of a lower orifice after the time it takes to eat a meal. If the transference succeeds, [762] one will go up to a pure realm by way of the crown of one's head. If one is to go to a formless realm, at the time of death one's mind remains in the intervening space at the level of one's heart; and for 80,000 years one remains comatose, with no mindfulness. Apart from those three cases, the transitional process will appear, and one remains for as long as it takes to milk a cow, for one day, or generally up to the morning of the third day. *The Kadam Volume* states that some people also remain for seven days, so it is appropriate to practice the transference until then.

– Even if a corpse has a luster or radiance about it, that is not necessarily an auspicious sign or an indication that the person attained a high state of realization; it may only imply that the person succumbed to grasping onto bliss, clarity, and nonconceptuality in the practice of quiescence.

Those who perform specific practices designed to stabilize awareness, such as focusing on a seed syllable in the heart during the stage of generation practice, or focusing on a stick as in quiescence practice, will be able to enhance their practice during the dying process.

In Tibet, some people would die with their bodies appearing very majestic and powerful. But this does not necessarily indicate spiritual realization. It may be that the person has been possessed by a malevolent entity such as a *gandharva*. There have also been reports of zombies, corpses that come back to life and walk around doing various things. Although they look impressive, this is not a sign of spiritual realization. One can be free of these dangers by engaging in the teachings and practicing with faith. Conversely, only listening to or reading the teachings will not help you during the dying process.

Rather than remaining for a few days following the cessation of the outer breath and before the cessation of the inner breath, nonvirtuous people linger for only the few moments it takes to eat a meal, and then they go directly to a hell realm through a lower orifice, without experiencing the intermediate state. If transference is performed successfully, one will go directly to a pure land without experiencing the intermediate state, and if one is to go to a formless realm, again the intermediate state will not be experienced. Other than those exceptions, one must experience the intermediate state. –

This is how appearances arise if one's spiritual practice is not maintained, as explained in *Avalokiteśvara's Instructions on the Natural Liberation from the Miserable States of Existence*:

> If self-mastery has not been achieved, after three days you become comatose, and with the thought, "What am I?" you do not believe in yourself. Erratic appearances arise, and you feel as if you have been placed in a cavern of lights, *bindus*, and rainbows. Upon suddenly generating your body as Avalokiteśvara and by resting your mind in the state of meditative equipoise, your own body will be adorned with [763] the signs and symbols of enlightenment, unlike its present appearance.[96] The entire phenomenal world will appear in the nature of the deity. In an instant, you will be perfectly enlightened....
>
> At that time you will have the inexpressible qualities of the three embodiments, all the natural radiance of the five primordial wisdoms, miraculous powers, and higher knowledge; so wherever you go among the pure realms, you will have attained self-mastery. You can arrive in Sukhāvatī, the Palace of Lotus Light, Abhirati, and so on, simply by bringing them to mind.

Avalokiteśvara's White Instructions on the Meaning of Daytime Contemplation states:

> O son of good family! If the first transitional process is not recognized, in the second transitional process the whole universe is filled with the five-colored lights of spontaneously present, primordial wisdom. All the lights are in motion, and rays appear to issue forth like weapons. Know those as the natural radiance of the primordial wisdom of your own awareness. By so doing, you will be Awakened during the second transitional process. [764]
>
> O son of good family, if that is not recognized, the third transitional process called "the threefold sounds, lights, and rays" will occur. Within those lights there will come peaceful and wrathful forms of Avalokiteśvara, with various faces and arms, to train sentient beings as needed. Know that they emerge from yourself. In the expanse of them there will arise the sounds of a thousand rolls

> of thunder, lights will move about, and rays will issue forth like a rain of weapons. Do not be alarmed at the embodiments. Do not fear the sounds. Do not be frightened at the lights. Do not be terrified of the rays. Recognize them as your own appearances.

Likewise, *Avalokiteśvara's Instructions on the Natural Liberation from the Miserable States of Existence* states:

> All your practices of the body, speech, and mind will be a hundred times clearer than they are now. Thus, in terms of your body, with the divine pride of your practice of deity *yoga* it will seem as if the entire phenomenal world is merged with light and light rays. In terms of your speech, all the sounds of *mantra yoga* will be empty, like echoes of the melodious sounds of the six syllables. [765] In terms of your mind, the *yoga* of reality-itself, entailing indivisible luminosity and emptiness, will be like the inseparability of the sun and its light. Whatever sounds, lights, rays, and various forms appear, without fear, you will be liberated as they naturally appear as yourself. Therefore, this is the foremost of all profound practical instructions and advice.
>
> If you are not liberated there, all the assemblies of a hundred kinds of sublime peaceful and wrathful beings, including peaceful, wrathful, and slightly wrathful deities, will gradually appear. Visions of emanations will appear for seven, fourteen, or twenty days. A time may come when you will flee from those forms, you may fear the lights, be frightened of the *bindus*, be alarmed at the sounds, and be unable to look at the rays. At that time meditate on Lord Avalokiteśvara. Recite the essential six syllables. Contemplate all lights as your own lights, all sounds as your own sounds, all forms as your own forms, appearing and empty, and contemplate all rays as your own naturally appearing rays. After two and a half weeks, you will not know that you have died, [766] and looking at your former corpse, you will not be able to return. Whatever you say to your relatives and friends, they will not respond. Then you may experience a sense of dejection and unbearable misery. At that time, if you bring to mind the deity Avalokiteśvara and the six-syllable *mantra*, your fear will naturally subside.

– In the intermediate state, you will actually see your previous corpse and may even want to go back into it, but you won't be able to. You will see your friends and relatives, but because they can't see or hear you, they will seem to ignore you. You will feel unbearable misery and suffer deep depression unlike any anguish you felt during your lifetime. You will have no freedom. However, right now you have the freedom to practice. Now is the time to prepare for the experiences of the intermediate state.

I once heard the story of a young boy who was extremely ill. One morning before dawn he had the sense of waking up, but he wasn't sure if he had truly awakened. A *lama* who was with him took his hand, saying that it was time to go. Wandering over rough terrain, they crossed several bridges, finally coming upon a cluster of houses and some wrathful beings, at which point the boy said he felt a terrible headache. Just then the *lama* lopped off the top of his head, and after vigorously stirring his brain, he offered it to the wrathful beings. He then immediately felt he should go to Buddha Śākyamuni, so they climbed upwards. Upon arriving, a deity, either Vajrasattva or Avalokiteśvara, met them and asked that he stay. The little boy replied that he couldn't, and so they left. As they retraced their steps, they again encountered the wrathful beings, and, once more, the spiritual mentor lopped off the top of his head and offered the boy's brain.

The boy later said that after awhile he saw what he thought was his body, which appeared completely rigid and without breath, and he felt that he had died. He called to his relatives to recite *Oṃ maṇi padme hūṃ*. Then feeling very thirsty, he came upon some people who offered him milk. Upon taking a few sips, he woke up and found that it was early evening and, in fact, he was still alive. He felt that his experience was so similar to the dying process that he should take it very seriously, so he earnestly prepared throughout his life for his death. –

Avalokiteśvara's Instructions of the Peaceful and Wrathful Lotus states:

> The best is the transference to the abode of the *ḍākinīs*. Make this resolution: "Alas! After long, countless, immeasurable eons since beginningless time, I am still left in this swamp of the cycle of existence. How miserable! How is it that I have not been liberated in the past, when there have been so many *buddhas*? Now I am nauseated and terrified by the cycle of existence. I must escape. Now I am ready to flee. I must take miraculous birth in the midst of a lotus blossom in the presence of Buddha Amitābha [767] in the *buddha*-field of Sukhāvatī to the west of me." By thinking in that way, powerfully focus your yearning for the western *buddha*-field of Sukhāvatī. Alternatively focus your yearning on a desired *buddha*-field, Abhirati, Ghanavyūha, Aṭakāvatī, Mount Potala, being in the presence of Orgyen in the Palace of the Lotus Light, or whatever other *buddha*-field you wish. Focus on it single-pointedly, without distraction, and you will immediately be born in that *buddha*-field. By focusing your aspiration with the thought, "On this occasion of the intermediate state, the time has come for me to go into the presence of the Dharma of Ajita in Tuṣita," you will be miraculously born in the heart of a lotus in the presence of Maitreya.

– Ask yourself, " How is it that I have been in the cycle of existence for so long and still have not become enlightened? How is it that all of the *buddhas* of the past have not been able to benefit me sufficiently so that I could achieve liberation?" This is the time, while still in the cycle of existence, that you can engage in practice and prepare for the intermediate state so that you can go to the *buddha*-field of your choice and receive teachings there. However, it is of the utmost importance that you practice now. It's simply not enough to hear and read the teachings, or we would already be liberated. You must think about them and, more importantly, engage in the actual meditation. That is what brings about the transformation. It's not enough to have the aspiration to go somewhere, you actually have to set out on the path. You must put one foot in front of the other. –

The Tantra of the Ocean of Primordial Wisdom states:

> These are the precious instructions for gaining firm realization
> In the face of the great fears of the intermediate state.
> These are the precious instructions for not blundering
> In the face of the great fears of the intermediate state. [768]

– In the intermediate state, there is great benefit to achieving firm realization in the union of the stage of generation and the stage of completion. These days, the teachings of many traditions are available—Hinduism, Bön, Christianity, Judaism, Tibetan Buddhism, and so on. Each of these views has its own value, but in order to benefit from them fully, it's crucial not to mix them up together. If you want to practice Hinduism, practice it properly according to the traditional teachings, otherwise your practice may be like pasting an arm onto a forehead or a toe onto a rib. If you haphazardly combine all these traditions together, you may derive no benefit, so I suggest that you focus on the specific tradition of your choice and follow exactly what it says. –

The Dawa Gyaltsen Tradition of *The Essential Instructions of Avalokiteśvara* states:

> In the contemplation of the transitional process of becoming
> You will have an unprecedented form of becoming,
> Your sense faculties will be complete, you will be able to move about without impediment;
> And with pure divine vision you will see those who are comparable to yourself...

During the transitional process, your body is the *maṇḍala* of the deity, your speech is the *maṇḍala* of the *mantra*, and your mind is the *maṇḍala* of *samādhi*. If you are not separated from these three *maṇḍalas*, you will be Awakened from the fears and so on of the intermediate state.

The Tshombu Tradition of *The Essential Instructions of Avalokiteśvara* states that by meditating on the stages of generation and completion at the door to the womb, there is no need to meditate on anything else.

– At the time of the transitional process of becoming, you are faced with conception, taking birth once again in one of the six states of existence. You will be desperate to take another body. At this point slow down! Visualize these beings, who appear as males and females and arouse your attachment and incite your anger, as the deity with consort—be it Vajrasattva, Avalokiteśvara, or Guru Rinpoche. Be it a peaceful or a wrathful deity, visualize your chosen deity with consort, and practice the stage of generation. If you are capable of practicing the stage of completion, as you encounter these beings, view them as the union of appearances and emptiness, with the male deity representing appearances, and the female, emptiness. In that way you will block the womb, and by not taking rebirth, you will be liberated. In some cases, such as a *tulku* who wishes to be of benefit to others, a person may seek out a male and female of a good background and a beneficial situation to oneself and others. With this sense of compassion, such a person enters the womb while imagining the mother to be the divine consort and her womb to be a palace. Then by generating oneself as the seed syllable of the chosen deity and entering into the palace of the womb, conception takes place. –

Avalokiteśvara's Instructions on the Natural Liberation from the Miserable States of Existence states:

> After six weeks, the mind becomes disturbed, and immeasurable, terrifying noises are heard. Sounds of earth, water, fire, and air, together with sounds of the combined five elements appear. At that time, if you bring to mind the sound of *maṇi padme hūṃ*, this will help.
>
> Then you will be overwhelmed with light rays, and you will have no sense of [769] there being a path. At that time, it will help to focus on the reality of unstructured meditative equipoise in reality-itself.
>
> Then the five lights and the six paths will appear. The pathways of the six states of existence are white, yellow, red, green, blue, and black. When you go to the white, appearances of *devas* will arise. Likewise, the green path is the pathway of the *asuras*, yellow is the pathway of humans, black is the pathway of animals, pale blue is the pathway of the *pretas*, and dark red is the pathway of hell beings. At that time, if you pray to your spiritual mentor, chosen deity, and the *ḍākinīs*, they will prophesy, "I am your chosen deity. Recite the essential [*mantra*]! Go to the white path! This will be your good place of birth, and your body will

be like this. This will be your Dharma." That prophesy will definitely come true.

Then you will experience a vision of a simultaneously arising god and demon arguing about your virtues and sins. At that time as well, if you bring Avalokiteśvara to mind, you will win and be able to take birth in a favorable state of existence. [770]

After seven weeks have passed, you will have a sense of taking a body, and you will wonder, "Where will I be reborn and into what kind of body?" By the power of your own vital energy, you will meet with the Dharma in your next life. The deity Avalokiteśvara bestows inconceivable, inexpressible blessings.

The Tantra of the Clear Expanse of the Quintessence of All the Ḍākinīs states:

> O you of pure *karma* and you who have received the instructions on identifying [awareness], from the very time that those visions occur, you will experience the western *buddha*-field of Sukhāvatī. There you will dissolve into the heart of Buddha Amitābha. Upon emerging from the lotus of his consort, you will be among the retinue of the Lord of the Lotus Family. Upon Awakening, you will empty out the cycle of existence.

Phagmo Drüpa's Verses on the Path of Skillful Means states:

> Form this thought:
> With the intention to be miraculously reborn
> In the pure land of Sukhāvatī,
> Or in the pure land of Padmāvatī,
> Make a firm resolve.

In that way, go to that *buddha*-field.

– People with "pure *karma*" are those who have purified their mind-streams of nonvirtuous habitual propensities by means of their spiritual practice of confession and so forth. All of us desire happiness for ourselves, but this desire is not enough. We need to engage in the practices of hearing, thinking, and meditation, with the emphasis on meditation. But even that is not enough; we must meditate with confidence and trust. We really must place our wholehearted trust in the enlightened beings who have revealed the Dharma to us. These omniscient beings, with complete knowledge of the nature of reality, as well as the full range of its diversity, are completely deserving of our trust. Only with such absolute trust can we really progress in meditation.

If we are interested in accomplishing our own self-interest, we must be utterly honest with ourselves. If we lie to ourselves and cheat others, we won't even be able to accomplish our own goals. So now is the time to practice! We have the freedom now, and if we want to be of benefit, this is the way to do it. If you have any doubt that you will be reborn in Sukhāvatī, you probably won't be. Whereas, if you cast aside all doubt and have utter faith that you will be reborn there, you will be. About that have no doubt! –

CHAPTER NINE

An Introduction to the Ground, Path, and Fruition

Homage to Avalokiteśvara!

[772] These are the profound practical instructions of Avalokiteśvara. Here is a concise explanation of the ground, path, and fruition, which are the methods for causal sentient beings to accomplish the fruition of spiritual awakening. In terms of the ground, the mind of the Buddha is realized and actualized by nondual *ārya* individuals. This is the character and natural appearance of the three realms of the cycle of existence. The original mode of being of all phenomena is innate primordial wisdom. It pervades all grounds. It is the pristine nature that is present in the mind-streams of all of us beings, from aphids up to *buddhas*, with no distinction as to good or bad, big or small, and so on. Thus, *The King of Samādhi Sūtra* states, [773] "The essence of the *sugatas* pervades all beings," and *The Smaller Sūtra on Nirvāṇa* concurs, "All sentient beings are endowed with the essence of the *tathāgatas*."

– Although Karma Chagmé Rinpoche could give a lengthy, scholarly presentation of the ground, path, and fruition, here he has chosen to give a concise version for those who prefer less elaborate explanations.

In terms of the ground, the mind of the Buddha is realized and actualized by nondual *āryas*, which refers to the fact that the mind-stream of an *ārya* is indivisible from the mind of the Buddha. Innate primordial wisdom pervades all grounds without partiality in terms of places or sentient beings. It is all-pervasive. –

The Great Sūtra on Nirvāṇa states:

> Just as butter saturates milk,
> So does the essence of the *tathāgatas* pervade all sentient beings.

The Sūtra on Nirvāṇa states:

> Suchness is pure,
> Everywhere, without distinction.
> Thus, all beings are endowed
> With the essence of the state of the *tathāgatas*.

The Vajra Pavilion Tantra states: [774]

> There are no *buddhas* and no sentient beings
> Who are excluded from the jewel mind.[97]

The Hevajra Tantra states:

> Sentient beings are in fact *buddhas*,
> But they are obscured by adventitious stains.[98]

You progress on the path by practicing this union of Mahāmudrā and Dzogchen, which is a method for becoming a *buddha* in one lifetime and with one body, once you have dispelled those adventitious stains. *The Great Instructions* states:

> Single-pointedness occurs when a contemplative focuses his experience, without being distracted from the immaculate, vivid clarity and nonconceptuality of the mind, and remains single-pointedly in the stream of unified quiescence and insight.

At the stage of small single-pointedness there are four applications of mindfulness: (1) the application of mindfulness of non-compositeness, free of any thought of the body as being either clean or unclean; (2) the application of mindfulness of taintless bliss, without regarding feelings as being either suffering or joy; (3) the application of mindfulness of the mind, free of conceptual elaborations concerning the mind being either permanent or impermanent; [775] (4) the application of mindfulness of mental objects, cutting off superimpositions concerning the reality of *nirvāṇa*, without thinking of mental objects as either having or not having an identity.

At the stage of middling single-pointedness, by abandoning complacency and sustaining single-pointedness, (1) you do not succumb to false views; (2) nonvirtuous behavior, such as holding false views, naturally ceases; as a result, (3) realizations arise naturally from within; and consequently, (4) excellent qualities increase.

At the stage of great single-pointedness, you practice the four foundations of miraculous powers: (1) the absence of distraction is the foundation of the miraculous power of aspiration, (2) the absence of lassitude is the foundation of zeal, (3) the abandonment of antithetic factors is the foundation of behavior; and (4) the foundation of the miraculous power of the mind is due to sustaining the attention. Lingje Repa says:

> The path of accumulation consists of three tetrads, equaling twelve.
> Progress is made with one realization.

– Of the five paths, the small stage of the path of accumulation, which marks the beginning of the *bodhisattva* path, is closely associated with the four applications of mindfulness. The four abandonments that pertain to the middling stage of the path of accumulation are also related to middling single-pointedness. The great stage of the path of accumulation is associated with the four foundations of miraculous power. However with the Dzogchen approach, you progress with one realization, which pertains to all the twelve subsections of the path of accumulation. –

Due to that realization, (1) the faculty of faith is uninterrupted; as a result, (2) the faculty of zeal is [776] constant; that results in (3) the faculty of mindfulness without forgetfulness; perpetual *samādhi* is the (4) faculty of *samādhi*; and (5) the reality of discerning wisdom is realized with *samādhi*. Those comprise the great single-pointedness of the path of preparation, and they are of the nature of the warmth, and pinnacle [stages of the path of preparation]. Thus it is said: "With the essential nature of those five faculties, the innate reality is observed."

As a result, (1) the power of faith overcomes false views; (2) the power of zeal overcomes spiritual sloth; (3) the power of mindfulness overcomes negligence; (4) consequently, the power of *samādhi* overcomes dualistic grasping onto subjects and objects; as a result, (5) the power of wisdom overcomes the signs of phenomena. They are of the nature of the patience and the supreme Dharma [stages of the path of preparation]. It is said:

> With the essential nature of those five great powers,
> Antithetic factors are overcome.
> With one realization you progress
> In the powers and faculties of the path of preparation.

The Great Instructions states:

> From the very nature of the arising of the clear, immaculate,

> unborn mind-itself of the mind, [777] perfect *samādhi* manifestly realizes the essential nature of your own mind, which is like space, free of the conceptual elaborations of the three constituents. The absence of effort is (1) the zeal factor of awakening; the absence of pain is the (2) delight factor of awakening; the absence of stains is (3) the purification factor of awakening; the absence of any distinction between *saṃsāra* and *nirvāṇa* is (4) the discrimination of phenomena factor of awakening; the maintenance of non-forgetfulness is (5) the mindfulness factor of awakening; and even-mindedness towards everything is (6) the equanimity factor of awakening. Thus it is said: "With one realization one progresses in the factors of awakening of the path of seeing."

– The essential nature of your own mind is free of conceptual elaborations concerning the three constituents, namely, the agent, the action, and the object of the actions. Due to our habitual propensities, when we sit down to meditate, we think, "I am meditating now." Grasping occurs together with this conceptual elaboration. In fact, whenever grasping occurs, conceptual elaborations are present!

In terms of the posture to adopt for meditation, the seven-point posture of Vairocana is recommended, but the *ṛṣi* posture is also satisfactory. A crucial aspect of the seven-point posture is holding the spine straight, for this causes the subtle channels in the body to become straight, which then allows the mind to settle naturally in its own state. The pith essential instruction on this meditation is to not follow after any phenomena that arise. The aspect of emptiness of all that appears to the mind is the *dharmakāya*; the aspect of the luminosity of phenomena is the *sambhogakāya*; and the aspect of the pervasive compassion implicit in phenomena is the *nirmāṇakāya*.

Listed above are six of the seven factors of enlightenment, which pertain to the third path, the path of seeing. In earlier stages of practice, as you cultivate the perfection of patience and zeal, effort is essential; but in this phase of practice, the very absence of effort is the zeal factor of enlightenment. The seventh factor, pliancy, which pertains closely to the effortlessness of simply being present, free of any type of conceptual elaboration, is omitted from this list. –

Although a variety of phenomena appear, they are of the "one taste" of your own mind-itself; and all dualities such as yourself and others and *saṃsāra* and *nirvāṇa* are of one taste. The realization of that one taste is (1) the perfect view, free of extremes; since it transcends the intellect, it is (2) perfect thought; as it is inexpressible, it is (3) perfect speech; because it is unceasing, it is (4) perfect mindfulness; freedom is one's sustaining (5) livelihood; [778] because of accomplishing the great goal, it is (6) effort; since one's task is complete, it is (7) the culmination of action; and as there is no distinction between meditative equipoise and the post-meditative state, it is (8) *vajra*-like perfect *samādhi*.

> With one realization one progresses
> Along the eight *ārya* grounds on the path of meditation.

– The preceding account is the Dzogchen interpretation of the Eightfold Noble Path as it pertains to the path of meditation, the fourth of the five paths. In terms of the one taste of all phenomena, you see all appearances as the display of your own awareness, indivisible from your own awareness. As an analogy, by knowing the wetness of a single drop of water, you implicitly know the nature of all water, whether it is water from a creek, rain, or an ocean. Its unceasing quality is called perfect recall, which implies that all fragmentation of awareness has completely vanished. The sustenance of your livelihood is nothing other than your own liberation.

Earlier phases of the path were characterized by an absence of effort, but at this stage effort is again evoked, but rather than conventional effort it is the spontaneous, natural display of activity arising from the state of awareness of meditative equipoise. That is called "ultimate effort" as opposed to relative effort. –

The Great Instructions states:

> Wherever you look in terms of "is" and "is not," your own mind-itself perpetually arises as the clear light, ungrounded in anything such as an object or agent of meditation. That is the contemplation of non-meditation....
>
> The fruitional *dharmakāya* of clear light,
> The two *rūpakāyas*, which emerge automatically,
> The indivisible *svabhāvikakāya*,
> And the taintless *mahāsukhakāya*[99]—
> The Buddha is of the nature of five embodiments....

Due to encountering one's spiritual mentor as the Buddha, one reaches (1) [the path of] accumulation. Due to the arising of certainty in one's supplications, there is (2) [the path of] preparation. The arising of realization due to blessings is (3) the path of seeing. Its increase is (4) the path of meditation. The absence of any distinction between meditative equipoise and the post-meditative state is (5) the culminating path.

The manifestation of one's own mind is (1) the Very Joyful [ground]; the resultant elimination of the stains of mental afflictions is (2) the second [*bodhisattva* ground, called the Stainless]; the innate clear light is (3) the Illuminating; [779] (4) the Radiant [ground] is so called because the qualities of a *buddha* occur here; (5) [the ground] Difficult to Purify is so called because it is profound and its depths are difficult to fathom; (6) the sixth ground, [the Manifesting,] is so called because the primordial wisdom of one's own mind becomes manifest; (7) [the seventh ground,] the Gone Afar, is so called because of crossing beyond the cycle of existence; (8) the eighth ground, [the Immovable,] is so called due to one's being unmoved by the stain of self-interest; (9) the ninth ground, [Fine Intelligence,] is so called due to the plenitude of one's wisdom; (10) the perfection of the might of one's realization is the tenth ground, the end of the continuum [called the Cloud of Dharma]; the arising of appearances as the *dharmakāya* is (11) the eleventh ground; serving the needs of the world without craving is (12) the twelfth ground; the plenitude of the ultimate is (13) the thirteenth ground; and the transcendence of the intellect, with non-mental-engagement, is (14) the fourteenth ground, great bliss.

Now this is the meaning of the teachings of one's earlier spiritual mentors on the individual occurrences of the experiences and realizations of the four *yogas*: (1) in the *yoga* of experience there is an integration of the bliss, clarity, and nonconceptuality of meditative stabilization. For as long as you apply yourself to this, you achieve empowerment, and that is the single-pointedness of experience. Within that state, while dwelling in the essential nature of emptiness, if your realization of emptiness is free of intellectual fabrication, that is experiential (2) freedom from conceptual elaborations. The homogeneous taste of your conduct during the post-meditative state, without interruption due to conditions, [780] is (3) the one taste of experience.

– Obstacles to one's practice inevitably arise when there is an imbalance among the three qualities of bliss, clarity, and nonconceptuality. All authentic meditative experience is imbued with each of these qualities. To the degree that your meditative practice is flawless and is imbued with insight into emptiness, the experiences of bliss, clarity, and nonconceptuality will arise. As you practice single-pointed meditative stabilization, you realize emptiness without any intellectual fabrication. You experience that which has been primordially empty, without involving yourself in conceptual elaborations, so you do not even have the thought that this is emptiness. In the post-meditative state, as you walk, eat, talk, and so forth, the emphasis should be on sustaining the experience of meditative equipoise. If the continuum of the meditative equipoise is not lost or interrupted by external influences, this is the one taste of experience. Bliss, clarity, nonconceptuality, and the one taste of experience pertain to the path of accumulation. –

Then before long, the occurrence of a constant state of (4) non-meditation is the path of preparation. Then the transcendence of the mundane is the path of seeing and the path of meditation. One is freed from eight flaws, including the previous authentic view of the fourth stabilization, investigation and analysis of the fourth [stabilization], likes and dislikes, joys and sorrows, fluctuations of mindfulness and awareness, and the movements of vital energy. One is merged with single-pointedness, and instantaneously and simultaneously one achieves direct perception of the Four Noble Truths. That is experiential non-meditation, and it is also the *yoga* of single-pointedness among the four *yogas* of realization.

At this time one attains the wisdom that discerns phenomena integrated with the essential nature of *samādhi*; and one uninterruptedly dwells in mindfulness until spiritual awakening, while engaged in enthusiasm for practice. The mind and its objects are highly purified. There is extraordinary delight in greatly fulfilling the needs of oneself and others. [781] One constantly participates in the experience of singular, great equanimity that is free of spiritual sloth. If one does not experience those [qualities], there may be experience, but it is not the realization of Mahāmudrā.

Then the path of seeing is reached, and the familiarization with that very seeing is the path of meditation. The essential nature of meditative equipoise appears, which is like the domain of space, in which the extremes of cyclic existence and peace have been eliminated. Composite phenomena appear like illusions and dreams, and one accomplishes nonconceptual, primordial wisdom. In the illusionlike post-meditative state one matures, purifies, and thoroughly refines sentient beings; and by so doing, one achieves phenomenological knowledge. When the might of the perfection of wisdom is perfected on the sixth ground, one is freed of conceptual elaborations, and one is divorced from the attitude of fearing and trying to ward off either cyclic existence or peace. When the stains of the mind have been utterly eradicated, one enters the secret abode of all the *buddhas*. [782] When the eighth ground is reached, one does not conceive of cyclic existence and peace as being dual, and one is unmoved by either the recognition of suchness or the signs of fruition; so this is called "the great single taste."

– In the illusionlike post-meditative state one purifies one's own perception of reality, so that the environment one experiences is viewed as a *buddha*-field, and the beings inhabiting the environment are seen as *vīras* and *ḍākinīs*. –

> The attainment of spiritual awakening is free of the previous mental formations of taintless *karma* in the mind, free of the malady of subtle habitual propensities, free of *karma* that is of the nature of the mind, and in an inconceivable transition it is free of the appearance of transference into death. That is non-meditation, and that is the culmination. When such a reality is reached, one may or may not give it the name of a path. It is discussed in terms of the names of the four *yogas*.

– When one attains the inconceivable state of Buddhahood, one is free of previous mental formations; one is free of taintless *karma* in the mind, so that one no longer has ideas of engaging in even pure activities. One's actions are not premeditated or conceptualized, and one is freed of the most subtle traces of the afflictions of habitual propensities. Since Buddhahood is completely beyond transference, one is also free of the appearance of transference into death, because this non-meditative state, Buddhahood, is the culmination of all of the paths. –

The Arising of the Precepts of Cakrasaṃvara states:

> One's abode is the Very Joyful ground;
> One's near abode, accordingly, is the Stainless;
> There is the ground Illuminating the pure lands,
> And the Radiance of the proximate pure lands.
> The Manifesting is called *chanda*,
> And the proximate *chanda* is the Difficult to Purify.
> The gathering of the Gone Afar,
> The close gathering known as the Immovable,
> Fine Intelligence, which is like a charnel ground, [783]
> The near charnel ground is the Cloud of Dharma –
> The purity of the abodes and so forth
> Is explained as they are known.

Those are also comparable to the progression of the four empowerments of the *mantra* path. Lord Naropa asserted this as well, and he taught this to Sandapa Rölpey Dorje:

> The first of the realizations of Mahāmudrā
> Entails observing
> Adventitious ideation.
> The departure from ignorance
> Entailing the realization of clear awareness
> Devoid of grasping is called the mastery of awareness.
> When the five poisons are present as the five primordial
> wisdoms,

> That is asserted to be the vase empowerment.
> Unceasing displays
> Appear without partiality.
> Thus, bliss arises from the state of emptiness,
> And that is asserted to be the empowerment of clarity, the second [empowerment].
> Innate primordial wisdom
> Is the state of space of indivisible bliss and emptiness.
> The great single taste of union
> Is experienced as the great bliss of appearances and the mind.
> That is explained as the empowerment of primordial wisdom.
> The third empowerment is synthesized
> In the indivisible mind. [784]
> When the mind-itself is pure like the sky,
> There is no distinction between meditative equipoise and post-meditative experience.
> The union of the two truths is the fourth [empowerment].

The Questions of Queen Kaparabhuja to the Great Brahmin Saraha states:

> Single-pointed awareness is the vase empowerment;
> Bliss, free of conceptual elaborations, is the secret empowerment;
> The third is the union with equality;
> And non-meditation is the fourth.

– One may view single-pointed awareness, associated with the vase empowerment, either as the realization of one's own awareness or as the union of quiescence and insight into the nature of awareness.

To receive the vase empowerment you should have completed the preliminary practices and have a strong foundation in the stage of generation, such that you see all appearances as being the pure land and all sentient beings as manifestations of your chosen deity. Likewise, you should maintain a "pure vision" of all speech and thoughts. Then you will be able to genuinely receive the vase empowerment. The spiritual mentor must also have pure vision. This empowerment plants the seeds for the *nirmāṇakāya* and the purification of the body.

To receive the second empowerment, in addition to the previous background in practice, you should have gained control over the channels, vital energies, and *bindus* within your body and see them in their pure form as the three *kāyas*. The second empowerment purifies speech and plants the seeds for achieving the *sambhogakāya*.

Some of the outer symbols used for the third empowerment are red powder, displaying a mirror, or showing a picture of a naked woman. Receiving the third empowerment is not simply a matter of engaging in sexual intercourse with the person of your choice. To receive this empowerment you should have accomplished pure vision and gained complete control over your channels, vital energies, and *bindus,* and then you may practice in union with a suitable partner. Such a consort should have completed the preliminary practices and be accomplished in the stages of generation and completion, but doing so prematurely or with an unsuitable consort may entail breaking one's vows of individual liberation, *bodhisattva* vows, and Vajrayāna *samayas,* resulting in rebirth in miserable states of existence. Receiving the third empowerment purifies the mind and sows the seeds for achieving the *dharmakāya.*

The fourth empowerment is the fruition of the previous three. It arises spontaneously and naturally without any special effort. It is simply the view of the *dharmakāya*—the one taste of the whole of *saṃsāra* and *nirvāṇa.* Why then is such an empowerment even needed? Because it acts to purify the body, speech, and mind. The fourth empowerment is the indivisibility of the three previous empowerments and purifies all mental afflictions and obscurations. –

The manner in which the four *yogas* of realization relate to the grounds and paths according to Lord Rangjung Dorje is taught in *The Great Instructions*:

> Single-pointedness is the [paths of] accumulation and preparation;
> Freedom from conceptual elaboration is the path of seeing;
> The path of meditation goes from the one taste up to the middling stage of non-meditation.
> The great stage of non-meditation is perfect spiritual awakening.

You may wonder, "If there have been many who have reached the grounds and paths, why is it that they seem to lack the characteristics and qualities of those states?" Even though realization has arisen, those qualities may be absent. As an analogy, inside its egg a *garuḍa* has grown its wings, but due to the shell it cannot fly. [785] Likewise, although those qualities do not appear to others, during the intermediate state, the *dharmakāya* fulfills one's own aspirations; and then it is certain that the two *rūpakāyas* will appear to others. For the contemplative, the body is the container; for the lion, the womb is the container; and for the *garuḍa,* the egg shell is the container. Although enlightened knowledge has grown from within, like an oil-lamp in a pot, extrasensory perception and so forth are veiled by the corruption originating from the body, which is like a rotten stalk. The slight confusion that is present now will vanish in the intermediate state.

That is the consensus among the Kagyü patriarchs. The Protector of the World Sakya Paṇḍita refutes them in a sarcastic manner:

> Some who are endowed with a little quiescence
> And minute insight into the emptiness of appearances
> Identify this as the path of seeing.
> They say that like the egg shell of a *garuḍa,*
> They are imprisoned by the container of the body,
> So excellent qualities do not arise.
> Thus, as soon as they die, upon the destruction of the container of the body,
> Excellent qualities later emerge.
> There are no references to such a spiritual tradition [786]
> In the Mahāyāna *sūtras* or *tantras.*
> It would be amazing if the sun were to rise today
> But its light rays were to shine tomorrow.
> The hypothesis of the path of seeing arising in this life,
> And its qualities occurring after death
> Is a fabrication of fools.
> It is out of accord with all *sūtras* and *tantras,*
> So such a spiritual tradition is rejected by the wise.

That is not the definitive meaning. It is widely proclaimed that Sakya Paṇḍita was actually Mañjuśrī, and in his own biography his mastery of the five fields of knowledge is discussed at length. But among non-Buddhist schools there have been many thousands of *paṇḍits* who have mastered the five fields of knowledge, so that does not prove that he was Mañjuśrī. If one is Mañjuśrī, one is on the tenth ground; and *A Guide to the Middle Way* explains the qualities of the tenth ground as follows:

> In an instant one is able to display
> From the pores of one's body countless perfected *buddhas,*
> With retinues of *bodhisattvas,* [787]
> *Devas,* humans, and *asuras.*

Not even a fraction of such qualities is mentioned in his biography. *The White Lotus Sūtra* states:

> Ānanda, here is one on the tenth ground but thinks he has not achieved anything. This *bodhisattva* does not know, for he has been blessed by a great mystery.

It is said that after the Buddha's *nirvāṇa,* there are no signs [of realization] until one becomes an *arhat. The Sūtra of the Maitreya Prophesy* states:

> The monks fell into uncertainty, saying "While this monk Ajita is prophesied to be the fifth Buddha of this fortunate eon, since he has no signs or excellent qualities, how is it possible that he will become the Jina Maitreya?"

Thus, the Lord taught *The Sūtra of the Maitreya Prophesy*. Therefore, it is clear that the degree of one's realization cannot be judged in terms of the presence or absence of signs and excellent qualities. Lord Jigten Sumgön says:

> There is a school that asserts that the path of seeing has been attained [788] if its signs and qualities are present in the midst of a massive gathering of people, but otherwise it has not been attained. If you find that assertion in the teachings of the Buddha and their authoritative commentaries, I will dress my horse in satin and give him to you.

He said this over a period of many days, but it is said that no one found such an assertion.

– It's very difficult for beings like ourselves to accurately evaluate other people's degree of realization. While many people nowadays brag about their realizations, when, in fact, they have none, the great beings of the past, such as the *mahāsiddhas* of India and Tibet, would never boast about their levels of realization. On the whole, they would conceal them from others. Although those on the tenth *bodhisattva* ground can miraculously display from every pore of their bodies all the *buddhas* and their retinues, many great *bodhisattvas* outwardly appeared as prostitutes, beggars, or other beings of low status. Thus, their outer appearance gives no indication of their inner realization. Some people believe that if a *bodhisattva* displays no external or public signs of realization, he or she has not achieved the path of seeing, but this assumption is not backed by the Buddha's teachings or any of the authoritative commentaries.

Often people have the impression that upon receiving Dzogchen instructions for identifying the nature of awareness, something amazing should happen. This may indeed occur, if you have previously accumulated much merit and purified your obscurations. But even if it does, that will not suffice. Whatever your initial insight may be, it's necessary to familiarize yourself with this insight by coming back to it again and again through hearing, thinking, and meditation. –

The definitive meaning is stated by Lord Phagmo Drüpa:

> There is no need to doubt this:
> The earth cannot be warmed
> As soon as the sun rises,
> But it is gradually warmed as the light rays shine forth.
> One's needs and desires are not fulfilled
> As soon as one finds a jewel,
> But they are granted if offerings and supplications are made.
> Although a child is none other than a human being,

It is not strong as soon as it is born;
Rather, it learns various things with gradual training.
Likewise, although the reality of truth is seen,
Without familiarization, excellent qualities do not arise;
But with familiarization the supreme is achieved.
All the eight great common *siddhis* and so forth
Arise in a dependently related fashion.
Under their influence, with the conceit of arrogance, [789]
One is destroyed by the arising of extrasensory perception;
Since one has not learned the supreme [*siddhi*], one is obscured by that.
All beings such as gods and so on
Have unimaginable, karmic, miraculous powers;
But none of those are said to be causes of liberation.
Where are there characteristics and signs
In the extinction of the distinction between real truth and deception?
Nevertheless, doubts arise about this.

Kyemé Zhang says:

Suffering does not go away
As soon as you realize nonduality.
And though excellent qualities and abilities have not yet arisen,
Who is to demean this by saying this is not the path of seeing?
A glacier cannot be melted
Nor can the earth and stones be warmed
With the rising of the morning sun.
But who is to say it is not the sun?

Since we are aspiring for spiritual awakening as the fruition of the *sūtras* and *tantras*, we should not have regard for the presence or absence of transient signs and qualities. Due to the power of *karma*, insignificant types of extrasensory perception and extraordinary powers are also found among some *pretas*, [790] elemental spirits, birds, and carnivores who fly in the sky. Thus, *The Commentary on Verifying Cognition* states, "Look at ordinary vultures!" and so on. The signs of having accomplished extrasensory perception solely in dependence upon quiescence are found even among non-Buddhists and Bönpos.

– Individuals can develop extrasensory perception and other extraordinary abilities simply by accomplishing quiescence. This is done by Buddhists, non-Buddhists, and Bönpos alike. Merely accomplishing these abilities is not an indication of having achieved the profound realization of the path of seeing. On the contrary, grasping onto the signs and qualities of extrasensory perception only perpetuates our suffering in the cycle of existence.

Nowadays, it is common to find both Western and Tibetan Dharma practitioners who do not even yearn for the achievement of liberation. Actually, they practice to achieve success in the eight mundane concerns and turn their backs on generating genuine altruism. Some think they will earn much praise by attaining *siddhis*. Others think their sexual life will be enhanced. Make no mistake: this approach to practice only perpetuates *saṃsāra*. Before encountering the Dharma, we had already amassed numerous causes of *saṃsāra*, so after learning about the Buddhadharma, there's no need to accumulate even more causes of *saṃsāra*. An essential point of the Buddha's teachings is to gain liberation from suffering and the sources of suffering. Without this aspiration, even if we practice for a thousand years, there will be no benefit! In fact, we are only wasting our time.

People who go to college generally have some reason or goal in mind for doing so, but some merely attend various classes without ever acquiring useful knowledge or skills or finally earning a degree. The ultimate aim of Buddhist practice is to accomplish the state of perfect enlightenment for the sake of oneself and others. However, some people attend many Buddhist teachings but never find time to practice. Although some blessings are received simply due to hearing the Dharma, with that alone one cannot actually taste the fruit of the practice and realize its benefits. This is like attending classes in college but never carrying through to a degree. In the end you have no degree and no real skills.

Right now, we have an extraordinary opportunity due to many dependently related events coming together, so it's very important not to squander that opportunity. By hearing, thinking, and meditation, devote yourself to practice like the great masters of the past, so that you can attain the same result of practice—Buddhahood. By realizing your own well-being, genuine altruism will naturally arise and you will serve the needs of others, just as rays from the sun naturally flow out and dispel the darkness.

Four of the Ten Innermost Jewels of the Kadampa Tradition are: Let the innermost reliance of your mind be the Dharma; let the innermost reliance of your Dharma be living as a beggar; let the innermost reliance of your life as a beggar be facing death; and let the innermost reliance of your death be dwelling alone in a dry cave. Practicing with that degree of purity and simplicity gives rise to authentic practice and genuine results. Otherwise we are bound to get caught up in the eight mundane concerns. –

Thus, Lingje Repa says:

> One may have gained mastery over the eight great *siddhis*,
> But apart from their sheer wonder,
> They have helped few to attain enlightenment.

Now in terms of the distinction between the fruition of the Sūtra[yāna] and Mantra[yāna], according to the assertions of some spiritual friends,

Buddhahood is not attained by the *sūtra* tradition alone, so from the eighth ground one must enter the Mantra[yāna]. Others say that following the tenth ground, it is enough to be empowered by the great light rays of the *buddhas* of the ten directions; [so] there are *buddhas* of the *sūtra* tradition who have not needed to enter the Mantra[yāna]. Yet others maintain that the teachings on realization in the *sūtras* are simply for the sake of generating interest, but it is impossible for genuine realization to arise without reliance on the Mantra[yāna]. Everything [791] taught in the *sūtras* must be related to the four empowerments. From the time of the great stage of the path of accumulation, one enters the Mantra[yāna]; and by encountering the Buddha, one is shown the pinnacle of the *yānas*.

Thus, the seventeen Mother and Son *Perfection of Wisdom Sūtras* and so on which constitute the intermediate teachings, *The Great Mound of Jewels Sūtra*, *The Nirvāṇa Sūtra* and so on which constitute the final teachings, *The Six Collections of Reasonings Concerning the Middle Way*, *The Five Dharmas of Maitreya*, and so forth, and all the words of the Buddha and the great commentarial treatises would all be refuted [by the previous assertion]; so it is incorrect. *The Concluding Treatise* composed by Mikyö Dorje states that according to our tradition, the spiritual awakening of the *mantra* tradition is not attained as a byproduct of achieving the spiritual awakening of the *sūtra* tradition; but it asserts that the spiritual awakening of the *sūtra* tradition is attained as a byproduct of achieving the spiritual awakening of the *mantra* tradition. Likewise, Orgyen Rinpoche says:

> You may wonder whether the same qualities are attributed to the Great Perfection extinction into reality-itself and to the culminating path among the five *sūtra* tradition paths, but they are not the same at all. One may have come [792] to the fulfillment in which the power of the six thousand qualities of the ten grounds and five paths of the *sūtra* tradition has been perfected. Nevertheless, the qualities and power of the Mantra[yāna] have still not been seen, nor have they been perfected. There are extremely important differences between the extinction into reality-itself and the culminating [*sūtra*] path.
>
> In this regard, some people say that the continuum of primordial wisdom in a *buddha* is cut off. Moreover, *The Perfection of Wisdom in Eight Thousand Verses* states, "A truly perfected *buddha* has attained primordial wisdom that is unobstructed with regard to all phenomena."

Why is one called a *buddha*? Because one has awakened from the sleeplike state of ignorance and one's mind has encompassed the two domains of knowledge, one is called a *buddha*. Thus,

> Because one has awakened from the sleep of ignorance,
> And because of the twofold expansion of the mind, one is a *buddha*.

The meaning of the phrase "awakened from the sleep of ignorance" is the perfect elimination [of obscurations], which has been explained previously. The phrase "the mind's encompassment of the objects of knowledge" refers to the [793] perfection of primordial wisdom, which also has been discussed earlier.

To explain the divisions, a *buddha* has three kinds of embodiments: the *dharmakāya*, the *sambhogakāya*, and the *nirmāṇakāya*. Thus, *The Sūtra of the Holy Golden Light* states, "All the *tathāgatas* possess three embodiments: the *dharmakāya, sambhogakāya*, and *nirmāṇakāya*." In some treatises there are references to two embodiments, four embodiments, and even five embodiments, but though they are discussed in those ways, all the embodiments are included in the three embodiments. *The Ornament for the Sūtras* states:

> The collection of a *buddha's* embodiments is to be known
> As having three embodiments.[100]

To give a presentation of the three embodiments, the *dharmakāya* is the actual Buddha, for *The Perfection of Wisdom in Eight Thousand Verses* states, "Do not regard the Tathāgata as a *rūpakāya*. The Tathāgata is the *dharmakāya*." [794] *The King of Samādhi Sūtra* also states, "Do not regard the Lord of the Jinas as a *rūpakāya*." The two *rūpakāyas* are embodiments produced by the blessings of the *dharmakāya*, the trainees' perception, and by previous prayers. Know that they occur due to the confluence of those three.

This treatise, *The Essential Instructions of Avalokiteśvara: The Union of Mahāmudrā and Dzogchen*, is complete in all the practices of the nine *yānas*. So in terms of the ground, path, and fruition, the Mahāsiddha Karmapakṣi says:

> With realization of the words and meanings of the nine *yānas*
> And with the blessings of the lineage of Naropa,
> The contemplative Rangjung Dorje
> Encountered Saraha in a pure vision.
> The revelation of the *buddhas*
> Is a limitless ocean whose depths are hard to fathom.

> A number of beings of superior, middling, and inferior faculties
> Have progressed and become manifestly enlightened.
> When they attain realization, simultaneous individuals
> Are comparable to Samantabhadra. [795]
> Whether or not one proceeds along the grounds and paths,
> The twenty-one stages of the grounds and paths
> Pervade the whole of *saṃsāra* and *nirvāṇa.*
> In Akaniṣṭa, the perfect reality,
> Everyone in general is perfected.
> The mode of being is Samantabhadra, the absolute space of phenomena.
> In the Great Perfection Atiyoga
> All the *yānas* are transcended.
> The sixteen stages of the grounds and paths
> Are all primordially, naturally perfected
> In Akaniṣṭa, the perfect reality.
> The specific signs of the path of the fruition
> Are effortlessly, spontaneously present,
> Perfected in the abode of the Akaniṣṭa of self-awareness.

The Quintessence of the Ḍākinīs states:

> This is striking the nail of the three attainments:
> By attaining the unborn *dharmakāya*
> Your own mind attains mastery of the *dharmakāya.*
> By attaining the unceasing *sambhogakāya,*
> Your own mind attains mastery of the *sambhogakāya.*
> By attaining the nondual *nirmāṇakāya,*
> Your own mind attains mastery of the *nirmāṇakāya.*
> The criteria are the *yogas* of the four confidences...

[796] You attain the confidence of not hoping for any spiritual awakening above. You ascertain that apart from the awareness of your own mind there is no other enlightenment. You attain confidence upon ascertaining that all the great qualities, the enlightened activities, and the merciful compassion of the *buddhas* are natural displays of the awareness of your own mind. You ascertain that all the sufferings of the hells in the miserable states of existence below are none other than delusions of your own mind. By ascertaining that the three miserable states of existence, the hot and cold hells, suffering and your life span are displays of the confusion of ignorance, you achieve the second and fourth confidence of not returning back to the cycle of existence. Upon actualizing the fruition that is devoid of hope and fear, you

awaken in the nature of the five embodiments, the five primordial wisdoms, and the four enlightened activities; and you are imbued with the ornamental wheel of an enlightened body, speech, mind, qualities, and activity. You unceasingly, spontaneously accomplish the needs of all sentient beings until the cycle of existence is empty.

[797] *The Great Instructions* states:

> Perfect awakening is attained in the culmination of non-meditation. In that regard, by accomplishing the supreme union of quiescence and insight in the reality of the four equalities of the taste of the absolute space and primordial wisdom, the fruition of the *dharmakāya* and the two *rūpakāyas* is actualized. The *dharmakāya* is the realization of the essential nature of insight, or the culminating fruition of the nature of nonconceptuality. The *rūpakāyas* arise from the facet of phenomenological knowledge, which in turn manifests from the illusionlike *samādhi* and so forth. Moreover, freedom from conceptual elaborations is the *dharmakāya*; and fulfilling the needs of sentient beings by whatever pure and impure means needed to train them is the *rūpakāya*. In this regard, it is appropriate to make the divisions among the three embodiments, the four embodiments, and so on. Then, without diverging from the *dharmakāya* for your own sake, the needs of sentient beings are fulfilled by the two *rūpakāyas*, which are for the sake of others. By way of the four kinds of enlightened activity, all the needs of all beings are vastly, pervasively, and limitlessly fulfilled. [798] In addition, the enlightened activity for the welfare of oneself as the agent is also brought to ultimate perfection. Constantly fulfilling the needs of sentient beings until the cycle of existence is empty by means of enlightened activity for the sake of others, they are gradually guided to the path in accordance with the degrees of perceptiveness of individuals. This is the supreme method for actualizing in one lifetime, with one body, and on one seat, the Mahāmudrā mode of being, innate primordial wisdom, which is of the nature of the three embodiments and the five primordial wisdoms. By revealing this method, all the supreme and common *siddhis* are effortlessly brought forth from the mind-streams of disciples. The primordial wisdom of Mahāmudā arises in their mind-streams; the state of perfect enlightenment is actualized; and by way of the Mahāmudrā of enlightened activity one attains spectacular power to bring all sentient beings to the path of maturation and liberation.

– In Gelugpa monasteries monks often debate whether there is anywhere that the Buddha is absent, and the answer is, of course, that the Buddha is present everywhere. This can imply that you are a *buddha*. If you ask yourself, "Am I a *buddha*?" doubt will probably arise. But then ask, "Do *buddhas* exist?" It's difficult to say either that they are existent or nonexistent. In terms of your own identity, do you exist or not? By following the implications of the view that the Buddha is present everywhere, you arrive at the Great Perfection, which is free of the constructs of both existence and nonexistence.

This view counteracts our tendency to judge others. We think we can size people up, even though we really aren't in a position to judge others. In reality, only a *buddha* is capable of truly evaluating another person's degree of spiritual maturity or realization. This view also counteracts our concepts of what is pure or impure. For example, among Tibetans, the head is thought to be pure, which might imply that the Buddha must be present in the head; and Tibetans also believe that shoes are dirty, so does this mean that no Buddha is present there? By recognizing that the Buddha is uniformly present everywhere and in everything, such conventional superimpositions upon reality are completely undermined.

Sentient beings are gradually guided to the path in accordance with the degree of perceptiveness of the individual. This emphasis on the gradual nature is found throughout all orders of Tibetan Buddhism. In addition each order emphasizes the importance of practicing in the proper sequence. In the West people tend to expect immediate results from whatever they do, which leads them to think they can just jump to enlightenment or up to the highest practices without gradually following the path, step by step, and we end up without any success at all.

The great Indian *mahāsiddhas* of the past attained enlightenment in caves, on riverbanks, at the foot of trees and so forth, not in palaces or large monasteries. Similarly, in Tibet many enlightened beings appeared, and they, too, gained realization in solitary places in the wilderness. Actually, such highly realized beings always reside in the midst of a pure land, no matter where they are, so they need no special environment to practice. Why then are there so many monasteries in India and Tibet, and why are Dharma centers even necessary? They have been founded by great beings of the past and present to preserve the Dharma and to provide places that facilitate the practices of hearing, thinking, and meditation. –

The Profound Inner Meaning states: [799]

> From the *maṇḍala* of the Jina's space[like] embodiment and sun[like] primordial wisdom
> Are displayed *rūpakāyas* in all the worlds in the ten directions.
> Your speech, which is like the sound of a celestial drum, never fails to resound;
> And it is effortlessly heard by all beings throughout the extent of space.

Your mind, like a wish-fulfilling jewel, with effortless primordial wisdom
Simultaneously, without conceptual elaborations, fulfills the hopes of those who are subject to conceptual elaborations.
Although you engage with sentient beings and mental afflictions, you are uncontaminated.
Thus, I reverently bow to you, the self-arisen Jina.

CHAPTER TEN

The Four Stages of Yoga

Homage to Avalokiteśvara!

[802] In accordance with the *sūtras, tantras,* and the teachings of the *siddhas,* I shall explain how to progress along the grounds and paths by meditating on these profound practical instructions of Avalokiteśvara. Both the ten grounds and five paths of the *sūtra* tradition as well as the four stages of *yoga* of the *mantra* tradition constitute the grounds and paths of the Sūtra[yāna] and Mantra[yāna]; so it is difficult to fit them together. Likewise, it is also hard to relate them to the four visions of the Great Perfection, for each of these paths is distinct.

– Here is a brief overview of the essential nature of the Four Yogas. The defining characteristic of the first *yoga,* single-pointedness, is recognizing the nature of your own mind. Further, you realize that appearances are none other than the nature of your own mind, and that nature is spacelike emptiness. Freedom from conceptual elaboration, the second *yoga,* entails recognizing that all appearances are adventitious; you realize that the very nature of the mind is empty and free from conceptual elaboration. Thirdly, in the *yoga* of the one taste, you recognize that *saṃsāra* and *nirvāṇa* are of the same nature, which is the key to attaining enlightenment. In the fourth *yoga,* the *yoga* of non-meditation, you recognize that the whole of *saṃsāra* and *nirvāṇa* is primordially unborn, ungrounded, and unceasing. The very duality of subjects and objects is primordially ungrounded and of one nature—the *dharmakāya.* Many points discussed in the fourth *yoga* pertain equally to the Breakthrough and Leap-over phases of Dzogchen practice.

While we are encouraged to first study and practice the Sūtrayāna and then enter the Mantrayāna, it is difficult to understand the Four Yogas of Mantrayāna in relationship to the five paths and ten grounds of the

Sūtrayāna. Likewise, it is difficult to relate the grounds and paths of the Sūtrayāna and the Four Yogas of the Mahāmudrā tradition to the four visions of Dzogchen.

Of the Four Yogas of the Mahāmudrā, two—single-pointedness and freedom from conceptual elaboration—are discussed at length in this chapter, and among Tibetan Buddhist contemplatives, a fair number have gained genuine experience in these two stages. The *yogas* of the one taste and non-meditation are extremely advanced stages of meditation, and for the sake of simplicity the author deals much more briefly with these in this text. –

Zhang Rinpoche says:

> Mahāmudrā is established as one,
> But fools become confused by trying to figure out the grounds and paths.

He [803] was referring to simultaneous individuals and those on the stage of the Leap-over. Gradual individuals practice in accordance with the ten grounds and five paths, so Naropa says, "First experience single-pointedness." *The Primary Words of the Great Instructions* states, "Abide in the reality of single-pointed, indivisible quiescence and insight." The meaning is that single-pointedness entails abiding in the spacelike reality of emptiness and luminosity. At that time, you realize the essential nature of meditation as spacelike emptiness and luminosity, but the insight of certain knowledge has not arisen from that spacelike emptiness and luminosity. Thus, with single-pointedness you pointlessly wander about in darkness. At that time, your subsequent [post-meditative] consciousness reifies phenomena by grasping onto them as ordinary and real. [804] Hence, even though you ascertain empty luminosity during meditative equipoise, your subsequent consciousness becomes confused concerning ordinary things, so there is the stain of grasping onto them as real, and the stains of *karma* are not purified.

If you are not mindful, you disengage from meditation, which brings about separation; and even if you are mindful, the essential nature is not seen [during the post-meditative state], so there is no attainment. You have not dispensed with superimpositions upon experience, and you still have the sense of an object and agent of meditation; so this is a time of meditation in which the mind-itself is reified. The form aggregate and the five avenues of consciousness are purified. They are cognized as naturally empty, ungrounded in an essential nature. Since you are inevitably subject to grasping, your experiential realizations are stained. In terms of the appearances to your limpid awareness, you precisely discern subtle and gross causality; but because this is grasped as being real, causality is reified. When you are undistracted, you are in meditative equipoise, and when you are distracted, you are in the post-meditative state.

At this time you disengage from characteristics, and you chiefly cultivate quiescence in a state that is free of the intellect. You know your own essential nature of empty luminosity.

– Rather than focusing on Mahāmudrā as one state, some people become confused by obsessively concerning themselves with the grounds and paths. Simultaneous individuals need not worry about following the gradual path of the ten grounds and five paths, because due to their past accumulation of great merit and purification, their practice is utterly simple and instantaneous. Those who have progressed through practice to the Leap-over stage of Dzogchen also do not need to concern themselves with the ten grounds and five paths. Gradual individuals, in contrast, must practice in accordance with these grounds and paths, proceeding through each of the *yānas*.

Among the Four Yogas, one must first achieve the state of single-pointedness, which entails a union of quiescence and insight, and therefore a high degree of attentional stability. Therefore, the first stage of single-pointedness occurs with the accomplishment of quiescence, wherein one single-pointedly attends to one's own awareness, which is primordially unceasing and luminous. This is realized when the mind is free of obscurations. Progressing to a more advanced stage of single-pointedness requires the cultivation of insight. Practicing without genuine quiescence or insight, while just being spaced out, is pointless. There are, of course, many methods to cultivate quiescence—such as attending to an object or simply meditating on the nature of awareness—but each method eventually culminates in the indivisibility of quiescence and insight, which has the spacious quality of both emptiness and luminosity. That constitutes the nature of the first of the four stages of *yoga*—single-pointedness. This is comparable to the Hīnayāna realization of identitylessness with traces of grasping still present, so this realization is not considered to be perfect, for the thought, "This is identitylessness," still remains. This state is analogous to the sun that has not completely risen over the horizon or a flower not yet in full bloom. You realize the essential nature of the meditative state, but you have not gained the certain knowledge that arises from spacelike emptiness and luminosity. That is because grasping is still present. After meditation sessions, your old habit of grasping onto the tangible, or substantial, existence of phenomena arises once again. As you sit in meditation, you may have a sense of the emptiness of phenomena, but if someone knocks on the door, your attention immediately becomes riveted on that, and then grasping has occurred. This is what is meant by the term *reify*—grasping onto phenomena as being substantial, or inherently existent.

Due to grasping, purification is not complete. You have gained realization of the various fields of consciousness and so forth as being empty, ungrounded in an essential nature, and you have a clear understanding of both subtle and gross causality, but you still grasp onto it as being real, rather than as dreamlike or illusory. Since you grasp onto the phenomena involved in causal relationships as being real, the causal relationships themselves are reified as well. –

Dagpo Rinpoche says, [805] "The *yoga* of single-pointedness is luminous and unceasing, and that is momentary consciousness." Saraha says:

> By holding firm without mindfulness, there is unceasing
> emptiness.
> If consciousness is left in its own mode, there will be stability.

And:

> If you remain there, a sense of bliss will occur.
> Experiencing the appearances of things as empty
> Is like recognizing water even though it appears as ice.

– Momentary consciousness is the interlude after thoughts of the past have vanished and before thoughts of the future have yet arisen. In this phase of practice, thoughts of the three times—of the past, present, or future—are not present. While in meditative equipoise, you are completely free of intellectual constructs or mental fabrications. In this state a sense of bliss may occur, and if you think, "I like this. This feels good," you only perpetuate your own cyclic existence. Among the three experiences of bliss, clarity, and nonconceptuality, not grasping onto bliss leads to the realization of the *nirmāṇakāya;* not grasping onto clarity leads to the *sambhogakāya;* and not grasping onto nonconceptuality leads to the attainment of the *dharmakāya.* –

The mental isolation discussed by Nāgārjuna in *The Five Stages,* the *yoga* of spontaneous presence taught by Lawapa, the *yoga* of the experience of *samādhi* taught by Nawaripa, cutting off superimpositions as explained by Maitrīpa, the *yoga* of identitylessness in *The Descent into Laṅkā Sūtra,* the meditative stabilization practiced by the childish, the dew-drops of *The Six Dharmas,* and the meaning of the vase empowerment are all said to be synonymous. *The Great Instructions* states:

> In the medium stage of single-pointedness, you occasionally enter into *samādhi* even when you are not meditating, and stability comes when you are meditating. [806] In the limpidity of training in the *samādhi* of bliss, clarity, and nonconceptuality you can display numerous kinds of tainted extrasensory perception and

> paranormal abilities. In that state ideation arises less than before, and whatever arises proceeds in its own limpidity. Afterwards, whenever you are mindful of spacious appearances that are imbued with a sense of empty luminosity, at times this arises as meditation, and at times it arises more substantially. Dreams occur less frequently than before. At times you have such an experience, and at times you do not, and you become fascinated with this meditation.

– In the medium stage of the *yoga* of single-pointedness, the stability of your *samādhi* may arise naturally even when you are not in formal meditation. But you cannot become complacent and stop applying yourself to rigorous meditation at this point. If so, you will be carried right back into *saṃsāra* because your many habitual propensities have not been dispelled, and they will simply re-emerge. The qualities of bliss, clarity, and nonconceptuality are in fact of one nature; they are primordially of the very nature of your own awareness. You do not develop or attain them by means of this practice. Rather through the stages of this practice these intrinsic qualities become more and more manifest.

One result of this practice is the achievement of extrasensory perception and paranormal abilities, but because they are not completely free of mental afflictions or obscurations, they are said to be tainted. It is inappropriate and even harmful to respond to these abilities with attachment or amazement, because that throws you off the path. However, the untainted extrasensory perception and paranormal abilities of a perfectly awakened being are certainly worthy of aspiration. Being both taintless and ultimate, they are of the nature of perfect enlightenment.

These paranormal abilities, like buried treasures, arise from time to time, and many people are profoundly misled by them, whether they achieve them themselves or witness them in others. Being fascinated with them only indicates an improper relationship with one's spiritual mentor and a lack of understanding of the stages of practice.

These days, more and more people are drawn to Dzogchen, and many try to practice and even teach it without establishing a sufficient foundation by completing the preliminary practices. These people are like little children who do whatever they like at the dinner table, stuffing food in their mouths—whatever and however much they want. We can't practice everything at once any more than a child can eat everything on the table. If parents are conscientious, they give only the amount of food that their child can properly digest; and if the child listens to the parents, he or she will take only what is given. In this way the child will be well nourished, grow well, and be free of illness. We should follow the same model in our practice of Dharma. If you don't, but rather leap into the more advanced stages of practice with an insufficient foundation, it will drive you crazy.

Recently, when I was interviewed about Buddhism in America, I was asked whether I thought Buddhism was flourishing and asked about my view on the relation between Buddhist teachers and students. In the West, there is a tradition of reading and relying on books rather than an actual teacher. It is quite common for people to hold a book up as the final authority. This tendency occurs in school systems and the government as well. If an issue is in debate, someone will point to a book as a final authority. In certain cases this is very helpful, but if something goes wrong in your practice and you experience ill effects, would it be proper to blame some author? Generally speaking, it is important to rely on a qualified spiritual mentor and not simply on a book. You need to listen to the spiritual mentor and then put his or her advice into practice. Both the spiritual teacher and the student need to have two eyes—the eye of wisdom and the eye of skillful means.

In this stage of single-pointedness, all that arises to the mind appears in its own luminosity, displaying no essence, or substantial nature. The contents of the mind arise like small clouds in the sky or like ripples on the ocean's surface. Fluctuations still occur, and by the power of previous habituation, phenomena appear concretely at times. You have fewer, more lucid dreams, and your interest in meditation will become stronger. In previous stages you tended to become easily tired, now you yearn to practice. –

Gyalwa Yang Gönpa says:

> In dependence upon that, the stillness whenever you rest in luminous, immaculate, nonconceptual consciousness without recognition constitutes mastery over the *samādhi* of middling single-pointedness.

Phagmo Drüpa says, "You attain mastery over the *samādhi* of the middling stage of single-pointedness." This accords with the assertion in *The Oral Transmission of the Lineage of Siddhas* that the bliss, clarity, and nonconceptuality of meditative stabilization are thus integrated, and the mastery of remaining therein for any duration is experiential single-pointedness. [807] The middling stage of single-pointedness, in which the facsimile of empty luminosity is maintained with mindfulness—although there may be occasional distraction during which it is not maintained continually—is called the warmth and the pinnacle [stages] of the path of preparation. Once the experience has become stable, if that empty luminosity is maintained with mindfulness, it will become constant, even if at times it is not intentionally maintained. This is also called warmth and the pinnacle. That is the teaching of Götsangwa.

Phagmo Drüpa says, "The great stage of single-pointedness entails continuity of experience." Yang Gönpa says:

> Once that has arisen uninterruptedly, all ideation is pacified in that state. Even sleep takes place in that state, and the four kinds of activities are not separated from it. When that happens, that is called the continuity of experience of the great stage of single-

> pointedness. Then you feel a strong conviction that this is non-meditation, and it is said that experiential realization has arisen.

– At this point, although your actual degree of realization is the stage of great single-pointedness, you may feel you have reached the culminating stage of the Four Yogas, namely non-meditation. In other words, you exaggerate the actual nature of your realization.

Throughout this chapter and the next, a distinction is made regarding meditative experience and actual realization. The former entails a lingering sense of grasping, whereas the latter is genuine insight. The term *experiential realization* refers to a realization and the subsequent grasping onto it, in which one may think, "This is my meditation. I have arrived at such and such a level." –

When this is said of partial realization, Zhang Rinpoche comments [808]:

> It is said that you realize the essential nature at the time of great single-pointedness, and that essential nature is said to be clear and unceasing. You have confidence in clear and unceasing consciousness, which is like the center of limpid space; and you nonconceptually ascertain the essential nature of single-pointedness. In the state of mental bliss, clarity, and nonconceptuality you may be present simply in brilliance and stillness; but if definite ascertainment does not arise, that is unrelated to the experience of insight. By failing to confront the nature of being, you wander in the midst of single-pointed darkness.

Thus, the essential nature is not seen. As a result of the mind not knowing its own essential nature, the distinction between meditative experience and realization is not made. Meditative stabilization in which there are appearances but not ascertainment is like a small child seeing the moon, or a fool looking at a temple. Such ascertainment is tainted experiential realization that is contaminated by grasping onto objects. Up until single-pointedness, primordial wisdom that realizes the path has not arisen, so that is not genuine meditative equipoise. Thus, as subsequent appearances do not appear as illusions, [809] there is no genuine post-meditative state.

Meditative equipoise and the post-meditative state occur according to your own level of practice. The mind nonconceptually remains in empty luminosity, but since the mental engagement of grasping onto objects has not been purified, this is nominal meditative equipoise. Afterwards, since you still grasp onto reality, this is a nominal post-meditative state, for it is like following a dog as if it were a human.

When you rest in the meditative equipoise of bliss, clarity, and nonconceptuality, that is the culmination of the power of single-pointedness. If at times this does not happen even while meditating, and at times it does occur even while not meditating, the power of single-pointedness has still not been perfected.

Once all ideation is pacified in the state of meditation simply by being mindful of it, and once even the sleeping state takes place in the experiential clear light, ideation arises as meditation. If ideation cannot be pacified with mindfulness and you have to draw it in with the hook of meditation, ideation has not yet arisen as meditation. If awareness is not maintained with mindfulness, it is disengaged from the meditative state. [810] Even though awareness is maintained, if the essential nature of ideation is not seen while resting in the previous continuum, there is no attainment.

– Ideation is of the nature of meditation, but if you still need to draw the mind back because of a sense of being distracted by thoughts, you have not actually realized the nature of ideation. If you still need to maintain your awareness with mindfulness, some effort is required, but in the natural state, you do not need to draw in the mind again or deal with ideation as something separate from the meditation. In the natural state, ideation simply flows from the meditative state like rays of light from the sun. –

By cultivating that meditation for a long while, your mind will turn away from the eight mundane concerns, you will be freed from outer and inner parasites, and you will be able to display paranormal abilities such as meditative manipulation and domination of the elements and so forth. When that happens, the qualities of single-pointedness have arisen. If the mind is not serviceable, if the essence and the dross of meditation are not differentiated due to a lack of mental peace, and if you are incapable of bringing forth the common signs of warmth, those qualities have not arisen.[101]

In the perception of limpid *samādhi*, upon precisely discerning pure subtle and coarse causality, if you understand causality while reifying the created and its creator, you have comprehended conventional reality [alone]. On that defiled, mundane path you cannot disengage your own mind-stream and so on from habitual tendencies. Even with the *samādhi* of realizing emptiness, if you do not understand appearances as dependently related events, you have not comprehended conventional reality.

[811] Due to the clear luster of your meditation, if sympathy naturally arises for sentient beings who are exhausted by various types of

ideation, you have attained the seed of the *rūpakāya;* and you are able to serve beings according to your own ability. If the power of your experience blocks the expression of compassion, you have not achieved the seed of altruism, and that is comparable to the *śrāvakas'* state of cessation. *The Great Instructions* states:

> In the great stage of single-pointedness, meditative equipoise, the post-meditative state, and the four kinds of activity constantly proceed day and night without interruption in the state of empty luminosity. All ideation as well as subsequent appearances and dreams also proceed in that state. The mind-itself is imbued with a sense of emptiness, including empty bliss, empty awareness, empty appearances, and empty luminosity; and everything arises chiefly as myriad illusionlike and dreamlike experiences. Since there are said to be many qualities [of *samādhi*], and you think there is no finer meditation that this, you may conclude this is great non-meditation. However, without clinging to those experiential realizations, recognize ideation as empty luminosity and as empty appearances. [812] You will achieve mindfulness that compellingly ascertains everything as the mind and ascertains the mind as unborn and naturally free. Manifestly roving thoughts will cease, and you will experience your spiritual mentor as the Buddha. You will proceed constantly day and night in that state of empty luminosity, and your craving for the cycle of existence will cease.
>
> If you proceed into non-meditation upon nonconceptually seeing the essential nature, the power of single-pointedness is perfected, its qualities are sustained, and you see its essential nature. Until that happens, generate enthusiasm and practice!
>
> The five fields of sensual experience are to be rejected here, so abandon craving for this life, for possessions, for *samādhi*, and so on. Maintaining good hygiene, you should dwell in solitude.
>
> Here the difference between meditative equipoise and the post-meditative state is made in terms of dwelling and non-dwelling. Dwelling in bliss, clarity, and nonconceptuality is meditative equipoise. Not dwelling therein is the post-meditative state. In great single-pointedness all realizations and related experiences dissolve into that state, and day and night they arise [813] as spacelike, empty luminosity. The stage when you think you have achieved non-meditation consists of the patience and supreme Dharma stages of the path of preparation.

– Abandon craving for this life, yourself, and your own well-being, which implicitly leads to attachment for your friends and family and aggressive feelings toward your enemies. Counteract attachment until compassion arises spontaneously even for your greatest enemy. One common method to accomplish this is to completely surrender your body, speech, and mind to your spiritual mentor, and to the Three Jewels—the Buddha, the Dharma and Saṅgha. The practice of Severance is especially helpful in this regard.

Even having all the money in the world won't bring satisfaction, and the remedy for such craving is to offer up our wealth. While it is fine to make offerings to the objects of refuge or make donations to charities, what is most important is the *spirit of generosity* with which you give your possessions to your spiritual mentor, the Three Jewels, your chosen deity, your *vajra* brothers and sisters, or a charity. In addition, recognizing that all that you enjoy is the direct result of your previous merit, you can offer up that merit, and by so offering, the merit is not used up, but increases further. Craving for anything, even *samādhi*, is like putting on a pair of handcuffs, so relinquish craving so that compassion may arise spontaneously.

Dwelling in alone in a meditation cell is thought to be the pinnacle of solitude. In very strict retreats practiced in Tibet, contemplatives were sealed in caves. Dispensing with all mundane speech did help them to disengage from the attachment and anger induced by mundane speech. But do you believe you cannot practice just because you live in a city? Imagine sealing yourself in a meditation cell in a city. Eventually, your neighbors would find out and they would probably think you were crazy, and you might even be committed to a mental hospital. Since this does not seem a very viable choice in our present situation, we can at least diminish our idle gossip. If we just talk less, nobody can accuse us of being crazy. We can maintain the silence of not engaging in mundane talk; we can avoid nonvirtue; we can practice virtue.

You may think that is pretty straightforward and easy, but it's not. To disengage from craving for your own life, your possessions, and so forth, you must know the nature of cyclic existence, and the Four Noble Truths, particularly the truth of suffering. Mere lip service is not enough, you must actually know that the nature of cyclic existence is suffering. The best way to gain such understanding is by discursive meditation. For example, you can imagine you are on the edge of a precipice, holding onto strands of grass for dear life. Then image first a white rat and then a black rat nibbling on these strands of grass over and over until nothing is left to hold. That's the type of crisis that we need to recognize. Only by knowing that the nature of the cycle of existence is suffering can craving be averted. Once you recognize that the nature of *saṃsāra* is suffering, you can begin to understand that nonvirtues committed with the body, speech, and mind simply lead to miserable states of existence. Your nonvirtuous activities are the source of your own suffering, so don't point the finger at anyone else.

By listening to the Dharma and following the preliminary practices to their culmination, you can attain *samādhi* without hindrances or problems. Taking refuge and engaging in the other preliminary practices is like clearing a field of sticks, thorns, and rocks so the seeds that are sowed can yield a rich harvest. You may even have craving not only for mundane things but for spiritual accomplishments, such as success in the stages of generation and completion, and realization of emptiness itself. Is it wrong to want to be free of suffering and its causes, and to yearn for and actually crave liberation? For the time being it is alright, but when you reach the highest stages of practice, such craving naturally drops away, just as craving naturally vanishes once you fulfill your desire to acquire a certain body of knowledge.

Initially, you must recognize the preciousness of this human life with which you are presently endowed. This human life is the means by which it is possible for you to attain Buddhahood in one lifetime and thereby fulfill the needs of yourself and others. This is the reality of our present existence, but we tend to overlook the value of this human life, falling back into our cravings and affairs of this life. What is an example of the craving of this life? If you were to lose ten dollars, wouldn't you be upset? Or if someone gave you one hundred dollars, wouldn't that make you really happy? In the meantime your own mind is imbued with the qualities of a *buddha,* with all of the causes for manifestly bringing forth perfect enlightenment, yet you're not amazed at all. We are not even astonished at being able to attain enlightenment in one lifetime—now that's amazing! -

The Oral Transmission of the Lineage of Siddhas states:

> At this point you attain discerning wisdom integrated with *samādhi* that ascertains the essential nature. This is related to the following experiential signs: while abiding in mindfulness with continuous enthusiasm for contemplation until achieving enlightenment, physical and mental pliancy, an extraordinary joy of fulfilling the vast needs of yourself and others, and great equanimity free of spiritual sloth all arise simultaneously. If your meditative state lacks those signs, it may be meditative experience, but it is not the realization of Mahāmudrā.

And:

> Although it is experienced as non-meditation, it is the single-pointed *yoga* among the Four Yogas of realization.

My teacher, the great sage Gyal Rongwa, says:

> At the supreme Dharma stage of the path of preparation, [814] you have the sense that you have perceptually realized emptiness, but you have still not realized emptiness.

Those statements seem to have the same meaning.

The difference between single-pointedness and freedom from conceptual elaboration is that in the former ideation does not arise as the *dharmakāya,* and in the latter it does. *The Tantra of the Great Āli Kāli River* states:

Secondly, due to the illusionlike *samādhi*
In great meditative equipoise that is free of conceptual
elaboration
The power of inconceivable *samādhi* arises.
Upon attaining warmth, you gain mastery over rebirth.

– At this point, you are no longer thrown by your previous *karma*, but can simply choose where you take rebirth. In your next life you no longer need to strive for certain qualities, which, like a spiritual inheritance, arise as the result of your previous life. –

In the realization of equality the great severance of superimpositions is free of conceptual elaboration, and the nature of the mind is realized without conceptual elaborations. If you think, "This is emptiness. There is nothing at all," and you dismiss conventional reality, that is called pseudo-emptiness that is not free of conceptual elaboration. Objects or things that appear as objects have no intrinsic nature, so your subsequent consciousness is like an illusion. Although you do not grasp onto the true existence of things, if appearances arise without ascertainment, there is the stain of non-recognition, and the stains of mental afflictions are not purified. If awareness is not maintained with unwavering mindfulness, [815] there is disengagement from meditation. By sustaining [mindfulness] and seeing the essential nature of whatever arises, there is both disengagement and attainment. Meditative equipoise and the post-meditative state are differentiated as (1) nonconceptual, primordial wisdom that realizes the nature of being, arising without an object, and (2) illusionlike, subsequent consciousness. In meditative equipoise you nurture nonconceptual, primordial wisdom that realizes the essential nature without an object; and in subsequent consciousness you meditate on the illusionlike absence of true existence. This is a time for meditating on the mind-itself both while in meditative equipoise and afterwards.

By purifying the grasping of experiential awareness, the aggregate of feelings is purified. As there is nothing that is conventionally designated, the aggregate of recognition is purified. With the realization of the mind and mental objects as being free of conceptual elaboration, the aggregate of mental consciousness is purified. Having purified your meditative experience, realization arises without an object. By knowing that meditative experience and realization are unmixed, you distinguish between meditative experience and realization. By understanding the power of emptiness as dependent origination and illusionlike causality, [you realize] that causes and effects are like illusions. [816] At this point, you renounce this life, and you meditate chiefly on emptiness while in a state in which thoughts of signs are naturally released. Recognizing the essential nature of ideation, it is important that your consciousness be potent and not drift off into equanimity.

– When we speak of bliss, clarity, and nonconceptuality, there is a sense of a meditative experience that we recognize as such. In this way meditative experience has at least a trace of grasping even in the more subtle states. One of the salient characteristics of meditative experience in this context is that it arises in accordance with our previous habitual propensities. In other words, it comes from the seeds of our own minds, predilections and habits, whereas realization stems from knowing reality, as opposed to merely having an experience of something.

While recognizing the essential nature of ideation, it is important at this stage not to drift off into a passive, or spaced out, state. Consciousness needs to be empowered. –

Lord Dagpo Rinpoche says:

> In the *yoga* free of conceptual elaboration, by seeing the unborn essential nature of awareness, you have no hopes above for spiritual awakening; you have no anxiety about the cycle of existence below; you do not grasp at appearances in-between; and you cannot be affected by anything else.

The Great Brahmin [Saraha] says:

> Like recognizing water even when it appears as ice,
> In the second [*yoga*], without impeding the appearances of mindfulness,
> Emptiness and bliss arise without differentiation.
> This is [like] ice melting into water.

The clear light as taught in *The Five Stages*, the inconceivable taught by Lawapa, the *yoga* as taught by Śawaripa, the occasion of attaining empowerment as taught by Maitrīpa, the *yoga* without an apprehended object as taught in *The Descent into Laṅkā Sūtra*, [817] the meditative equipoise that discerns reality, and the reality of the secret empowerment are all said to be synonymous.

Gyalwa Yang Gönpa says:

> By sustaining single-pointed meditation in that way, without craving, after awhile in the state of that pure experience you will see the truth of reality-itself, free of conceptual elaboration. What is seen? You see yourself. What is it that sees? You yourself see.

> This is seeing without an object and without a subject. In between the cessation of the stream of past consciousness and prior to the arising of future consciousness, there is either the momentary ideation of the consciousness of the present, or the essential nature of nonconceptuality, which recognizes its own nature without an object. At this time you distinguish the demarcation between *saṃsāra* and *nirvāṇa*. All your previous understanding and experiences of Dharma conversations which you held so dear are seen as outer husks. As the mind looks outwards, it is free of conceptual elaboration, and as it looks inwards, it is free of conceptual elaboration. The recognition of seeing the essential nature of freedom from conceptual elaboration is ungrounded. [818] No conventional designation for it can be found, and it cannot be an object of the mind. Without an object, you recognize yourself. The nonconceptual severance of superimpositions is seeing the essential nature that is free of conceptual elaboration.

The Condensed Perfection of Wisdom states the meaning of that:

> Forms are not seen, nor are feelings seen. Recognitions are not seen, nor are volitions seen. Consciousness of anything, mind, and cognition are not seen. The Guide declares that this is seeing reality. No other analogy to seeing can be found. If this is put into words of sentient beings by saying, "Space is seen," ponder the meaning of the manner in which space is seen. The Tathāgata has taught seeing reality in that way.

Thus, this goes beyond the scope of meditative experience. That realization that is congruent with ordinary consciousness is free of the five aggregates. It is ungrounded as a substantial entity, so it is free of the aggregate of form. [819] Due to the purification of grasping onto experiential awareness, it is free of the aggregate of feelings. Due to the absence of conventional designations, it is free of the aggregate of recognition. Due to the absence of a fettered sentient being, it is free of the aggregate of compositional factors. Due to the absence of apprehension of an ascertained object, it is free of the aggregate of consciousness. That realization that is free of the five aggregates is established as contemplative perception, which is what the Buddha intended. *The Essence of Amoghapāśa Sūtra* states the meaning: "This contemplation that is free of the five aggregates is reminiscent of the Buddha." *The Great Instructions* states:

> Whatever you meditate on, without reliance on the effort of mindful apprehension, there is realization of the nature that is free of

> the extremes of both stillness and movement, and of the nature of connate, primordial wisdom, which is the essential nature of the mind, and the arising, cessation, and presence of ideation. There is the uncontrived understanding that all phenomena are free of conceptual elaboration. All experiences are understood to be empty and without an object. Like peeling off the husk of the essential nature of awareness, or like finding a treasure, there is a naked, vivid realization, free of conceptual elaboration. [820] You think that you have attained mastery over the mind, and that this alone is it. From the outset, there is homogeneous recognition. Fluctuations in the experience do not occur, or even if they do, there is no gladness or sorrow. Upon directing the mind towards outer phenomena, everything appears like an illusion and proceeds into emptiness. And even if it does not, there is no incongruity. Thus, appearances are indeterminate, and recognition arises, free of superimpositions. You realize that reality is like that, and in that integration of quiescence and insight the signs of ideation are released right where they are. Thoughts arise as the *dharmakāya*. Appearances are realized as your own mind. By knowing the mind-itself to be the *dharmakāya*, your view is saturated by emptiness. Thus, these appearances, too, are ascertained solely as empty, nonexistent, and ungrounded. There is bliss in the emptiness. The dominant realization of causality and emptiness is called "the yoga that is free of conceptual elaboration."

Yang Gönpa says: [821]

> Even though the essential nature of luminosity and emptiness is seen, if you are not free of all traces of the grasping of the recognition of emptiness, you have not differentiated between meditative experience and realization; so that is the small stage of freedom from conceptual elaboration.

The Great Instructions states:

> There are small, medium, and great stages. Among them, in the first, you realize that appearances and the mind are simply of the essential nature of awareness, free of arising and cessation. However, a trace of grasping of the recognition of the facet of emptiness has crept in; and since you are not free of that, you have not really differentiated between meditative experience and realization. In subsequent consciousness, when this is not sustained with mindfulness, grasping onto friends and foes will not cease, and grasping onto objects is not severed. Thus, virtuous as well as nonvirtuous grasping occur, for the disengagement from the practice of Mahāmudrā is nonvirtue, and not disengaging from

> it is virtue. [822] The scriptures do not speak much of seeing the truth in this phase.

There is also a considerable degree of confusion while sleeping and dreaming, and there are little ups and downs in your spiritual practice. Lord Phagmo Drüpa says, "With the medium stage rootlessness is realized." Gyalwa Yang Gönpa says:

> At that time, the realization that the mind is free of arising and cessation is naked, ordinary consciousness; and appearances due to ideation and habitual propensities are bright and vivid. Awareness is empty, and movement is empty. They do not arise as real phenomena, they do not cease as unreal phenomena; and they do not remain as conventional phenomena. So they are free of arising, cessation, and remaining. The meaning of the three doors of liberation is seen. Due to the absence of mentally engaged nonvirtue, it is said there is genuine spiritual practice. Since this brings you to the undefiled path, it is the actual path of liberation. That realization becomes stable, and the degenerative stain of the element of recognition of grasping onto emptiness is utterly purified. Ordinary consciousness becomes objectless and lucid. [823] You are freed from the basic root of grasping onto appearances and grasping onto emptiness; so the medium stage of freedom from conceptual elaboration is said to be a rootless realization.

- Appearances do not truly arise—which counteracts the extreme of substantialism—nor do they cease as unreal phenomena—which counteracts the extreme of nihilism. Since the mind no longer engages with its objects by way of grasping, there is no nonvirtue, so genuine spiritual practice takes place. At this stage of practice, there are appearances, but due to the absence of grasping, there is no longer a sense of a subject/object duality. -

A *Doha* states:

> Who knows that very rootlessness?
> It is the foremost attainment due to the spiritual mentor's
> kindness.

The Great Instructions states:

> The medium stage of freedom from conceptual elaboration entails a coarse, experiential sense of the mind's freedom from arising, cessation, and remaining. Coarse stains of grasping onto emptiness are purified, and you are freed from the sense of purity or

> craving. Ordinary consciousness becomes objectless and resplendent. All ideation and all mental afflictions of grasping onto appearances and emptiness are groundless and rootless, and it is enough simply for them to recognize their own nature in their own state. External objects are still not quite fathomed, so there is a little unease with respect to appearances. You wonder, "Whence do these arise? They are empty, but these appearances cease, and they no longer act as dependently related events." When such thoughts, entailing slight hopes and fears, arise during subsequent consciousness and while dreaming, various states of confusion and non-confusion occur. [824] The consciousness subsequent to that is called recognition. You then remain effortlessly in the state of recognition in meditative equipoise.

– In terms of the five paths, the culmination of the first of the four *yoga*s, single-pointedness, corresponds to the four stages of the path of preparation. At this stage, there is not yet a direct realization of ultimate truth. Freedom from conceptual elaboration, the second *yoga*, corresponds to the path of seeing, which is the third path, as well as the path of meditation, the fourth path. –

Götsangwa says:

> In the first stage of freedom from conceptual elaboration you realize that all phenomena are free of arising, cessation, and remaining. That serves as the basis for all excellent qualities. Extraordinary gladness arises, so the first ground is called the Very Joyful.

And:

> By realizing all phenomena as being free of conceptual elaborations, you are freed from the stains of mental afflictions that are eliminated on the path of meditation; so the second ground is called the Stainless.

And:

> Due to the blessing of your spiritual mentor, you realize that the mind is primordially free of all arising and cessation; so the third ground is called the Illuminating.

And:

> In this rootless realization the great qualities of the Buddha emerge, and the needs of sentient beings are fulfilled; so the fourth ground is called the Radiant.

And:

> Due to purifying the stains of habitual propensities, which are difficult to cleanse, the fifth ground is called Difficult to Purify. [825]

Lord Phagmo Drüpa says, "The great stage of freedom from conceptual elaboration cuts off superimpositions upon outer and inner phenomena." Gyalwa Yang Gönpa says:

> At that time the nature of conceptualization is bliss in the cessation of the stream of [impure] consciousness. Grasping onto joy and sorrow arises with respect to appearances. From this point, you differentiate between meditative experience and realization. Realization and meditative experience are mixed, and without the two being separate, realization purifies meditative experience. The benefits of realization are brought forth and sustained by means of meditative experience. Thus, that realization is ultimate. You realize that every possible outer and inner phenomenon included in *saṃsāra* and *nirvāṇa* is free of conceptual elaboration, and you comprehend that there is not even a tip of a hair that is not empty. Thus, phenomena appear to be identityless. Appearances and your own mind are realized by way of generic ideas, and you realize that appearances are not outside, but are your own mind. That is also the meaning of the assertion of the Cittamātrins. By realizing the nature of the spirit of awakening, which is free of conceptual elaboration, [826] you cut off superimpositions upon emptiness. That is ultimate wisdom. All phenomena are devoid of an inherent nature, and are unborn and ungrounded. At one time you are happy, but when there is a decline of the freshness of whatever ideation arises, you are a little unhappy. You have not realized more than one aspect of Mahāhudrā. The one taste arises, and there is no distinction between freedom and no freedom from conceptual elaboration or between emptiness and non-emptiness. Appearances are fresh, realization is fresh, and you are satisfied with whatever occurs, whatever appears, and whatever arises. That is the first realization of genuine Mahāmudrā. The clear light and freedom from conceptual elaboration are realized.

The Great Instructions states:

> In the great stage of freedom from conceptual elaboration, you cut off superimpositions upon all outer and inner phenomena. You know that appearances are your own mind. The mind and

appearances have no inherent nature, and you are free of any object on which to focus. This homogeneously joyful realization is like the center of space. Previously you were unhappy with respect to appearances, but happy with respect to awareness, and you engaged in practice with respect to awareness. Now you know that appearances are the mind. You know that the mind is empty. [827] That is the usefulness of emptiness. Emptiness is the foremost of meditations. Superimpositions with respect to emptiness are cut off and are seen as having no inherent nature, or as being ungrounded. The slight unhappiness due to the decline of freshness with respect to present appearances is asserted to be a groundless, delusive appearance.

At this point, meditation is unceasing during the daytime; and at night, at times realization arises and at times confusion arises in the subsequent consciousness involved with grasping onto dreams. That happens because of letting your mindfulness and aspiration decline during sleep. When there is agitation due to long-term, violent conditions, subsequent consciousness may carry on for a little while. From this point on, if meditation proceeds without the sense of an agent, you should never at any time be separated from it.

Unceasing mindfulness depends a little on undistracted, mindful apprehension, so mindfulness is important. Mindfulness is the criterion for differentiating between meditative equipoise free of conceptual elaboration on the one hand and subsequent consciousness on the other. The only thing standing between freedom from conceptual elaboration and both *saṃsāra* and *nirvāṇa* is the presence or absence of mindfulness. I say mindfulness is the most important. [828] If grasping does not intrude on anything, even constant hatred is empty of itself. If grasping intrudes without recognition being present, mental afflictions and ideation appear as if they were nonexistent, and that is ignorance.

When you are not separated from recognition, the stream of appearances as mental afflictions comes to a stop, and yet there is nothing to reject or affirm. As an indication of that, you have no sense of seeking emptiness apart from whatever appears. The appearances to consciousness subsequent to pure realization are limpid and immaculate. You will not always remain in that state, so rely on mindful apprehension. It is difficult to apprehend each thought with mindfulness, so rely on unceasing mindfulness.

If you are not harmed by daily circumstances, that is called the realization of the great stage of freedom from conceptual

> elaboration. Then you realize that the essential nature of the mind is free of arising, cessation, and remaining. You see beyond the intellect. You renounce the world. You feel no jealousy for others. Many qualities such as extrasensory perception arise. [829] During the post-meditative state, appearances arise as illusions. The nature of the spirit of awakening is realized. You are free of hopes and fears. The root of grasping is cut. The eighty-two obscurations on the path of seeing are eliminated. You do not return to the cycle of existence. Apart from the power of prayers, you do not take birth in cyclic existence due to the influence of *karma*. When that happens, the essential nature of freedom from conceptual elaboration is seen, and that is called the perfection of ability and the achievement of excellent qualities. Here, too, the three cravings are cast off. You resort to solitude, a sealed meditation cell, and to the wilderness, and you cease speaking.

– Prior to this state, in meditation you had a sense of yourself as the person doing the meditation. Once you no longer have a sense of yourself as the agent, simply carry on and never be separated from that. As long as you are still on the path, you must exert some effort to maintain mindfulness so that the practice can progress. At this point, if grasping intrudes, afflictions will arise: they arise as if they were nonexistent, yet they are of the nature of ignorance.

We can resort to solitude and silence in a sealed meditation cell in the wilderness, but on the other hand, if we follow the practice of Dudjom Rinpoche, all appearances will be the pure appearances of the *nirmāṇakāya*. All sounds will be like the echoes of the Buddha's speech, and all thoughts will be expressions of the *dharmakāya*. If you can practice in that way throughout the course of the day and night, you will experience everything as one taste. Nothing must be abandoned, and nothing is to be sought.

With this reference to Dudjom Rinpoche's practice, you might think he was just a practitioner on the stage of generation, but this would be incorrect. In fact, he was an extraordinary Dzogchen practitioner. But how do these relate? First of all we cultivate a pure vision of appearances, sounds and mental events. With regard to each of these three, we can speak of the essence, the nature, and the pervasive compassion of all appearances, sounds, and mental activity. This ninefold practice stems from one essential nature, namely the nature of your own awareness. The nature of your own awareness is the essence of all these teachings on the Mahāmudrā and Dzogchen. –

Götsangwa says:

> With the mature realization of the small stage of freedom from conceptual elaboration, both *saṃsāra* and *nirvāṇa* are manifestly unborn, so the sixth ground is called the Manifesting.

And:

> The demarcation between the defiled and undefiled path of meditation is the medium stage of freedom from conceptual elaboration, so the seventh ground is the Gone Afar.

And:

> Being like the earth, the eighth ground is the Immovable Ground.

– The focus of the great Kagyü *siddhas*, who gained deep insight into Mahāmudrā, was not a conceptual understanding of the relationship between the ten grounds and the Four Stages of Yoga. However, many did gain thorough understanding, through practice, of the Four Yogas, particularly the first two. The fourth *yoga*, the *yoga* of non-meditation, is not discussed at much length because it is difficult to attain. Rather than concerning ourselves with a realization that we haven't accomplished and may be far off, it is better to turn our attention to that which we have a good chance of realizing. This also holds true for the fourth vision of the Leap-over, extinction into reality itself. Those who practice Dzogchen often do not discuss that stage because just from listening to teachings people can become pompous, thinking they have completely understood it or even attained it already! Since that level of attainment is so advanced, it is not important to gain a precise conceptual understanding of it, when, in fact, our own experience lags far behind. –

Gyalwang Chöjey says:

> The single-pointedness of freedom from conceptual elaboration is undistracted mindfulness of the essential nature of whatever appears; and that is the view of single-pointedness. The freedom from conceptual elaboration of the freedom from conceptual elaboration is the ungroundedness of any extreme of conceptual elaborations when you are observing anything. The one taste of the freedom from conceptual elaboration is the one taste in the state of the emptiness of everything. The non-meditation of the freedom from conceptual elaboration is achieving confidence in that and maintaining it constantly day and night.

– In terms of the single-pointed facet of the second *yoga*, freedom from conceptual elaboration, whatever experience you may have, whether it is in relationship to the arising of appearances or your practice of quiescence and insight, this very facet of undistracted mindfulness is the single-pointedness of freedom from conceptual elaboration. The facet of the freedom from conceptual elaboration of the freedom from conceptual elaboration implies that you realize emptiness in everything that is experienced or observed. In the mode of experience of the one taste of freedom from conceptual elaboration, you recognize the one nature of all dualities. In the course of mundane experience, we come across many dualities: *saṃsāra* and *nirvāṇa*, joy and sorrow, peacefulness and agitation, and so forth. The one taste doesn't imply that these experiences are nonexistent, but that they have one nature. In essence, those things we label as *saṃsāra* and *nirvāṇa*, joy and sorrow, and so on are essentially of the same nature. The non-meditation of the freedom from conceptual elaboration is achieving confidence in the previous realization and maintaining it constantly day and night. –

There are many people who have achieved the great and medium stages of experiential freedom from conceptual elaboration. Therefore, recognize your own experiential realization as if you were recognizing your own bowl. I encourage you to apply yourself to the practices taught for your own level.

CHAPTER ELEVEN

How to Progress Along the Grounds and Paths

Homage to Avalokiteśvara!

[832] These are the profound practical instructions of Avalokiteśvara on how to progress along the grounds and paths by practicing the Breakthrough to the ground and Mahāmudrā. From this point on, it is difficult to teach from experience, and those with experiential realization of the following stages are rare. Therefore, even if I do not explain this at great length, this will have to suffice. Be that as it may, some people with enthusiasm and good karmic fortune who meditate for a long time may be able to experience the one taste of experience. For their sake, and for the completeness of the Dharma for the general public, and for the benefit of hearing these teachings, I shall explain this in brief.

– The grounds refer to the ten *bodhisattva* grounds, and the paths are the five sequential paths to enlightenment. Since so few have attained the higher levels of such realization, it is difficult to find those who are qualified to teach from this stage forward. Moreover, the very nature of the realization itself is beyond concept and beyond articulation, so it is even difficult for those who have gained realization to speak about it. This is like giving a mute person a spoonful of sugar: such a person can't verbalize how it tastes even though it is directly experienced. –

The Tantra of the Great Āli Kāli River states: [833]

> Thirdly, due to the *samādhi* of proceeding with valor, there arise the realizations of the ten grounds, in which the manifold world is known to be of one taste. The Sons of the Jinas of the three times serve the needs of sentient beings. Upon achieving single-pointedness, your progress is unceasing.

Naro Paṇchen says, "Thirdly, the *yoga* of the one taste arises." Everything that appears arises as meditation, so it is all of one taste, with nothing to be rejected or accepted. You realize the characteristic of the mind-itself appearing as the array of *saṃsāra* and *nirvāṇa*.

Once you realize identitylessness, if you are dismissive of such things as reverence, veneration, and compassion, you have been carried away by waves mixed with the one taste. [834] Since you have not nondually recognized your own essential nature, only one aspect of emptiness has arisen, so your subsequent consciousness is empty. The limpid apprehension of emptiness has not been recognized with respect to objects, so there is the stain of meditative experience. The stains of habitual propensities have not been purified. When your awareness is not maintained with mindfulness, there is no realization and no apprehension, so you are not free.

By maintaining mindfulness with the appearance of the natural luminosity of the essential nature, there is attainment. Once thoughts and memories arise as meditation, nothing is apprehended as being separate from meditation, so [everything] is merged homogeneously. The two truths are integrated, as are meditative equipoise and the post-meditative state. So this is a time of meditating on the union of the mind-itself. Due to the absence of fettered volition, the aggregate of recognition is purified. You realize that grasping onto "I" and "mine" has no basis, so the afflicted mind is purified. Once meditative experience itself arises as realization, there is no distinction between meditative experience and realization, so the two are unified. From the empty absolute space of phenomena dependently related events arise as empty phenomena, so they are immaterial like space. The difference between meditative equipoise and the post-meditative state is that in the latter grasping occurs and in the former it does not. [835]

At this time generic ideas, as objects of understanding, are mistaken for experiences of realization, so it is important not to mix them together. In a state of expansive unity in which the six collections of consciousness are openly spacious, meditate chiefly on unity, and you will recognize the self-nature of appearances. Dagpo Rinpoche says,

"The *yoga* of one taste entails realizing the indivisibility of appearances and emptiness." The Great Brahmin [Saraha] says:

> Thirdly, you dissolve into the unmindful and the unborn.
> Nothing is different, and everything is one as great bliss.
> Thatness is indivisible like ice and water.

The Five Stages states:

> The union of a trainee, the union taught by Lawapa, the occasion of attaining confidence taught by Maitrīpa, the non-grasping *yoga* taught in *The Descent into Laṅkā Sūtra*, the meditative stabilization focused on suchness, and the meaning of the third empowerment are all synonymous.

– The third empowerment, the wisdom/gnosis empowerment, refers to both wisdom that is acquired and connate, primordial wisdom. One cultivates wisdom as well as the other perfections, whereas primordial wisdom is inborn. The crucial point of the third empowerment is the experience of the nonduality of connate bliss and emptiness. The significance of each empowerment is to purify mental afflictions. In our present state we tend to follow our habitual propensities with our body, speech, and mind. Because we act habitually, we really don't have freedom, so the purpose of the empowerments is to imbue us with the power to attain the four *kāyas* of the Buddha, which allows us to break out of our habitual propensities. The empowerments remove the stains of the body, speech, and mind, and they mature the mind, elements, and so forth. Finally, by being blessed by the *samayasattvas*, you arise as a *jñānasattva*.

The purpose of the first empowerment is to transform your body into the body of an enlightened being. With this vase empowerment, there is a maturation such that your ordinary body is purified and can arise as the deity's body. The second empowerment, the secret empowerment, enables you to transform your channels and vital energies through practices that purify the speech and ripen your experience, such that you hear all sounds as *mantras*. The purpose of the third empowerment is to yield the experience of connate bliss and emptiness. This wisdom/gnosis empowerment purifies all latent and residual impurities of the basic elements of the body. It also purifies the essential fluids of the body, and you are matured so that you experience great bliss and connate primordial wisdom. The fourth empowerment is the attainment of the union that transcends the intellect, and you are matured so that you can experience the expansive purity of the *dharmakāya*. –

Phagmo Drüpa says, "The small stage of the one taste unifies *saṃsāra* and *nirvāṇa*. [836] *The Great Instructions* states:

> At the stage of the one taste there is bliss regarding the emptiness, or the ungroundedness in any inherent nature, of all the phenomena arising on the stage of freedom from conceptual

> elaboration. Once all thoughts that arise are fresh, and the slight discomfort concerning appearances has been relieved, one enters the state called "the merging of *saṃsāra* and *nirvāṇa*." The reality of that does not cease, and there is no reification of these fresh appearances. Nor is there any grasping onto emptiness. There is no intellectual meditation on these external appearances as having no inherent nature, nor are there any dualistically appearing phenomena. In a manner that is not simply an intellectual conclusion, you realize that all dualities—including appearance and non-appearance, perceived appearances and emptiness, the stage of generation and the stage of completion, conventional and ultimate truth, *saṃsāra* and *nirvāṇa*, and joy and sorrow—are not different, but are indivisibly of the one taste of unity; and connate, primordial wisdom arises. Whatever fresh appearances and fresh thoughts arise, they are free of rejection and affirmation. [837]
>
> With self-cognizing, self-luminous, effortless, perfect mindfulness, the mind, mindfulness, and appearances manifest as causally related interdependent events, like fire and heat. The bliss regarding appearances is called "the *yoga* of the one taste."

– Prior to this stage, when you are actually meditating, dwelling in the emptiness of phenomena, your mind is peaceful and contented. But when you need to engage with the appearances, you may be somewhat disturbed. However, at this stage one is beyond that: the stains giving rise to such discomfort have been purified, and so one attains the state called "the merging of *saṃsāra* and *nirvāṇa*." At this point one transcends all contrived, intellectual understanding of appearances and emptiness; all appearances of duality have vanished. –

Gyalwa Yang Gönpa says:

> Thus, upon sustaining the realization of freedom from conceptual elaboration, you recognize your own essential nature as naturally liberated right where it is, with no distinctions between freedom and non-freedom from conceptual elaboration, emptiness and non-emptiness, auspicious and non-auspicious occasions, or negation and affirmation with respect to anything in the entire phenomenal world of *saṃsāra* and *nirvāṇa*. Although manifold phenomena appear, they are realized as the essential nature of a single realization. This is the *yoga* of the one taste of the manifold world.

In the small stage of the one taste there is a unification of *saṃsāra* and *nirvāṇa*: all dualities—including appearances and emptiness, the ultimate and the conventional, the stage of generation and the stage of completion, and so on—manifest as the union of the indivisible essential nature of a single realization. Appearances and emptiness have never been separate, [838] so all the qualities of the path are complete in either appearances or in emptiness, and they are nondually unified. So that is the great union.

Even though the manifold world is thus realized to be of one taste, if there is still a semblance of grasping onto that, or if there is a slight stain of a recognition of that experience of integration, that is the small stage of the one taste. *The Great Instructions* states:

> In the small stage of the one taste, appearances and emptiness are indivisibly merged, and everything is realized as the innate nature. Fresh consciousness of whatever arises, with no distinction between emptiness and non-emptiness, is enough. You realize that all the qualities of the path are complete in either the appearance or the emptiness of whatever is known as a phenomenon; and the body, appearances, and the mind are indivisible. Even though you ascertain your mind at times, there is still a slight sense of an object of experience and the apprehension of it. Afterwards, the ground and so on appear to be firm and solid, and there is discomfort in your practice concerning the appearances of the six collections of consciousness that are disturbed by violent, objective circumstances. At times there are fragmented appearances of a duality between the apprehended and the apprehender; [839] and it is as if there is a slight inability to practice Dharma in secret. Even in "illusionlike" subsequent appearances and in the dream-state there is occasional, fragmented confusion and grasping. At times you experience a sense of the indivisibility of the body, appearances, and the mind; you may not concern yourself with causality, and your reverence, veneration, and compassion may be somewhat feeble. So do not go that way.

– The reference to "fresh consciousness" means that this state of consciousness is unmixed with any fabrications or artificial contrivances of the conventional mind. It is free of conceptual elaboration and adulteration; this is the innate nature. Where is this nature found? It is already present, but thus far we have failed to recognize it, so it is like the sky obscured by the clouds or ice covered water. As soon as the clouds vanish into the sky, you clearly see they were none other than the sky. The ice may cover up the water below, yet when it melts, it is seen to be the same as the water below.

Within the context of Mahāmudrā and Dzogchen, the term "fresh" when modifying consciousness or appearances doesn't mean "new." Rather it indicates primordial purity. Even if gold is buried in the ground, its nature remains primordially pure. Similarly, the sun's primordial nature of luminosity cannot be obscured or tainted by anything else. So too, fresh consciousness, our own innate nature, may be obscured, but it cannot be stained. It is not that obscurations somehow influence that which is obscured. Even if the whole of *saṃsāra* tried to sully the innate nature of your own consciousness, it could not, but that innate nature can be hidden. Similarly, even if you piled all the dirt in the world on a piece of gold, it wouldn't affect its nature; and even if the entire sky is covered with clouds, the sun is in no way affected.

At this stage of the third *yoga*, there may still be some trace of craving, some trace of meditative experience, some dualistic grasping onto experience. In this context, the objects of the six senses of consciousness may still appear to have their normal qualities of firmness and solidity. Fire will still appear to be hot; wind will still appear to be light and motile. Again, if reverence and compassion begin to wane and one's conscientiousness regarding actions and their consequences diminishes, these should be regarded as flaws in one's practice. Proper practice actually enhances devotion, compassion, and conscientiousness. –

Yang Gönpa says:

> At the medium stage of the one taste, the root of subject/object dualism is completely cut, but that realization has not become stable. Thus, the one who realizes that unifies the manifold world as one taste, and the tendency to grasp onto objects is utterly purified. Thus, material phenomena are not left over outside, awareness is not left over inside, and appearances and the mind are simply one. The mental engagement of the medium stage of the one taste manifests those characteristics.

The Great Instructions states:

> At the medium stage of the one taste, the reified recognition of your earlier experience is merged into one. Thus, once that is purified, material phenomena are not left over outside, [840] and awareness is not left over inside. Appearances and the mind are simply unified, and the root of subject/object duality is completely cut. Such grasping arises in dependence upon objects, but now all apprehended objects arise in their own innate luminosity. When they are nonexistent [as external objects], consciousness no longer grasps onto them. With one consciousness to which apprehended objects appear, everything arises as one's aid. Due to objects such as forms appearing nonconceptually, the apprehension of forms arises objectively.
>
> Although there is no difference between the small stage of the one taste and the essential nature of union, the experience has become more stable. There arises a sense of the unification of the body, appearances, and the mind. There is less confusion than

> before during subsequent consciousness and dreams, and the grasping of reification does not occur strongly.
>
> Nevertheless, while dreaming and on other occasions, depending on whether or not perfect mindfulness is distracted, illusion-like, grasped appearances become indistinct. Here is the difference between [841] mindfulness of an apprehended object and perfect mindfulness: [in the former case] when there is distraction, you sense that there is distraction; and afterwards, even though your spiritual practice is vividly present in your mindstream, that is mindfulness of an apprehended object; and that is a sign that earlier grasping has returned. The occurrence of vigilance in your practice of simple mindfulness without grasping onto realization is called *perfect mindfulness of realized phenomena;* and even if earlier recognition is not maintained, this is a sign that grasping has not intruded.

Lord Phagmo Drüpa says, "From the great stage of the one taste, phenomena are calmed in equality."

– What type of phenomena are calmed in equality? Everything other than fresh consciousness is calmed leaving only the appearance of the mind as totally fresh. –

Gyalwa Yang Gönpa says:

> At the great stage of the one taste, all possible phenomena are calmed in the unborn state, and that is the realization of the one taste. Due to the arising of manifold appearances, all the phenomena of *saṃsāra* and *nirvāṇa* are present as instances of emptiness. That is called "the manifold one taste," and it is a realization of the indivisibility of the profound and the vast. That is the *samādhi* which in the *sūtras* is called "the appearance of profound phenomena" and "the *samādhi,* free of conceptual elaboration, of the equality of all phenomena." [842]
>
> All phenomena included in the phenomenal world of *saṃsāra* and *nirvāṇa* are present in the essential nature of the nondual realization of them just as they are in their own state, with undiminishing freshness and unchanging radiance. Therefore, whether in meditative equipoise or in the attainment of freedom, there is not a trace of alteration by antidotes; and that is the great stage of the one taste.

– Just as all the water in the world, whether from a mountain brook, a river, or a lake, flows into the ocean and becomes of one taste, so, too, when one gains realization of emptiness, the emptiness of each individual phenomenon is but one emptiness. This is the manifold one taste. The attainment of freedom does not refer to *nirvāṇa,* but freedom from hindrances such as grasping and craving. You are free of them, yet nothing has really been remedied or altered. This is the great stage of the one taste. –

The Great Instructions states:

> At the great stage of the one taste, all possible phenomena within *saṃsāra* and *nirvāṇa* are realized to be unborn in the state of equality. Appearances and the mind are known to be one, and the experience of your earlier recognition becomes stable. Then reification of these unceasing appearances is purified. As a result, that nondual realization constantly arises throughout the day and night. Occasionally a slight experience of non-ascertaining perception occurs with respect to the sheer luminosity of nonconceptual appearances. There is no cessation of luminous appearances free of grasping, and at times realization arises in the nature of the entirety of phenomena within *saṃsāra* and *nirvāṇa.* The continuum of dualistic grasping is cut, [843] and merely illusionlike subsequent appearances are present without any recognition entailing grasping. Rather, they are like apparitions created by an illusionist.
>
> Subtle dualistic appearances may not stop, even though you know they do not exist, or indistinct dreams entailing dualistic grasping may occur. At times you may not dream at all. These subtle dualistic appearances indistinctly occur as the displays, appearances, or empty visions of purification in the experience of your practice. They are said to appear as the empty, subsequent consciousness of the one taste. In reality, they are residual displays of antidotes. Furthermore, as long as there is an experiential sense of meditating, other events will automatically occur as a result. Subtle dualistic appearances are impurities. Nevertheless, some nonconceptual appearances arise as manifold, natural displays which appear but are not ascertained. Depending on whether or not mindfulness is distracted, you may feel discomfort in sustaining the sense of stillness, and fragmented feelings of sheer luminosity may occur. They are residues of that which is to be eliminated. [844] As long as they are present, events other than those subtle [dualistic appearances] may automatically take place as a result. They are called the subtle illusions of the great stage of the one taste.
>
> Therefore, whatever appearances arise, there is nothing to eliminate or accept and nothing to negate or affirm. You know your own essential nature as empty luminosity, as innate equality without an object. All phenomena included among dualities such as

> *saṃsāra* and *nirvāṇa* are realized to be of one taste. The eight mundane concerns are equalized, and all dependent relationships become apparent. As for the understanding regarding appearances, this is called "the arising of the vision and qualities of the perfected power of the essential nature of the one taste." [845]

– At this stage, subtle appearances may occasionally arise, but you don't actually ascertain them. From an illusionist's perspective, the magical displays of elephants, tigers, and so forth that he creates appear, yet he knows they are not truly existent. For spectators, though, they appear to be real, and they respond to them as such. Even if you know that an illusionist is conjuring up a tiger and you aren't taking it to be real, out of habit you may still respond with some fear. This indicates that there is still a trace of your previous habit patterns. Similarly, recognizing a dream as a dream and still responding with attachment and anger to objects and events within the dream is an indication that apprehending the dream as a dream alone is not sufficient. Only by completely realizing the nature of the dream do attachment and anger cease.

In different phases of dream *yoga*, you practice transforming events and objects in the dream. For example, if there are many things, you change them into one. You may be dreaming that a tiger is crouching ready to attack you, but you transform it into a purring kitten. As soon as you no longer feeling threatened, fear and anger vanish. Likewise, while practicing the stage of generation, if something threatening arises, you simply transform it into your chosen deity. However, upon attaining the complete realization of the empty nature of the phenomena in the dream, there is no need to implement any change whatsoever. You let whatever arises arise, because you've realized the utter lack of true existence of phenomena. Therefore, there is no incentive to change it; instead you've realized its actual nature.

What is the nature of dualistic grasping of the post-meditative state or dream state? It is the residue of your previous application of antidotes applied in your spiritual practice. For example, in the stage of generation when there is grasping, you apply the antidote of trying to see everything as pure. That is an antidote that lingers on. –

Gyalwang Chöjey says:

> In the single-pointedness of the one taste you cut off superimpositions upon all appearances and sounds in the state of equality. In the freedom from conceptual elaboration of the one taste there is no separation in the state of equality among all the conceptual elaborations of grasping onto things as being different or dual. In the one taste of the one taste that equality completely pervades all experience and involvement with all phenomena. In the non-meditation of the one taste when stability is attained in that, it continues throughout the day and night.

The meaning of Lord Naropa's statement that fourthly there arises the *yoga* of non-meditation is stated in both *The Tantra of Inconceivable Mysteries* and *The Tantra of the Great Āli Kāli River*:

> Fourth, by applying yourself to the practice of non-meditation
> With the *vajra*-like *samādhi*,
> Incalculable omniscient *buddhas* and pure realms are seen,
> And, without seeking it, that is the great, supreme, spontaneous Dharma. [846]

The Great Brahmin's *Vajra Song of Immortality* states:

> The fruition that transcends the intellect is accomplished without desiring it.
> Among the best of medicines, it is like *soma*.[102]

All experiential feelings of meditating on emptiness and so forth are purified, so the purification of experience is non-meditation. There is a constant realization that the mind-itself variously appears as *saṃsāra* and *nirvāṇa*. If the lack of recognition of nonconceptuality is not purified, that is a cloudlike obscuration over the sun of non-meditation. Moreover, subsequent consciousness arises as objectless compassion. The lack of recognition of nonconceptuality obscures the innate reality, so that is a stain of subsequent consciousness. With the purification of the stain of cognitive [obscurations] there is no difference between maintaining mindfulness and either seeing or not seeing the essential nature; so the duality of separation and attainment becomes one. The primordial wisdom of insight becomes constant, so one abides solely in meditative equipoise. At all times there is indivisible insight into the absolute space of innate equality, so this is a time when the mind-itself becomes manifest. Ethically neutral non-conceptuality is purified, [847] so the stream of the aggregate of consciousness, the ground consciousness, and nondual primordial wisdom are uninterrupted. Thus, realization is constant. The dependently related events of the nondual absolute space and primordial wisdom, as well as the entire array of phenomena are perceived as they are. However, due to the absence of dualistic appearances, one knows dependently related events to be groundless.

The difference between the one taste and non-meditation has to do with whether or not subtle dualistic appearances have been purified and whether or not you exert the effort of mindfulness. At this point there is no distinction between meditative equipoise and subsequent consciousness. The most subtle of dualistic appearances and dysfunctions are purified. It is important not to be stuck in evaluations of experience. Meditate chiefly on nonduality in a state in which the grasping of mindfulness has vanished. It is said that your own spontaneous, essential nature is known.

The details concerning the four stages are found in the annotations by Gyatönpa Chökyi Zangpo, [848] which were cited by Drungchen Kün-ga Namgyal in his written commentary. I have unraveled them so that they can be easily understood. In the *yoga* of non-meditation of Lord Dagpo Rinpoche, whatever appears and whatever arises is seen to be of one essential nature, so he says that all thoughts and memories turn into meditation. *The Five Stages* states:

> The union of non-trainees, the complete purity taught by Lawapa, the great *yoga* taught by Śawaripa, the time at which awareness is liberated into thatness as taught by Maitrīpa, the *yoga* free of conceptual elaboration, the meditative stabilization of the Tathāgata taught in *The Descent into Laṅkā Sūtra,* and the meaning of the fourth empowerment are all said to be the same.

– The fourth empowerment enables us to enter into a state of meditation beyond intellect. Furthermore, this empowerment of the precious word is meant to enable us to realize the pervasive purity of all phenomena, as nothing other than the *dharmakāya*.

In the general context of *tantra,* there is the basis of purification, that which is to be purified, that which purifies, the purifier, and the fruit of the purification. The basis of purification is your own *buddha*-nature. What is to be purified? Everything that obscures your *buddha*-nature. The four empowerments are the purifiers. For the first empowerment, the vase empowerment, the basis of purification is our own aggregates and the surrounding environment, which are in fact primordially pure. For the speech empowerment the basis is all speech, letters, syllables, and the vital energies. The basis of purification for the wisdom/gnosis empowerment is the male and female elements and the *bindus*. The basis of purification for the fourth empowerment is the nature of your own awareness, which is as yet unknown, but is actually present as the *dharmakāya*. –

The Great Instructions states:

> Concerning the *yoga* of non-meditation, by familiarizing yourself with that, the mere illusions of dualistic appearances to subsequent consciousness that occur until the great stage of the one taste are purified. There is simple non-distraction of perfect mindfulness of the phenomena that are realized; and the slight stains of grasping onto emptiness, the maintenance of the effort of perfect mindfulness, and all subtle dualistic appearances are purifed. [849] Then a state of spontaneity is maintained. There is joy in

> the realization that is no object of meditation and no act of meditating. Even without meditating, everything unceasingly arises as meditation. Everything arises as meditation whether or not you are in meditative equipoise, whether or not phenomena are sustained with mindfulness, and whether or not there is distraction.
>
> The clear light of meditation regarding the character of the mind and the clear light of death—that is, the mother and child clear light—are unified. This is like the sky clear of clouds, or like water free of ripples. In the clear light, the two are unified, and they are the *dharmakāya* alone. This is free of anything to be rejected or accepted and free of any object or action. You sense that there is no difference between dying and not dying, and you suddenly gain certain knowledge of there being no difference between meditative equipoise and subsequent consciousness.
>
> Others see you as being surrounded by *ḍākinīs* and you are seen in multiple bodies. To reverent and devout individuals you appear in the very form of a *buddha*. Whatever you say becomes Dharma. Whatever you do with your body, it instills faith in sentient beings. Wherever you stay, blessings arise. Even if you remain alone, you feel no depression or fatigue. Whatever land you visit, you experience joy and goodness. [850] At times it may appear to others that you are attracted to external activity and to mundane things, but you are actually displaying your spirit of awakening. You realize the causal relations between actions and their consequences, and you know that everything is unborn. You have no craving for any location, and you have no more thoughts of embarrassment or of things being either clean or dirty. All *vīras* and *ḍākinīs* make offerings to you, and they help you fulfill the needs of sentient beings. You become a wish-fulfilling jewel for everyone.

Lord Phagmo Drüpa says, "With the small stage of non-meditation, you are free of an object of meditation and the act of meditating." Gyalwa Yang Gönpa says:

> Thus, the one taste is the union of a trainee. Non-meditation is the union of a non-trainee. Beyond that realization, there is nothing with which you need to be acquainted, so you inwardly realize non-meditation. The absence of an object of meditation and the act of meditating in the small stage of non-meditation entails the utter purification of the agent who meditates, or the agent who gains realization. Thus, there is no object of meditation or act of meditating, no object of realization or act of realizing, no

> object of knowledge or act of knowing, [851] and no object of mindfulness or act of being mindful. There are no such things on which to meditate, and after completely purifying the stains of experience, there appears to be no distinction between meditative equipoise and subsequent consciousness throughout the day and no distinction between distraction and non-distraction. In the small stage of non-meditation, at night there remains a slight stain of the grasping of non-recognition.

The Great Instructions states:

> In the small stage of non-meditation, everything you do arises as meditation, without needing to maintain it with mindfulness. You are free of an object of meditation and the act of meditating. Everything arises as meditation without reliance upon whether or not you remain in meditative equipoise. The previous illusionlike, subsequent appearances at the time of the great stage of the one taste become more subtle. Then it is not necessary to maintain perfect mindfulness. They becomes purified by themselves.
>
> The mental affliction called "the non-recognition of the nonconceptuality of subsequent appearances" and all thoughts that are residues of ignorance are purified by the stage of the one taste. The ethically neutral, nonconceptual ground consciousness does not transform into primordial wisdom. [852] That mere non-recognition of nonconceptuality itself is the only thing to be eliminated, and it is an aspect of ignorance. Due to that, illusionlike [appearances] occasionally occur for brief moments. Your own essential nature is nonconceptually present, so there is no need to apply antidotes. It is possible that slight stains of grasping may occur occasionally while you are sleeping; and since they are not recognized as your own luminosity, they are cognitive obscurations.

Lord Phagmo Drüpa says, "With the medium stage of non-meditation, a state of spontaneity is reached." Lord Götsangwa says:

> During the daytime as well, the mere illusions of subsequent appearances last for just the duration of a finger snap. The essential nature of that is naturally purified, without reference to anything being maintained with mindfulness.

Yang Gönpa says:

> In the medium stage of non-meditation, a state of spontaneity is reached. Here the fruition returns to the ground, there is a meeting

> with the mother, the three embodiments, and your wishes are fulfilled. There is no difference whatever between day and night, being asleep or not asleep, [853] maintaining something with mindfulness or cultivating recognition. In the one great meditative equipoise, there is a self-obscuration of primordial wisdom and a dewdrop of ignorance, together with a slight stain that obscures knowledge. That is the medium stage of non-meditation.

– Even at this advanced stage, there is the most subtle trace of ignorance that obscures primordial wisdom. When one has reached the medium stage of the *yoga* of non-meditation, obscurations still remain. We still fail to recognize our own nature fully, and this ignorance is the stain that obscures primordial wisdom. The actual nature of primordial wisdom itself is, of course, unstained, but it is our failure to recognize our own nature that creates the stain.

As Andzom Rinpoche, one of the great Dzogchen masters of Eastern Tibet, declared: the primordial nature of being is not grounded substantially in any kind of reality; it is of the very nature of spontaneous presence. However, at this medium stage of the practice of non-meditation, you may momentarily fail to recognize your own nature, and this implies that phenomenological knowledge is obscured. This is like a subtle trickle of water running under a sheet of ice. Once this subtle obscuration is dispelled in meditative equipoise, you achieve the *vajra*-like *samādhi*, in which the mind is self-purified. This purified state remains constant throughout the day and night. It is as natural and spontaneous as the blossoming of a flower. –

The Great Instructions states:

> In the medium stage of non-meditation, you firmly reach a state of spontaneity. Your experience becomes more stable than before, and you realize the primordial, spontaneous presence of both *saṃsāra* and *nirvāṇa*. Free of all grasping, once you reach that innate state, the wheel of the primordial wisdom of meditative equipoise turns day and night. The subtle traces of nonconceptual non-recognition of subsequent appearances that emerge by the power of that primordial wisdom of meditative equipoise become more subtle than before. They appear for just the duration of a finger snap, with no time to engage with objects, and they are released in the illusionlike natural luminosity. At all times, the nonconceptual essential nature appears as its own natural luminosity. [854] As a result, all states of meditative equipoise bearing the stains of dysfunction and their most subtle residues become undefiled, while subsequent appearances, such as the eightfold path of the *āryas*, remain defiled.

– In this medium stage, subsequent appearances arise in the post-meditative state, but they are very subtle and fleeting like the snap of a finger. In fact, they appear so briefly that there is no time to grasp onto them. This nonconceptual non-recognition is neutral. At this stage there is still a distinction between meditative equipoise, which is undefiled, and the post-meditative state, which, at this point, still has a very subtle defilement. –

Lord Phagmo Drüpa says, "With the great stage of non-meditation, the two clear lights are merged." Gyalwa Yang Gönpa says:

> In the great stage of non-meditation, the clear lights are united as one. The primordial wisdom of the absolute space of phenomena and the absolute space of the reality of the *sugatas* are indivisible, so the clear light of the path and the natural clear light are united as one. Then in the great clear light, primordial wisdom free of conceptual elaboration, ignorance, knowledge, and the stains of knowledge are utterly purified. Thus, neither in this life nor afterwards is there even subtle grasping onto karmic causes and effects. You and others and *saṃsāra* and *nirvāṇa* are unified. In the great stage of non-meditation, the clear lights are united as one, so that is the union of a non-trainee.

– The primordial wisdom of the absolute space of phenomena, which refers to the nature of reality as a whole, and the absolute space of the reality of the *buddhas* are indivisible. This implies the indivisibility of *saṃsāra* and *nirvāṇa*. *Saṃsāra* and *nirvāṇa* are unified, but it's not as if you transform two separate substances into one. Rather, neither has ever been grounded in any kind of separate reality. Therefore, if *saṃsāra* is primordially ungrounded in reality, it goes without saying that *nirvāṇa* is also ungrounded. And this pertains to all other dualities as well. If one element of a duality is ungrounded in reality, its opposite must be equally ungrounded. This is the recognition of primordial unity. –

The Great Instructions states:

> In the great stage of non-meditation, all consciousness is transformed into primordial wisdom. [855] The sword of primordial wisdom utterly cuts through the cognitive obscurations, together with the stains of dysfunctions. The immaculate, absolute space of phenomena, which is the mother clear light, and the son clear light of mirrorlike primordial wisdom are united. The union of a non-trainee and supreme enlightenment become manifest. There is no distinction between meditative equipoise and the post-meditative state. By coming to uncontrived, innate reality, the natural potency of the connate *dharmakāya* is wholly perfected

for your own sake. As a result, the two *rūpakāyas*, which are for the sake of others, fulfill the needs of the world until the cycle of existence is empty. Thus, the culminating path becomes manifest.

In non-meditation, meditative equipoise opens up vastly. For the most part there is no fluctuation away from meditative equipoise. Thus, with nothing of which to be mindful and nothing on which to meditate, experience is purified. You are free of the effort of mindful apprehension including recognition. You achieve the state of extinction into reality-itself, and you are freed from reified appearances.

When non-meditation is first realized, [856] all the great qualities of a *buddha* converge like clouds, so the tenth ground is called "the Cloud of Dharma." In the medium stage of non-meditation, a state of spontaneity is firmly reached, and it is said that one's experience becomes more stable than it was before. The liberation that arises as natural luminosity is said to be the special path of the end of the continuum of the ten grounds.

– In the earlier phases of the *yoga* of non-meditation there is a distinction between meditation and non-meditation, but in the culmination of this *yoga*, there is no distinction at all. As one progresses along the path by developing quiescence and insight, the various afflictive and cognitive obscurations are purified. Then the child clear light, which is the clear light of the path, comes to its culmination; it becomes manifest and is directly realized. At that point, one recognizes that the clear light of the path is nothing other than the clear light of the ground, the mother clear light—this is recognizing one's own nature. There has never been any obscuration in the eternally pure motherlike clear light. Implicit within it are the two *kāyas*—the *dharmakāya*, for yourself, and the *rūpakāya*, for others. But at this point of the practice, the great stage of non-meditation, these manifest in the recognition of the unity of the clear light: the path clear light and the ground clear light. This is transforming the *buddha*-nature, or the fruition, into the path.

The distinction of the child and mother clear lights can be understood in the context of the four visions of the Leap-over—the direct perception of reality, progress in meditative experience, consummate awareness, and finally, the extinction into reality-itself. Of the four, the first three correspond to the progression of the child clear light, which becomes more and more manifest. With the fourth vision, there is nothing more for the child to do. Or to use the analogy of the sun and the clouds, the clouds that have obscured the sun have completely vanished and the sun blazes forth clearly. The clear light that becomes manifest in the fourth stage is nothing other than the child clear light; and that is nothing other than the mother clear light. This is the recognition of the identity of the ground clear light and path clear light. –

In the great stage of non-meditation, once the mother [and child] clear lights are unified, there is no distinction between meditative equipoise and the post-meditative state. By coming to the uncontrived, innate reality, the *dharmakāya* is achieved for your own sake. Due to perfecting the natural potency of innate reality, the two *rūpakāyas*, which are for the sake of others, fulfill the needs of the world until the cycle of existence is empty. This is the eleventh ground, the Universal Light. Chöjey says, "Non-meditation, the eleventh ground, is the culminating path," and "That is the culminating path among the five paths." Gyalwang Chöjey says:

> The single-pointedness of non-meditation is the meditative equipoise of single-pointedness in a state that is free of an object of meditation and the act of meditation. [857] The freedom from conceptual elaboration of non-meditation transcends the intellect and is free of all conceptual elaborations of the intellect. The one taste of non-meditation is the one taste of the whole of cyclic existence and peace in the absolute space of non-meditation; and there is not the slightest trace of differentiation in that. The non-meditation of non-meditation is the attainment of stability in that. The attainment of stability in the one taste and lower stages entails temporary integrations of meditative equipoise and the post-meditative state. The attainment of stability of non-meditation is the ultimate integration of meditative equipoise and the post-meditative state. This is comparable to the attainments of stability in the stage of generation and the stage of completion.

CHAPTER TWELVE

Conclusion

Homage to Avalokiteśvara!

[860] These are the profound practical instructions of Avalokiteśvara. At the end of these thirty chapters of instructions on the union of Mahāmudrā and Dzogchen I should synthesize the meaning of these teachings. Orgyen Rinpoche says, "The synthesis of the meaning is for the sake of bringing delight in the teachings." The way to synthesize the meaning is suggested by Orgyen Rinpoche's prophecy, "My speech emanation by the name of Dīpaṃkara will be a *bodhisattva* who will purify the land of Tibet." In accordance with that prophecy, the venerable lord, the glorious Atiśa, who was like the crown jewel among five hundred *paṇḍits* in India, came to Tibet.

At that time, the great translator Rinchen Zangpo, [861] who was an emanation of Mañjuśrī, had studied and trained under more than twenty *paṇḍits;* and he was like the snowy source of all the streams of Dharma of the New Translation School. He thought, "Nowadays there is no one with greater qualities than mine, and I have nothing to ask the Paṇḍit [Atiśa]. However, due to an auspicious sign in a dream, I shall simply pay my respects." In a dream that night a white man appeared and told him, "You are being very pompous about your service to sentient beings. There are still many questions for you to ask. Even if you combined all the translators and *paṇḍits* in one, this single individual would not have all the excellent qualities of this *paṇḍit.* Tibet has not received all the oral instructions." He then disappeared.

[862] Rinchen Zangpo then took the long journey to meet Atīśa and invited him to his place, where he gave him a seat equal in height to his own. In his shrine room on the ground floor were the deities of the common [Hīna]yāna, in a room on the second floor were those of the Mahāyāna, and on the third floor were images of deities of the Mantrayāna. Atīśa composed verses of praise for all of them. For the first time experiencing faith in Atīśa's words, poetry and so on, the translator removed the three layers of his own seat so that he had no cushion at all. The translator asked him many questions, and hearing many things for the first time, he was struck by Atīśa's knowledge, and his pride collapsed. To all the questions Atīśa asked of the translator, he replied only that he knew.

Atīśa was also pleased with the translator, and he commented, "With someone like you in Tibet, there was no need for anyone to ask me to come to Tibet." He then asked, "Translator, if you combine all those teachings in one meditation session and practice them, how can you do it?" The translator replied, "I do not combine the *yānas*. Rather, I keep each one distinct, and without mixing them, I practice each one by itself." [863] Lord Atīśa then remarked, "This indicates that you, the translator, are wrong. There is a need for me to be in Tibet after all!"

That night the translator meditated during three sessions, visualizing the three *yānas* in progressive order in three places in his body. The Paṇḍit knew what he was doing and told him, "Translator, that's no good. You won't get anywhere!" Rinchen Zangpo asked him, "Well then, how do you do it?"

"Whatever I say, wherever I am, whomever I accompany, whatever I am doing, I make the ethical discipline of the *vinaya* my foundation. Since all sentient beings have been my mother, I must meditate on them as such. I train in the pure view of seeing them as my mother. As the deities are unborn, I meditate on them as such. If you do not know how to combine those, you will not obtain the essence."

Lord Atīśa also said:

> Our Teacher has well taught
> That ethical discipline is the basis of all excellent qualities.
> The spirit of awakening, which is linked with great
> compassion,
> Is praised above all. [864]
> Enlightenment is certain with the union of the stages of
> generation and completion,
> Which are not fettered by the signs of good thoughts.

These are the tasks of individuals of small and great capacity
And medium capacity as well:
Emphasize [meditation on] impermanence, making offerings, and requesting [that the wheel of Dharma be turned].
If you abandon selfishness, you are following the Jina's counsel.
Extensive discussions of this are for the learned.
Righteous are those individuals who synthesize the essence
And practice it.
Noble, I say, are those conscientious people
Who are not dismissive of actions and their consequences.
Knowing everything, but clinging to one thing is a flaw of scholars.
Not engaging in practice is a mistake.
Not adopting [the good] and rejecting [evil]
Makes for an empty facade of nobility.
Live with wisdom, Rinchen Zangpo!
This is the admonishment of the Great Compassionate One.

Certainty arose in the mind of the translator Rinchen Zangpo, and he made a vow to spend the rest of his life in meditative retreat. As a result of his practice, he moved on to Khasarpaṇa without leaving his body behind. Lord Atiśa also gave practical instructions on practicing the four classes of *tantras* on a single cushion, [865] and he composed Indian treatises on the fivefold practice. Accordingly, the glorious Phagmo Drüpa had 5,800 illustrious disciples, all of whom were liberated solely by means of the fivefold practice. The Protector Jigten Sumgön says:

Mahāmudrā is like a lion,
But without the fivefold practice it is like a blind man.

– The fivefold practices are: (1) cultivating the spirit of awakening, (2) meditating on your own body as being that of a deity, (3) meditating on your spiritual mentor as the deity, (4) cultivating the view of non-conceptuality, and (5) sealing your practice with prayers of dedication. Practicing the four classes of *tantras* on a single cushion means to do so in a single meditation session. –

It is reported that by training his disciples by way of the fivefold practice, 180,000 of them attained extrasensory perception and supernormal abilities. Regarding that practice it is said:

Cultivate the spirit of awakening and your chosen deity,
Meditate on your spiritual mentor and Mahāmudrā,
And practice the Dharma of dedication.

There are no kinds of practices of the Sūtrayāna or Mantrayāna according to the New Translation School that are not included among those five topics.

The tradition of these instructions adds onto them the Leap-over of the Great Perfection, thereby completing the practices of the nine *yānas*. You should practice them upon a single cushion, or within a single session. [866] I shall give a concise account of their meaning as taught in *The Design of Mahāmudrā* composed by Lord Phagmo Drüpa and Jigten Sumgön's *Three Dharmas*.

If you do not meditate on a deity, there will be obstacles. Mistaking your own identity, even if you practice for your whole life, your practice is said to be lacking in gratitude, and it will go astray. Without a chosen deity, you remain an ordinary person; and without meditating on a deity, you will not attain spiritual awakening no matter what practice you do. That is the *sūtra* tradition, and it requires three countless eons to reach spiritual awakening. By meditating on a deity, *piśācīs*[103] are pacified, all lusty people are brought under your influence, appearances are mastered, the primordial wisdom of discernment arises, passions are sublimated, you attract followers of others, and you do not mistake your own identity.

– Years ago the Dalai Lama counseled me to practice Vajrakīlaya as my chosen deity, commenting that he also engaged in this practice, and he gave me some blessed pills associated with this chosen deity. I followed his advice. Sometime later when I was in Nepal, I met with H.H. Dudjom Rinpoche, and he gave me the same instructions. I replied that His Holiness had suggested this earlier and that I had followed his advice, to which Dudjom Rinpoche told me I was doing just what was needed.

Meditation on a chosen deity in general, and on Vajrakīlaya in particular, is very important. It's indispensable for counteracting the obstacles that are bound to arise in the course of your practice due to insufficient merit and your own past obscurations and karmic imprints. To ward off these obstacles so that you aren't thrown off the path, it's very helpful to meditate on a chosen deity. But make sure that you do not imagine the deity as being material and substantial as if it were a statue. As you bring your chosen deity to mind, think of it as appearing, yet lacking any kind of substantial or inherent existence. Meditate on this deity as being a pure expression of primordial wisdom. In this way, your deity practice will be a union of the stages of generation and completion, with the appearance of the deity corresponding to the stage of generation and the facet of emptiness corresponding to the stage of completion. But remember that the appearance isn't one thing and emptiness another. Rather they are of one nature. The deity appears, and yet it is empty.

According to the *sūtra* tradition, you don't generate yourself as the deity; rather you worship and make offerings to the deity visualized in front of you. By practicing in this way, it takes three countless eons to attain Buddhahood. By meditating on the deity, your passions, desires, and cravings are sublimated, rather than leading you further into *saṃsāra*. –

Without Mahāmudrā, there is no liberation from the cycle of existence; even though you strive in Dharma and spiritual practice, you achieve nothing more than the mere pleasures of gods and humans. That is practicing the *yāna* of gods and humans, [867] and by so doing you are unable to be a blessing to others. By meditating on Mahāmudrā, delusion is sublimated; *nāgas* are pacified; you are liberated from the cycle of existence; the primordial wisdom of the absolute space of phenomena is realized; you become a master of *saṃsāra* and *nirvāṇa*; and the *dharmakāya* and *svabhāvakāya* are attained.[104]

Thus, the meditations on the bodily stage of generation of your chosen deity and the mental stage of completion concerning the meaning of emptiness are to be practiced by a novice during the earlier and later phases of the meditation session. Once you are accustomed to that, meditate on them in union, for that is the main practice taught in the Secret Mantra Vajrayāna.

– Beginners should first practice the stage of generation and then move on to the stage of completion during the latter phase of their meditation session. How is this done? The very nature of your mind is the chosen deity, and the essential nature of that is emptiness. As a beginner, you may find it hard to hold this in mind all at the same time. When you are visualizing the face, you may forget about the hands and the torso; your visualization may be nebulous and fragmented. You may not even be sure whether you are a male or a female. Eventually, when you are able to maintain a strong visualization, recall that the essential nature of the mind is emptiness, which introduces the stage of completion. The generation of the deity stems from the mind and dissolves completely back into the mind, and the essential nature of that mind is empty. The major point of this practice is to perceive all appearances, especially all visual appearances, as being the body of the deity, all sounds as being the speech of the deity, and all mental events as being the mind of the deity. –

Thus it is said:

> Equally establishing the two stages
> Of the stage of generation
> And the stage of completion
> Is the teaching of the Buddha.

The best way to dispel interferences and enhance the main practices of the stages of generation and completion is *guruyoga*, so this is crucial. If you do not meditate on this, you will not realize the mind-state of your spiritual mentor; [868] you will not receive blessings; you will not have experiential realizations; and even your own followers will have no reverence or devotion. By meditating on your spiritual mentor, pride is sublimated; *devaputras* are pacified; jealous people are brought under your influence; awareness is apprehended and you are blessed; the primordial wisdom of equality arises; you are honored by everyone, and you attain the state of the spiritual mentor.

The cultivation of the spirit of awakening is initially important for the attainment of enlightenment, so it is like a seed. In the interim it is like water and fertilizer, and finally it is like a bountiful harvest. If this is not cultivated, even if you devote your whole life to Dharma, you veer off to the Hīnayāna states of the *śrāvakas* and *pratyekabuddhas*; you do not attain the fruition of spiritual awakening; you do not attract a monastic following; and even if you do attract followers, they get involved in quarrels, strife, and bickering. Due to cultivating the spirit of awakening, hatred is sublimated; *pārthivas*[105] and *grahas*[106] are pacified; all hateful people are brought under your influence; the needs of the world are fulfilled; mirrorlike primordial wisdom arises; your followers come together in harmony; [869] and you accomplish the result of various *nirmāṇakāyas*.

Spiritual practice is like a fine horse on which you place a saddle and bridle, and the dedication is like directing the horse with the reins, so that it goes wherever you wish. So this is important. Without the dedication, you do not attain the results that you desire. Even if you briefly attract a following, they fall under someone else's influence. If you practice the dedication, jealousy is sublimated; *nāgas*[107] and *tsän*[108] are pacificed; jealous people are drawn under your influence; the roots of your virtue are not misdirected; the primordial wisdom of accomplishment arises; and your followers do not fall under the influence of others.

– If you engage in spiritual practice, you acquire causes for rebirth in the pure land of Sukhāvatī. Although the cause is there, without dedicating the practice it's possible for other obstacles to intervene, so that seed will not bear that fruit. By dedicating the merit of your practice to be reborn in Sukhāvatī, it will definitely bear that fruit. This is like pouring the tiny cup of water of your virtue into the ocean, where it can't vanish until the whole ocean evaporates. Similarly, by dedicating the roots of virtue, you protect them, and they grow until enlightenment is achieved. It's just like watering the tree of enlightenment. Without the dedication of merit, the roots of virtue will never become strong, and even a single outburst of anger can destroy them.

One general dedication of merit is simply the prayer that however the *sugatas* of the past dedicated their merit, so, too, do I direct my virtue. This brings about both temporary joy as well as ultimate happiness for all beings within the cycle of existence. –

If you do not meditate on the clear light Leap-over, the practice of the nine *yānas* is not complete; the practical instructions on liberation through observation are not received; you are left with a view entailing the grasping of mental analysis; and when the delusive appearances of the intermediate state arise, it will be difficult to recognize them. If the clear light Leap-over is constantly observed, your view is not left in mental analysis; the five primordial wisdoms are directly perceived; [870] in the best of cases, you directly encounter the assembly of the peaceful and wrathful deities; even if you do not meet them, when you encounter them in the intermediate state, you will identify them and certainly be liberated; the practice of the nine *yānas* is thoroughly complete; planetary spirits are pacified; the *ḍākinīs* and Dharma protectors take care of you as if you were their own child; and finally you attain the rainbow body, specifically the great transference body of the *dharmakāya*. You soon see extraordinary radiant, lustrous *bindus* of rainbow light; and when you see them, that is the vision of the direct perception of reality-itself.

– When you are still involved in the grasping of mental analysis, you continue to label and classify your practices, thinking, "This is the deity. This is the pure land. This is the palace. This is appearance. This is emptiness." In this way you construct layer upon layer of conceptual grasping.

You may think you are familiar with *saṃsāra*, while *nirvāṇa* may seem to be very distant from you, almost out of reach. In reality, it's really not. Failing to recognize the nature of *nirvāṇa* is failing to recognize our own nature. The entire phenomenal world consists of five elements: earth, fire, water, air, and space. Their pure nature is the five consorts, the five female expressions of enlightenment, closely conjoined with the five primordial wisdoms, or the five *buddha*-families. All sentient beings are composed of the five elements. The blood, bones, tissues, and so forth consist of the five elements. From the Dzogchen perspective all of these are creative expressions of the nature of awareness. When the actual nature of the five elements is not recognized, they then constitute *saṃsāra*.

When we recognize the actual nature of the five elements, they are *nirvāṇa*. The appearances we experienced yesterday are nothing other than the mind. The dream experiences we will have tonight are nothing other than the mind. The agent who engages in virtue and nonvirtue is the mind. The experiences of joy and sorrow are none other than the mind. –

The benefits of that are taught in *The Secret Tantra of the Sun of the Blazing Clear Expanse of the Ḍākinīs*:

> All the *buddhas* of the three times,
> The five families of *sugatas*, the three families of protectors,
> And peaceful and wrathful *ḍākinīs* and *vīras*
> Are seen by means of direct perception.
> Karmic obscurations and habitual propensities are
> extinguished.
> A contemplative who sees this
> No longer has the names of the three realms of *saṃsāra*,
> And the three worlds are ascertained.
> For you who see this place of liberation just once,
> As soon as the transitional process of becoming arises,
> You will undoubtedly take miraculous rebirth
> In a natural *nirmāṇakāya* realm. [871]

Thus, it is crucial to engage in constant practice of these six: your chosen deity, Mahāmudrā, your spiritual mentor, the spirit of awakening, the clear light, and the dedication. Whether you remain in retreat for thirteen years, six years, a three-year and three-fortnight cycle, a month, three weeks, two weeks, or even one week, this is the practice. In terms of your regular schedule, whether you have each day four sessions, three sessions, two sessions in the morning and evening, or even one session per day, you should meditate on this.

In what way do you engage in that meditation? It is best to sit upon a comfortable cushion in the posture bearing the seven attributes of Vairocana. If you cannot do so, it is enough to sit in the "sixfold fastened stove" posture. Consider, "Alas! Everything is of the nature of impermanence. Today I must engage in truly satisfying spiritual practice. What does tomorrow hold in store?" Cultivate a fine motivation, thinking, "For the sake of all sentient beings I shall attain perfect spiritual awakening. In order to do so, I shall practice the profound stages of generation and completion." [872] With that motivation, clearly visualize your body in the form of the Great Compassionate One. The color of your body is white like an autumnal moon. Your one face is calm and smiling. You are adorned with a precious crown of jewels and your spiritual mentor Amitābha is present on the top of your head. You have four hands, the first two pressed together at your heart, your lower right hand holding a rosary of white crystal, and your lower left hand holding an eight-petalled, white lotus blossom. You wear a shawl, lower garment, and skirt of various silks, and the hide of a *kṛṣṇaśāra* antelope is draped over your left shoulder. Imagine that you are seated upon a moon-disk in the center of a variegated lotus, with your legs in the *vajrāsana*. A white syllable *Hṛīḥ* stands upright in the center of a full-moon disk at your heart inside your body, which is inwardly hollow and immaculate. On the periphery of that disk the white six syllables circle about in a clockwise direction.

From them, rays of light of various colors are emanated out in the ten directions like rays of a rainbow. [873] All the spiritual mentors, chosen deities, *buddhas*, and *bodhisattvas* dwelling in the ten directions and the three times come floating in like snowflakes in a blizzard. All your primary and lineage spiritual mentors dissolve into the Lord of the Family Amitābha, thereby synthesizing all your spiritual mentors. All the chosen deities, *buddhas*, and *bodhisattvas* dissolve into yourself as the Great Compassionate One, thereby synthesizing all the chosen deities. Their root *mantras*, essential syllables and secondary syllables all dissolve into the six syllables at your heart, thereby synthesizing all *mantras*, *vidyāmantras*, and *dhāraṇīs*. Meditate on this not just once, but with great earnestness. This is practical advice for accomplishing everything with one spiritual mentor, one deity, and one *mantra*.

– From the outset of your practice cultivate a pure motivation by thinking, "For the sake of all sentient beings I shall obtain perfect Buddhahood!" Do this regardless of the depth of your practice, regardless of the duration of your practice. If you are self-deprecating and think that your practice is insignificant, superficial, and so short that it would be embarrassing to think of dedicating your effort, you will ruin your practice. It is very important to cultivate a proper motivation—not contrived and artificial, not simply mimicking others, but rather doing all you can to bring forth a virtuous motivation unmixed with the eight mundane concerns. Here is a way to synthesize all the teachings into one simple practice, all spiritual mentors into one spiritual mentor, all deities into one deity, all *mantras* into one *mantra*. –

Then the seed syllables emit rays of light while they are circling about, transforming the entire external universe into the realm of

Sukhāvatī, and transforming all the sentient beings who dwell in the six states of existence into forms of the Great Compassionate One. Gloriously visualize everyone you see as being in the form of the Great Compassionate One. Even if you cannot maintain that clearly, imagine that they are the Great Compassionate One. [874] That is the transformation of appearances into the divine body, and if that is clear, it is alright even if you do not complete your retreat. With regard to seeing other people and so on while in retreat, this is practical advice for not incurring the fault of breaking your retreat.

Then if you recite the six syllables in a very loud voice, this will not do, and it will take a long time to accomplish anything; and if malevolent local spirits are present, they may harm you. If your voice is too soft, the syllables will be unclear, so their power will not emerge. Recite them clearly and purely with the humming sound of a bee. Imagine that while you are chanting your song on your own, all sentient beings of the six states of existence are reciting together with you. Imagine that all sounds of fire, of wind, of movement, and all voices are sounds of the six syllables. That is the transformation of sounds into the divine speech. If that is clear, even a single voice is multiplied many hundreds of millions of times. This is practical advice for accomplishing the state of an *ārya* with a hundred *mantras*. If that is clear, it is alright even if you are not able to maintain silence. [875] While you are in retreat, it is alright even if it is mixed with talking, for all speech is the *mantra*. It is said that even if you are practicing with a rosary, this will make up for omissions and excesses.

If your practice is good, when you meditate on those points without wavering from the essential nature of your mind, that is the supreme union of the stages of generation and completion. That will happen once ideation arises as meditation. The stage of generation is ideation; ideation is the mind; and the mind is emptiness. The mind and ideation are like water and waves, so when that very movement arises as meditation, that is the union. If that union is beyond the capacity of novices, you should first meditate single-pointedly on the visualizations of the stage of generation.

You may get a little tired of those visualizations. The stillness of the mind with respect to the visualization is quiescence. By mentally, vividly observing the mind of the meditator, you will have a special vision of emptiness that is ungrounded in anything; [876] and that is insight. Evenly settle your mind as stably as possible in that state. If thoughts flow out again, observe their essential nature and let them release themselves. That is the technique for experiential novices.

– If you tire of those visualizations, take a little rest and simply settle your mind in emptiness or quietly and gently bring Avalokiteśvara to mind. Some people feel that if they see all appearances as a pure land with themselves and all sentient beings as deities, they hear all sound as the speech of the deity, and all mental events as the mind of the deity, they can do anything they like, because they are transmuting everything with this pure vision. They believe they can just engage in chit chat and let their mind rove through the three times, thinking about anything that comes up. That attitude really constitutes abandoning the Dharma. Instead, be clear about what you do. Know and practice according to your own level. Some people have cultivated very fine external qualities, talents and so forth, but have failed to cultivate fine inner qualities. If you want to see how the cultivation of inner qualities gives rise to a sense of joy in one's life, look to His Holiness the Dalai Lama. Among Tibetan *lamas*, there is none finer. He walks around as a simple monk, meeting people with warmth and openheartedness. The same was true of His Holiness Dudjom Rinpoche. He was gentle, always affirming and encouraging people. Likewise, Gyalwa Karmapa was known for his compassion. This is the conduct one sees in great spiritual mentors.

The crucial element of the practice should be to recognize and to abandon our own mental afflictions. If our practice does not focus on that, which is the very root of Buddhist practice, how can we say we are Buddhists? This holds true for spiritual mentors as well, because a spiritual mentor who does not counteract his or her mental afflictions is not a genuine *lama*. You may think that when you really practice the Dharma, you must always be externally gentle and loving, but that is not always the case. Those who apply themselves to practice are opened to the four types of enlightened activity: peaceful, expansive, powerful, and ferocious. Therefore, all of these are possibilities for a person deeply involved in practice, but only when they are motivated by pure altruism.

It's good to acquire learning, to study, and understand many things, but most importantly, we must apply the essence of whatever we have understood to ourselves, to take it to heart. The crucial point that characterizes a genuine Dharma practitioner is recognizing and abandoning even the most subtle nonvirtue. That is the gist of the 84,000 collections of the Buddha's teachings: to subdue our mental afflictions. Many great beings in India were able to do this by practicing these teachings. This has also been true of many beings in Tibet. Many did attain perfect enlightenment. This has happened in the past, and it will happen in the future. –

Once you are accustomed to that, there is no need to watch the flow of the essential nature of thoughts. Just as you might enjoy gazing at a sparkling clear lake in the springtime, restfully observe the essential nature of the mind, simply and without distraction. Just as the waves emerge from the water and merge back into the lake, without harming the lake, even if a little movement emerges from the state of stillness, it does not harm the stillness; and it merges back into the state of stillness. Once you are accustomed to that, however many thoughts occur, they do not impair the stillness; but like snowflakes drifting down upon a lake, they merge into the experience of stillness. By acquainting yourself with that, thoughts will appear as meditation. When ideation does arise as meditation, that is the union of the stages of generation and completion, for the stage of generation is ideation. [877]

If the mind still has something to observe, it is not seeing its essential nature. Then unify the person who is observing and that which is being observed. You will then gain certain knowledge of a brilliant, serenely joyful, homogeneous emptiness, and there will no longer be anything onto which to grasp. There is nothing of which you can say, "This is it," and there is nothing of which you can say, "This is the meditation." This will be unlike anything you have experienced before, and doubts may arise. Be quiet, stop trying, and simply be undistracted, without having anything to do. When that happens, the essential nature of ordinary consciousness will be seen. If the sentinel of mindfulness is lost, you will wander off into confusion as usual. Simply do not lose the sentinel of undistracted mindfulness. That is the meaning of Tilopa's statement:

> If the mind has no intentional object, that is Mahāmudrā.
> If you become accustomed and well acquainted with that,
> supreme awakening will be attained.

– The term "intentional object" means a referential object of awareness, in which case you are the subject, and the object you are looking at is called the intentional object.

Many meditators sit in an uptight, frozen posture with glazed eyes, meditating with the strong sense of thinking that they are now in meditation. How can they get any benefit from this? Specifically, some people practicing the stage of generation visualize themselves, their environment, and the deities as real, substantial entities; then during the stage of completion, they demolish everything they've visualized. To such a practitioner the two stages of meditation are analogous to building a mansion, and then demolishing it with a bulldozer; then, just to make sure not even a speck is left, they bomb it. This is a misguided approach to these two stages of practice. In reality, these two practices are of the same nature. The phenomena in these practices appear, yet they are devoid of any intrinsic nature. Their appearance and their absence of an inherent nature are themselves of the same nature, with the stage of generation corresponding to the facet of appearances, and the stage of completion corresponding to the absence of an intrinsic existence. In fact, this is true of all phenomena—they appear, yet lack an intrinsic nature.

The progression of the two approaches of quiescence practice is to meditate with and then without signs. Initially, you cultivate and grow accustomed to practicing quiescence with signs, while having as the higher goal the practice of quiescence without an object and without signs. The meditator—that which is meditating—is you; and that upon which you are meditating is you. Both are ungrounded in any kind of intrinsic, or inherent, reality. In this regard the three times—past, present, and future—appearance and disappearance are all ungrounded in any substantial reality.

The fact that the mind no longer has an intentional object does not imply a mere vacuity or a nihilistic perspective. You don't space out, rather the mind that is meditating must be imbued with the power of wisdom—the very nature of awareness itself is wisdom. As a result of becoming well acquainted with that, you will attain the fruition of Dzogchen, which is Buddhahood. –

If you meditate without losing the sentinel of mindfulness, that is meditative equipoise. If the sentinel of mindfulness is lost, that is the post-meditative state.

The best way to counteract obstructive forces, avoid pitfalls, and enhance your practice is *guruyoga*. [878] Visualize Amitābha, the Lord of the Family, as the sentinel of mindfulness on the crown of your head as the Great Compassionate One. His body is red in color like coral, and has all the signs and symbols of enlightenment, including an *uṣṇīṣa* on his head. His hands are in the *mudrā* of meditative equipoise, holding an almsbowl filled with ambrosia. Imagine him upon a lotus and moon seat, with his legs in the *vajrāsana*. Invite all your primary and lineage spiritual mentors, and dissolve them into him. Make whatever supplications you know, or recite, "I pray to the *dharmakāya* Amitābha. I pray to the *sambhogakāya* the Great Compassionate One. I pray to the *nirmāṇakāya* Padmasambhava. I pray to my kind primary and lineage spiritual mentors." Recite the six syllables as a way of supplication, or recite one rosary of the *vajraguru mantra*, for this is the essence of supplications. From the depths of your heart, and not with mere lip-service, completely place your trust in him with the conviction, "You know whatever is to be done in this life, future lives, and the intermediate state." [879] Do so with such heartfelt reverence and devotion that your hairs stand on end and you are moved to tears.

– How do we succumb to pitfalls? Primarily due to grasping and clinging. Then we succumb to the mental afflictions of attachment, hatred, and delusion. As we practice the stage of generation, if we reify the objects of our visualization, we will never realize emptiness. That approach cannot lead to Buddhahood. Similarly, practicing the stage of completion with craving does not lead to genuine realization of emptiness with compassion, just to nihilism.

Just as in Tibet, many Buddhists in the West don't want to practice stage by stage. We would much rather leap to the most advanced stages of Dzogchen and Mahāmudrā without first laying a suitable foundation. We leap up to these advanced practices, only to fall down again and again. This reminds me of the story of a man who accumulated a big bag of grain. To keep it away from rodents he suspended it on a rope hung from the ceiling. In the evenings, he would sit beneath the bag admiring it and wondering what he could acquire with it. This one bag represented his entire life's wealth. One evening he thought, "With this much grain I could find a wife and we could have children. Maybe we will have a son. But what will I name him?' Just then the moon rose up and shone through his window. "Oh, I'll give my son the auspicious name of Dawa Dragpa, the Moon of Renown." Unbeknownst to him a rat had climbed up the rope and chewed through it, and just as he had this thought, the big bag of grain fell down, landing on his head and killing him. In a similar way, we get caught up in our fantasies about the future, which only revolve around the eight mundane concerns, and we get nowhere at all.

Mahāmudrā and Dzogchen are indeed very swift paths to enlightenment, but in order for them to be effective, we need to accumulate merit and purify our mind-streams of obscurations, because our lack of success is due simply to an insufficient accumulation of excellent qualities and insufficient merit. –

Each time you make this supplication, do so in the manner of calling your spiritual mentor from afar. By so doing, scattered, outer thoughts will swirl away, and inner thoughts will nakedly arise as empty luminosity. Whatever experience arises due to the power of blessings from praying in that way, sustain it. It is said that as a result, there will not be a single obstructing force or pitfall.

Then this is the way to enhance your practice in reliance upon the spirit of awakening, love, and compassion. All sentient beings in the six states of existence have been very kind to you in that they have all been your parents many times. This being the case, generate powerful compassion as you consider that they have had no opportunity to escape from the suffering of the six states. Then, while you are exhaling through your nostrils, imagine that all your merit and roots of virtue gently dissolve into all sentient beings; and imagine them finding immeasurable joy and happiness and possessing incalculable merit as the cause of joy. [880] Either verbally or mentally recite, "May all sentient beings be endowed with joy and the causes of joy."

– For this practice recall specific ways your parents have shown you kindness from the moment you were born. Recall how they changed your dirty diapers and gave you the best food and clothing they could afford. Most importantly, we have this precious fully endowed human life due to the kindness of our own parents. However, all our parent sentient beings continue in the cycle of existence just as we have done for eons. By pondering their state of entrapment in the suffering of the six states of cyclic existence, develop great compassion for them.

Why do we perpetuate *saṃsāra*? Because we do just the opposite of what needs to be done to free ourselves. There is a well-known fable about a flock of birds who decided they needed to choose a king. One bird proposed that the first bird that saw the sun come up in the morning should be named king. As the sun was about to rise, all but one of the birds turned toward the east, while one of them gazed steadfastly toward the west. We are like the bird looking west. –

While you are inhaling, imagine all the suffering, evil, and obscurations of all sentient beings converging and dissolving into yourself. Your own form as Avalokiteśvara blazes with greater splendor, like wood added to fire, and all sentient beings are freed from the sufferings of each of the six states of existence. Imagine that they are freed from all evil and obscurations, which are the causes of suffering. Verbally or mentally recite, "May all sentient beings be freed from suffering and the causes of suffering." That is the cultivation of compassion. If you are moved to tears due to love and compassion, that is great love and great compassion. If you have a sense of equality, without bias, towards all sentient beings, that is immeasurable love and immeasurable compassion. Moreover, if you can meditate while in a state of undistracted practice on the essential nature of the mind, that is the innate *samādhi* of great love and emptiness bearing the essence of compassion. This is the root of Dharma of the *sūtra* tradition of the Mahāyāna. [881]

Moreover, it is said that there is nothing more profound than this in terms of perfecting your own merit, purifying obscurations, and as a wheel of protection. There are said to be 640,000 Atiyogatantras, among which seventeen are presently available. There are seventeen "little child" *tantras*, seventeen mother and child *tantras* of the Mind Class, *The Quintessence of the Ḍākinīs, The Quintessence of the Clear Expanse, The Quintessential Commentary of the Spiritual Mentor*, and so on. The primary meaning of all of them is this clear light Leap-over. This is the practical instruction on awakening without meditating, and it is the profound practical instruction on liberation by means of observation. This vision of the five-colored lights is not like seeing a rainbow; it is a direct, perceptual vision of the five primordial wisdoms. It is said that there is no difference between this and actually encountering the five families of *jinas*. Unlike when you make your first observations, you will see an amazing brilliance. It is said that if that is witnessed, when the assemblies of peaceful and wrathful deities appear in the intermediate state, you will surely be liberated in that state. [882] There is no shorter path than this. If you watch constantly, you will directly see many peaceful and wrathful deities, including the five families of *jinas*. It is said that if they are seen, there is no need to go through the intermediate state. Therefore, it is important that you watch constantly throughout the morning and evening.

– If you wish to accumulate greater merit to empower and enhance your spiritual practice, there is nothing more profound than this *tonglen* practice of *guruyoga*, in which the *guru* is indivisible from your chosen deity and you take on the suffering of others and give them happiness. If you wish to eliminate the obscurations of your mind-stream, there is no method more powerful. If you are concerned about obstructions and malevolent forces, no wheel of protection is more effective.

Once again, the reference to enlightenment without meditating doesn't mean that no meditation is needed at all. Rather, it means that you can attain enlightenment very swiftly. Also, as you practice the Leap-over, the visions come gradually as you become more and more familiar with the practice. –

In the evening when you are about to fall asleep, you should seal with prayers of dedication whatever virtue you have accomplished that day. If you make this dedication by reifying the person doing the dedication, the object of dedication, and the dedication itself, that dedication is poisonous; so it will not lead to the path of awakening. Performing a dedication in a state that is undistracted from the essential nature of the mind is perfect dedication concerning the agent, object, and act; so that leads to the path of awakening.

Whatever Dharma and spiritual practices are performed, any concluding prayer of dedication that is made with an undistracted mind will later certainly come true. Therefore, it is important that there is no misunderstanding concerning prayers of dedication. Consider what you want in the future as a result of receiving these instructions and engaging in this spiritual practice. [883] It is best to surrender yourself, and pray to serve the needs of sentient beings for as long as the cycle of existence persists.

It is said that among the *buddhas*, there is no one but Buddha Śākyamuni, and among the *bodhisattvas*, there is no one but the Protectors of the Three Families.[109] Might we become them? Do we fear the miseries of the cycle of existence? One who has no qualms or dismay at the prospect of experiencing the miseries of birth and death many hundreds of millions of times, but who attains spiritual awakening while in a state of joy and happiness is called a slothful *bodhisattva*.

He is the least among *bodhisattvas*, and the Jina Maitreya is said to be such a one. I think there is nothing wrong with our turning out like him. To do so, eventually we would have to be born in a pure realm. Even if we are born in Potala, Tuṣita, or the Glorious Copper-colored Mountain, there is no guarantee that we will not fall back. It is said that one cannot take birth in other pure realms such as Abhirati until one reaches at least the first ground. [884] So even if one prays, one will not get there, for that is analogous to not reaching one's destination.

Bodhisattvas who voluntarily serve the needs of sentient beings do not cringe at the miseries of the cycle of existence. We, on the other hand, fear the suffering of *saṃsāra*, so if we wish to attain spiritual awakening in a state of joy and happiness, without experiencing suffering, we should pray to be born in the realm of Sukhāvatī. If we pray to be born there—except in cases of sins of immediate retribution and the abandonment of Dharma—our birth there will be due to the power of Amitābha's prayers. If we are reborn there, we will not have even the slightest suffering, and our joy and happiness will be abundant. We will be able to go miraculously to Abhirati, the Glorious Copper-colored Mountain, and Tuṣita, meet [the *buddhas* there] and receive the Dharma. With unimpeded extrasensory perception and paranormal abilities, we will be able to lead those with whom we have a connection out of the intermediate state. For countless hundreds of millions of eons, there will be no illness, no aging, and no death. We will behold the face of Buddha Amitābha and listen to Dharma. [885] Incalculable clouds of offerings will be emanated from the palms of our hands and be offered to the *buddhas*. Thus, the qualities of the grounds and paths will be perfected, and we will become enlightened.

How easy is it to be born there? It is said that if one earnestly prays ten times, one will take birth there. There is no point is doubting whether or not you will be born there. If you nurture doubts, you will be born in that pure realm, but the lotus flower [in which you are born] will not open for five hundred years. It is said that during that time, you will experience joy and happiness, and you will hear the voice of the Buddha; but unfortunately there will be a delay in seeing his face. Therefore, without harboring doubts, tonight when you are about to sleep, you should dedicate whatever spiritual practice you have done today to be reborn there. If you know them, recite *The Prayer of Fine Conduct* and *The Sukhāvatī Prayer*, but if you do not know them, it is enough to say, "May I be born in Sukhāvatī!" By so doing, when you die—whether or not you are able to sustain your spiritual practice, or succeed in the practice of transference, or recognize the assemblies of peaceful and wrathful deities in the transitional process of reality-itself—[886] two weeks after your death, you will determine that you have died; and before the messengers of Yama arrive, and before the verdict is made concerning your actions and their karmic consequences, with defiled extrasensory perception you will be aware of your past and future lives and the intermediate states. You will be able to demonstrate various paranormal abilities, and you will have great freedom to go where you will. At that time, hold Buddha Amitābha in mind, and go to Sukhāvatī. There is no doubt that you will go there simply by thinking of it.

Try hard not to forget the meaning of the Dharma you have received now. Everyone can certainly practice this, for this is an unsophisticated discussion of the Dharma. This is the essence of the Buddha's words, the *sūtras, tantras,* the New Translation School, the Old Translation School, and the treasure teachings. Oh, now in this one-month teaching we have well completed eighteen primary Dharma sessions and twelve supplementary Dharma sessions.

– Throughout this text there have been many complex, difficult, and lofty discussions of Dzogchen and Mahāmudrā. However, these teachings concerning rebirth in Sukhāvatī entail simple, easily performed practices.

We have now completed the supplementary chapters among the thirty sessions of teachings of Karma Chagmé, and I would like to make a few concluding remarks. Do not try for practices that are beyond your reach. It is important to realize what level of practice you are on and then to engage in it. This practice of praying to be born in Sukhāvatī falls into that category. Simply by praying to be reborn in Sukhāvatī, we are guaranteed that this will come true. The four traditions within Tibetan Buddhism are in agreement about this, and it is a widely accepted truth in Chinese and Japanese Buddhism. It is pointless to doubt this. By making such prayers, when we die at the very least we can accomplish our own well-being, and may even be able to accomplish the welfare of others. Whether you are a teacher or a scholar, of high or low social status, rich or poor, a beggar or even an idiot, there is no one who can say you cannot go to Sukhāvatī. These days there is much discussion about human rights. Of all human rights, the right to go to Sukhāvatī is the greatest! –

May there be the good fortune of Ācārya Padmasambhava!
May there be the good fortune of the Great Compassionate
One! [887]
May there be the good fortune of the ocean of *vīras*!

May there be the good fortune of the ocean of *ḍākinīs*!
May there be the good fortune of the ocean of oath-bound protectors!

Then make extensive prayers of dedication. Utter verses of good fortune, scatter grain from your hands. This concludes this Dharma session.

Amazing! This is a synthesis of the meaning of all the *sūtras* and *tantras* of the New and Old Translation schools.
This is a synthesis of the blessings of the New and Old Translations and the treasure teachings.
This is a synthesis of practices of all the essential instructions on Mahāmudrā and Dzogchen.
This is a synthesis of citations from the entire ocean of the *sūtras* and *tantras*.
This is a synthesis of the contemplations of all the *vidyādharas* and *siddhas*.
This is a synthesis of practices of all superior and inferior people.
This is a synthesis of all philosophical systems, surpassing them all.
Although this is the Secret Mantra[yāna], these are teachings that help everyone.
Due to the power of the compassion of Avalokiteśvara,
This has been well compiled by Rāga Asey,
The contemplative of the Great Compassionate One during these degenerate times.
Bhikṣu Tsöndrü has written it down.
Whatever inconsistencies, mistakes, or flaws there may be in this,
[888] I confess them to the assembly of deities of the Three Roots.
By the virtue of this composition, may I, the scribe,
And everyone who has found a connection with these instructions
Enjoy longevity and good health in this life, and may our experiential realizations increase.
When the time comes to move on from this life,
May we be miraculously reborn in the realm of Sukhāvatī,
Without any other lifetime coming inbetween.
Then may we please the Protector Amitābha by making offerings,
And in that corporeal existence may we manifestly become enlightened.

Once we have become perfectly enlightened,
May we emanate to fulfill the needs of the world for as long as space endures.
As for the qualities of each emanation,
May we have might like a billion Vajrapāṇis,
Supreme wisdom like a billion Mañjuśrīs,
Paranormal abilities like a billion Padmasambhavas,
And the unified capacity to fulfill the needs of the world like a billion Avalokiteśvaras.
May the continuum of teaching of these instructions and their oral transmission, [889]
And the stream of meditative accomplishment, experience, and realization
Increase; and for six hundred years
May they never degenerate, but grow and flourish.
May the oceanic assembly of oath-bound Protectors, including Ekajāti and Mahākala,
Increase this Dharma and make it flourish.
Protect those who practice this!
May the oceanic assembly of wealth deities, including Vaiśravaṇa,
Provide the necessities of life for those who practice this.
May the assemblies of the [twelve] *dṛḍhās*, the [thirteen] brother sylvan gods, the [twenty-one] *upāsakas*, and local gods
Increase this Dharma and help it flourish.
Do not transgress your earlier oath and *samaya*.
With regards to teaching, attending, and meditating on this Dharma,
If there are any enemies, obstructive forces, or false guides who create interferences,
And anyone who adulterates this with their own fabrications,
Punish them immediately and severely!
Does the power of the ocean of oath-bound Protectors exist or not? [890] At that time I shall watch, so bear that point in mind.
In these instructions do blessings exist or not?
Practice as you are taught in the treatises, and this will be evident.
Is this compatible with the meaning of the *sūtras* and *tantras* or not?
Look extensively into the New and Old Translations and the treasure teachings.

Look in terms of the practice of the stages of generation and
completion.
A few friends who are prejudiced and have partial knowledge
Might possibly disparage this,
But I have no remorse, for the *sūtras* and *tantras* are my
witness.
May the glory of good fortune shine on, and may this be an
ornament for the world!

Maṅgalam!

Notes

1 The meditations on the human life of leisure and endowment, impermanence and death, the miserable nature of the cycle of existence, and the nature of actions and their ethical consequences.

2 Tib. *byang chub sems dpa'*. A being in whom the spirit of awakening has effortlessly arisen and who devotes himself or herself to the cultivation of the six perfections in order to achieve spiritual awakening for the benefit of all beings.

3 Tib. *'pho ba*. According to the Great Perfection, the unsurpassed "transference" is the realization of the pristine absolute nature of phenomena, the *sugatagarbha*.

4 Tib. *sgrub thob*. One who has accomplished one or more *siddhis*, or paranormal abilities.

5 Tib. *mchod rten*. A reliquary which holds sacred objects, such as the remains of an enlightened being; its form symbolizes the mind of a *buddha*.

6 Tib. *dkyil 'khor*. A symbolic representation of the world, which is ritually offered.

7 These instructions are presented in the opening chapters of his work, which have not been translated either here or in his work entitled *A Spacious Path to Freedom: Practical Instructions on the Union of Mahāmudrā and Atiyoga*, commentary by Gyatrul Rinpoche, trans. by B. Alan Wallace (Ithaca, NY: Snow Lion, 1998).

8 Tib. *theg pa*. A vehicle for spiritual practice leading to varying degrees of spiritual liberation and awakening.

9 Tib. *longs spyod rdzogs pa'i sku*. A "full enjoyment embodiment" of an enlightened being, which is accessible only to *āryabodhisattvas* and *buddhas*.

10 Tib. *bka' ma*. The canonical teachings of the Buddha, according to the Tibetan tradition.

11 Tib. *gter ma.* "Treasure teachings" hidden for later generations by enlightened beings of the past.

12 Tib. *nyan thos.* A disciple of the Buddha who is committed to his own individual liberation by following the path set forth by the Buddha.

13 Tib. *dpa' bo.* A highly realized male *bodhisattva* who manifests in the world in order to serve sentient beings. Literally the term refers to a "heroic being," who shows great courage in not succumbing to the mental afflictions and in striving diligently in spiritual practice.

14 Tib. *mkha' 'gro ma.* A highly realized female *bodhisattva* who manifests in the world in order to serve sentient beings. Literally the term means a female "sky-goer," referring to the fact that such beings course in the expanse of the absolute space of phenomena.

15 Tib. *dngos sgrub.* A paranormal ability.

16 Tib. *rgyal ba.* A "victorious one," who has conquered cognitive and afflictive obscurations; an epithet of a *buddha*.

17 Tib. *lha.* A "god" within the cycle of existence, who experiences great joy, extrasensory perception, and paranormal abilities, but who suffers greatly when faced with death.

18 Tib. *sgrub pa.* A matrix of meditative practices designed to purify the mind, accumulate merit, and bring spiritual awakening.

19 Tib. *phyag rgya.* A gesture usually symbolizing some form of enlightened activity.

20 Tib. *'phags pa.* A being who has gained direct realization of ultimate reality.

21 Tib. *'khor ba.* The cycle of existence, qualified by compulsively taking rebirth after rebirth due to the power of one' s mental afflictions and *karma*.

22 Tib. *sāts tsha.* Small images (pronounced in Tibetan as "sa tsa"), of enlightened beings usually formed of clay and produced in large quantities.

23 Tib. *thang ka.* A Tibetan scroll painting with a religious subject.

24 Tib. *ma hā yo ga.* The "Great Yoga," which is perfected by realizing the nondual reality of the deity and one's own appearance.

25 Tib. *a nu yo ga.* The stage of Vajrayāna practice corresponding to the stage of completion, following Mahāyoga.

26 Tib. *shin tu rnal 'byor.* The "extraordinary yoga," which is equivalent to the Great Perfection, the highest of the nine spiritual vehicles.

27 Tib. *rang sangs rgyas.* A person who is committed to his own individual spiritual liberation won through solitary practice.

28 Tib. *rgyal ba'i sras.* An epithet of a *bodhisattva*, literally meaning "a son of the victorious ones."

29 The most basic of these twenty-two levels of the spirit of awakening is likened to the earth, while the highest level is likened to a cloud.

30 Tib. *slob dpon*. An accomplished teacher, especially of Dharma.

31 Tib. *bde bar gshegs pa*. An epithet of a *buddha*, a "well-gone one," meaning one who has gone to the far shore, achieving liberation from *saṃsāra* and the fulfillment of one's own and other's needs by achieving perfect spiritual awakening.

32 Tib. *lha ma yin*. A titan, or demigod, whose existence is characterized by aggression and conflict with the *devas*.

33 Tib. *bdud*. A demonic force that manifests as all kinds of grasping involving hopes and fears.

34 Tib. *dge bshes*. Literally, "a spiritual friend," but here referring to Buddhist scholars who have completed a lengthy monastic training in Buddhist doctrine and have taken the final examination conferring upon them the title of "*geshe*."

35 *A Guide to the Bodhisattva Way of Life*. Trans. by Vesna A. Wallace & B. Alan Wallace (Ithaca: Snow Lion, 1997) I: 9.

36 Ibid. I: 19.

37 Ibid. IV: 4.

38 Tib. *dgra bcom pa*. An individual who has completely overcome all mental afflictions and has thereby gained irreversible freedom from the cycle of existence.

39 Tib. *phur ba*. A ritual dagger used in certain tantric meditations. This ritual instrument is not actually used as a physical weapon to inflict injury or death, but is purely symbolic.

40 The account on which this narrative is based is presented in Chapter Eighteen of *The Sutra of the Wise and the Foolish* or *The Ocean of Narratives*, trans. from the Mongolian by Stanley Frye (Dharamsala: Library of Tibetan Works and Archives, 1981).

41 I surmise that the Tibetan phrase "*smon chul log pa'i mna' skyel*" refers to making a false oath together with a mock prayer, such as "If I'm not telling the truth, may I be struck by lightning!"

42 This refers to the four states of stream entry, once-returner, non-returner, and the state of an *arhat*.

43 See *The Sutra of the Wise and the Foolish*, Ch. 52.

44 See *The Sutra of the Wise and the Foolish*, Ch. 29.

45 See *The Sutra of the Wise and the Foolish*, Ch. 3.

46 Literally meaning "God of Flowers."

47 Tib. bSod nams skyabs

48 See *The Sutra of the Wise and the Foolish*, Ch. 19.

49 See *The Sutra of the Wise and the Foolish*, Ch. 20.

50 See *The Sutra of the Wise and the Foolish*, Ch. 21.

51 See *The Sutra of the Wise and the Foolish*, Ch. 22.

52 See *The Sutra of the Wise and the Foolish*, Ch. 25.

53 See *The Sutra of the Wise and the Foolish*, Ch. 43.

54 See *The Sutra of the Wise and the Foolish*, Ch. 35.

55 See *The Sutra of the Wise and the Foolish*, Ch. 38.

56 Maudgalyāyana was the disciple of the Buddha who had the greatest paranormal abilities, making it all the more remarkable that he could not blow out the lamp.

57 See *The Sutra of the Wise and the Foolish*, Ch. 41.

58 See *The Sutra of the Wise and the Foolish*, Ch. 47.

59 See *The Sutra of the Wise and the Foolish*, Ch. 49.

60 See *The Sutra of the Wise and the Foolish*, Ch. 50.

61 The term "without leisure" refers to being reborn without the eight leisures and ten endowments.

62 Bodhisattva Supuṣpacandra knew of a king's animosity and yet did not avoid his own suffering as a sacrifice for many people in misery, as recounted in the *Samādhirājasūtra*, Buddhist Sanskrit Texts Series, no. 2, pp. 160-161.

63 VIII: 129-130.

64 It is especially important to note that the prince did not have to lose his identity as a beggar, or have to continue living as a beggar.

65 The text reads *rtogs te sangs ma rgyas, ma rtogs te 'khor*, so I assume that the negative participle in the initial phrase is a scribal error (trans.).

66 That is to say that the entirety of *saṃsāra* and *nirvāṇa* is of the same essence as emptiness.

67 The name Ākāśagarbha literally means the essence, or womb, of space.

68 The six fields of experience are those of the five physical senses and of mental awareness.

69 Tib. *zha nas*. This term is unclear to me (trans.).

70 The preceding questions refer to the threefold analysis of the arising, location, and dispersion of thoughts.

71 Translated in Karma Chagmé's *A Spacious Path to Freedom: Practical Instructions on the Union of Mahāmudrā and Atiyoga*, Ch. 5.

72 This *māra* represents doubt and laziness.

73 Cf. Karma Chagmé's *A Spacious Path to Freedom: Practical Instructions on the Union of Mahāmudrā and Atiyoga*, Ch. 4.

74 Sentient beings are called causal, while *buddhas* are called fruitional.

75 The term "fresh" means unadulterated by conceptual grasping.

76 In the phrase "emptiness and luminosity," the latter term refers to appearances, and the former term refers to the emptiness of appearances.

77 In this context, "to bow" actually means "to recognize."

78 The Sanskrit term *kīla* means "dagger," but this also refers here to the chosen deity Vajrakīlaya.

79 This quote appears earlier in the text on p. 679 of the Tibetan.

80 If there are many people practicing together, it is sufficient for them all to practice in the *nirmāṇakāya* posture alone.

81 Thatness refers to space.

82 These three directions of the gaze pertain respectively to the *dharmakāya, sambhogakāya,* and *nirmāṇakāya* postures.

83 According to the *Bod rgya tshig mdzod chen mo* (Tse tan zhab drung, Dung dkar blo bzang phrin las, & dMu dge bsam gtan. Mi rigs dpe skrun khang, 1984), Vol III, p. 2783, the Tibetan term *lu gu rgyud* literally means a rope tying together lambs in a row. This would seem to be used here as a metaphor for a strand, or series, of interconnected components. This meaning reflects the etymology of the term, for *lu gu* is a variant spelling of *lug gu*, meaning "lamb" (Ibid., pp. 2781 & 2782); and *rgyud* means "continuum." I am translating *lu gu rgyud* here simply as "strand" to accord with earlier translations by contemporary scholars.

84 This does not refer to a point on your forehead, but to the space in front of you at the level of your eyebrows.

85 The bracketed phrase does not appear in this version of Karma Chagmé's text, but it does appear in another version of *Zab chos zhi khro dgongs pa rang grol gyi rdzogs rim bar do drug gi khrid yig*, as translated by myself in *Natural Liberation: Padmasambhava's Teachings on the Six Bardos* (Boston: Wisdom, 1998), p. 247.

86 The bracketed term does not appear in this version of Karma Chagmé's text, but it does appear in another version of *Zab chos zhi khro dgongs pa rang grol gyi rdzogs rim bar do drug gi khrid yig*, as translated by myself in *Natural Liberation: Padmasambhava's Teachings on the Six Bardos*, pp. 246-248.

87 "Casting off the shell" refers to discarding the aggregates of the conventional body and mind.

88 The "synthesis *bindu*" is the single nature of the whole of *saṃsāra* and *nirvāṇa*.

89 Make your hand into a fist and place it on the middle of your forehead. When you look straight ahead, if you cannot see your wrist, then there is said to be "an absence of a life-form in the space in front of you."

90 To test for the inner hum in the ears, place your hands over your ears. If there is an absence of sound, you are close to death.

91 Cf. *Natural Liberation: Padmasambhava's Teachings on the Six Bardos*, p. 283.

92 The Sanskrit word *cakṣu* means "eye."

93 This refers to the great *siddhi* of Mahāmudrā.

94 Tib. *gtum mo.* A meditative practice designed to bring forth realization of emptiness by way of igniting the "psychic heat" at the navel *cakra.*

95 Cf. *Natural Liberation: Padmasambhava's Teachings on the Six Bardos*, p. 165-166.

96 This occurs only if you have previously engaged in the practice of Avalokiteśvara.

97 The jewel mind refers to the *buddha*-nature.

98 Sentient beings wander in *saṃsāra* because we have not recognized our own nature, whereas *buddhas* are free because they have recognized their nature.

99 Literally, the body of great bliss.

100 IX:65A.

101 "The common signs of warmth" should not be confused with the stage of warmth on the path of preparation, for here these are simply signs of success in the practice.

102 The text reads "*seta,*" instead of "*soma,*" but we have found no meaning in Tibetan or Sanskrit for "*seta.*"

103 Tib. *'dre mo = bsen mo.* A demoness whose actual nature is that of negative thoughts, rooted in ego-grasping, who causes *saṃsāra* to come into existence.

104 Without Mahāmudrā, it is difficult to receive blessings, which makes it impossible to be a conduit of blessings for others. Becoming a master of *saṃsāra* and *nirvāṇa* means that you realize the indivisibility of the two.

105 Tib. *rgyal po.* Demonic forces that emerge from the aggregates of grasping onto the *I,* and consist of the conceptual mental factors that reify appearances. Such beings are created by conceptually focusing on them, and they arise as apparitions of hatred.

106 Tib. *'gong = gdon.* Malevolent demonic forces that torment one in lifetime after lifetime.

107 Tib. *klu.* A serpentlike creature whose actual nature is that of delusions produced by the causes and conditions of ignorance. Such beings may be called into the service of the Dharma.

108 Tib. *btsan.* A class of evil demons.

109 The "Protectors of the Three Families" are Mañjuśrī, Avalokiteśvara, and Vajrapāṇi.

Buddhist Sanskrit and Tibetan Terms

Abhirati (Tib. *mngon par dga' ba*) The *buddha*-field of Akṣobhya in the eastern direction.

ācārya (Tib. *slob dpon*) An accomplished teacher, especially of Dharma.

ārya (Tib. *'phags pa*) A being who has gained direct realization of ultimate reality.

asura (Tib. *lha ma yin*) A titan, or demigod, whose existence is characterized by aggression and conflict with the *devas*.

Atiyoga (Tib. *shin tu rnal 'byor*) The "extraordinary yoga," which is equivalent to the Great Perfection, the highest of the nine spiritual vehicles.

bhikṣu (Tib. *dge slong*) A fully ordained Buddhist monk.

bhikṣuṇī (Tib. *dge slong ma*) A fully ordained Buddhist nun.

bindu (Tib. *thig le*) An orb of light; the red and white essential drops of vital fluids within the body, included within the triad of channels, *bindus*, and vital energies; the dot, or small circle, above Tibetan and Sanskrit syllables such as *Hūṃ*; the "sole bindu" is the one *dharmakāya*, which is replete with all the qualities of all the *buddhas* and which encompasses the entirety of *saṃsāra* and *nirvāṇa*.

bodhicitta (Tib. *byang chub kyi sems*) The red and white *bodhicittas* are the female and male regenerative fluids, which are composed of the red and white *bindus*; see "spirit of awakening."

bodhisattva (Tib. *byang chub sems dpa'*) A being in whom the spirit of awakening has effortlessly arisen and who devotes himself or herself to the cultivation of the six perfections in order to achieve spiritual awakening for the benefit of all beings.

buddha (Tib. *sangs rgyas*) A spiritually awakened being in whom all afflictions and obscurations are dispelled and all excellent qualities brought to perfection.

cakra (Tib. *rtsa 'khor*) A "wheel" of channels through which course vital energies. The fivefold classification of the *cakras* includes the *cakra* of great bliss at the crown of the head, the *cakra* of enjoyment at the throat, the *dharmacakra* at the heart, the *cakra* of emanation at the navel, and the *cakra* of sustaining bliss at the genital region.

ḍākinī (Tib. *mkha' 'gro ma*) A highly realized female *bodhisattva* who manifests in the world in order to serve sentient beings. Literally the term means a female "sky-goer," referring to the fact that such beings course in the expanse of the absolute space of phenomena.

ḍāmaru (Skt.) A ritual hand-drum used, for instance, in the practice of Severance (Tib. *gCod*).

deva (Tib. *lha*) A "god" within the cycle of existence, who experiences great joy, extrasensory perception, and paranormal abilities, but who suffers greatly when faced with death.

devaputra (Tib. *lha'i bu*) Literally, a "son of the *devas*," referring to one of the four *māras*, especially associated with sensual desire.

Dharma (Tib. *chos*) Spiritual teachings and practices that lead one irreversibly away from suffering and the source of suffering and to the attainment of liberation and enlightenment.

dharmakāya (Tib. *chos kyi sku*) The "Truth Embodiment," which is the mind of the Buddha.

dhāraṇī (Tib. *gzungs*) A spell, or sequence of syllables believed to be imbued with transformative blessings.

doha (Skt.) A song of contemplative realization.

dṛḍhā (Tib. *brtan ma*) Twelve female protectors.

gandharva (Tib. *dri za*) Ethereal beings who are said to subsist on fragrances.

garuḍa (Tib. *bya khyung*) The mythical king of birds, like a great eagle.

graha (Tib. *gdon*) Malevolent demonic forces that torment one in lifetime after lifetime.

guruyoga (Tib. *bla ma'i rnal 'byor*) Meditation on one's spiritual mentor as indivisible from one's chosen deity.

Hīnayāna (Tib. *theg pa dman pa*) Literally, "the inferior vehicle" of Buddhist theory and practice, aimed at one's own liberation.

jina (Tib. *rgyal ba*) An epithet of a *buddha*, meaning a victorious one who has overcome all obscurations.

jinaputra (Tib. *rgyal ba'i sras*) An epithet of a *bodhisattva*, meaning a child of the victorious ones.

jñānasattva (Tib. *ye she sems dpa'*) A "primordial wisdom being," whose essential nature is primordial wisdom and who appears as an emanation of Samantabhadra.

karma (Tib. *las*) An action that is tainted by mental afflictions, especially the delusion of self-grasping.

kāya (Tib. *sku*) An embodiment of enlightenment.

kīla (Tib. *phur ba*) A sacred, three-sided, ritual dagger that may be used as an object of devotions such as prostrations, offerings, and circumambulations, and is also used in various magic rituals.

kṛṣṇaśāra (Skt.) A species of spotted antelope.

lama (Skt. *guru*) A spiritual mentor capable of leading others along the path to spiritual awakening.

Mahāmudrā (Tib. *phyag rgya chen po*) The "Great Seal," which is a synonym for emptiness, the absolute space of phenomena.

mahāsiddha (Tib. *sgrub chen*) A "great adept," who has accomplished mundane and supramundane abilities and realizations.

Mahāyāna (Tib. *theg pa chen po*) The "Great Vehicle," by which one proceeds to the state of the perfect spiritual awakening of a *buddha*.

maṇḍala (Tib. *dkyil 'khor*) A symbolic representation of the world, which is ritually offered; a representation of the pure abode of a deity.

mantra (Tib. *sngags*) An incantation of Sanskrit letters or syllables imbued with special symbolic significance or spiritual blessings.

māra (Tib. *bdud*) A demonic force that manifests as all kinds of grasping involving hopes and fears.

nāga (Tib. *klu*) A serpentlike creature whose actual nature is that of delusions produced by the causes and conditions of ignorance. Such beings may be called into the service of the Dharma.

nirmāṇakāya (Tib. *sprul pa'i sku*) An "emanation embodiment" of the *buddhas*, which may appear anywhere in the universe in order to benefit sentient beings.

nirvāṇa (Tib. *mya ngan las 'das pa*) Spiritual liberation, in which one is forever freed from delusion and all other mental afflictions, which give rise to suffering.

piśāca (Tib. *'dre*) A demon whose actual nature is that of negative thoughts, rooted in ego-grasping, who causes *saṃsāra* to come into existence.

prāṇāyāma (Tib. *srog rtsol*) Meditation techniques involving the regulation of the breath in order to control the vital energies.

pratyekabuddha (Tib. *rang sangs rgyas*) A person who is committed to his own individual spiritual liberation won through solitary practice.

preta (Tib. *yi dvags*) A spirit whose existence is dominated by unsatiated hunger, thirst, and craving.

ṛṣi (Tib. *drang srong*) An accomplished contemplative.

rūpakāya (Tib. *gzugs kyi sku*) A form embodiment of an enlightened being, including *nirmāṇakāyas* and *sambhogakāyas*.

sādhana (Tib. *sgrub pa*) A matrix of meditative practices designed to purify the mind, accumulated merit, and bring spiritual awakening.

samādhi (Tib. *ting nge 'dzin*) Meditative concentration.

samaya (Tib. *dam tshig*) A solemn pledge made to the *buddhas.*

samayasattva (Tib. *dam tshig sems dpa'*) Literally, a "pledge being," meaning the form of the chosen deity whom one visualizes and with whom one merges the *jñānasattva.*

sambhogakāya (Tib. *longs spyod rdzogs pa'i sku*) A "full enjoyment embodiment" of an enlightened being, which is accessible only to *āryabodhisattvas* and *buddhas.*

saṃsāra (Tib. *'khor ba*) The cycle of existence, qualified by compulsively taking rebirth after rebirth due to the power of one' s mental afflictions and *karma.*

Saṅgha (Tib. *dge 'dun*) Technically, the assembly of *āryas,* but more generally the congregation of Buddhist practitioners.

siddha (Tib. *sgrub thob*) One who has accomplished one or more *siddhis.*

siddhi (Tib. *dngos sgrub*) A paranormal ability.

śrāvaka (Tib. *nyan thos*) A disciple of the Buddha who is committed to his own individual liberation by following the path set forth by the Buddha.

stūpa (Tib. *mchod rten*) A reliquary which holds sacred objects, such as the remains of an enlightened being; its form symbolizes the mind of a *buddha.*

sugata (Tib. *bde bar gshegs pa*) An epithet of a *buddha,* meaning a "well-gone one," meaning one who has gone to the far shore, achieving liberation from *saṃsāra* and the fulfillment of one's own and others' needs by achieving perfect spiritual awakening.

sugatagarbha (Tib. *bde gshegs snying po*) The essence, or womb, of the *sugatas,* which is synonymous with the *buddha*-nature.

Sukhāvatī (Tib. *bde ba can*) The *buddha*-field of Amitābha in the western direction.

svabhāvakāya (Tib. *ngo bo nyid kyi sku*) The "natural embodiment" of the buddhas, which is the one nature of the *dharmakāya, sambhogakāya,* and *nirmāṇakāya.*

tantra (Tib. *rgyud*) A scripture belonging to the class of Vajrayāna Buddhism.

terma (Tib. *gter ma*) A "treasure" hidden by great adepts of the past, to be revealed when humanity is ready to receive the spiritual teachings preserved in them.

tertön (Tib. *gter ston*) A "treasure revealer" who discovers and makes known *termas* hidden by earlier spiritual adepts.

tulku (Tib. *sprul sku,* Skt. *nirmāṇakāya*) A realized being who is either firmly on the path to spiritual awakening or who has already achieved enlightenment and incarnates for the sake of the world.

tummo (Tib. *gtum mo*) A meditative practice designed to bring forth realization of emptiness by way of igniting the "psychic heat" at the navel *cakra.*

upāsaka (Tib. *dge bsnyen*) A Buddhist layperson who has taken the five basic vows of individual liberation.

upavāsa (Tib. *bsnyen gnas*) A Buddhist fast.

uṣṇīṣa (Tib. *gtsug tor*) A protrusion on the crown of a *buddha's* head, which is one of the major thirty-two marks of an enlightened being.

utpala (Skt.) A rare lotus.

vajra (Tib. *rdo rje*) A symbol of ultimate reality, bearing the seven attributes of invulnerability, indestructibility, reality, incorruptibility, immutability, unobstructedness, and invincibility.

vajraguru (Tib. *rdo rje'i bla ma*) A spiritual mentor who is qualified to lead one in the practices of Vajrayāna.

vajrāsana (Tib. *rdo rje skyil krung*) A cross-legged meditation posture.

Vajrayāna (Tib. *rdo rje'i theg pa*) Esoteric Buddhist teachings and practice aimed at bringing one swiftly to a state of spiritual awakening.

vidyādhara (Tib. *rig pa 'dzin pa*) A "holder of knowledge," who has ascertained the nature of awareness.

vidyāmantra (Tib. *rig pa'i sngags*) A *mantra* for inducing spiritual knowledge.

vinaya (Tib. *'dul ba*) Monastic ethical discipline, and Buddhist scriptures on that topic.

vīra (Tib. *dpa' bo*) A highly realized male *bodhisattva* who manifests in the world in order to serve sentient beings. Literally the term refers to a "heroic being," who shows great courage in not succumbing to the mental afflictions and in striving diligently in spiritual practice.

yāna (Tib. *theg pa*) A vehicle for spiritual practice leading to varying degrees of spiritual liberation and awakening.

yoga (Tib. *rnal 'byor*) A meditative practice explicitly involving the mind and frequently the body as well.

Buddhist Terms in English Translation

absolute space (Tib. *dbyings,* Skt. *dhātu*) The ultimate nature of reality, often referred to as emptiness.

absolute space of phenomena (Tib. *chos kyi dbyings,* Skt. *dharmadhātu*) The essential nature of the whole of *saṃsāra* and *nirvāṇa.*

awareness (Tib. *rig pa,* Skt. *vidyā*) The comprehension of *saṃsāra* and *nirvāṇa* as being totally subsumed within great spiritual awakening, which entails a natural liberation in the ground absolute space, the great, pure equality of *saṃsāra* and *nirvāṇa.*

Breakthrough (Tib. *khregs chod*) The first of the two major phases in the practice of the Great Perfection, in which one seeks to break through to the primordial purity of awareness.

***buddha*-field** (Tib. *zhing khams,* Skt. *kṣetra*) A "pure realm," which is brought forth spontaneously from a *buddha's* mind.

***buddha*-nature** (Tib. *sangs rgyas kyi rigs,* Skt. *buddhadhātu*) The primordially pure, essential nature of the mind, equivalent to awareness, which is none other than the *dharmakāya,* but may be regarded provisionally as one's capacity for achieving spiritual awakening.

chosen deity (Tib. *yi dam,* Skt. *iṣtadevatā*) The enlightened manifestation, or embodiment, which one chooses as one's primary object of refuge and meditative practice.

***citta* lamp of the flesh** (Tib. *tsiitta sha'i sgron ma*) The "lamp" located at the heart and included among the six lamps discussed in the teachings on the Leap-over.

cognition (Tib. *yid,* Skt. *manas*) The mind of every sentient being, which serves as the basis for the emergence of all ideation, and which transforms into the objects of all appearances.

cognitive obscuration (Tib. *shes bya'i sgrib pa,* Skt. *jñeya-āvaraṇa*) The subtle obscurations of the mind, specifically the habitual propensities of mental afflictions and the appearance of true existence, which impede the experience of omniscience.

conceptual elaboration (Tib. *spros pa,* Skt. *prapañca*) Conceptual constructs such as those of existence, nonexistence, birth, and cessation.

consciousness (Tib. *shes pa, rnam par shes pa,* Skt. *jñāna, vijñāna*) The clear and knowing qualities of the mind that emerge in the aspect of the object and are bound by reification.

creative display (Tib. *rtsal*) An effulgence, or manifestation, such as the creative displays of primordial wisdom.

cultivation of the spirit (Tib. *sems bskyed,* Skt. *cittotpāda*) The ultimate cultivation of the spirit entails knowing one's own essential nature as the homogeneous, pervasive nature of being of *saṃsāra* and *nirvāṇa,* while the Mahāyāna, relative cultivation of the spirit is developing an altruistic aspiration to achieve spiritual awakening for the benefit of all beings. The cultivation of the spirit for Hīnayāna practitioners entails developing motivations for spiritual practice appropriate to their respective paths.

definitive meaning (Tib. *nges don,* Skt. *nītārtha*) The meaning of ultimate reality.

delusion (Tib. *'khrul ba*) Principally the delusion of reifying oneself and other phenomena, which acts as the root of all other mental afflictions.

delusive appearance (Tib. *'khrul snang*) The reified appearance of phenomena arising due to delusion.

direct vision of reality-itself (Tib. *chos nyid mngon sum gyi snang ba*) The first of the four visions that arise in the course of the Leap-over practice, in which one directly ascertains the nature of existence of suchness, or ultimate truth. This realization corresponds to the attainment of the first *āryabodhisattva* ground, and provides one the confidence of never returning to *saṃsāra.*

ego-grasping (Tib. *ngar 'dzin,* Skt. *ahaṃkāra*) Reification of one's own identity.

eight aggregates of consciousness (Tib. *rnam shes kyi tshogs brgyad,* Skt. *aṣṭavijñāna-kāya*) The five kinds of sensory consciousness, mental consciousness, total-ground consciousness, and the consciousness of afflicted cognition.

eight mundane concerns (Tib. *'jig rten chos brgyad*) Material gain and loss, pleasure and pain, praise and abuse, and good and bad reputation.

embodiment (Tib. *sku,* Skt. *kāya*) An aspect of a buddha, including the *dharmakāya, sambhogakāya,* and *nirmaṇakāya.*

emptiness (Tib. *stong pa nyid,* Skt. *śunyatā*) The absence of true existence of all phenomena, which itself is not objectively or truly existent.

enlightenment (Tib. *byang chub,* Skt. *bodhi*) Spiritual awakening.

essential nature (Tib. *ngo bo*) The fundamental nature of a phenomenon, as in the case of awareness being the essential nature of the mind.

ethically neutral (Tib. *lung ma bstan*, Skt. *avyākṛta*) Neither virtuous nor nonvirtuous.

expression (Tib. *rtsal*) A creative display, or manifestation, such as *saṃsāra* and *nirvāṇa* being the expression of awareness.

extinction into reality-itself (Tib. *chos nyid zad pa*) The fourth, and final, vision on the path of the Leap-over, in which all phenomena indescribably dissolve into the absolute space. This stage corresponds to the attainment of the supreme ground of a spontaneously present *vidyādhara* on the *mantra* path, which surpasses the tenth ground known as the Cloud of Dharma.

extrasensory perception (Tib. *mngon par shes pa*, Skt. *abhijñā*) Exceptional modes of perception that arise along the path to enlightenment.

five deeds of immediate retribution (Tib. *mtshams med pa lnga*) Killing one's father, killling one's mother, killing an *arhat*, maliciously drawing the blood of a *buddha*, and causing a schism in the Saṅgha. If one commits any such deed, one immediately falls to hell upon death, without spending any time in the intermediate state.

five poisons (Tib. *dug lnga*) Delusion, hatred, pride, attachment, and jealousy.

five primordial wisdoms (Tib. *ye shes lnga*, Skt. *pañcajñāna*) Mirrorlike primordial wisdom, primordial wisdom of the absolute space of phenomena, primordial wisdom of equality, primordial wisdom of discernment, and primordial wisdom of accomplishment.

fluid lasso lamp (Tib. *rgyang zhags chu'i sgron ma*) In the Leap-over terminology, this is the lamp of the eyes, which are fluid and are able to apprehend objects far away, as if they were caught with a lasso. This lamp is like the flowers of a tree that has the *citta* lamp of the flesh as its root, and the hollow crystal *kati* channel as its trunk; the term *fluid lasso lamp* is collectively given to all three, which are known as the three lamps of the vessel.

Four Immeasurables (Tib. *tshad med bzhi*, Skt. *caturapramāṇa*) Loving-kindness, compassion, empathetic joy, and equanimity.

Four Thoughts that Turn the Mind (Tib. *blo ldog rnam pa bzhi*) Meditations on the precious human life of leisure and opportunity, death and impermanence, the miserable nature of *saṃsāra*, and the nature of actions and their ethical consequences.

freedom from conceptual elaboration (Tib. *spros pa dang bral ba*) The second of the four stages of Mahāmudrā meditation.

gaining confidence (Tib. *gding thob pa*) Identifying awareness, then bringing forth spacious awareness, free of activity, and by practicing that uninterruptedly, finally achieving stability within oneself.

Great Perfection (Tib. *rdzogs pa chen po*, Skt. *mahāsandhi*) The clear light absolute space of phenomena, having no center or periphery, from which all phenomena of *saṃsāra* and *nirvāṇa* spontaneously arise as its creative displays.

great transference rainbow body (Tib. *'ja' lus 'pho ba chen po*) The highest-level achievement of the rainbow body, associated with the *dharmakāya*, in which all the material aggregates of one's body are extinguished while one is still living, leaving only a body of light that is unperishing. With the achievement of the second level of the rainbow body, associated with the *sambhogakāya*, at death one's body dissolves into rainbow light, leaving only one's hair and nails behind. With the achievement of the third level of the rainbow body, associated with the *nirmāṇakāya*, at death one's body shrinks considerably in size, sometimes down to the size of an infant.

ground (Tib. *gzhi*, Skt. *āśraya*) The ground of the whole of *saṃsāra* and *nirvāṇa*, which is the *dharmakāya*.

grounds and paths (Tib. *sa lam*, Skt. *bhūmimārga*) The stages along which one progresses to spiritual awakening.

habitual propensity (Tib. *bag chags*, Skt. *vāsanā*) A mental imprint accumulated as a result of previous experiences or actions, which influences later events and conduct.

hollow crystal *kati* channel (*ka ti shel gyi sbu gu can*) Among the six lamps, this is a single channel, one-eighth the width of a hair of a horse's tail, with two branches that stem from inside the heart, curve around the back of the ears, and come to the pupils of the eyes.

insight (Tib. *lhag mthong*, Skt. *vipaśyanā*) Contemplative realization of the nature of phenomena.

intermediate state (Tib. *bar do*, Skt. *antarābhava*) The transitional process of becoming, following death and prior to one' next rebirth.

introspection (Tib. *shes bzhin*, Skt. *saṃprajanya*) The mental faculty by which one ascertains how the mind is functioning, which is crucial to all forms of meditation.

karmic energy (Tib. *las rlung*) A vital energy coursing through the body which is propelled by one's previous *karma*.

lamp of self-arisen wisdom (Tib. *shes rab rang byung gi sgron ma*) One's own awareness, the *sugatagarbha*, which witnesses the displays of primordial wisdom.

lamp of the empty *bindus* (Tib. *thig le stong pa'i sgron ma*) The appearance of the five quintessences in luminous, spherical forms called *bindus*.

lamp of the pristine absolute space (Tib. *dbyings rnam par dag pa'i sgron ma*) The pristine expanse of the sole *bindu* inside the *citta* lamp of the flesh, which appears as the space in which the *bindus* and *vajra*-strands appear.

Leap-over (Tib. *thod rgal*, Skt. *vyutkrāntaka*) The second of the two phases of the practice of the Great Perfection, which is aimed at realizing the spontaneous manifestations of the *dharmakāya*.

meditative experience (Tib. *nyams*) Mundane experiences produced by one's previous behavioral patterns, and occurring within the context of one's familiar conceptual framework. The normal response to such experiences is to grasp onto them by conceptually identifying and classifying them.

meditative stabilization (Tib. *bsam gtan*, Skt. *dhyāna*) An advanced state of meditative concentration included in the form realm, including the four meditative stabilizations.

mental cognition (Tib. *yid*, Skt. *manas*) See cognition.

mindfulness (Tib. *dran pa*, Skt. *smṛti*) The mental faculty of attending continuously, without forgetfulness, to an object with which one is already familiar.

mind-itself (Tib. *sems nyid*, Skt. *cittatā*) The essential nature of the mind, which is awareness, also known as the *sugatagarbha*.

mirrorlike primordial wisdom (Tib. *me long lta bu'i ye shes*, Skt. *ādarśajñāna*) A primordial wisdom that is of a limpid, clear nature free of contamination, which allows for the unceasing appearances of all manner of objects.

mundane existence (Tib. *srid pa*, Skt. *bhava*) The cycle of existence, in which one is propelled from life to life by the force of one's mental afflictions and *karma*.

nature of existence (Tib. *gnas lugs*) The fundamental mode of existence of all phenomena, which is emptiness.

one taste (Tib. *ro gcig*) The third of the four stages of Mahāmudrā meditation.

ornamental wheel (Tib. *rgyan gyi 'khor lo*) A metaphor for the qualities of a *buddha*. The term *ornament* refers to those excellent qualities, and the term *wheel* refers to the all-encompassing, inexhaustible nature of those outer, inner, and secret qualities.

personal identity (Tib. *gang zag gi bdag*, Skt. *pudgalātmya*) An intrinsically existent self, which is actually nonexistent but which is grasped as real by the deluded mind.

phenomenal identity (Tib. *chos kyi bdag*, Skt. *dharmātmya*) An intrinsically existent identity of phenomena other than the self, which is actually nonexistent but which is grasped as real by the deluded mind.

primordial wisdom (Tib. *ye shes*, Skt. *jñāna*) The manifest state of the ground, which is self-arisen, naturally clear, free of outer and inner obscuration, and is the all-pervasive, limpid, clear infinity of space, free of contamination.

primordial wisdom of accomplishment (Tib. *bya ba sgrub pa'i ye shes*, Skt. *kṛtyānuṣṭhānajñāna*) The primordial wisdom by which all pure, free, simultaneously perfected deeds and activities are accomplished naturally, of their own accord.

primordial wisdom of discernment (Tib. *so sor rtog pa'i ye shes*, Skt. *pratyavekṣaṇājñāna*) The primordial wisdom that is an unceasing avenue of illumination of the qualities of primordial wisdom.

primordial wisdom of equality (Tib. *mnyam pa nyid kyi ye shes*, Skt. *samatājñāna*) The primordial wisdom that equally pervades the nonobjective emptiness of the whole of *saṃsāra* and *nirvāṇa*.

primordial wisdom of knowing reality as it is (Tib. *ji lta ba mkhyen pa'i ye shes*, Skt. *yathāvidjñāna*) The primordial knowledge of the ultimate nature of existence.

primordial wisdom of seeing the full range of reality (Tib. *ji snyed pa gzigs pa'i ye shes*, Skt. *yāvadvidjñāna*) The primordial knowledge of all phenomena throughout space and time.

primordial wisdom of the absolute space of phenomena (Tib. *chos kyi dbyings kyi ye shes*, Skt. *dharmadhātujñāna*) Primordial wisdom, the essential nature of which is primordial, great emptiness, and which realizes the absolute nature of the whole of *saṃsāra* and *nirvāṇa*.

progress in meditative experience (Tib. *nyams gong 'phel ba*) The second of the four stages on the path of the Leap-over, in which all appearances during and after meditation transform into displays of light and rainbow *bindus* with ever-increasing clarity, until finally all ordinary appearances vanish and dissolve into continuous, omnipresent displays of visions of light. This stage corresponds to the attainment of the fifth ground known as the Difficult to Practice.

provisional meaning (Tib. *drang don*, Skt. *neyārtha*) The symbolic, relative, or contextual meaning, as opposed to the actual, ultimate, or absolute meaning.

quiescence (Tib. *zhi gnas*, Skt. *śamatha*) An advanced degree of meditative concentration in which attentional stability and vividness have been developed to the point that one can fully engage in the cultivation of insight.

reaching consummate awareness (Tib. *rig pa tshad phebs*) The third of the four stages on the path of the Leap-over, in which the entire universe appears to be totally pervaded with rainbow light and blazing fire, and everything appears as *bindus* in which the five families of male and female peaceful and wrathful divine embodiments appear in union. This stage of spontaneous manifestation corresponds to the attainment of the eighth ground known as the Immovable.

reality-itself (Tib. *chos nyid*, Skt. *dharmatā*) The essential nature of phenomena, which is emptiness, also known as the absolute space.

realization (Tib. *rtogs pa*) The subtle, exact knowledge of how all appearing phenomena are nonobjective and empty from their own side, culminating in the decisive knowledge of the one taste of great emptiness, the fact that all of *saṃsāra* and *nirvāṇa* naturally arises from the expanse of the ground and is not established as anything else.

Severance (Tib. *gcod*) A meditative practice of imaginitively offering up one's entire being as a means to realizing the empty nature of all phenomena, severing all clinging onto the appearances of the three realms, and realizing that all gods and demons are none other than one's own appearances.

sign (Tib. *mtshan ma*, Skt. *nimitta*) An object grasped by the conceptual mind.

sin (Tib. *sdig pa*, Skt. *pāpa*) A nonvirtue that karmically ripens in this or future lifetimes as misery and adversity.

six lamps (Tib. *sgron me drug*) The three lamps of the vessel—namely, the *citta* lamp of the flesh, the hollow crystal *kati* channel, and the fluid lasso lamp—and the three lamps of the vital essence—namely, the lamp of the pristine absolute space, the lamp of the empty *bindus*, and the lamp of self-arisen wisdom.

spirit of awakening (Tib. *byang chub kyi sems*, Skt. *bodhicitta*) In the context of the Great Perfection, the primordial, originally pure ground, which pervades the whole of *saṃsāra* and *nirvāṇa*. The nominal cultivation of the spirit of awakening entails bringing forth the motivation to liberate all sentient beings of the three worlds from the ocean of suffering of mundane existence and bring them to the state of omniscience.

spiritual awakening (Tib. *byang chub*, Skt. *bodhi*) Enlightenment in which all obscurations are purified and all excellent qualities are brought to fulfillment.

spiritual mentor (Tib. *bla ma*, Skt. *guru*) A spiritual teacher who leads one to the state of liberation and spiritual awakening.

spiritual vehicle (Tib. *theg pa*, Skt. *yāna*) A theoretical and practical system of spiritual development leading to spiritual awakening.

stage of generation (Tib. *bskyed rim*, Skt. *utpattikrama*) A Vajrayāna system of practice, corresponding to Mahāyoga, in which one's own body, speech, and mind are regarded as displays of the *vajra* body, speech, and mind of one's chosen deity. As a result of such practice, one achieves stability upon one's own awareness; ordinary appearances and clinging are transferred to the nature of *buddha*-fields; and one's body, speech, and mind are transformed into the three *vajras*.

three doors of liberation (Tib. *rnam thar sgo gsum*) Emptiness, signlessness, and desirelessness.

Three Jewels (Tib. *dkon mchog gsum*, Skt. *trīratna*) The Buddha, Dharma, and Saṅgha.

three realms (Tib. *khams gsum*, Skt. *tridhātu*) The desire realm, form realm, and formless realm.

three roots (Tib. *rtsa ba gsum*) The spiritual mentor, the chosen deity, and the *ḍākinī*.

total-ground (Tib. *kun gzhi*, Skt. *ālaya*) A vacuous, immaterial, nonconceptual state—experienced in deep, dreamless sleep, when one faints, and when one dies—in which appearances to the mind are impeded.

total-ground consciousness (Tib. *kun gzhi rnam shes*, Skt. *ālayavijñāna*) An ethically neutral, inwardly-directed state of consciousness free of conceptualization, in which appearances of oneself, others, and objects vanish.

transference (Tib. *'pho ba*) According to the Great Perfection, the unsurpassed "transference" is the realization of the pristine absolute space of phenomena, the *sugatagarbha*.

transitional process (Tib. *bar do*, Skt. *antarābhava*) Any one of the six transitional processes of living, dreaming, meditative stabilization, dying, reality-itself, and the transitional process of becoming.

transitional process of becoming (Tib. *srid ba bar do*) The dreamlike intermediate state immediately following the transitional process of reality-itself, in which one is on one's way to one's next rebirth.

treasure-revealer (Tib. *gter ston*) A highly realized being who reveals precious spiritual teachings concealed either in the ground by path enlightened beings or reveals such teachings from the nature of his or her own awareness.

vice (Tib. *sdig pa*, Skt. *pāpa*) A nonvirtuous deed of the body, speech, or mind.

vital essence (Tib. *bcud*) The vital core of such phenomena as the five elements.

wisdom (Tib. *shes rab*, Skt. *prajñā*) The knowledge that determines everything included in the phenomenal world of *saṃsāra* and *nirvāṇa* as being empty, identityless, and nonobjective, such that all appearances and mental states are gradually extinguished in the absolute space.

Glossary of Names

Ajita
Mi pham

Chökyi Wangchuk
Chos kyi dbang phyug

Dagpo Rinpoche
Dvags po rin po che

Dawa Gyaltsen Tradition
Zla ba rgyal mtshan gyi lugs

Dezhin Shekpa
De bzhin gshegs pa
The Fifith Karmapa

Dölpupa
Dol pu pa

Draklha Gönpo
Grags lha mgon po

Drakpa
Grags pa

Dram Gyalwey Lodrö
'Bram rgyal ba'i blo gros

Drenpa Namkha
Dran pa nam mkha'

Drungchen Kün-ga Namgyal
Drung chen kun dga' rnam rgyal

Drungkyi Kün-ga Namgyal
Drung skyid kun dga' rnam rgyal

Düsum Khyenpa
Dus gsum mkhyen pa

Gampopa
sGam po pa

Garab Dorje
dGa' rab rdo rje

Gongchik Dorje
dGongs cig rdo rje

Go Phodrang Phardey
mGo pho brang phar 'das

Götsangwa
rGod tshang ba

Gyal Rongwa
rGyal rong ba

Gyalsey Thogmé
rGyal sras thogs med

Gyalwa Gyatso
rGyal ba rgya mtsho
Jinasāgara

Gyalwa Yang Gönpa
rGyal ba yang dgon pa

Gyalwang Chöjey
rGyal dbang chos rje

Gyarey
rGya ras

Gyatönpa Chökyi Zangpo
rGya ston pa chos kyi bzang po

Jigten Sumgön
'Jig rten gsum mgon

Karma Lingpa
Kar ma gling pa

Karma Pakṣi
Kar ma pak ṣi

Khachö Wangpo
mKha' spyod dbang po

Khamgya
Khams mrgya

Kharchen Palgyi Wangchuk
mKhar chen dpal gyi dbang phyug

Kyemé Zhang Rinpoche
sKye me zhang rin po che

Lang Palgyi Sengge
gLang dpal gyi seng ge

Langdarma
gLang dar ma

Langdro Könchok Jungney
Lang gro dkon mchog 'byung gnas

Lasum Gyalwa Jangchup
La gsum rgyal ba byang chub

Lawapa
La ba pa

Lhalung Palgyi Dorje
hLa lung dpal gyi rdo rje

Lingje Repa
gLing rje ras pa

Lorey
Lo ras

Ma Rinchen Chok
rMa rin chen mchog

Machig
Ma gcig

Maitripa
Me tri pa

Marpa Lotsawa
Mar pa lo tsva ba

Milarepa
Mi la ras pa

Nagpopa
Nag po pa

Nanam Dorje Düdjom
sNa nam rdo rje bdud 'joms

Naro Paṇchen
Na ro paṇ chen

Natsok Rangdröl
sNa tshogs rang grol

Nawaripa
Na ba ri pa

Neudzok Nakpa
Ne'u rdzogs nag pa

Ngenlam Gyalwa Chog-yang
Ngan lam rgyal ba mchog dbyangs

Nup Namkhey Nyingpo
gNubs nam mkha'i snying po

Nup Sang-gye Yeshe
gNubs sangs rgyas ye shes

Ö Palgyi Chungwa
'Od dpal gyi chung ba

Ödren Palgyi Wangchuk
'Od dran dpal gyi dbang phyug

Orgyenpa
O rgyan pa

Palmo Tradition
dPal mo lugs

Pal Yeshe Yang
dPal ye shes dbyangs

Phagmo Drüpa (Phagdrup)
Phag mo grus pa

Potowa
Po to ba

Rangjung Dorje
Rang byung rdo rje

Ratna Lingpa
Rat na gling pa

Rechenpa
Ras chen pa

Rechungpa
Ras chung pa

Rendawa Zhönnu Lodrö
Re mda' ba gzhon nu blo gros

Rinchen Tsukpü
Rin chen gtsug phud

Rinchen Zangpo
Rin chen bzang po

Rölpey Dorje
Rol pa'i rdo rje

Sakya Paṇdita
Sa skya paṇ di ta

Sakyapa Dragpa Gyaltsen
Sa skya pa grags pa rgyal mtshan

Sandapa Rölpey Dorje
San da pa rol pa'i rdo rje

Serlingpa
gSer gling pa

Śākya Ö
Śākya 'od

Sogpo Lha Palgyi Yeshe
Sog po lha dpal gyi ye shes

Trisong Deutsen
Khri srong lde'u btsan

Tromdragpa
sProm brag pa

Tshombu Tradition
Tshom bu lugs

Vidyādhara Kumāraja
Rig 'dzin ku mā ra dza

Yeshe Dey
Ye shes sde

Yeshe Tsogyal
Ye shes mtsho rgyal

Zhang Rinpoche
Zhang rin po che

Index of Texts Cited by the Author

The Advice to a King Sūtra 32
rGyal po la gdams pa'i mdo
Rājādeśasūtra

An Analysis of Actions 58, 59, 60, 62
Las rnam par 'byed pa
Karmavibhaṅga

The Arising of the Precepts of Cakrasaṃvara 208
bDe mchog sdom pa 'byung ba

Avalokiteśvara's Instructions of the Peaceful and Wrathful Lotus 190, 196
Thugs rje chen po pad ma zhi khro

Avalokiteśvara's Instructions on the Natural Liberation from the Miserable States of Existence 190, 194, 195, 198
Thugs rje chen po ngan song rang grol

Avalokiteśvara's Tantra Identifying the Secret Path of the Supreme Light of Primordial Wisdom 166, 172
Thugs rje chen po ye shes 'od mchog gi gsang lam ngo sprọd rgyud

Avalokiteśvara's White Instructions on the Meaning of Daytime Contemplation 160, 169, 171, 173, 176, 177, 189, 194
Thugs rje chen po don tig gi dkar khrid nyin mo'i rnal 'byor

Avalokiteśvara's White Instructions on the Supreme Light of Daytime Contemplation 155
Thugs rje chen po 'od mchog gi dkar khrid nyin mo'i rnal 'byor

The Blazing Lamp 158
sGron me 'bar ba

The Chapter on the Cycle of Existence of Birth and Death 58
sKye shi 'khor ba'i le'u

The Collected Teachings of the Lady Labdrön 147
Ma rje mo lab sgron gyi bka' tshom

The Commentary on Verifying Cognition 213
Tshad ma rnam 'grel
Pramāṇavārttika

The Concluding Treatise 215
mJug ṭi ka

The Condensed Perfection of Wisdom 234
Shes rab kyi pha rol tu phyin sdud pa
Prajñāpāramitāsañcayagāthā

The Cultivation of the Spirit of Awakening 127
Byang chub sems bsgom pa
Bodhicittabhāvanā

Dechen Lingpa's Letter 144
bDe chen gling pa'i spring yig

The Descent into Laṅkā Sūtra 224, 245
Lang kar gshegs pa'i mdo
Laṅkāvatārasūtra

The Design of Mahāmudrā 264
Phyag chen re'u mig

The Disclosure of the Secrets of Songtsen Gampo 143
Srong btsan sgam po'i gab pa mngon phyung

The Doha Treasury Treatise in One Hundred and Ten Verses 137
Do ha mdzod brgya bcu pa'i gzhung

The Eight Verses 147
Tshig su bcad pa brgyad pa

The Essence of Amoghapāśa Sūtra 234
Don yod zhags pa'i snying po'i mdo
Amoghapāśahṛdaysūtra

The Essence of the Self-arisen View 129
lTa ba rang byung gi snying po

The Essence of the Tantras 128
rGyud kyi snying po

The Essence of the Tathāgata Sūtra 98
De bzhin gshegs pa'i snying po'i mdo
Tathāgatagarbhasūtra

The Essential Instructions of Avalokiteśvara 179, 197, 198
Thugs rje chen po'i dmar khrid

An Explanation of Severance 193
gCod kyi rnam bshad

The Five Dharmas of Maitreya 215
Byams chos sde lnga

The Five Stages 135, 224, 233, 245, 253
Rim pa lnga pa
Pañcakrama

The Four Dharmas for Subduing the Borderlands 147
mTha' 'khob 'dul ba'i chos bzhi

The Four Syllables of Mahāmudrā 116
Phyag rgya chen po yi ge bzhi pa

The Fulfillment of the Power of Primordial Wisdom 160
Ye shes rtsal rdzogs

The Glorious Bhairava Tantra 123
dPal 'jigs byed kyi rgyud

The Glorious Tantra of Royal Ambrosia 136
dPal bdud rtsi rgyal po'i rgyud

The Glorious Tantra of Secret Activity 135, 136
dPal gsang ba spyod pa'i rgyud

The Glorious Tantra of Vajra Delight 128
dPal dgyes pa rdo rje'i rgyud

The Great Exposition of the Six Dharmas 192
Chos drug chen mo

The Great Instructions 202, 203, 205, 210, 218, 224, 234, 235, 236, 238, 245, 247, 248, 250, 253, 256, 257
Khrid chen

The Great Mound of Jewels Sūtra 215
'Phags pa dkon mchog btsegs pa'i mdo
Āryamahāratnakūṭasūtra

The Great Nirvāṇa Sūtra 71
Yongs su mya nga las 'das pa chen po'i mdo
Mahāparinirvāṇasūtra

The Great Synthesis Sūtra 122
'Dus pa chen po'i mdo
Mahāsamayasūtra

The Guhyasamāja Tantra 136
gSang ba 'dus pa'i rgyud

A Guide to the Middle Way 211
dBu ma la 'jug pa
Madhyamakāvatāra

The Hevajra Tantra 202
Kye rdo rje'i rgyud

The Immaculate Thought Sūtra 99
bSam pa rnam par dag pa'i mdo

An Introduction to the Quintessence of the Clear Expanse 185
kLong gsal snying thig gi ngo sprod

The Jewel Inlay 165
Nor bu phra bkod

The Jewel Meteor Spell Sūtra 27
dKon mchog ta la la'i gzungs kyi mdo
Ratnolkādhāraṇisūtra

The Kadam Volume 193
bKa' gdams glegs bam

The King Doha 137
rGyal po'i do ha

The King of Dharma Sūtra 97
Chos kyi rgyal po'i mdo

The King of Samādhi Sūtra 201, 216
Ting nge 'dzin rgyal po'i mdo
Samādhirājasūtra

The King of Tantras Equal to Space 103
Nam mkha' dang mnyam pa'i rgyud
Khasamatantrarāja

The Lamp of the Moon Sūtra 98
Zla ba sgron ma'i mdo

A Letter to a Friend 70
bShes pa'i spring yig
Suhṛllekha

The Mahāmudrā Gaṅgāma 142
Phyag rgya chen po gang ga ma

The Mahāmudrā Precipitance 116
Phyag rgya chen po'i thog bab

A Mound of Jewels: Instructions on the Quintessence of the Ḍākinīs 163, 170
mKha' 'gro snying thig gi khrid yig rin chen spungs pa

The Mound of Jewels of the Great Perfection 173
rDzogs chen rin chen spungs pa

The Mound of Jewels Sūtra 122, 123
Rin po che'i phung po'i mdo
Ratnarāśisūtra

The Natural Liberation of Seeing: Experiential Instructions on the Transitional Process of Reality-Itself 163, 167, 171, 174
Chos nyid bar do'i ngo sprod mthong ba rang grol

Nine Seeds of the Precious Practical Advice of Paṇchen Śākyaśrī 143
Paṇ chen Śā kya śrī'i gdams ngag rin po che'i 'bru dgu

No Letters 157, 159
Yi ge med pa

Non-mental-engagement of the Three Embodiments 140
sKu gsum yid la mi byed pa

One Hundred and Sixty Verses of the Public Doha 139
'Bang do ha brgya drug cu pa

The Oral Transmission of the Lineage of Siddhas 231
Grub thob brgyud pa'i zhal lung

The Ornament for Higher Realization 27, 137
mNgon rtogs rgyan
Abhisamayālaṃkāra

The Ornament for the Sūtras 21, 27, 216
mDo sde rgyan
Mahāyānasūtrālaṃkāra

The Pearl Garland 155, 157
Mu tig phreng ba

The Perfect Expression of the Names of Mañjuśrī 160
'Jam dpal gyi mtshan yang dag par brjod pa
Mañjuśrīnāmasaṃgīti

The Perfection of the Lion's Might 165
Seng ge rtsal rdzogs

The Perfection of Wisdom in Eight Thousand Verses 216
Shes rab kyi pha rol tu phyin pa brgyad stong pa
Aṣṭasāhasrikāprajñāpāramitā

The Perfection of Wisdom Sūtra 70, 102
Shes rab kyi pha rol tu phyin pa'i mdo
Prajñāpāramitāsūtra

Phagmo Drüpa's Verses on the Path of Skillful Means 199
Phag gru'i thabs lam tshigs bcad ma

The Prayer of Fine Conduct 277
'Phags pa bzang po spyod pa'i smon lam gyi rgyal po
Āryabhadracāryapraṇidhānarājā

The Primary Tantra 136
rTsa ba'i rgyud

The Primary Tantra on the Penetration of Sound 155, 157, 158, 159, 164, 170, 172, 175, 189
sGra thal 'gyur rtsa ba'i rgyud

The Primary Words of the Great Instructions 222
Khrid chen rtsa tshig

The Profound Inner Meaning 95, 219
Zab mo nang don

The Questions of Brahmā Sūtra 100, 102
Tshang pas zhus pa'i mdo
Brahmaparipṛcchāsūtra

The Questions of Brāhman Tsangpa Sūtra 102
Bram ze tshang pas zhus pa'i mdo [?]

The Questions of Dewa Lodrö Sūtra 101
bDe ba blo dros kyi zhus pa'i mdo

The Questions of King Dejin Sūtra 102
rGyal po bde byin gyis zhus pa'i mdo

The Questions of King Dewa Lodrö Sūtra 124
rGyal po bde ba blo gros gyi zhus pa'i mdo

The Questions of King Dewa Sūtra 102
rGyal po bde bas zhus pa'i mdo

The Questions of King Katsal Sūtra 101
rGyal po bka' rtsal gyi zhus pa'i mdo

The Questions of King Miyowa Sūtra 100
rGyal po mi g.yo bas zhus pa'i mdo

The Questions of Madröpa Sūtra 136
Ma gros pas zhus pa'i mdo

The Questions of Maitreya Sūtra 101
Byams pas zhus pa'i mdo
Maitreyaparipṛcchāsūtra

The Questions of Nairātmya Sūtra 123
bDag med pa dris pa'i mdo
Nairātmyaparipṛcchāsūtra

The Questions of Ngangpa Giryin Sūtra 100
Ngang pa gir yin gyis zhus pa'i mdo [?]

The Questions of Queen Kaparabhuja to the Great Brahmin Saraha 209
rGyal po'i btsun mo ka pa ra bhu dza yis bram ze chen po sa ra ha la zhus pa

The Questions of Śrīmatībrāhmaṇī Sūtra 101
Bram ze mo dpal ldan mas zhus pa'i mdo
Śrīmatībrāhmaṇīparipṛcchāsūtra

The Questions of Śūradatta Sūtra 34
dPal sbyin gyi zhus pa'i mdo

The Questions of the Girl Regöma Sūtra 102
Bu mo ras gos mas zhus pa'i mdo

The Questions to Chen-ngawa 79
sPyan snga ba la zhu gtugs zhus pa

The Quintessence of the Ḍākinīs 217
mKha' 'gro snying thig

The Quintessential Commentary of the Spiritual Mentor ???
bLa ma yang tig

The Secret Tantra of the Sun of the Blazing Clear Expanse of the Ḍākinīs 154, 268
mKha' 'gro klong gsal 'bar ma nyi ma'i gsang rgyud

The Secret Vajra Ḍāka Tantra 135
rDo rje mkha' 'gro gsang ba'i rgyud
Vajraḍākaguhyatantra

The Set of Aphorisms 70
Ched du brjod pa'i tshom
Udānavarga

The Six Collections of Reasonings Concerning the Middle Way 215
dBu ma rigs tshogs drug

The Six Dharmas 193, 224
Chos drug

The Smaller Sūtra on Nirvāṇa 201
mDo sde mya ngan 'das chung ba

The Splendid Assemblage Sūtra 123
dPung pa bkod pa'i mdo

The Stages of the Path of Secret Mantra 115
gSang sngags lam rim

The Sukhāvatī Prayer 35, 277
bDe ba can gyi smon lam

The Sūtra of Individual Liberation 79
So sor thar pa'i mdo
Prātimokṣasūtra

The Sūtra of Liberated Primordial Wisdom 131
Ye shes rnam par grol ba'i mdo

The Sūtra of the Great Liberation 22
Yongs su mya ngan las 'das pa chen po'i mdo
Mahāparinirvāṇasūtra

The Sūtra of the Holy Golden Light 216
gSer 'od dam pa'i mdo sde'i dbang po'i rgyal po
Suvarṇaprabhāsottamasūtrendrarāja

The Sūtra of the Maitreya Prophesy 211, 212
Byams pa lung bstan gyi mdo

The Sūtra of the Wise and the Foolish 44, 48
mDo mdzangs blun
Damamūkasūtra

The Sūtra on Dependent Origination 45
rTen cing 'brel bar 'byung ba'i mdo (rTen cing 'brel bar 'byung ba bcu gnyis kyi mdo)
Pratityasamutpadasutra

The Sūtra on Possessing the Roots of Virtue 101
dGe ba'i rtsa ba yongs su 'dzin pa'i mdo
Kuśalamūlasaṃparigrahasūtra

The Sūtra on Unraveling the Intention 27
dGongs pa nges par 'grel pa'i mdo
Saṃdhinirmocanasūtra

The Synthesis of Maitripa's Words on Mahāmudrā 143
Mai tri pa'i phyag rgya chen po'i tshig sdus

The Synthesis of Naropa's View 142
Na ro pa'i lta ba mdor sdus

The Tantra Equal to Space 127, 129, 132
Nam mkha' dang mnyam pa'i rgyud
Khasamatantra

The Tantra Free of Contention 129
rTsod pa bral ba'i rgyud

The Tantra of All Views 128
lTa ba thams chad kyi rgyud

The Tantra of Entering into the Renunciate Life 124
mNgon par 'byung ba'i rgyud
(Possible reference to *The Sūtra of Entering into the Renunciate Life*
mNgon par 'byung ba'i mdo
Abhiniṣkramaṇasūtra)

The Tantra of Great Space 129
Nam mkha' chen po'i rgyud (Nam mkha' che)
Mahākhatantra

The Tantra of Identifying Self-arisen Awareness 127
Rang byung rig pa ngo sprod kyi rgyud

The Tantra of Inconceivability 134
bSam gyis mi khyab pa'i rgyud

The Tantra of Inconceivable Mysteries 131, 135, 252
gSang ba bsam gyis mi khyap pa'i rgyud

The Tantra of Naturally Arising Awareness 158, 159, 165, 176
Rig pa rang shar gyi rgyud

The Tantra of Nonabiding 104
Rab tu mi gnas pa'i rgyud

The Tantra of Nonconceptuality 133
rTog pa med pa'i rgyud

The Tantra of Nondwelling 134
Rab tu mi gnas pa'i rgyud

The Tantra of Saṃbhuṭa 135
Saṃ bhu tri'i rgyud

The Tantra of Self-arisen Bliss 127, 130
Rang byung bde ba'i rgyud

The Tantra of Supreme Meditative Stabilization 131
bSam gtan mchog gi rgyud

The Tantra of the Black Skull of Yama 127
gShin rje thod nag gi rgyud

The Tantra of the Blazing Clear Expanse of the Ḍākinīs 143
mKha' 'gro klong gsal 'bar ma'i rgyud

The Tantra of the Blood-drinking Manifestation 187
Khrag thung mngon 'byung rgyud

The Tantra of the Clear Expanse of the Quintessence of All the Ḍākinīs 199
mKha' 'gro kun gyi snying tig klong gsal rgyud

The Tantra of the Compendium of the Contemplations of Samantabhadra 154, 179, 183
Kun bzang dgongs pa kun 'dus rgyud

The Tantra of the Ḍākinī Realizations 182
mKha' 'gro kun tu rtogs pa'i rgyud

The Tantra of the Exposition of Meditative Stabilization 127
Lung bsam gtan gyi rgyud

The Tantra of the Full Enlightenment of Vairocana 126
rNam snang mngon par byang chub pa'i rgyud
Vairocanābhisaṃbodhitantra

The Tantra of the Full Enlightenment of Vajrasattva 126
rDo rje sems dpa' mngon par byang chub pa'i rgyud

The Tantra of the Gathering of Mysteries on Non-mental-engagement 131
gSang ba 'dus pa yid la byed pa'i rgyud

The Tantra of the Great Āli Kāli River 231, 244, 252
Āli kāli chu klung chen po'i rgyud

The Tantra of the Great Perfection Inquiry into Deceptive Appearances 154
rDzogs pa chen po 'khrul snang rtsad gcod kyi rgyud

The Tantra of the Ocean of Primordial Wisdom 197
Ye shes rgya mtsho'i rgyud

The Tantra of the Sole Bindu 125, 128
Thig le nyag gcig gi rgyud

The Tantra of the Supreme Class of Kila 128
Phur pa rigs mchog gi rgyud

The Tantra of the Synthesis of Awareness 129
Kun 'dus rig pa'i rgyud

The Tantra of the Two Bindus 124
Thig le gnyis pa'i rgyud

The Tantra of the Vast Expanse of Space 130
Nam mkha' klong yangs kyi rgyud

The Tantra of Treasures 154
gTer rgyud

The Tantra Synthesizing the Quintessence of Great Compassion 119
Thugs rje chen po yang snying 'dus pa'i rgyud

The Tantra that Liberates the Whole World: A Commentary on the Meaning of Great Compassion 105
Thugs rje chen po don trig 'gro ba kun sgrol rgyud

Three Dharmas 264
Sum chos

The Transference of the Primordial Wisdom of Great Bliss: Instructions on Emptying the Cycle of Existence 183
bDe chen ye shes kyi 'pho ba 'khor ba dong sprugs kyi gdams ngag

The Treasury of Secret Mind 140
Thugs gsang ba mdzod

The Treasury of Secret Speech 140
gSung gsang ba mdzod

The Treasury Treatise of the Secret Embodiment 139
sKu gsang ba mdzod gzhung

A Treatise of Instruction of the Greatly Compassionate Supreme Light 106
Thugs rje chen po 'od mchog gi khrid gzhung

The Treatise on Discipline 68
'Dul ba lung
Vinayaśāstra

A Treatise on the Six Dharmas 187
Chos drug gi gzhung

The Vajra Pavilion Tantra 124, 135, 202
rDo rje gur gyi rgyud

A Vajra Song of Immortality 252
'Chi med rdo rje'i glu

The Vajra Stanza of Avalokiteśvara 182
sPyan ras gzigs kyi tshig khang

The White Lotus Sūtra 211
mDo sde padma dkar po
Puṇḍarīkasūtra

The Wish-fulfilling Gem Instruction on the Mind 117
Sems khrid yid bzhin nor bu

The Wish-fulfilling Gem: Instructions on the Quintessence of the Clear Expanse 161, 177
kLong gsal snying thig gi khrid yig yid bzhin nor bu

The Zhijepa Tradition of Phadampa 143
Pha dam pa'i zhi byed pa lugs

General Index

Akyong Khenpo 181
Amitābha 8, 17, 20, 166, 183, 184, 190, 191, 196, 199, 269, 273, 277, 278, 280
Amoghasiddhi 166
Āryamitra 54
Andzom Rinpoche 256
Atiśa 33, 193, 261, 262, 263
Avalokiteśvara 183, 184, 185, 190, 194, 195, 196, 198, 199, 271, 275, 279, 280

bliss 100
bliss, clarity, and nonconceptuality 134, 152, 169, 187, 189, 193, 206, 224, 225, 226, 229, 233
bodhisattva grounds 176, 205–206, 221, 223, 237–238, 241, 243
bodhisattva training 32–33
Breakthrough 15, 153, 154, 186, 221, 243
buddha-nature 90, 98, 132, 137, 253, 258

Chökyi Wangchuk 187
consciousness of the present 103–104

Dagpo Rinpoche 224, 233, 244, 253
Dalai Lama 32, 55, 75, 89, 181, 264, 271
Dawa Gyaltsen Tradition 179, 183, 197
dedication of merit 29, 59, 62, 65, 263, 266–267, 276, 277, 279
definite action 58
Dezhin Shekpa 72
dharmakāya 56, 88, 89, 90, 95, 107, 112, 130, 133, 134, 141, 166, 173, 188, 204, 206, 216, 218, 224, 258, 290
Dölpupa 191
Düdjom Lingpa 9, 102, 119, 177
Dudjom Rinpoche 9, 68, 71, 89, 98, 101, 181, 240, 264, 271
Düsum Khyenpa 149

Eightfold Path 205
empowerment 15
extinction into reality-itself 174, 177

five paths 203–205, 205, 210, 221, 223, 237, 243
five primordial wisdoms 139, 159, 161, 166–167, 173, 194, 208, 218, 267, 275
fivefold practices 263
four empowerments 208–210, 245, 253
Four Immeasurables 33, 35, 64, 111, 125
four negative deeds 31
Four Noble Truths 24, 25, 26, 56, 207, 230
Four Thoughts that Turn the Mind 13–16, 24, 25, 26, 111, 119, 297
four visions 160, 258

Gampopa 149
Garab Dorje 176
generation and completion stages 15, 72, 76, 95, 210, 231, 246, 264–265, 272, 273
Gongchik Dorje 59
Götsangwa 71, 226, 237, 240, 255
great equality 112
Gyal Rongwa 231
Gyalsey Thogmé 117, 148
Gyalwa Yang Gönpa 226
Gyalwang Chöjey 241, 251, 259
Gyatönpa Chökyi Zangpo 117, 253

ideation 99, 100, 108, 117, 118, 125, 169, 228, 233
insight 153, 192, 202, 209, 218, 222, 223, 235, 241, 258
intentional object 272
intermediate state 166, 167, 169, 170, 172, 189, 194–198, 210, 267, 275

Jigten Sumgön 212, 263, 264

Kalu Rinpoche 71
karma 48–49, 55–56, 57–80, 162; arousal of *karma* 71; collective *karma* 78; completed *karma* 68; propulsive *karma* 68; uncontaminated *karma* 76
Karma Chagmé 7–8, 9, 10, 20, 38, 110, 206, 285
Karma Lingpa 163
Karmapa 7, 8, 71, 89, 187, 276
Karmapakṣi 150, 183, 216
Khachö Wangpo 151
Kumāraja 167
Kün-ga Namgyal 7, 151, 187, 253
Kyemé Zhang 213

Lawapa 224, 233, 245, 253
Leap-over 15, 122, 153, 154, 162, 167, 178, 185, 186, 221, 222, 223, 241, 258, 264, 267, 275, 276
letting be 132–133
Lingje Repa 203, 214
Longchen Rabjampa 138

Mahākāpina 51
mahāsukhakāya 205
Maitrīpa 142, 224, 233, 245, 253
Marpa 148
Mikyö Dorje 215
Milarepa 138, 148
Min-gyur Dorje 8

Nagpopa 142
naked awareness 107, 149, 191
Naropa 208, 216, 222, 252
nature of awareness 109–110
Nawaripa 224
New Translation School 193, 261, 264, 278
Nāgārjuna 29, 224
nine *yānas* 99, 154, 162, 216, 264, 267
nirmāṇakāya 56, 107, 112, 133, 134, 141, 166, 173, 188, 204, 209, 216, 224, 291
non-meditation 187, 205, 207, 208, 209, 210, 218, 221, 222, 227, 229, 231, 241, 242, 252–259

offering 16, 19, 21, 22, 29, 30, 32, 53–54, 61, 64, 65, 181, 182, 230
one taste 57, 152, 186, 187, 204, 210, 221, 222, 241, 242, 244–254, 259
Orgyen Rinpoche (Padmasambhava) 7, 15, 20, 71, 108, 110, 115, 154, 167, 179, 180, 183, 188, 192, 198, 204, 222, 272, 273, 278, 280

Palmo Tradition 179, 183
Phagmo Drüpa 212, 226, 236, 238, 245, 249, 254, 255, 257, 263, 264
postures 155–157, 169, 171, 173, 204, 268

quiescence 105, 106, 115, 116, 122, 125, 145, 153, 169, 193, 202, 209, 211, 213, 218, 222, 223, 235, 241, 258, 270, 272, 273

Rangjung Dorje 150, 210, 216
Ratna Lingpa 7, 8, 65, 161
Ratnasambhava 166

Rechenpa 149
Rechungpa 149
refuge 16–26, 111, 188; corresponding disciplines of 21–23; eight benefits of 24
rejoicing 29, 30, 77
Rinchen Zangpo 261, 262, 263
Rölpey Dorje 151, 208
rūpakāya 205, 216, 218, 229, 258

Sakya Paṇḍita 210, 211
Sakya Trizin 181
Sakyapa Dragpa Gyaltsen 147
Samantabhadra 29, 173, 178, 189, 217
sambhogakāya 56, 107, 112, 133, 134, 141, 166, 171, 173, 188, 204, 209, 216, 224
Saraha 141, 216, 224, 233, 245
Śawaripa 233, 253
sending and receiving (*tonglen*) 35, 39, 274–276
sevenfold devotion 29
Severance 71, 72, 169, 230
single-pointedness 57, 151, 186, 187, 202, 203, 206, 207, 210, 221–229, 223, 229, 231, 237, 241, 244, 251, 259
six states of existence 66
six-syllable mantra 75, 184, 185, 195, 196, 198
sole bindu 57, 123, 133, 161, 164
spirit of awakening 5, 13, 14, 16, 24, 25, 26–36, 66, 108, 111, 113, 115, 127, 128, 141, 160, 178, 245, 250, 265, 272, 275, 277, 287, 295, 297, 300, 302; divisions of 27
Śrī Siṃha 176
sugatagarbha 121, 132; causal *sugatagarbha* 94
svabhāvikakāya 205

tathāgatagarbha 98, 99
ten nonvirtues 25, 49
tertöns 65
Tilopa 67, 103, 141, 272
Trisong Deutsen 108
Tromdragpa 149
Tshombu Tradition 179, 183, 198
Tulku Natsok Rangdröl 73
two types of knowledge (ontological and phenomenal) 22, 56, 133, 163

Vairocana 166
vajra-strands 159, 161, 162, 163, 164, 165, 167, 171, 173, 174
Vajrakīlaya 264
Vajrasattva 15, 105, 166, 172, 185, 186, 196, 198
Vimalamitra 175
Virupa 141
vital energies 84, 86, 157, 158, 159, 160, 170, 171, 172, 180, 209, 210, 245, 253

Yang Gönpa 226, 233, 235, 236, 238, 246, 248, 249, 254, 255, 257
Yeshe Rabsel 181
Yeshe Tsogyal 110, 138

Zhang Rinpoche 146, 222, 227